Steven Holzner

P9-CAO-375

Microsoft Visual C# .NET 2003

KICK START

SAMS

201 West 103rd Street, Indianapolis, Indiana 46290

Microsoft Visual C# .NET 2003 Kick Start

International Standard Book Number: 0-672-32547-0

Library of Congress Catalog Card Number: 2003092630

Printed in the United States of America

First Printing: July 2003

06   05   04   03   4   3   2   1

Sams Publishing offers excellent discounts on this book when ordered in quantity for bulk purchases or special sales. For more information, please contact

U.S. Corporate and Government Sales

1-800-382-3419

corpsales@pearsontechgroup.com

For sales outside of the U.S., please contact

International Sales

1-317-581-3793

international@pearsontechgroup.com

Trademarks

Warning and Disclaimer

Associate Publisher
Michael Stephens

Acquisitions Editor
Neil Rowe

Development Editor
Songlin Qiu

Managing Editor
Charlotte Clapp

Project Editor
George E. Nedeff

Copy Editor
Kezia Endsley

Indexer
Ken Johnson

Proofreader
Juli Cook

Technical Editor
Doug Holland

Team Coordinator
Cindy Teeters

Multimedia Developer
Dan Scherf

Interior Designer
Gary Adair

Cover Designer
Gary Adair

Page Layout
Michelle Mitchell

Contents at a Glance

Table of Contents

About the Author

Steven Holzner is an award-winning author of 78 books on computing. He did his undergraduate work at MIT and got his PhD from Cornell University. While a graduate student at Cornell, he was also a contributing editor at PC Magazine. He's been on the faculty of both MIT and Cornell, teaching classes of up to 450 students, but prefers writing. Many of his books have been bestsellers; they've sold nearly two million copies, and have been translated into 16 languages around the world. He's written about Visual Studio programming since before Visual Studio was even released. He also teaches corporate programming seminars around the nation and runs his own online business.

Dedication

To Nancy, the best of the best (as everybody knows).

Acknowledgments

A book like the one you're reading is the product of many people's hard work. I'd especially like to thank Neil Rowe, the acquisitions editor; Songlin Qiu, the development editor; George Nedeff, the project editor; Kezia Endsley, the copy editor; and Doug Holland, the tech editor.

Foreword

The .NET Framework and Visual Studio .NET were officially released in early 2002. Since that time, Microsoft has received an overwhelmingly positive response about the newest member of the language family, Visual C# .NET. C# is a modern, innovative, object-oriented programming language with a clean and elegant syntax that is instantly familiar to both the C++ and Java developer. C# strikes the perfect balance between the power that C++ developers demand, with language features like "unsafe" code and operator overloading, as well as productivity features like the foreach statement, indexers, enumerations, switch on string, and XML comments.

It's this balance of power and productivity that has lead to the popularity of C# both inside and outside of Microsoft, with the .NET Framework and future versions of Microsoft Windows, Microsoft Office, and the Microsoft Server System incorporating C#, and enterprise customers like AllState Insurance, 7-Eleven, and Xerox Corporation writing mission-critical applications in C#.

With the release of Visual Studio .NET 2003, the C# developer can create a diverse set of applications ranging from mobile Web applications to rich client applications to XML Web services and everything in between. This book, aptly titled *Visual C# .NET 2003 Kick Start*, will guide you from building your first "Hello World" application in C# to discussing advanced topics like multithreaded application development and .NET Remoting. Armed with the knowledge and insight found in this book, you can become a more powerful, productive, and capable programmer.

Dan Fernandez

Product Manager

Visual C# .NET

We Want to Hear from You!

As the reader of this book, *you* are our most important critic and commentator. We value your opinion and want to know what we're doing right, what we could do better, what areas you'd like to see us publish in, and any other words of wisdom you're willing to pass our way.

As an associate publisher for Sams Publishing, I welcome your comments. You can email or write me directly to let me know what you did or didn't like about this book—as well as what we can do to make our books better.

Please note that I cannot help you with technical problems related to the *topic* of this book. We do have a User Services group, however, where I will forward specific technical questions related to the book.

When you write, please be sure to include this book's title and author as well as your name, email address, and phone number. I will carefully review your comments and share them with the author and editors who worked on the book.

Email: feedback@sampublishing.com

Mail: Michael Stephens
            Associate Publisher
            Sams Publishing
            201 West 103rd Street
            Indianapolis, IN 46290 USA

For more information about this book or another Sams Publishing title, visit our Web site at www.samspublishing.com. Type the ISBN (excluding hyphens) or the title of a book in the Search field to find the page you're looking for.

Introduction

Welcome to C#, today's premiere programming language for the .NET platform, and the most exciting one. We're going to push the C# envelope in this book, working from the ground floor up through the advanced levels. This book has been designed to open up C# and make it more accessible than any other book can.

This is a programmer-to-programmer book, written to bring you up to speed in C# by giving you what you need without wasting time. Because this discussion is targeted to programmers, we're going to skip the in-depth explanations of elementary programming constructs like variables that you'd skip anyway. If you're a programmer, this book is written to give you exactly what you want to see when moving to C#—the good stuff, and only the good stuff.

There's as much C# crammed into this book as you need to get truly proficient. And getting you there is this book's goal.

What's in This Book

From cover to cover, this book is pure C#. It covers the full C# language and hundreds of skills from using visual tools when dropping data adapters into windows to remoting C# objects and classes across process boundaries. Here are a few of the topics we're going to see:

- The complete C# syntax
- Creating console applications
- Abstract classes
- Sealed classes
- Boxing and unboxing types
- Delegates and events
- Asynchronous I/O
- Network I/O
- Stream classes
- Web streams
- Serialization
- Indexers

- Creating Windows forms
- Showing/hiding forms
- Handling events
- Showing dialog boxes
- Working with multiple forms
- Creating Multiple Document Interface (MDI) forms
- Creating always-on-top forms
- Creating owned forms
- Creating Web forms
- Setting Web control layout
- Forcing event handling on the server
- Redirecting Web browsers
- Detecting browser type and capabilities
- Saving program data across Web server round trips
- Adding controls to forms at runtime
- ADO.NET
- Creating data connections
- Data access using data adapters
- Using relational databases
- Adding multiple tables to a dataset
- Using data views
- Creating three-tier data applications
- Binding data to controls
- Simple and complex binding
- Creating custom user and Web user controls
- Creating a Windows service
- Creating a Windows Service Installer
- Creating a Web service

- Deploying your applications
- Assemblies
- Assembly manifests
- Versioning
- Private and shared assemblies
- Security boundaries
- Code-access security
- Encrypting and decrypting files
- Using intrinsic attributes
- Creating custom attributes
- Handling reflection
- Discovering types at runtime
- Discovering type information
- Late binding versus reflection
- Creating types at runtime
- Using multithreading
- Using locks and monitors
- Synchronizing threads
- Remoting

You can also download the code for this book from Sams Web site at www.samspublishing.com. All the code in this book has been tested on at least two separate computers, and verified to work as it should. (Note that in the past, Microsoft has made unannounced changes to Visual Studio products without changing the version number, which has made previously working code stop

NOTE

To download the code on the Sams Web site at www.samspublishing.com, enter this book's ISBN (without the hyphens) in the Search box and click Search. When the book's title is displayed, click the title to go to a page where you can download the code.

working. If you have problems with the code or get errors when you try to run it, be sure to check whether Visual C# itself has changed. Check the book's Web site for updates.)

Conventions Used in This Book

The following typographic conventions are used in this book:

- When we've added a new piece of code and are discussing it, it'll appear shaded, and when there's more code to come, you'll see three dots. Here's what that looks like:

```
class ch01_07
{
 static void Main()
 {
  long source = 5;
  int target;
  target = (int) source;

   .

   .

   .

 }
}
```

- Occasionally, we'll discuss C# syntax in the compact form you'll see in the Microsoft documentation, and you should know how to decipher that. For example, check out this description showing how to create a method:

```
[attributes] [modifiers] type identifier ([[out][ref]
type parameter, [[out][ref]type parameter, ...]]) statement
```

  In descriptions like this one, items in brackets ([and]) are optional, vertical bars, |, mean "or", curly braces ({ and }) indicate that you select only one of the enclosed items, and the items in italics are not keywords built into C#, but are meant to be replaced with your own terms.

- Code lines, commands, statements, variables, and/or code-related terms appear in a monospace typeface.

- We'll also refer to the items in menus the same way you'll see in many computer books. For example, the File, New Project menu item refers to the New Project item in the File menu.

- You'll see sidebars throughout the book, which are meant to give you something more, such as a little more insight or some new technique. Here's what a sidebar looks like:

- Also, if you're a C++ programmer, take a look at the "For C++ Programmers" sidebars in the first few chapters; these sidebars are there to let you skim through the more basic material faster because you already know C++. They're often designed to give you information at a more advanced programming level than the surrounding text.

- The "Shop Talk" sidebars are designed for more professional discussion about what's going on behind the scenes in programming these days. They go into more depth, and hit topics harder, than the sidebars.

> **BACKGROUND THREADS**
>
> You can also set a thread's `IsBackground` property to `true`, making it a background thread. Background threads are the same as foreground threads, except that an application doesn't need to wait for background threads to terminate before finishing.

What You'll Need

To use this book, you'll need C#, and as discussed in Chapter 1, you can get the free C# command-line compiler by installing the .NET Framework's Software Development Kit (SDK), which you can find at `http://msdn.microsoft.com/downloads` as of this writing. We're going to be using C# version 2003 in this book, but if you have an earlier version, you're also OK, because the C# will be the same (be sure to read the directions in readme.txt in the code download for this book on converting Visual Studio .NET projects to earlier versions of Visual Studio).

You can also use the Visual Studio Integrated Development Environment (IDE) to create C# programs. In fact, we'll be using the IDE almost exclusively when we create Windows and Web applications (you can create these applications with the command-line compiler, but the process can become extraordinarily tedious).

Besides C# itself, there are some additional software packages you might want. To create Web applications and Web services, you'll need access to a Web server that runs the Microsoft Internet Information Server (IIS). If you choose, you can run IIS on the same machine the IDE is on, and IIS comes with many Windows versions (although you might have to install it from the CDs that come with Windows).

We'll also work with databases in this book. To work with a database, you need a data provider like SQL Server. You can use other data providers, but C# is most often connected to SQL Server, so we'll use that data provider here. A knowledge of Structured Query Language (SQL) also helps.

And that's about it—just about everything else that you need comes with the C# command-line compiler or the Visual Studio IDE itself.

C# Online Resources

There are plenty of C# resources online that you can turn to for additional information and to stay in touch with the C# community. For example, the official C# group on Usenet is `microsoft.public.dotnet.languages.csharp`. As you'd expect, there are many Web pages out there on C#; a casual search turns up 1,830,000 pages on the subject. Here's a starter list of pages hosted by Microsoft:

- http://msdn.microsoft.com/vcsharp/—The main C# page

- http://msdn.microsoft.com/vstudio/techinfo/articles/upgrade/Csharpintro.asp—Microsoft's overview and introduction to C#

- http://msdn.microsoft.com/library/default.asp?url=/library/en-us/vcedit/html/vcorivisualcmainnode.asp—The C# documentation online

- http://msdn.microsoft.com/downloads—The .NET Framework's Software Development Kit (SDK), which includes csc, the C# command-line compiler

- http://msdn.microsoft.com/vcsharp/community/default.asp—A list of C# online communities

- http:msdn.microsoft.com/vcsharp/productinfo/—The C# Product Info page

- http://msdn.microsoft.com/vcsharp/productinfo/faq/default.asp—The C# Frequently Asked Questions (FAQ) page

- http://msdn.microsoft.com/vcsharp/downloads/default.asp—Free downloads for C#

And there are plenty of C# tutorials available from others as well; here's a starter list of online tutorials:

- http://www.c-sharpcorner.com/Tutorials/CSTutorial1AN.asp

- http://www.csharphelp.com/archives2/archive402.html

- http://www.simonrobinson.com/DotNET/Articles/Languages/IntroCSh.aspx

- http://www.mantrotech.com/technology/csharp/tutorial_csharp_1.asp

- http://tutorials.findtutorials.com/index/category/87

- http://www.managedworld.com/articles/0002/article.aspx

- http://www.andymcm.com/csharpfaq.htm A C# FAQ for C++ programmers

That's all the introduction you need. You have all you need to get your kick start in C#. If you have comments, suggestions, or problems, please email them to me, Steve Holzner, at feedback@samspublishing.com. I want to make sure this book stays at the top of the field, and I'll implement your suggestions in upcoming editions.

Essential C#

Creating Our First C# Program

Welcome to C#. This is a programmer-to-programmer book, so we're going to pack in the code, pushing the envelope—and not wasting much space. In this book, we're assuming you know programming already, but are new to C#. In these early chapters, we're going to cover the C# basics—not because you're unfamiliar with elementary constructs like variables and if statements, but because there are substantial differences between C# and languages like C++ and Java that can trip you up unless you know what's going on. Please feel free to skim this early material and press on to the later chapters if you want. If you're a C++ programmer, you might take a look at the "For C++ Programmers" sidebars as you skim; these sidebars assume you know C++ and often give you information at a more advanced programming level than the surrounding text. In the following chapters, we're going to break C# wide open as we see what it can do for you.

We'll get our start with the code immediately, digging right into things. You can see our first C# application, ch01_01.cs, in Listing 1.1 (all the code in this book is available for download—see the Introduction for the details). As you can surmise from this code, this little application displays the friendly greeting "Hello from C#." when it runs.

LISTING 1.1   The First C# Application (ch01_01.cs)

```
class ch01_01
{
  static void Main()
  {
    System.Console.WriteLine("Hello from C#.");
  }
}
```

Let's get this application to run and then we'll take it apart line by line.

Compiling the First Program

There are two ways to compile our first C# application—using the C# command-line compiler, csc.exe, and using the Visual Studio .NET development tool. We'll take a look at both techniques here. Because csc is free from Microsoft—it's built into the .NET Framework—it's an attractive option for many programmers. On the other hand, building Windows and Web services is very difficult using only csc, so we will use Visual Studio .NET primarily to build those kinds of applications later in the book. Until that point, our code can be used with either csc or Visual Studio .NET—just download the code samples from the Sams Web site at http://www.samspublishing.com. You also can type it into a text editor like WordPad, or copy and paste it directly into Visual Studio .NET, as we're about to see.

To use the C# command-line compiler, csc, you need to install the .NET Framework's Software Development Kit (SDK), which you can download for free at http://msdn.microsoft.com/downloads.

WARNING ON MICROSOFT URLS

Note that Microsoft has the regrettable habit of changing their URLs every few months, so by the time you read this, you might have to go to a different URL than http://msdn.microsoft.com/downloads to download the .NET Framework SDK. In that case, search the http://msdn.microsoft.com site for ".NET Framework Software Development Kit."

After you've installed this download, you can find the csc command-line compiler in your system's root directory; for example, in Windows 2000, for example, that is C:\WINNT\Microsoft.NET\Framework\ xxxxxxxx\csc, where xxxxxxxx is the version of the .NET Framework that you've downloaded. You can add csc to your computer's path so that you can type it directly at the command line, or you can enter its full path (that is, C:\WINNT\Microsoft.NET\ Framework\xxxxxxxx\csc) each time you run it.

To compile our first program, enter the code in Listing 1.1 into a text file named ch01_01.cs, or download it from the Web site for this book. Then open a command-line window (that is, a DOS window—in Windows 2000, you do that with the Start, Programs, Accessories, Command prompt; in Windows XP, it's Start, All Programs, Accessories, Command prompt). Assuming you've added csc to your computer's path, you can simply move to the directory that holds ch01_01.cs and compile it like this (for a list help topics, type csc /?):

```
C:\>csc ch01_01.cs
Microsoft (R) Visual C# .NET Compiler
version xxxxxxxxxxx
for Microsoft (R) .NET Framework version
xxxxxxxx
Copyright (C) Microsoft Corporation 2001-
2002. All rights reserved.
```

SETTING THE PATH VARIABLE

To set your system's Path variable, open the Control panel, double-click System, click the Advanced tab, and then click the Environment Variables button. Double-click the entry for the Path system variable and add the directory that holds csc to that variable (note that paths are separated by semicolons).

RUNNING THE VISUAL STUDIO GROUP COMMAND PROMPT

Alternatively, if you have Visual Studio installed and want to run the command-line compiler, you can run the Visual Studio command prompt, which already has the environment variables set correctly. Just select Start, Start, Programs, Microsoft Visual Studio .NET, Visual Studio .NET Tools, Visual Studio .NET Command Prompt menu item.

This compiles ch01_01.cs into ch01_01.exe, which is what we'll need.

If you have it, you can also use Visual Studio .NET to compile ch01_01.cs into ch01_01.exe. To do that, start Visual Studio .NET now and select the File, New Project to open the New Project dialog box you see in Figure 1.1.

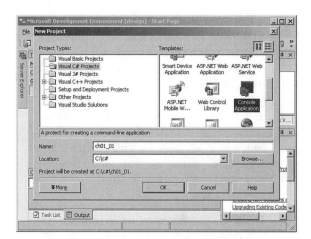

FIGURE 1.1   Creating a new project in Visual Studio .NET.

In the New Project dialog box, select the Visual C# Project folder in the Project Types box, and the Console Applications item in the Templates box. Then enter the name of the new project, ch01_01, in the Name text box and the location where you want to store the project files in the Location box, as you see in Figure 1.1. Click OK to create the new project.

This opens the Visual Studio Integrated Development Environment (IDE), which you see in Figure 1.2. We'll see more on the IDE when it's time to start building Windows applications in Chapter 7, "Creating C# Windows Applications."

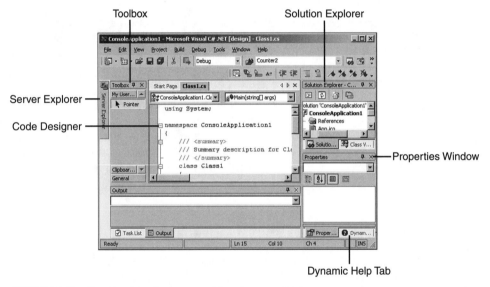

FIGURE 1.2   The Visual Studio Integrated Development Environment.

NAMING SOURCE CODE FILES

Here, we've changed the name of the .CS file to match the name of the class contained in it, ch01_01. That's not necessary in C#, as it is in Java—we could have left the filename as Class1.cs. It's often good programming practice to make a .CS filename match the class it contains, but you don't have to do it that way. For the console applications we develop in this book, all you really have to do is replace the default code Visual Studio supplies and then run the project.

When the IDE appears, the code designer window in the center will hold some skeleton code for a console application. Just replace that code with the first application's code, as you see in Figure 1.3. Next, in the Solution Explorer window, shown in the upper-right corner in Figure 1.2, find the entry for the default .CS file in this project, which will be Class1.cs, and change it to ch01_01.cs by editing that name directly (as you would edit a filename in the Windows Explorer). See Figure 1.3.

That's all it takes—now we're ready to run this new project.

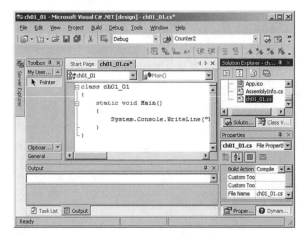

FIGURE 1.3   The code in the IDE.

Running the First Program

To run ch01_01.exe after compiling it with the command-line compiler, just enter ch01_01 at the command prompt. The new application will run and display its message like this:

```
C:\>ch01_01
Hello from C#.
```

That's how you run console applications (if you have problems ending a C# console application, type ^C to break out of it).

To run the example from the Visual Studio .NET IDE, select the Debug, Start Without Debugging menu item, which displays the example at work in a DOS window, as you see in Figure 1.4. Note that the application also automatically displays the prompt "Press any key to continue"; when you do press a key, the DOS window closes.

FIGURE 1.4   Running the first application.

On the other hand, if you select Debug, Start (not Debug, Start Without Debugging), or run the ch01_01.exe file created by Visual Studio .NET outside Visual Studio (by double-clicking ch01_01.exe in the Windows Explorer, for example), that prompt isn't displayed. The DOS window appears only briefly, flickering onscreen and then immediately closing. To display a prompt to the users and wait until the users type a key, you can add this code, which uses ReadLine to wait for user input:

```
class ch01_01
{
  static void Main()
  {
    System.Console.WriteLine("Hello from C#.");
    System.Console.WriteLine("Press any key to continue");
    System.Console.ReadLine();
  }
}
```

When you add this code, you can select Debug, Start in the IDE to run the example. You can also create ch01_01.exe as a stand-alone executable by selecting Build, Build Solution, and then creating ch01_01.exe in a subdirectory of the ch01_01 project directory. (The actual subdirectory depends on several Visual Studio settings, such as whether you're creating a debug-enabled version of your program.) Then you can run ch01_01.exe at the command prompt—the result is the same as when you use the command-line compiler.

And that's it—your first C# program is running.

The next step is to understand C#'s place in the programming world. That programming world starts with the .NET Framework, of which C# is a part.

The .NET Framework in Overview

C# is a big part of the .NET Framework, and you can run C# programs only on computers that have the .NET Framework installed. As you know, .NET is a huge initiative from Microsoft. It creates an entirely new set of Application Programming Interfaces (APIs). It brings together and improves on many older technologies such as COM+, ASP, XML, OOP, SOAP, WSDL, and so on.

.NET provides the platform on which our applications will run, and that platform runs on top of the underlying operating system. There are many components to the .NET Framework, and from our point of view, here are the most important ones:

- Four standard programming languages—C#, Visual Basic .NET, Managed C++, and J#. (If you include languages from other vendors, there are now more than 25 .NET compliant languages.)

- The *Common Language Runtime* (CLR)—An object-oriented platform for Windows and Web development. This is what actually runs your code.

- The *Framework Class Library* (FCL)—An enormous amount of pre-written code that provides built-in support for creating objects such as windows, buttons, list boxes, and thousands more.

The Common Language Runtime is much like the Java virtual machine, which is to say that it provides the environment in which programs execute. The CLR starts programs, checks security issues, manages program execution, assigns memory for programs, and manages that memory through automatic *garbage collection*, a process that disposes of objects no longer being used.

From a programmer's point of view, the Framework Class Library is a major asset, because it contains tens of thousands of pre-written classes, ready for you to use. You can use those classes to create windows and controls like buttons and check boxes, as well as handle strings, security issues, threads, network communications, Web forms, Windows services, and more. Because all that code is already written for you, you have to use only a few lines to put it all to work.

When you compile a program like the first example into an .EXE file, you're not actually creating the machine code that the computer will run. The .EXE file is actually written in Microsoft Intermediate Language (MSIL, also called IL). .NET programs are compiled into MSIL (much like the bytecodes used in Java), and the CLR converts that MSIL into the actual machine code the computer runs using a just-in-time (JIT) compiler (also like Java).

Take a look at how the first example looks in MSIL. Note that the Main method is marked as the program's entry point:

```
.method private hidebysig static void Main() cil managed
{
 .entrypoint
 // Code size    11 (0xb)
 .maxstack 1
 IL_0000: ldstr    "Hello from C#."
 IL_0005: call     void [mscorlib]System.Console::WriteLine(string)
 IL_000a: ret
} // end of method FirstApp::Main
```

In fact, there's often more to a program than just the executable code. For example, you can have image files, help files, other code modules, and so on. In .NET, these files can be packaged together into an *assembly*, which is the .NET unit of deployment. Assemblies appear to the user like single .EXE or .DLL files, but can contain many internal files. They're used for

CROSS-LANGUAGE PROGRAMMING

Because the MSIL created by a C# program is the same type as, say, that created from a Visual Basic .NET program, the CLR can run either without problem. MSIL makes cross-language programming possible, a major asset of .NET programming. You can develop part of your program in C#, and part in Visual Basic .NET, for example. .NET defines its own types using the Common Type System (CTS), which is common to all .NET programming. The CTS prevents the variables defined in different languages from clashing in your application. Any .NET language must adhere to the Common Language Specification (CLS), which sets up the rules for .NET Framework languages and makes sure they don't clash, even when used in the same program.

deployment, security (providing boundaries between different assemblies and between their internal files), versioning, and code reuse. The CLR has a great deal of support for manipulating assemblies, and we're going to be working with assemblies starting in Chapter 13, "Understanding C# Assemblies and Security."

Visual C# .NET

C# is an important aspect of the .NET Framework; it was announced in July 2000, and is built on the shoulders of not only C++, but also Java. Java programmers will find a lot that's familiar in C. Perhaps the most important aspect of Java that came over to C# is the emphasis on security,

particularly on the use of pointers. Although C# still supports pointers, their use is highly restricted, making the old hacker's trick of using pointers to rewrite code impossible to implement. We'll see more on pointers and their place in C# (you have to designate code with pointers in it as "unsafe") in Chapter 13.

FOR C++ PROGRAMMERS

Note the following discussion on C#'s differences from C++.

C# itself was developed by a small team, led by Anders Hejlsberg (who was a major player in the development of both Turbo Pascal and Borland Delphi) and Scott Wiltamuth. There are many differences between C++ and C#. For example, C# does not use header

files as C++ does; it supports an XML style of documentation comments marked with ///, and supports declarative constructs called *attributes*, which add metadata indicating how to handle methods. C# de-emphasizes pointers (sometimes by inventing new safe types, such as *delegates*, which act much like function pointers to let you set up callbacks), implements structs as a lightweight type very different from classes (structs and classes are very close in C++), supports reflection for handling metadata, and more. These are only a few examples.

There are also many small differences that we'll encounter throughout the book—for example, the C# entry point is Main(), not main(), and, unlike ANSI C++, it can return either void or int. Conditional statements such as if are restricted to Boolean operands, which, as we'll see, avoids the confusion between a statement like if(temperature = 212).. and if(temperature == 212)....

C# is an amazingly simple language, and consists of 77 keywords (only a few more than ANSI C++), listed in Table 1.1. All these keywords are reserved words in C#, and cannot be used as identifiers in your code unless you implement them with an ampersand, @ (such as @class). You'll become very familiar with these keywords in the following chapters.

TABLE 1.1

The C# Keywords

KEYWORDS

abstract	event	new	struct
as	explicit	null	switch
base	extern	object	this
bool	false	operator	throw
break	finally	out	true
byte	fixed	override	try
case	float	params	typeof
catch	for	private	uint
char	foreach	protected	ulong
checked	goto	public	unchecked
class	if	readonly	unsafe
const	implicit	ref	ushort
continue	in	return	using
decimal	int	sbyte	virtual
default	interface	sealed	volatile
delegate	internal	short	void
do	is	sizeof	while
double	lock	stackalloc	
else	long	static	
enum	namespace	string	

Now that you've been introduced to .NET and C#'s place in it, you can start dissecting the first example. We'll do that next, taking it apart line by line. Understanding this first simple program will give us the framework we need to run example code over the next 10 chapters.

Dissecting the First Program

Take a look at the first example's code:

```
class ch01_01
{
  static void Main()
  {
```

```
    System.Console.WriteLine("Hello from C#.");
  }
}
```

If you're a C++ programmer, you're probably familiar with what's going on here (with the notable exception that Main is capitalized in C#). Everything begins, as it usually does in C#, with a class statement. A class named ch01_01 is created, whose body will appear inside the curly braces:

```
class ch01_01
{
    .
    .
    .

}
```

C# code is case-sensitive, so class ch01_01 is not the same as class CH01_01. As programmers familiar with object-oriented programming (OOP) know, classes create new *types*, and creating new types is the very heart of OOP. All code must be enclosed in a class (or a similar construct like a struct) in C#. You put code into a class's *methods*; the term method simply refers to a procedure that is a member of a class. In this example, the single method is called Main:

```
class ch01_01
{
  static void Main()
  {
      .
      .
      .
  }
}
```

C# will call the method named Main in your code automatically as soon as the program starts, thus transferring execution to that method. In other words, Main is your program's *entry point*, andyou put the code you want to run first in this method. Declaring Main as static void Main() means we do not need to create an object of this new class in order to call this method (which allows C# to call the method when the program starts). This declaration also specifies void as this method's return type, which means this method does not return any value to the code that calls it. The empty parentheses after its name indicate that you do not pass any data to it.

The code in the Main method is enclosed in the curly braces, which form the body of that method. In this case, that's the single line of code, `System.Console.WriteLine("Hello from C#.");`:

```
class ch01_01
{
  static void Main()
  {
    System.Console.WriteLine("Hello from C#.");
  }
}
```

This line of code is a C# statement, and all statements must end with a semicolon, as in C++ and Java. This statement calls the WriteLine method of the Console class, passing that method the text "Hello from C#.". When you execute this text, "Hello from C#." will appear in the DOS window.

The Console class that supports the WriteLine method is one of the classes built into the Framework Class Library, the FCL. Instead of writing all the code to display text in a DOS window yourself, you can simply call the Console.WriteLine method. Note the dot operator (.) here—Console.WriteLine indicates that we're calling the WriteLine method of the Console class in this case. Console.WriteLine is referred to as System.Console.WriteLine because the Console class is part of the FCL.

When you develop your own classes, it's possible to create one with the same name as one in the FCL, because there are tens of thousands of classes in the FCL. To avoid those kinds of clashes, C# uses *namespaces*, which, as the name implies, define a separate space for named elements. System is the namespace used for most FCL classes, which means that you refer to Console.WriteLine as System.Console.WriteLine.

There's another way to handle the namespace issue. You can add a using statement such as using System; to the beginning of your code, and when C# can't find a method you're calling in your code, it will search the System namespace as well—note that after you indicate you're using the System namespace, you can refer to System.Console.WriteLine simply as Console.WriteLine:

```
using System;

class FirstApp
{
  static void Main()
  {
```

```
    Console.WriteLine("Hello from C#.");
  }
}
```

As we're developing examples in the next few chapters, input and output will be an issue, so it's worth taking a closer look at WriteLine. You've seen how you can use it to display quoted text. You can also use it to display numbers, like this:

```
System.Console.WriteLine(32);
```

This simply displays the number 32 and skips to the next line in the output. Sometimes, you don't want to skip to the next line in the output, as when you display a prompt where the user is supposed to enter some data on the same line and then press <Enter>. You can use the Console.Write method for that, which is the same as Console.WriteLine, except that it doesn't skip to the next line:

```
System.Console.Write("Please enter a number: ");
```

Both Write and WriteLine let you embed values in a quoted string of text. To do so, you use {0} as a placeholder for the first item to be embedded, {1} for the next, and so on, and follow the quoted text with the items you want to embed. Here's an example (note that this example also shows you can break a single C# statement over more than one line, because C# will know the statement is done when it reaches the terminating semicolon—just don't break quoted text this way or you'll introduce extra spaces and a carriage return into the text):

```
class FirstApp
{
  static void Main()
  {
    System.Console.WriteLine("The temperature is between {0} and {1}",
      32, 212);
  }
}
```

The output of this code is as follows:

```
The temperature is between 32 and 212
```

What about reading data in from the user using `ReadLine` and working with that data? To do that, we'll need some way of working with and storing data. Although this is basic stuff, it's worth taking a look at how C# addresses it.

Data Types

Data handling is one of the most important tasks you'll perform in C#. Some data handling is rudimentary, as when you place a quoted string of text in your code, which is called a *literal*:

```
Console.WriteLine("Hello from C#.");
```

Numerical values can also be literals, as when we used 32 and 212 like this:

```
Console.WriteLine("The temperature is between {0} and {1}", 32, 212);
```

When it comes to manipulating your data under programmatic control, you have to go further than that. In general, C# data types fall into the following categories:

- Value types
- Reference types
- Pointer types

We'll take a look at each of these categories in turn.

Value Types

When you copy value types, a copy is made of their *values* (hence the name). Value types are broken into two categories:

- Enumeration types
- Struct types

Enumeration types are created with the `enum` keyword, as we'll see later in this chapter. The struct types contain the user-defined types you create with the `struct` keyword that we'll see in Chapter 3, "C# Object-Oriented Programming," as well as the following built-in simple types:

- Integral
- Floating-point
- Decimal
- Boolean

These simple types are often what people mean when they talk about data storage.

Integral Types

Integral types hold numbers such as -1 or 15. These types include integers (referred to as `int` types) and longs (called `long` types, which have twice the storage capacity of `int` types). You can see the data capacities of the various integral types in Table 1.2.

TABLE 1.2

The C# Integral Types

TYPE	RANGE	SIZE
sbyte	−128 to 127	Signed 8-bit integer
byte	0 to 255	Unsigned 8-bit integer
char	U+0000 to U+ffff	Unicode 16-bit character
short	−32,768 to 32,767	Signed 16-bit integer
ushort	0 to 65,535	Unsigned 16-bit integer
int	−2,147,483,648 to 2,147,483,647	Signed 32-bit integer
uint	0 to 4,294,967,295	Unsigned 32-bit integer
long	−9,223,372,036,854,775,808 to 9,223,372,036,854,775,807	Signed 64-bit integer
ulong	0 to 18,446,744,073,709,551,615	Unsigned 64-bit integer

FOR C++ PROGRAMMERS

In C#, the `long` data type is 64 bits, whereas in C++, it is often 32 bits.

Floating-Point Types

Floating-point types hold data like 3.14159 and -1.503. There are only two built-in floating-point data types in C#, `float` and `double`, as you can see in Table 1.3.

TABLE 1.3

The C# Floating-Point Types

TYPE	APPROXIMATE RANGE	PRECISION
float	$\pm1.5 ? 10^{-45}$ to $\pm3.4 ? 10^{38}$	7 digits
double	$\pm5.0 ? 10^{-324}$ to $\pm1.7 ? 10^{308}$	15-16 digits

Decimal Types

The `decimal` type is a 128-bit data type. Compared to floating-point types, the `decimal` type has greater precision and a smaller range, which makes it suitable for financial and monetary calculations. You can see the range for this type in Table 1.4.

TABLE 1.4
The Decimal Type

TYPE	APPROXIMATE RANGE	PRECISION
decimal	±1.0×10–28 to ±7.9×1028	28–29 significant digits

Boolean Types

Boolean values are used to declare variables to store the Boolean values, true and false.

Here's an important point—all of the simple types are aliases of the .NET Framework types. For example, int is really just another name for the .NET Framework's System.Int32. For a complete list of aliases, see Table 1.5.

> ### FOR C++ PROGRAMMERS
>
> Unlike in C++, data conversions between the bool type and other types (in particular, int) are not allowed in C#.

TABLE 1.5
The .NET Types Corresponding to the C# Simple Types

C# TYPE	.NET FRAMEWORK TYPE
bool	System.Boolean
byte	System.Byte
sbyte	System.SByte
char	System.Char
decimal	System.Decimal
double	System.Double
float	System.Single
int	System.Int32
uint	System.UInt32
long	System.Int64
ulong	System.UInt64
object	System.Object
short	System.Int16
ushort	System.UInt16
string	System.String

Reference Types

Reference types are not as simple as value types. When you create an object of a reference type, that object is stored in general memory allocated for the program, the heap (value types are stored on the stack). When you create an object of a reference type, you use the `new` operator, which returns a reference to that object. When you pass an object of a reference type to a method, you actually pass that reference, not a copy of the object itself (as you do with value types). Here are the keywords you use to declare reference types in C#, and we'll see them all in this book:

- `class`
- `interface`
- `delegate`

There are also some built-in reference types in C#:

- `object`
- `string`

The `string` type is a reference type, but it's so popular that it shares many aspects of value types in C#—for example, you don't have to use the `new` operator when declaring a new string.

Pointers

Pointers are the third data type in C#, and they're strongly discouraged, used only if there's no other way (as when you have to pass a pointer to a Windows API function). You use pointers to "point" to locations in memory, and although pointers are a big part of C++, they've been put on the back burner in C# for security reasons. Although C# can still support pointers, they can only be used in C#'s "unsafe" mode, as we'll see in Chapter 13.

That covers the C# data types and their capabilities—now it's time to put them to work by creating variables.

Variables

You declare variables like this in C# (the syntax we'll use is standard for C# documentation—items in square brackets are optional, and items in italics are placeholders for your own identifiers):

`[attributes] [modifiers] type declarators;`

Here are the parts of this statement:

- *attributes* (optional)—Holds optional declarative meta-information, as we'll discuss in Chapter 14, "Using Attributes and Reflection."

- *modifiers* (optional)—Optional modifiers that include the new modifier and one of the four access modifiers like public and private that we'll see in Chapter 3.

- *type*—One of the C# types—byte, char, short, int, long, float, double, decimal, bool, string, an enum—or a reference type.

- *declarators*—A comma-separated list of declarators. A declarator takes the form *identifier* [= *constant-expression*].

For example, to declare an integer variable named temperature, you can use the statement int temperature; and then assign it a value of 32 like this:

```
int temperature;
temperature = 32;
System.Console.WriteLine("The temperature is {0}.", temperature);
```

You can also initialize variables when you declare them, as in this case, where we're declaring a string variable and assigning it a value in the same step:

```
string greeting = "Hello from C#.";
System.Console.WriteLine(greeting);
```

When you assign literals to variables, C# ensures that the type matches. That means statements like these work to declare variables:

```
int temperature = 32;
double data = 1.53322;
```

However, the default type for floating point literals is double, so statements like these seem like errors to the compiler, because you're assigning what it thinks is a double value to decimal and float variables:

```
decimal dough = 300.5;
float data = 1.53322;
```

To set the type of these literals, you can use the m (or M) suffix for decimal literals and the f (or F) suffix for float literals, like this:

```
decimal dough = 300.5m;
float data = 1.53322f;
```

You can assign values of true or false to Boolean variables this way:

```
bool day = true;
bool night = false;
```

Now that you have a grip on working with variables, it's time to use the Console.ReadLine method to read text, store it, and display it, as you see in Listing 1.2. In ch01_02.cs, the Console.ReadLine method returns the text typed by the user, which we store in a variable named text and then display that text using Console.WriteLine. That's all there is to it.

LISTING 1.2   Reading Text and Displaying it (ch01_02.cs)

```
class ch01_02
{
  static void Main()
  {
    string text;
    System.Console.Write("Type some text: ");
    text = System.Console.ReadLine();
    System.Console.WriteLine("You typed {0}", text);
  }
}
```

Here's what you see when you run ch01_02 and type Hello C#!:

```
C:\>ch01_02
Type some text: Hello C#!
You typed Hello C#!
```

C# uses *definite assignment*, which means that you must initialize a variable before using it (there are a few exceptions to this rule, as you'll see when creating methods). That means that this code will *not* compile:

```
int value;
System.Console.WriteLine(value);
```

FOR C++ PROGRAMMERS

In C#, you must initialize a variable before using it (although an exception is made for "out" parameters used in methods, as we'll see in the next chapter).

There's no official recommendation on how to name variables, but you'll usually see "Camel" notation used for variables (Microsoft no longer recommends its earlier "Hungarian" notation); in this notation, you can make up a variable name of several words, each of which begins with a leading capital letter except the first, like this:

dayOfTheMonth, monthOfTheYear, and so on. For all other identifiers, you usually use Pascal notation, where all the words that make up an identifier begin with a leading capital letter, such as the methods CalculateCompoundInterest, WriteLine, ConnectToInternet, and so on.

Constants

Variables are great for storing values, but sometimes you don't want a value to change, and as in C++, you can make such values into constants. Declaring a constant works just as declaring a variable, except that you also use the const keyword:

```
[attributes] [modifiers] const type declarators;
```

The parts of this statement are just the same as for variables; in fact, declaring a constant is like declaring a variable, but you just use the const keyword. Take a look at ch01_03.cs in Listing 1.3, where we're declaring a constant named pi and displaying its value.

LISTING 1.3 Using a Constant (ch01_03.cs)

```
class ch01_03
{
  static void Main()
  {
    const float pi = 3.14159f;
    System.Console.WriteLine("Pi = {0}", pi);
  }
}
```

Here's what you see when you run this code:

```
C:\>ch01_03
Pi = 3.14159
```

If you try to assign a new value to our constant named pi, your code won't compile. Here's an example, where we're trying to change the value of pi:

```
class ch01_03
{
  static void Main()
  {
    const float pi = 3.14159f;
    pi = 3.14f;
    System.Console.WriteLine("Pi = {0}", pi);
  }
}
```

Here's the error message you get when you try to compile:

```
ch01_03.cs(6,9): error CS0131: The left-hand side of an assignment must be a
    variable, property or indexer
```

Enumerations

Enumerations are an alternative to constants, and provide a way of grouping constants together logically. For example, say you're using a lot of constants like this:

```
const int Sunday = 1;
const int Monday = 2;
const int Tuesday = 3;
const int Wednesday = 4;
const int Thursday = 5;
const int Friday = 6;
const int Saturday = 7;
System.Console.WriteLine("Sunday is day {0}", Sunday);
```

This code will give you this output:

```
Sunday is day 1
```

However, all the constants you've created can be put into an enumeration, which groups them together logically. Here's how you create an enumeration, using the enum statement:

```
[attributes] [modifiers] enum identifier [:base-type] {enumerator-list};
```

Here are the parts of this statement:

- *attributes* (optional)—Holds optional declarative meta-information.

- *modifiers* (optional)—Optional modifiers that include the new modifier and one of the four access modifiers like `public` and `private`.

- *identifier*—The enumeration name.

- *base-type* (Optional)—The underlying type that specifies the storage allocated for each enumerator. It can be any of the integral types except `char`. The default is `int`.

- *enumerator-list*—The enumerators' identifiers separated by commas, optionally including a value assignment.

Enumerations act like groups of constants, which can be any of the built-in signed or unsigned integer types (such as `int`, `Byte`, or `UInt64`, but not `char`). You can see an example in ch01_04.cs, in Listing 1.4, which declares an enumeration named Days (unless you declare a type like this, enum Days :uint {...}, the underlying type used for the constant in enumerations is int). (Note that the values in that example ascend smoothly from 1–7, but enumeration values can take any values consistent with their underlying type.)

LISTING 1.4   Using an Enumeration (ch01_04.cs)

```
class ch01_04
{
  enum Days
  {
    Sunday = 1,
    Monday = 2,
    Tuesday = 3,
    Wednesday = 4,
    Thursday = 5,
    Friday = 6,
    Saturday = 7,
  }

  static void Main()
  {
    System.Console.WriteLine("Sunday is day {0}", (int) Days.Sunday);
  }
}
```

The code in Listing 1.4 will also give you this output:

```
Sunday is day 1
```

Note that we specify the type for constants in the Days enumeration by prefacing them with the cast (int), which casts the member of the enumeration to its underlying type:

```
System.Console.WriteLine("Sunday is day {0}", (int) Days.Sunday);
```

We'll cover casts in a few pages; the upshot is that if you omit that cast, the value of Days.Sunday would be its symbolic name, "Sunday", the value of Days.Monday would be "Monday" and so on, not the integers 1, 2, and so on. That's because in C#, enumerations are formal data types, which means you have to convert them to their underlying types if you want to access the values each enumeration member stands for.

FOR C++ PROGRAMMERS

Whereas C# enumerations are formal types, C++ is a little more loose—in C++, for example, you can assign a member of an enumeration whose base type is int to an integer variable without a type cast.

Arrays

Just as enumerations group constants together, so arrays can be thought of as grouping variables together. There's a lot of support for arrays built into C#, and we'll take a look at it in Chapter 6. As you know, arrays store data values by index. In C#, arrays are reference types, so you can create a new array with the `new` operator. You declare an array as *type*[], where *type* is the data type of each element. For example, here's how to declare an array of five integer elements:

```
int[] array1 = new int[5];
```

FOR C++ PROGRAMMERS

In C#, you need to declare arrays as `type[] name`; the optional C++-style declaration `type name[];` isn't available in C#.

These elements can be addressed with index values 0 to 4, as `array1[0]`, `array1[1]`, up to `array1[4]`. You can see this at work in Listing 1.5, where we've created a C# array, placed data in one of its elements, and displayed that data.

LISTING 1.5   Using an Array (ch01_05.cs)

```
class ch01_05
{
  static void Main()
  {
    int[] array1 = new int[5];
    array1[0] = 1;
    System.Console.WriteLine("The first element holds {0}.", array1[0]);
  }
}
```

You can also initialize each element in an array when you declare the array by assigning it a list of values

```
int[] array1 = {1, 2, 3, 4, 5};
array1[0] = 1;
System.Console.WriteLine("The first element holds {0}.", array1[0]);
```

One common use of arrays is for reading arguments typed on the command line when your code is invoked. If you declare an array of type `string[]` in the parentheses following the `Main` method, C# will fill that array with any command-line arguments. You can see an example in Listing 1.6, set up to take exactly four command-line arguments (any more or any less will cause an error in this example).

LISTING 1.6   Using an Array (ch01_06.cs)

```
class ch01_06
{
  static void Main(string[] args)
  {
    System.Console.WriteLine("You entered: {0} {1} {2} {3}.",
      args[0], args[1], args[2], args[3]);
  }
}
```

Here's what you see when you run this example and type the command-line arguments "Now is the time" into this code:

```
C:\>ch01_06 Now is the time
You entered: Now is the time.
```

FOR C++ PROGRAMMERS

Note that the first element in the command-line argument array holds the first argument passed to the program in C#, not the name of the program as in C++.

Type Conversions in C#

C# is a strongly typed language, and that makes mixing data stored in variables of different data types a process that requires thought. For example, look at this code:

```
int source = 5;
long target;
target = source;
System.Console.WriteLine(target);
```

Here, we're creating an `int` variable, `source`, and a `long` variable, `target`, and assigning the value in `source` to `target`. Although these variables are not of the same data type, no data will be lost, because this is a *widening conversion*, where we're moving from a smaller container (`int`) to a larger one (`long`). Because data is not lost in a widening conversion, C# has no problem making this conversion, and will do so automatically—this is called implicit conversion.

On the other hand, look at this code, where we've switched the data types of the `source` and `target` variables:

```
long source = 5;
int target;
target = source;
System.Console.WriteLine(target);
```

Now it looks to C# as if we're trying to cram a long into an int, and that implies a possible loss of data accuracy. This is a *narrowing conversion*, and you'll see an error message like this when you try to compile:

```
conversion.cs(7,18): error CS0029: Cannot implicitly convert type 'long' to 'int'
```

On the other hand, we happen to know that the long only contains 5, which means you can assign it to an int without loss of accuracy, so we can use an explicit *cast*, (int), to let the compiler know that we really do want to read the value in source, convert that value to an int, and assign that value to target, as you see in ch01_07.cs, in Listing 1.7.

LISTING 1.7   Using an Explicit Type Case (ch01_07.cs)

```
class ch01_07
{
  static void Main()
  {
    long source = 5;
    int target;
    target = (int) source;
    System.Console.WriteLine(target);
  }
}
```

Now the code compiles and runs without problem. Explicit casts, which you create with (*type*), where type is the *type* you're casting to, can be made between many different types in C#. Table 1.6 shows the possibilities for numeric conversions.

TABLE 1.6

Allowed Explicit Type Conversions for C# Numeric Types

FROM	TO
sbyte	byte, ushort, uint, ulong, or char
byte	sbyte or char
short	sbyte, byte, ushort, uint, ulong, or char
ushort	sbyte, byte, short, or char
int	sbyte, byte, short, ushort, uint, ulong, or char
uint	sbyte, byte, short, ushort, int, or char
long	sbyte, byte, short, ushort, int, uint, ulong, or char
ulong	sbyte, byte, short, ushort, int, uint, long, or char
char	sbyte, byte, or short
float	sbyte, byte, short, ushort, int, uint, long, ulong, char, or decimal
double	sbyte, byte, short, ushort, int, uint, long, ulong, char, float, or decimal
decimal	sbyte, byte, short, ushort, int, uint, long, ulong, char, float, or double

What if you're not working with a numeric type? What if you want to convert a string to a number, for example? It's clear that there's more going on here than an explicit cast can handle. In this case, C# supports a `Parse` method for each numeric type, enabling you to convert strings to numbers. For example, `int.Parse` parses strings and returns an `int`, `float.Parse` does the same for `float` values, and so on. You can see an example in ch01_08.cs, Listing 1.8, where we're reading in an integer as a string, parsing it, and displaying it.

LISTING 1.8   Parsing Integers from Strings (ch01_08.cs)

```
class ch01_08
{
  static void Main()
  {
    System.Console.Write("Please enter an integer: ");
    int value = int.Parse(System.Console.ReadLine());
    System.Console.WriteLine("You entered: {0}", value);
  }
}
```

Here's what you might see when you run ch01_08.cs:

```
C:>ch01_08
Please enter an integer: 5
You entered: 5
```

How about going the other way and converting a number to a string? Every object in C# supports the `ToString` method, and you can always call that method to get a string representation of that object. Here's all you need to do to convert an integer to a string:

```
int intNumber = 5;
string text = intNumber.ToString();
```

The .NET Framework also provides the heavy-duty `Convert` class, which can convert most types to other types. For example, here's how you convert a `string` to a C# `int` type (which is an `Int32` type as far as the .NET Framework is concerned):

```
int value = Convert.ToInt32(Console.ReadLine());
```

Unlike the `Parse` method, which only handles strings, the `Convert` class methods can accept all kinds of data—for example, you can pass a `string` to `Convert.ToInt32`, or a `long`, a `float`, and so on. Here are the conversion methods of the `Convert` class:

- Convert.ToBoolean

- Convert.ToByte

- Convert.ToChar

- Convert.ToDateTime

- Convert.ToDecimal

- Convert.ToDouble

- Convert.ToInt16

- Convert.ToInt32

- Convert.ToInt64

- Convert.ToSByte

- Convert.ToSingle

- Convert.ToString

- Convert.ToUInt16

- Convert.ToUInt32

- Convert.ToUInt64

Comments in C#

As you know, commenting your code helps make it a good deal clearer. C# supports three types of comments, C++-style // comments, C-style /*...*/ comments, and XML-style /// comments.

// Comments

The // style of comments are the most commonly used in C#, as in C++. These comments are single-line comments, making the compiler ignore the text following the //:

```
class ch01_01
{
// Display the message.

  static void Main()
  {
```

```
    System.Console.WriteLine("Hello from C#.");
  }
}
```

These comments don't have to be on their own line, of course; you can add them to any line, and the compiler will stop looking for code when it reaches the // on a line:

```
class ch01_01
{
  static void Main()
  {
    System.Console.WriteLine("Hello from C#."); // Show message.
  }
}
```

/*...*/ Comments

/*...*/ comments are multi-line comments; when the compiler reaches /*, it stops reading and compiling code until it reaches the */. Here's an example:

```
class ch01_01
{
  /*
    Display the message.
  */

  static void Main()
  {
    System.Console.WriteLine("Hello from C#.");
  }
}
```

Multi-line comments like this are often used to create documentation blocks, which are usually outlined in asterisks like this:

```
class ch01_01
{
  /*                    *
   *  Display the message.      *
   *                    */

  static void Main()
  {
```

```
     System.Console.WriteLine("Hello from C#.");
   }
}
```

/// Comments

/// comments are *XML documentation
comments*. These comments are stripped out
by various C# tools and treated as XML-style
documentation, stored in an XML file. You
write your comments as XML elements, like
this:

```
class ch01_01
{
   /// <summary>
   ///    Display the message.
   /// </summary>

   static void Main()
   {
     System.Console.WriteLine("Hello from C#.");
   }
}
```

You can then use the /doc switch with the command-line compiler to strip the XML documentation out of your source code and into a file (named doc.xml here) like this:

```
C:\>csc ch01_01.cs /doc:doc.xml
```

Here's what doc.xml looks like:

```
<?xml version="1.0"?>
<doc>
  <assembly>
    <name>t</name>
  </assembly>
  <members>
    <member name="M:ch01_01.Main">
      <summary>
        Display the message.
```

```
      </summary>
    </member>
  </members>
</doc>
```

In this way, you can make your source code almost self-documenting.

You can also create XML documentation in Visual Studio by clicking the project's icon in the Solution Explorer (see Figure 1.2), selecting the View, Property Pages menu item, clicking the Configuration Properties folder, and then clicking the Build item in that folder. Enter a name for the XML Documentation File property and click OK.

Besides creating XML documentation files, you can also create *Web reports* that present the documentation in your code as a clickable set of nodes. When you're creating a Web report, you can use these XML elements in your /// comments:

- <summary></summary> provides a summary.

- <remarks></remarks> gives overview information.

- <param></param> describes a parameter for a method call.

- <returns></returns> Describes the return value of a method.

- <newpara></newpara> starts a new paragraph.

To build a Web report for your project in Visual Studio .NET, select Tools, Build Comment Web Pages; you can see a Web report for the example in Figure 1.5 (where the text from the XML comment appears in the lower-right corner in the center window).

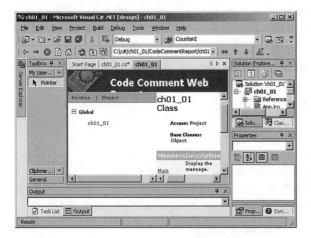

FIGURE 1.5   Creating a Web report from XML comments.

You can also create XML-style documentation comments with `/**...*/` multi-line comments, not just the `///` single-line style, like this:

```
class ch01_01
{
    /**
        <summary>
            Display the message.
        </summary>
    */

    static void Main()
    {
        System.Console.WriteLine("Hello from C#.");
    }
}
```

Creating Expressions and Statements

It's now time to start actually *doing* something with the data discussed so far. The first essential topic in C# coding is the *expression*. An expression can be evaluated and it yields a single value. At the most basic, literals are expressions, because they evaluate to a value. Variables are also expressions, because they evaluate to the value they contain.

Here's another expression—`5 + 3`—which evaluates to 8. In fact, `int1 = 1`, where you assign 1 to the variable `int1`, is an expression, and its value is 1. Because `int1 = 1` is an expression yielding 1, it's legal in C# to create expressions like this: `int3 = int2 = int1 = 1`. We'll be using the term expression frequently throughout this book, and the thing to remember is that an expression is something the C# compiler can evaluate to produce a value.

The next step is to create whole C# statements. C# code consists of statements, not just expressions, and each statement ends with a semicolon. Here are three statements:

```
int int1;
int1 = 5;
System.Console.WriteLine("Hello from C#.");
```

You can also create *compound statements* if you enclose a set of statements in curly braces, `{` and `}`. In C#, you can use a compound statement wherever you'd use a single statement. For example, the `if` statement we're about to take a look at in a few pages works as `if` statements usually do, evaluating an expression and executing a statement if that expression evaluates to true:

```
if(expression)
  statement;
```

Although `if` statements are technically defined to only execute a single statement if their test expression is true, you can make that single statement a compound statement made up of many single statements:

```
if(expression)
  {
    statement1;
    statement2;
    statement3;
      .
      .
      .
  }
```

With the concepts of expressions and statements under our belts, it's time to turn to the next step in C# coding—the C# operators.

Using the C# Operators

C# has the standard set of operators to manipulate your data, and you can see the C# operators arranged by category in Table 1.7. Operators work on *operands* and yield a value. For example, in the expression 5 + 3, 5 is the first operand, + is the operator, 3 is the second operand, and this expression yields a value of 8. Just about all these operators are the same as in other languages, with some exceptions that we'll be seeing throughout the book.

OVERLOADING OPERATORS

As in C++, nearly all of the C# operators can be overloaded—that is, redefined for your own user-defined data types. More on this in Chapter 3.

FOR C++ PROGRAMMERS

Note that C# supports more operators than C++, such as `is` and `typeof`.

TABLE 1.7

The C# Operators by Category

CATEGORY	OPERATORS
Arithmetic	`+ - * / %`
Logical	`&	^ ! ~ && ||` `true false`
String concatenation	`+`

TABLE 1.7

Continued

CATEGORY	OPERATORS
Increment, decrement	++ --
Shift	<< >>
Relational	== != < > <= >=
Assignment	= += -= *= /= %= &= |= ^= <<= >>=
Member access	.
Indexing	[ ]
Cast	( )
Conditional	?:
Delegate concatenation and removal	+ -
Object creation	new
Type information	is sizeof typeof
Overflow exception control	checked unchecked
Indirection and Address	* -> [] &

Assignment Operators

We've already seen the most basic assignment operator at work, the = operator. This operator simply assigns a value to an *lvalue* (an lvalue is an element that corresponds to a location in memory that you can assign a value to, such as a variable):

```
class Assigner
{
  static void Main()
  {
    string text = "Hello from C#.";
    System.Console.WriteLine(text);
  }
}
```

Besides the simple = assignment operator, C# also supports these compound assignment operators: +=, -=, *=, /=, %=, &=, |=, ^=, <<=, and >>=. As in C++ and Java, these operators combine an operation with an assignment. For example, the statement int1 += 5; adds 5 to the current value in int1, and in logical terms is the same as the statement int1 = int1 + 5;.

Arithmetic Operators

The C# arithmetic operators are the same as you've seen elsewhere: + (addition), - (subtraction), * (multiplication), / (division), and % (modulus, which returns the remainder after a division—for example, 16 % 3 equals 1). You use these operators as you would in other languages:

```
class Adder
{
  static void Main()
  {
    int value1 = 5, value2 = 10, result;
    result = value1 + value2;
    System.Console.WriteLine(result);
  }
}
```

Increment and Decrement Operators

As in C++ and Java, the increment and decrement operators, ++ and --, take a little extra discussion, because they're different depending on whether you use them as *prefix* or *postfix* operators. You can use them as prefix operators as in ++variable, which increments the value in a variable before the rest of the statement is executed, or as postfix operators, as in variable++, which increments the value in a variable after the rest of the statement has been executed. You can see an example showing both prefix and postfix usage in ch01_09.cs, Listing 1.9.

LISTING 1.9   Prefix and Postfix Incrementing (ch01_09.cs)

```
class ch01_09
{
  static void Main()
  {
    int value1 = 5, value2 = 5, result1, result2;
    result1 = value1++;
    result2 = ++value2;
    System.Console.WriteLine(result1);
    System.Console.WriteLine(result2);
  }
}
```

The code in ch01_09.cs gives you this result, where you can see that value1 wasn't incremented before its value was assigned to result1, whereas value2 *was* incremented before the assignment:

```
C:\>ch01_09
5
6
```

We'll also take a look at the relational and logical operators when discussing the C# conditional statements later in this chapter.

Operator Precedence

Say you wanted to add 10 to 15 and multiply the result by 4; you might use this expression:

```
10 + 15 * 4
```

And you might expect the result to be 100. Unfortunately, C# will give you a value of 70. What happened? Instead of adding 10 to 15 and multiplying the result by 4, C# performed the multiplication first, multiplying 15 and 4 and adding the result (60) to 10 to get 70. That's because multiplication has higher *precedence* than addition, so the multiplication operation in this example was performed first. You can see the C# operator precedence in Table 1.8, from highest to lowest.

TABLE 1.8

C# Operators Precedence from Highest to Lowest

CATEGORY	OPERATORS
Primary	x.y f(x) a[x] x++ x-- new typeof checked unchecked
Unary	+ - ! ~ ++x --x (T)x
Multiplicative	* / %
Additive	+ -
Shift	<< >>
Relational and type testing	< > <= >= is as
Equality	== !=
Logical AND	&
Logical XOR	^
Logical OR	|
Conditional AND	&&
Conditional OR	||
Conditional	?:
Assignment	= *= /= %= += -= <<= >>= &= ^= |=

You can force C# to ignore the rules of precedence by using parentheses; for example, in the expression (10 + 15) * 4, the addition is performed first, followed by the multiplication, giving you the expected result of 100.

The next step in C# programming is the use of *conditional statements*, also called *branching statements*, which let you make decisions and execute code according to the results of those decisions. There are two conditional statements in C#—the `if` statement and the `switch` statement.

The if Statement

The if statement selects a statement for execution based on the value of a Boolean expression. Here's what this statement looks like formally:

```
if (expression)
  statement1
[else
  statement2]
```

Here are the parts of this statement:

- *expression*—An expression that can be implicitly converted to a bool value. If true, *statement1* is executed, otherwise, *statement2* (if present) will be executed.

- *statement1*—The statement(s) to be executed if *expression* is true. Can be a compound statement.

- *statement2*—The statement(s) to be executed if *expression* is false. Can be a compound statement.

You can see an example in ch01_10.cs, Listing 1.10, where we're playing Blackjack with a user. As long as the value the user enters beats or is equal to our value (18), but doesn't exceed 21, they win; otherwise, we win. To decide the outcome of the game, we use an if statement, as you can see in the code.

LISTING 1.10 Using the if Statement (ch01_10.cs)

```
class ch01_10
{
  static void Main()
  {
    int myNumber = 18;
    System.Console.WriteLine("BlackJack!");
    System.Console.Write("Can you beat my number? Enter 1-21: ");
    int theirNumber = System.Convert.ToInt32(System.Console.ReadLine());
    if (theirNumber >= myNumber && theirNumber <= 21)
    {
      System.Console.WriteLine("You win.");
    } else {
      System.Console.WriteLine("You lose.");
    }
  }
}
```

Take a look at the if statement in this example:

```
if (theirNumber >= myNumber && theirNumber <= 21)
{
  System.Console.WriteLine("You win.");
} else {
  System.Console.WriteLine("You lose.");
}
```

The expression that this if statement tests, theirNumber >= myNumber && theirNumber <= 21, uses the relational operators >= (greater-than-or-equal-to) and <= (less-than-or-equal-to) to create two logical clauses, theirNumber >= myNumber and theirNumber <= 21. The logical operator && (the logical And operator) connects these clauses, insisting that the overall expression is true only if both these clauses are true. In this way, the number the user entered has to beat our number *and* be less than 21. If we had used the logical || operator (the logical Or operator) instead, either of the two clauses could be true for the overall expression to be true.

Here's what you see when you run ch01_10:

```
C:\>ch01_10
BlackJack!
Can you beat my number? Enter 1-21: 17
You lose.


C:\>ch01_10
BlackJack!
Can you beat my number? Enter 1-21: 20
You win.
```

FOR C++ PROGRAMMERS

By demanding that the conditional expression in if statements be of a bool data type, C# goes a long way in eliminating the confusion between == and =.

A popular relational operator is the == operator, which tests for equality. For example, the expression variable == 5 is true if variable holds 5, false otherwise. In C++, confusing == and = in if statements is a classic mistake—for example, instead of writing if(temperature == 32)...., one might write if(temperature = 32)...., and that's a problem because the second version assigns temperature a value of 32, no matter what its original value was. In addition, the expression temperature = 32 evaluates to 32, and because non-zero values evaluate to true in C++, the if statement's enclosed statement would be executed. C# solves this problem to a great extent by insisting that the conditional expressions evaluated by if statements must be of type bool, so if(temperature = 32)... wouldn't compile.

Like C++, C# also makes its logical operators, such as && and ¦¦, *shortcut* operators. If you use these operators to connect two logical clauses in an expression and the overall Boolean value of the expression becomes clear by evaluating the first clause, the second clause will not be evaluated (short-circuiting the evaluation of the entire expression).

For example, if in the expression `theirNumber >= myNumber && theirNumber <= 21`, `theirNumber` is not greater than or equal to `myNumber`, the first clause is `false`, which means the Boolean value of the whole expression must be `false`. This in turn means that C# will not evaluate the second clause because it already knows the answer. That's something to remember in case the second clause does something vital you'll need later, like open a file.

The switch Statement

Besides the `if` statement, the other conditional statement in C# is the `switch` statement. This statement acts much like an extended `if` statement; it can handle multiple tests in a single statement, checking a test expression against various values and executing code when the test expression matches one of the values you've tested it against. Here's what the `switch` statement looks like formally in C#:

```
switch (expression)
{
  case constant-expression:
   statement
   jump-statement
  [default:
   statement
   jump-statement]
}
```

Here are the parts of this statement:

- *expression*—An integral or string type expression used to test against.

- *statement*—The embedded statement(s) to be executed if the test expression matches the current case statement's *constant-expression*.

- *jump-statement*—A jump statement that transfers control out of the `case` body.

■ *constant-expression*—Control is transferred to the body of a case statement according to the value of this expression. A `switch` statement can include any number of `case` statements, but note that no two `case` statements inside the same `switch` statement can have the same *constant-expression*.

FOR C++ PROGRAMMERS

C# case statements work differently than in C++; if you want control to fall through from statement `case1` to statement `case2` in C#, `case1` cannot have *any* executable statements in its body. C++ switch statements don't support the `goto` statements we're about to see.

Here's how it works: Control is transferred to the case statement whose *constant-expression* matches *expression*. If no case statement matches the test expression, the code in the default statement (if present) is executed.

You can see an example, ch01_11.cs, in Listing 1.11. This program asks the user to guess a number (5), and it checks the user's guess against the mystery number with a switch statement.

LISTING 1.11 Using the switch Statement (ch01_11.cs)

```csharp
using System;

class ch01_11
{
  static void Main()
  {

    Console.Write("Guess my number (1-5): ");
    int input = Convert.ToInt32(Console.ReadLine());

    switch (input)
    {
      case 1:
        Console.WriteLine("Wrong, sorry.\n");
        break;
      case 2:
      case 3:
        Console.WriteLine("Neither 2 nor 3 is correct.\n");
        break;
      case 4:
        goto case 1;
      case 5:
        Console.WriteLine("Right!\n");
```

LISTING 1.11   Continued

```
      break;
    default:
      Console.WriteLine("Not a valid guess!\n");
      break;
  }
 }
}
```

If the user guesses 1, the first `case` in the `switch` statement will be executed—note the `break` statement at the end, which terminates the `switch` statement:

```
case 1:
  Console.WriteLine("Wrong, sorry.\n");
  break;
```

If the user guesses 2, control will *fall through* to `case` 3, because there is no code for `case` 2 (note that if you place *any* code in `case` 2, but omit a `break` or `goto` statement, you'll get a compilation error):

```
case 2:
case 3:
  Console.WriteLine("Neither 2 nor 3 is correct.\n");
  break;
```

If the user guesses 4, we send them to the code for `case` 1 with a `goto` statement, which transfers control to the code in the case we specify:

```
case 4:
  goto case 1;
```

And if the user guesses 5, they're right, and we admit the fact:

```
case 5:
  Console.WriteLine("Right!\n");
  break;
```

We've taken care of the numbers 1–5, and if we still haven't left the `switch` statement, the user must have entered an invalid guess. We can handle that error with the (optional) `default` statement, which (if present) is executed if no `case` statement matches:

```
default:
  Console.WriteLine("Not a valid guess!\n");
  break;
```

Preprocessor Directives

The last topic discussed in this chapter is using *preprocessor directives*. These are directives to the compiler, not C# statements, and they enable you to skip compilation of sections of your code that you specify.

Here are the C# preprocessing directives:

- #define and #undef are used to define and undefine, respectively, conditional compilation symbols.

- #if, #elif, #else, and #endif are used to conditionally skip sections of source code.

- #error and #warning are used to display errors and warnings, respectively.

- #region and #endregion are used to mark sections of source code.

- #line is used to control line numbers for errors and warnings.

FOR C++ PROGRAMMERS

In C++, preprocessor directives are evaluated in a preliminary run-through of your code first, and then the code itself is compiled. In C#, on the other hand, all this takes place in the same pass through your code (in fact, it's not "preprocessing" at all).

You can see an example in ch01_12.cs, Listing 1.12. In that example, it's the user's birthday, so we'll display a birthday greeting. To do that, we define a symbol named Birthday and expressly undefine a symbol named NormalDay. Then we can use #if statements to indicate which code we want compiled and which we want to omit, and in this case, we'll only compile a statement to display the birthday greeting.

LISTING 1.12   Using Preprocessor Directives (ch01_12.cs)

```
#define Birthday
#undef NormalDay

using System;

class ch01_12
{
  static void Main()
  {
    #if Birthday
      Console.WriteLine("Happy Birthday!");
    #else
      Console.WriteLine("It's not your birthday.");
```

LISTING 1.12 Continued

```
    #endif

    #if NormalDay
      Console.WriteLine("It's just a normal day.");
    #endif
  }
}
```

Because we've defined the symbol `Birthday`, this code in Listing 1.12 makes the compiler compile the statement `Console.WriteLine("Happy Birthday!");`, but not the statement `Console.WriteLine("It's not your birthday.");`:

```
#if Birthday
  Console.WriteLine("Happy Birthday!");
#else
  Console.WriteLine("It's not your birthday.");
#endif
```

When you compile ch01_12.cs, the only `WriteLine` statement that is actually compiled is `Console.WriteLine("Happy Birthday!");`, so here's the result when you run this program:

```
C:\>ch01_12
Happy Birthday!
```

In Brief

In this chapter, we got our start with C#. Here's an overview of the topics we've covered:

- Visual C# .NET is part of the Microsoft .NET initiative. It's a CLR-compliant language that you can use either in Visual Studio .NET or at the command line.

- The C# data types are fairly standard for programming languages, and they're based on the .NET data types.

- All variables must be declared before use in C#. C# also supports an extensive range of operators for use with your data.

- C# supports conditional or branching statements to allow decision-making in code. We saw the `if` and `switch` statements in this chapter.

- C# also supports a number of preprocessor directives, much like C++, which let you compile your code conditionally, omitting and including sections as you like. You can define or undefine symbols using preprocessor directives, and use those symbols to designate sections of code you want the compiler to see—or ignore.

Basic C# Programming

Loops

Loop constructs are all about executing code iteratively, and as you'd expect, C# supports the standard loops—`for`, `while`, and `do...while`. It also includes another loop construct you might not expect—the `foreach` loop, which lets you loop over C# collections (coming up in Chapter 6) and arrays. We'll see all these loops in this chapter.

The for Loop

The `for` loop is the most basic loop, and it's a programmer favorite. It simply executes a statement (or a block of statements) repeatedly until a test expression evaluates to `false`. Here's what it looks like:

```
for ([initializers]; [expression]; [iterators]) statement
```

Here are the parts of this statement:

- *initializers*—A comma-separated list of expressions (possibly including assignment statements) used to initialize the loop indices or set other starting conditions.

- *expression*—An expression that can be implicitly converted to `bool`. This expression is used to test the loop-termination criteria—when it's false, the loop terminates.

- *iterators*—Expression statement(s) to increment or decrement the loop counters and/or perform other actions after the body of the loop executes.

- *statement*—The embedded statement(s) to be executed.

In this statement, the *initializers* are evaluated first, and you can declare a loop variable that will keep track of the number of iterations there. When the *expression* evaluates to true, the statement(s) are executed and the iterators are evaluated. When *expression* becomes false, the loop terminates. Typically, the statement is a compound statement, enclosed in curly braces.

You can see an example in ch02_01.cs, Listing 2.1. This program asks the user how many pats on the back they require and uses a for loop to display the text "Good work!" that many times. Note that this example declares the loop index variable, loopIndex, in the for loop's parentheses (which means, by the way, that it isn't available outside the loop).

LISTING 2.1   Using the for Loop (ch02_01.cs)

```
class ch02_01
{
  static void Main()
  {
    System.Console.Write("How many pats on the back" +
      " do you require? ");
    int Max = int.Parse(System.Console.ReadLine());

    for (int loopIndex = 1; loopIndex <= Max; loopIndex++)
    {
      System.Console.WriteLine("Good work!");
    }
  }
}
```

Here's the output from ch02_01.cs:

```
C:\>ch02_01
How many pats on the back do you require? 3
Good work!
Good work!
Good work!
```

There are all kinds of `for` loops, of course. For example, because all the expressions in a `for` statement are optional, you can even omit them all to get an infinite loop: `for(;;){}`. You can also use multiple loop indices, like this:

```
for(int x = 1, y = 2; x < 10 && y < 12; x++, y++){...}
```

The while Loop

Another popular loop in C# is the `while` loop, which executes a statement (or a block of statements) until a specified expression evaluates to `false`. Here's what this loop looks like in C#:

```
while (expression) statement
```

Here are the parts of this statement:

- *expression*—An expression that can be implicitly converted to `bool`. The expression is used to test the loop-termination criteria, and the loop terminates when *expression* is false.

- *statement*—The embedded statement(s) to be executed.

While loops keep executing the *statement* as long as *expression* is true. Note that the test of *expression* takes place before execution of the loop, unlike the do...while loops (discussed next). You can see an example, ch02_02.cs, in Listing 2.2. This program just prompts the user to type quit to quit, and uses a while loop to keep reading text until the user types quit.

LISTING 2.2   Using the while Loop (ch02_02.cs)

```
class ch02_02
{
  static void Main()
  {
    System.Console.Write("Type quit to quit: ");
    string text = System.Console.ReadLine();

    while (text != "quit")
    {
      System.Console.Write("Type quit to quit: ");
      text = System.Console.ReadLine();
    }
  }
}
```

Here's what you see when you run this code:

```
C:\>ch02_02
Type quit to quit: stop
Type quit to quit: end
Type quit to quit: terminate
Type quit to quit: quit
C:\>
```

Note that because the loop's test is made at the beginning of the `while` loop, the code has to get the user's first response before even starting the loop, which means duplicating the code in the body of the loop outside the loop. You can fix that with a `do...while` loop, coming up next.

The do...while Loop

The `do...while` loop executes a statement (or a block of statements) repeatedly until a specified expression evaluates to `false`. Unlike the `while` loop, it makes its test *after* the loop body is executed, so it always executes one or more times (that's the difference between these loops). Here's what the `do...while` loop looks like:

```
do statement while (expression);
```

Here are the parts of this statement:

- *expression*—An expression that can be implicitly converted to `bool`. The expression is used to test the loop-termination criteria; when it's `false`, the loop ends.

- *statement*—The embedded statement(s) to be executed.

You can convert the `while` example in Listing 2.2 to use the `do...while` loop, making the example much cleaner because you don't have to artificially summon the first response from the user before the loop begins. The new version appears in ch02_03.cs, Listing 2.3.

LISTING 2.3   Using the do...while Loop (ch02_03.cs)

```
class ch02_03
{
  static void Main()
  {
    string text;

    do
    {
```

LISTING 2.3 Continued

```
        System.Console.Write("Type quit to quit: ");
        text = System.Console.ReadLine();
    } while (text != "quit");
  }
}
```

This example gives the same results as the `while` example shown in ch02_02.cs.

The foreach Loop

The `foreach` statement iterates over all members of a collection or array automatically. Here's what the `foreach` statement looks like:

```
foreach (type identifier in expression) statement
```

Here are the parts of this statement:

- *type*—The type of *identifier*.

- *identifier*—The iteration variable that represents the successive elements in the collection. Note that if the iteration variable is a value type, it is read-only in the body of the loop.

- *expression*—A collection or array.

- *statement*—The embedded statement(s) to be executed.

You use `foreach` to iterate over collections and arrays, and it's very handy, because it iterates over all elements in the collection or array automatically. You don't have to know how many elements there are and keep track of them with your own loop variable. Each time through the loop, *identifier* refers to the current element in the collection, giving you access to each element successively. For example, in the loop `foreach (int element in collection)` `{...}`, `element` will refer to the first item in collection in the first iteration, the second item in the second iteration, and so on.

You can see an example in Listing 2.4, ch02_04.cs, which uses `foreach` to iterate over an array, displaying each element in the array.

FOR C++ PROGRAMMERS

The `foreach` loop is a C#, not C++, construct.

LISTING 2.4   Using the foreach Loop (ch02_04.cs)

```csharp
class ch02_04
{
  static void Main()
  {
   int[] array1 = {0, 1, 2, 3, 4, 5};

   System.Console.Write("Here are the array elements: ");

   foreach (int element in array1)
   {
     System.Console.Write("{0} ", element);
   }
  }
}
```

Here's what you see when you run ch02_04. As you can see, foreach has iterated over all elements in the array:

```
C:\>ch02_04
Here are the array elements: 0 1 2 3 4 5
```

The break and continue Statements

You have more control over loops in C# using the break and continue statements. The break statement lets you break out of a loop, and the continue statement lets you skip to the next iteration of a loop.

Say, for example, that you wanted to display the reciprocals (the reciprocal of 10 is 1/10) of various integers with a for loop, from –3 to 3. However, trying to take the reciprocal of 0 is a problem, because 1/0 is infinite (the result you'll get in C# is the constant NaN, "not a number"). To avoid taking the reciprocal of 0, you can use the break statement to break out of the loop, as you see in ch02_05.cs, Listing 2.5.

LISTING 2.5   Using the break Statement (ch02_05.cs)

```csharp
class ch02_05
{
  static void Main()
  {
   for(int loopIndex = -3; loopIndex <= 3; loopIndex++)
   {
```

LISTING 2.5   Continued

```
      if(loopIndex == 0){
         break;
      }
      System.Console.WriteLine("The reciprocal of {0} is {1}",
         loopIndex, 1/(float) loopIndex);
   }
  }
}
```

Here's what you see when you run this program:

```
C:\>ch02_05
The reciprocal of -3 is -0.3333333
The reciprocal of -2 is -0.5
The reciprocal of -1 is -1
```

That's fine as far as it goes, but that's not very far. The loop simply ended when it encountered a value of 0. We can do better in this case with the continue statement, which just skips the troublesome 0 by continuing to the next iteration of the loop. You can see how this works in Listing 2.6, ch02_06.cs.

LISTING 2.6   Using the continue Statement (ch02_06.cs)

```
class ch02_06
{
  static void Main()
  {
   for(int loopIndex = -3; loopIndex <= 3; loopIndex++)
   {
      if(loopIndex == 0){
         continue;
      }
      System.Console.WriteLine("The reciprocal of {0} is {1}",
         loopIndex, 1/(float) loopIndex);
   }
  }
}
```

Here's what you see when you run ch02_06.cs. Note that the problematic reciprocal of 0 was skipped:

```
C:\>ch02_06
The reciprocal of -3 is -0.3333333
The reciprocal of -2 is -0.5
The reciprocal of -1 is -1
The reciprocal of 1 is 1
The reciprocal of 2 is 0.5
The reciprocal of 3 is 0.3333333
```

The goto Statement

The goto statement has long been a pariah among programmers because of its capability to produce unstructured code, but it does have its uses (or it wouldn't have been included in C#). In fact, we saw the primary use for goto in Chapter 1, "Essential C#," where we used it in a switch statement to transfer control to another case statement:

```
using System;

class ch01_13
{
  static void Main()
  {

    Console.Write("Guess my number (1-5): ");
    int input = Convert.ToInt32(Console.ReadLine());

    switch (input)
    {
      case 1:
        Console.WriteLine("Wrong, sorry.\n");
        break;
      .
      .
      .
      case 4:
        goto case 1;
      .
      .
      .
    }
  }
}
```

You can use goto in these three forms in C#:

- goto *identifier*;

- goto case *constant-expression*; (in switch statements)

- goto *default*; (in switch statements)

In the goto *identifier* form, you need to label a line of code with an identifier, followed by a colon. That looks like this:

```
Top: System.Console.WriteLine("Welcome!");
.
.
.
//Let's start over
goto Top;
```

The general use of goto in cases like this is, of course, strongly discouraged, because it creates unstructured *spaghetti code*—code that jumps all over the place, which is very hard to deal with and debug.

Creating Methods

The next step in coding is to divide your code into *methods*. Methods are members of classes that hold code and can be *called* to execute that code. We've already seen how to write and work with the Main method, so this idea should be somewhat familiar. Here's how you declare a method in C#:

```
[attributes] [modifiers] type identifier ([[out][ref]
type parameter, [[out][ref]type parameter, ...]]) statement
```

Here are the parts of this declaration:

- *attributes* (Optional)—Hold additional declarative information, as we'll see in Chapter 14, "Using Attributes and Reflection."

- *modifiers* (Optional)—The allowed modifiers are new, static, virtual, abstract, override, and a valid combination of the four access modifiers we'll see in the next chapter.

- *type*—The return type of the method.

- *identifier*—The method name.

- *parameter*—A parameter passed to the method.

- *statement*—The statement(s) that make up the body of the method.

Let's take a look at an example. Like the Main method, you can simply add another method to a class. This new method is called DisplayMessage, and, when called, simply displays the customary greeting:

```
class ch02_07
{
  void DisplayMessage()
  {
    System.Console.WriteLine("Hello from C#.");
  }

  static void Main()
  {
    .
    .
    .
  }
}
```

FOR C++ PROGRAMMERS

Methods in C# are like methods in C++, except that they can use ref and out keywords, can use attributes, and do not support default values. See the upcoming "For C++ Programmers" sidebars for more information.

That was simple enough. Unfortunately, actually calling DisplayMessage from the code executing in the Main method is a little trickier. It's tricky because Main is declared static so that C# doesn't have to create an object to call Main. However, the new method, DisplayMessage, is not static, so you *do* need an object to call it. We can solve this problem by creating a new object of the entire class (that's ch02_07 here) and calling the DisplayMessage method of that object, as you see in Listing 2.7 (Chapter 3 covers the difference between static and non-static class members in depth).

LISTING 2.7 Creating a Method (ch02_07.cs)

```
class ch02_07
{
  void DisplayMessage()
  {
    System.Console.WriteLine("Hello from C#.");
```

LISTING 2.7   Continued

```
    }

    static void Main()
    {
        ch02_07 obj = new ch02_07();
        obj.DisplayMessage();
    }
}
```

Now when you run ch02_07, you see that the method was indeed called, because you see the message:

```
C:\>ch02_07
Hello from C#.
```

Passing Data to Methods

You can also pass data to methods. There are a few differences here between C# and C++ as well, in order to avoid the use of pointers and enable you to avoid having to initialize variables before passing them by reference.

You pass arguments to methods as in other languages—as a comma-separated list—and you must declare those arguments and their types in the argument list of the method when you declare that method. You can see an example in ch02_08.cs, Listing 2.8, where the DisplayMessage method is passed one argument, which holds the text the method should display.

LISTING 2.8   Passing Data to a Method (ch02_08.cs)

```
class ch02_08
{
    void DisplayMessage(string text)
    {
        System.Console.WriteLine(text);
    }

    static void Main()
    {
        ch02_08 obj = new ch02_08();
        obj.DisplayMessage("Hello from C#.");
    }
}
```

This example gives you the same output as ch02_07.cs.

Returning Data from Methods

Besides passing data to methods, you can also return data, of course, and you use the `return` statement for that purpose. Here's what that looks like:

```
return [expression];
```

If the return type of a method is `void`, you can omit a `return` statement. You can only return single values, although that value can be an array or other collection. Here's an example, a method named `Addem`, which takes two `int` values and returns their sum as a `long`:

```
long Addem(int value1, int value2)
{
  return value1 + value2;
}
```

You can see this method at work in Listing 2.9, where `Addem` is used to add 2 and 3.

LISTING 2.9   Returning Data from a Method (ch02_09.cs)

```
class ch02_09
{
  long Addem(int value1, int value2)
  {
    return value1 + value2;
  }

  static void Main()
  {
    ch02_09 obj = new ch02_09();
    System.Console.WriteLine("2 + 3 = {0}", obj.Addem(2, 3));
  }
}
```

Here's what you see when you run ch02_09:

```
C:\>ch02_09
2 + 3 = 5
```

Passing Data By Reference

If you pass a reference object, like an array, to a method, C# will pass that reference, which means you can change the values in the original object. For example, take a look at ch02_10.cs in Listing 2.10. It passes an array whose elements are 1, 2,

FOR C++ PROGRAMMERS

C# uses ref and out instead of pointers to pass value types by reference, as discussed in this section.

and 3 to a method named ChangeElement, which changes the last element to 4. Because arrays are passed by reference, we have access to the original, passed array, so ChangeElement changes the last element in that array as well.

LISTING 2.10   Passing an Array (ch02_10.cs)

```
class ch02_10
{
  void ChangeElement(int[] passedArray)
  {
    passedArray[2] = 4;
  }

  static void Main()
  {
    ch02_10 obj = new ch02_10();
    int[] array1 = {1, 2, 3};
    obj.ChangeElement(array1);
    System.Console.WriteLine("array1[2] = {0}", array1[2]);
  }
}
```

Here are the results. As you can see, the last element was indeed changed to 4:

```
C:\>ch02_10
array1[2] = 4
```

That works if you pass reference types, but not if you pass value types. For example, if you simply passed an integer to a method and wanted that method to fill that integer with a value accessible back in the calling code, you'd have to indicate that you want to pass that integer by reference. You can do so with the `ref` keyword (which C# uses so you don't have to pass a pointer to the item you're passing by reference).

You can see an example in ch02_11.cs, Listing 2.11. This example passes an integer by reference to a method named `GetTemperature`, which places the current temperature into that integer:

```
obj.GetTemperature(ref temperature);
```

Note the `ref` keyword here—you must use it in the method declaration as well as when you pass the integer variable (making the formal type of that argument `ref int`), as you see in Listing 2.11.

LISTING 2.11   Passing a Value Type by Reference (ch02_11.cs)

```
class ch02_11
{
  void GetTemperature(ref int temp)
  {
    temp = 32;
  }

  static void Main()
  {
    ch02_11 obj = new ch02_11();
    int temperature = 0;
    obj.GetTemperature(ref temperature);
    System.Console.WriteLine(
      "The current temperature is = {0}", temperature);
  }
}
```

Here's what you see when you run this code:

```
C:\>ch02_11
The current temperature is = 32
```

Note that because you must use a definite assignment in C#, we have to assign a value to the temperature variable in ch02_11.cs before using it—even though it simply needs to be filled with a value from the `GetTemperature` method:

```
int temperature = 0;
obj.GetTemperature(ref temperature);
```

C# actually provides for this case with the out keyword, which works like ref except that you don't have to initialize an out parameter before passing it to a method. You can see an example in ch02_12.cs, Listing 2.12. Note that in that example, we don't have to initialize temperature before passing it to the GetTemperature method. This example gives you the same results as ch02_11.

LISTING 2.12 Passing a Value Type As an out Argument (ch02_12.cs)

```
class ch02_12
{
  void GetTemperature(out int temp)
  {
    temp = 32;
  }

  static void Main()
  {
    ch02_12 obj = new ch02_12();
    int temperature;
    obj.GetTemperature(out temperature);
    System.Console.WriteLine(
      "The current temperature is = {0}", temperature);
  }
}
```

So, you can pass value items by reference with the ref keyword, and you can avoid having to initialize them before passing them if you use the out keyword. (Technically speaking, value items you pass by value are called "in" parameters, although there is no in keyword for this purpose.)

Passing a Variable Number of Arguments

You can also set up methods to accept variable numbers of arguments. Although this functionality has been largely replaced by overloading methods, as we'll see in Chapter 3, it still has its uses. To declare a method so that it can accept a variable number of parameters, you can use a parameter array, which you create with the params keyword. You use this keyword in the declaration of an array in the method's argument list, and that array must be the last item in the argument list (if you mixed the varying number of values intended for the parameter array and standard parameters, C# would have no idea where the parameter array ended).

THE PARAMETER ARRAY NEED NOT BE THE ONLY ITEM PASSED

Note that it wasn't necessary to pass the actual number of parameters in the parameter array to Addem (in fact, it would have been far easier to loop over that array with a `foreach` statement). This example uses this approach simply to emphasize that the parameter array need not be the only item you can pass when passing multiple parameters.

You can see an example in ch02_13.cs, Listing 2.13. Here, the Addem method is set up to add values—you pass it the number of integer values you want to add, followed by the actual integers to add. As you can see, you can call this method with a variable number of arguments. In the method itself, you need only to loop over the passed parameter array:

```
System.Console.WriteLine("1 + 2 = {0}", obj.Addem(2, 1, 2));
System.Console.WriteLine("1 + 2 + 3 = {0}", obj.Addem(3, 1, 2, 3));

long Addem(int numberParams, params int[] paramArray)
{
  for(int loopIndex = 0; loopIndex < numberParams; loopIndex++){
      total += paramArray[loopIndex];
  }
  .
  .
  .
}
```

LISTING 2.13   Passing a Variable Number of Arguments (ch02_13.cs)

```
class ch02_13
{
  long Addem(int numberParams, params int[] paramArray)
  {
    int total = 0;
    for(int loopIndex = 0; loopIndex < numberParams; loopIndex++){
      total += paramArray[loopIndex];
    }
    return total;
  }

  static void Main()
  {
    ch02_13 obj = new ch02_13();
    System.Console.WriteLine("1 + 2 = {0}", obj.Addem(2, 1, 2));
```

LISTING 2.13 Continued

```
        System.Console.WriteLine("1 + 2 + 3 = {0}", obj.Addem(3, 1, 2, 3));
    }
}
```

Here's what you see when you run this example:

```
C:\>ch02_13
1 + 2 = 3
1 + 2 + 3 = 6
```

Scope

Now that we're dividing our code into methods, *scope* becomes an issue. As you know, an identifier's scope is its region of visibility in your code. We'll discuss this more in Chapter 3 when we discuss object-oriented programming, because OOP is largely about scoping issues, but it's an issue when writing methods as well.

For example, a variable that you declare in a method—a *local* variable like `total` in the `Addem` method in Listing 2.13—is not available to the code in other methods unless you make special provisions. In fact, this is one of the major reasons to create methods: to compartmentalize your code. If you declare a variable outside any method (making it a *field* of the enclosing class, as we'll discuss in the next chapter), that variable is available to the code in any of the class's methods. You can see an example of this in ch02_14.cs, Listing 2.14. In this case, the variable `text` is declared outside any method, making it available to the code in all methods. In this example, the code in `Main` and `DisplayMessage` accesses this variable.

LISTING 2.14 Setting a Field's Scope (ch02_14.cs)

```
class ch02_14
{
    string text;

    void DisplayMessage()
    {
        System.Console.WriteLine(text);
    }

    static void Main()
    {
        ch02_14 obj = new ch02_14();
        obj.text = "Hello from C#.";
        obj.DisplayMessage();
```

LISTING 2.14   Continued

```
    }
}
```

Recursion

It's also worth noting briefly that C# supports *recursion*, the capability of a method to call itself. The usual example showing recursion is a factorial program (for example, `factorial(6)` = 6! = 6 x 5 x 4 x 3 x 2 x 1 = 720), and you can see our factorial program in ch02_15.cs, Listing 2.15. This example calculates and displays the value of 6!. Note in particular that to find the value of *x*!, the `factorial` method calls itself to get the value of (`--x`)!.

LISTING 2.15   Using Recursion (ch02_15.cs)

```
class ch02_15
{
    long factorial(int value)
    {
        if(value == 1){
            return 1;
        } else {
            return value * factorial(--value);
        }
    }

    static void Main()
    {
        ch02_15 obj = new ch02_15();
        System.Console.WriteLine("6! = {0}", obj.factorial(6));
    }
}
```

Here's what you see when you run this example, where we see that 6! = 720:

```
C:\>ch02_15
6! = 720
```

Exception Handling

An *exception* has come to stand for almost any type of error, but that's not how the word was originally intended. For example, *bugs* are errors in the logic of your code, but they're not exceptions. Similarly, the term *error* is often reserved for a problem in user input—the user might have entered an out-of-bounds number, for example. However, you are supposed to handle such errors with validation code that checks input and other user actions without resorting to the special kind of code meant to handle exceptions.

Exceptions are not preventable in the same way as errors. They're the problems that occur because of runtime conditions—you might be out of memory, for example, or there might not be a disk in a drive.

In C#, as in many other languages, you handle exceptions with `try-catch` statements. The `try-catch` statement is made up of a `try` block followed by one or more `catch` clauses, which are the actual handlers for different exceptions. The `try-catch` statement looks like this:

```
try try-block
catch (exception-declaration-1) catch-block-1
     .
     .
     .
catch (exception-declaration-n) catch-block-n
```

Here are the parts of this statement:

- *try-block*—Contains the sensitive code that can cause an exception.

- *exception-declaration-1, exception-declaration-n*—An exception object declaration used to filter the exceptions this `catch` block will handle.

- *catch-block-1, catch-block-n*—Contains exception handler code.

The exceptions you use in C# use objects based on the `System.Exception` class. C# itself bases several class in the `System.Exception` class, as you see here:

```
System.Object
  System.Exception
  System.ApplicationException
  System.IO.IsolatedStorage.IsolatedStorageException
  System.Runtime.Remoting.MetadataServices.SUDSGeneratorException
  System.Runtime.Remoting.MetadataServices.SUDSParserException
  System.SystemException
  System.Windows.Forms.AxHost.InvalidActiveXStateException
```

Each of these classes in turn has many exception classes based on it; for example, the most common types of exceptions to use in your own programming are based on the `SystemException` class. Here are those exceptions (many of which have other exceptions based on them as well):

```
System.Object
  System.Exception
    System.SystemException
      System.AppDomainUnloadedException
      System.ArgumentException
      System.ArithmeticException
      System.ArrayTypeMismatchException
      System.BadImageFormatException
      System.CannotUnloadAppDomainException
      System.ComponentModel.Design.Serialization.CodeDomSerializerException
      System.ComponentModel.LicenseException
      System.ComponentModel.WarningException
      System.Configuration.ConfigurationException
      System.Configuration.Install.InstallException
      System.ContextMarshalException
      System.Data.DataException
      System.Data.DBConcurrencyException
      System.Data.Odbc.OdbcException


      System.Data.OracleClient.OracleException
      System.Data.SqlClient.SqlException
      System.Data.SqlServerCe.SqlCeException
      System.Data.SqlTypes.SqlTypeException
      System.Drawing.Printing.InvalidPrinterException
      System.EnterpriseServices.RegistrationException
      System.EnterpriseServices.ServicedComponentException
      System.ExecutionEngineException
      System.FormatException
      System.IndexOutOfRangeException
      System.InvalidCastException
      System.InvalidOperationException
      System.InvalidProgramException
      System.IO.InternalBufferOverflowException
      System.IO.IOException
      System.Management.ManagementException
      System.MemberAccessException
      System.MulticastNotSupportedException
      System.NotImplementedException
      System.NotSupportedException
      System.NullReferenceException
      System.OutOfMemoryException
      System.RankException
      System.Reflection.AmbiguousMatchException
```

```
System.Reflection.ReflectionTypeLoadException
System.Resources.MissingManifestResourceException
System.Runtime.InteropServices.ExternalException
System.Runtime.InteropServices.InvalidComObjectException
System.Runtime.InteropServices.InvalidOleVariantTypeException
System.Runtime.InteropServices.MarshalDirectiveException
System.Runtime.InteropServices.SafeArrayRankMismatchException
System.Runtime.InteropServices.SafeArrayTypeMismatchException
System.Runtime.Remoting.RemotingException
System.Runtime.Remoting.ServerException
System.Runtime.Serialization.SerializationException
System.Security.Cryptography.CryptographicException
System.Security.Policy.PolicyException
System.Security.SecurityException
System.Security.VerificationException
System.Security.XmlSyntaxException
System.ServiceProcess.TimeoutException
System.StackOverflowException
System.Threading.SynchronizationLockException
System.Threading.ThreadAbortException
System.Threading.ThreadInterruptedException
System.Threading.ThreadStateException
System.TypeInitializationException
System.TypeLoadException
System.TypeUnloadedException
System.UnauthorizedAccessException
System.Web.Services.Protocols.SoapException
System.Xml.Schema.XmlSchemaException
System.Xml.XmlException
System.Xml.XPath.XPathException
System.Xml.Xsl.XsltException
```

Let's take a look at an example. Say that you create a new array with four elements and then try to access element 10. That will cause an IndexOutOfRangeException, which we can handle. First, we enclose the sensitive code that will cause an exception in a try block like this:

```
class ch02_16
{
  void Exceptor()
  {
    int[] array = new int[4];
    try
    {
```

```
      array[10] = 4;
      System.Console.WriteLine(array[10]);
    }
    .
    .
    .
  }

  static void Main()
  {
    ch02_16 obj = new ch02_16();
    obj.Exceptor();
  }
}
```

You can handle the exceptions that occur in this try block in a catch block that follows the try block, as you see in Listing 2.16. This catch block simply informs the user that an exception occurred by displaying the (unenlightening) message "Exception!".

LISTING 2.16   Using a try-catch Block (ch02_16.cs)

```
class ch02_16
{
  void Exceptor()
  {
    int[] array = new int[4];
    try
    {
      array[10] = 4;
      System.Console.WriteLine(array[10]);
    }

    catch
    {
      System.Console.WriteLine("Exception!");
    }
  }

  static void Main()
  {
    ch02_16 obj = new ch02_16();
    obj.Exceptor();
  }
}
```

Here's what you see when you run this example:

```
C:\>ch02_16
Exception!
```

This works, but it doesn't tell the user a heck of a lot about what's going on. Let's go deeper into this topic.

Filtering Exceptions

You can specify which type of exception a catch block is to catch in C#. The generic catch block we saw in Listing 2.16 looks like this:

```
catch
{
  System.Console.WriteLine("Exception!");
}
```

You can specify which type of exception you want a catch block to catch by enclosing that type in parentheses after the keyword catch. Because all exceptions are based on System.Exception, that means that this catch block is the same as the previous one:

```
catch(System.Exception)
{
  System.Console.WriteLine("Exception!");
}
```

This still doesn't tell us much, because this catch block will catch any exception, which means we still don't know which exception occurred. To catch only the IndexOutOfRangeException, we can use a catch block like this:

```
catch(System.IndexOutOfRangeException)
{
  System.Console.WriteLine("Array Index Exception!");
}
```

This catch block only catches IndexOutOfRangeException exceptions. To catch not only IndexOutOfRangeException, but also any other kind that occurs, you can use multiple catch blocks, as you see in ch02_17.cs, Listing 2.17. The first catch block in that example catches IndexOutOfRangeException exceptions, and the second catches any other exception.

LISTING 2.17   Filtering Exceptions (ch02_17.cs)

```
class ch02_17
{
  void Exceptor()
  {
    int[] array = new int[4];
    try
    {
      array[10] = 4;
      System.Console.WriteLine(array[10]);
    }

    catch(System.IndexOutOfRangeException)
    {
      System.Console.WriteLine("Array Index Exception!");
    }

    catch(System.Exception)
    {
      System.Console.WriteLine("Exception!");
    }
  }

  static void Main()
  {
    ch02_17 obj = new ch02_17();
    obj.Exceptor();
  }
}
```

Here's what you see when you run ch02_17:

```
C:\>ch02_17
Array Index Exception!
```

Catching specific exceptions allows you to filter your exception handling, responding to individual exceptions individually. You can use as many catch blocks as you like, all catching different types of exceptions from a single try block.

When you filter your exceptions, here's something to keep in mind—if exception A is based on exception B, and you want to catch both exceptions, make sure you catch exception B first. Here's an example to make this clear. The `DivideByZeroException` is based on the `ArithmeticException` class. If you arrange your `catch` blocks like this:

```
catch(System.ArithmeticException)
{
  System.Console.WriteLine("Arithmetic exception!");
}

catch(System.DivideByZeroException)
{
  System.Console.WriteLine("Divide by zero!");
}
```

when a `DivideByZeroException` occurs, the first `catch` block will catch it, because `DivideByZeroException` is based on the `ArithmeticException` class. In fact, no exception can reach the `DivideByZeroException` catch block here (the compiler will let you know of this problem). To do this right, make sure you catch the exception that other exceptions are based on last, like this:

```
catch(System.DivideByZeroException)
{
  System.Console.WriteLine("Divide by zero!");
}

catch(System.ArithmeticException)
{
  System.Console.WriteLine("Arithmetic exception!");
}
```

The finally Statement

Bear in mind that when an exception occurs in a `try` block, execution jumps from that `try` block to a `catch` block, which means that any code left in the `try` block won't execute. That can be a problem, because you might have done something in the `try` block that needs to be cleaned up. For example, you might have locked some resource or opened a file. That's where the `finally` block comes in. The code in the `finally` block is always executed (unless the program itself has halted) whether or not there has been an exception. In other words, the `finally` block is where you put your clean-up code, if you need it. You can use a `finally` block with or without `catch` blocks like so:

```
try try-block
[catch (exception-declaration-1) catch-block-1]
    .
```

.

.

```
[catch (exception-declaration-n) catch-block-n]
finally finally-block
```

Here are the parts of this statement:

- *try-block*—Contains the sensitive code that might cause an exception.

- *exception-declaration-1, exception-declaration-n*—An exception object declaration used to filter the exceptions this `catch` block will handle.

- *catch-block-1, catch-block-n*—Contains the exception handling code.

- *finally-block*—Contains the code you want executed whether or not there's been an exception.

You can see a `finally` block example in ch02_18.cs, Listing 2.18. In this example, the `finally` block ensures that the message `"Ending..."` is always displayed.

LISTING 2.18   Using a finally Block (ch02_18.cs)

```
class ch02_18
{
  void Exceptor()
  {
    int[] array = new int[4];
    System.Console.WriteLine("Starting...");

    try
    {
      array[10] = 4;
      System.Console.WriteLine(array[10]);
    }

    catch(System.IndexOutOfRangeException)
    {
      System.Console.WriteLine("Array Index Exception!");
    }

    catch(System.Exception)
    {
      System.Console.WriteLine("Exception!");
    }
```

LISTING 2.18   Continued

```
    finally
    {
        System.Console.WriteLine("Ending...");
    }
}

  static void Main()
  {
    ch02_18 obj = new ch02_18();
    obj.Exceptor();
  }
}
```

Here's what you see when you run this code. Even though an exception occurred, the code in the `finally` block was indeed executed:

```
C:\>ch02_18
Starting...
Array Index Exception!
Ending...
```

Working with Exception Objects

So far, we've used exceptions only in a simplistic way. We can filter various exceptions, but only to determine which one occurred. There is more to handling an exception, however. You can also use the *properties* of the `System.Exception` object to get more information.

Properties in C# are accessed with the dot (.) operator, just as methods are, but you specify them only by name, without passing arguments or using parentheses as you do with methods (although you *can* set up properties to take arguments). For example, the property `exception.Message` of the exception object `exception` holds a system message describing the exception. You can see the properties of exception objects in Table 2.1.

FOR C++ PROGRAMMERS

Handling exceptions in C++ can cause problems with memory leaks when objects aren't cleaned up correctly and aren't deallocated in the `finally` block. That's changed in C#, which implements first-rate garbage collection. In fact, many programmers think that the new garbage collection facilities in C# are C#'s biggest step forward. We'll read about these facilities in the next chapter.

FOR C++ PROGRAMMERS

Properties in C# are like fields in C++ with built-in accessor methods; these methods let you restrict access to the actual data stored for each property.

TABLE 2.1

Public Properties of Exception Objects

PROPERTY	PURPOSE
HelpLink	Returns or sets a link to a help file associated with this exception.
Message	Returns a message that describes the current exception.
Source	Returns or sets the name of the application or the object that causes the error.
StackTrace	Returns a string showing the call stack at the time the current exception occurred.
TargetSite	Returns the method that caused the current exception.

To be able to refer to the current exception object and so gain access to its properties, you must name it in the catch block's declaration, just as you do an argument passed to a method. For example, here we're naming the exception object e, making it accessible inside this catch block:

```
catch(System.IndexOutOfRangeException e)
{
  System.Console.WriteLine(e.Message);
}
```

You can see how this works in ch02_19.cs, Listing 2.19, which displays the Message property of an exception object.

LISTING 2.19   Using Exception Object Properties (ch02_19.cs)

```
class ch02_19
{
  static void Main()
  {
    ch02_19 obj = new ch02_19();
    obj.Exceptor();
  }

  void Exceptor()
  {
    try
    {
      int[] array = new int[4];
      array[10] = 4;
      System.Console.WriteLine(array[10]);
    }
```

LISTING 2.19   Continued

```
    catch(System.IndexOutOfRangeException e)
    {
        System.Console.WriteLine(e.Message);
    }
  }
}
```

You can see the system message for array index out-of-bounds exceptions when you run this
example, like this:

```
C:\>ch02_19
Index was outside the bounds of the array.
```

Throwing Exceptions

When an exception occurs, it is *thrown* (which is why you use `catch` blocks to catch it). Using
the `throw` statement, you can throw exceptions yourself; you don't need to rely on an actual
exception to occur in your code. The `throw` statement looks like this:

```
throw [expression];
```

whereby *expression* is the exception object (can be omitted when rethrowing the current
exception object in a `catch` clause).

You can see an example showing how this works in ch02_20.cs, Listing 2.20. In that example,
we're purposely throwing an `IndexOutOfRangeException` exception in the `try` block, which is
then caught in the following `catch` block.

LISTING 2.20   Throwing an Exception (ch02_20.cs)

```
class ch02_20
{
  static void Main()
  {
    ch02_20 obj = new ch02_20();
    obj.Exceptor();
  }

  void Exceptor()
  {
    try
    {
```

LISTING 2.20   Continued

```
      throw new System.IndexOutOfRangeException();
    }

  catch(System.IndexOutOfRangeException e)
    {
      System.Console.WriteLine(e.Message);
    }
  }
}
```

Here's what you see when you run this code:

```
C:\>ch02_20
Index was outside the bounds of the array.
```

You can also use the throw statement to *rethrow* an exception. For example, you might catch an exception in a nested try-catch statement and if you want an outer catch block to handle the exception, you can just rethrow it. You can see how this works in ch02_21.cs, Listing 2.21.

LISTING 2.21   Rethrowing an Exception (ch02_21.cs)

```
class ch02_21
{
  static void Main()
  {
    ch02_21 obj = new ch02_21();
    obj.Exceptor();
  }

  void Exceptor()
  {
    try
    {
      try
      {
        int[] array = new int[4];
        array[10] = 4;
      }

      catch(System.IndexOutOfRangeException e)
      {
```

LISTING 2.21   Continued

```
            //Rethrow the exception
            throw e;
        }
    }

    catch(System.IndexOutOfRangeException e)
    {
        System.Console.WriteLine(e.Message);
    }
    }
}
```

Here's what you see when you run ch02_21:

```
C:\>ch02_21
Index was outside the bounds of the array.
```

Note that if an exception handler cannot be found in the current method to handle an exception, C# automatically moves back to the method that called the present method to search for an appropriate catch block. If it can't find one there, it moves back one level again and keeps going until it does.

SHOP TALK

CATCHING EXCEPTIONS

It can be a pain trying to catch every possible exception your code can generate, but you should do it anyway. C# uses just-in-time debugging, and even if you compile your console applications so that they don't include debugging information, the user will still see a just-in-time debugger dialog box appear if there's been an unhandled exception. After dismissing that dialog box, the user will see a message about an unhandled exception and a stack trace, which is going to be very confusing and make you look unprofessional. So check on possible exceptions and handle them, even if only with a generic catch block.

Throwing Custom Exceptions

You can also create your own exception, based on the System.Exception class. We'll discuss how to derive classes from other classes in Chapter 4, but if you're familiar with the idea of inheritance, take a look at ch02_22.cs. In that example, we're creating a new exception class,

TooHotException, based on the System.Exception class. After you create this new class, you're free to throw exceptions of that class, as in this example.

LISTING 2.22   Throwing a Custom Exception (ch02_22.cs)

```
public class TooHotException :
  System.Exception
{
  public TooHotException(string text):
    base(text)
  {
  }
}

public class ch02_22
{
    public static void Main()
    {
      ch02_22 obj = new ch02_22();
      obj.Exceptor();
    }

    public void Exceptor()
    {
      try
      {
        throw new TooHotException("Temperature is 97F!");
      }

    catch (TooHotException e)
    {
      System.Console.WriteLine(e.Message);
    }
  }
}
```

When you create an object of your custom exception class, you install a message in that object, like this: throw new TooHotException("Temperature is 97F!"). You can see that message displayed when the example runs:

```
C:\>ch02_22
Temperature is 97F!
```

All the details on class inheritance and deriving one class from another, as we've done here, are covered in Chapter 4.

The final topic in this chapter is a big one in C#—string handling. This is the last basic programming topic we'll need to grasp before going on to OOP.

Working with Strings

FOR C++ PROGRAMMERS

C# strings are built on the .NET String type, which makes them quite different from C++ strings. For example, the C++ string class contains 24 methods (including overloaded versions) to search strings, all with the term find in their name. C# contains 18 methods (also including overloaded versions) to search strings, all with the term IndexOf in their names.

Strings in C# correspond to the .NET String type, and there's a great deal of functionality built into them. For example, you can append one string to another with the + operator:

```
string string1 = "Hello ";
string string2 = "there!";
string2 = string1 + string2;
```

This code leaves "Hello there!" in string2. You can also access the individual characters as if the string were an array, like this:

```
string string1 = "Hello ";
char char1 = string1[1];
```

This code leaves 'e' in char1 (note that, as in C++, character literals are enclosed in single quotes, like 'e', whereas string quotes are enclosed in double quotes, like "Hello!"). Strings come with many built-in methods as well. For example, take a look at the code in ch02_23.cs, Listing 2.23, which determines the length of a string and uses the IndexOf method to find the location of a substring in that string.

LISTING 2.23   Using String Methods (ch02_23.cs)

```
class ch02_23
{
  static void Main(string[] args)
  {
    string now = "Now is the time.";
    System.Console.WriteLine("In the string '{0}', which is " +
      "{1} characters long, 'the' begins at position {2}.",
      now, now.Length, now.IndexOf("the"));
  }
}
```

Here's what you see when you run this code:

```
C:\>ch02_23
In the string 'Now is the time.', which is 16 characters long, 'the' begins
at position 7.
```

You can find a summary of the more significant string methods in Table 2.2. All these methods can be applied directly to strings in C#.

TABLE 2.2

Significant String Methods

METHOD	PURPOSE
Compare	Compares two given String objects.
Concat	Concatenates one or more strings.
Copy	Copies the current string.
CopyTo	Copies a given number of characters from a given position in this string to a given position in an array of Unicode characters.
EndsWith	Determines whether the end of this string matches the given string.
IndexOf	Returns the 0-based index of the first occurrence of a string, or one or more characters within this string.
IndexOfAny	Returns the 0-based index of the first occurrence in this string of any character in a specified array of Unicode characters.
Insert	Inserts a given string at a given index position in this string.
Join	Concatenates a given separator string between each element of a given string array, resulting in a single concatenated string.
LastIndexOf	Reports the index position of the last occurrence of a given Unicode character or string within this string.
LastIndexOfAny	Reports the index position of the last occurrence in this string of one or more characters given in a Unicode array.
PadLeft	Right-aligns the characters in this string, padding the left with spaces or a given Unicode character.
PadRight	Left-aligns the characters in this string, padding the right with spaces or a given Unicode character.
Remove	Deletes a given number of characters from this string.
Replace	Replaces all occurrences of a given Unicode character or string in this string with another given Unicode character or string.
Split	Identifies the substrings in this string that are delimited by one or more characters given in an array, and stores the substrings into a string array.
StartsWith	Determines whether the beginning of this string matches the given string.
Substring	Returns a substring from this string.
ToCharArray	Copies the characters in this string to a Unicode character array.

TABLE 2.2
Continued

METHOD	PURPOSE
ToLower	Returns this string in lowercase.
ToUpper	Returns this string in uppercase.
Trim	Removes all occurrences of a set of characters you specify from the beginning and end of this string.
TrimEnd	Removes all occurrences of a set of characters in an array from the end of this string.
TrimStart	Removes all occurrences of a set of characters in an array from the beginning of this string.

As in other languages, you can also embed *escape sequences*, which start with a backslash, \, in strings. These escape sequences have these special meanings:

- \ordinary characters are characters other than . $ ^ { [(|) * + ? \ that stand for themselves.

- \a is a bell (alarm).

- \b is a backspace.

- \t is a tab.

- \r is a carriage return.

- \v is a vertical tab.

- \f is a form feed.

- \n is a new line.

- \e is an escape.

- \0XX is an ASCII character as octal (up to three digits).

- \xXX is an ASCII character using hexadecimal representation (exactly two digits).

- \cX is an ASCII control character (for example, \cC is ^C).

- \uXXXX is a Unicode character using hexadecimal representation (exactly four digits).

- \, when followed by a character that is not recognized as an escaped character, is the same as that character.

For example, the string "Now\tis\tthe\ttime." is interpreted to have three tab characters in it (and will appear that way if you display it with Console.WriteLine). And you can embed double quotation marks in string by escaping them like this: "He said, \"Now is the time.\"". If you display this string with Console.WriteLine, you'll see He said, "Now is the time."

Sometimes, however, escape characters get in the way, as when you want to use the string "c:\csharp\folder1\timer". In this case, you want the backslashes to stand for directory separators, not escape characters. You can escape each backslash to preserve it as a backslash, "c:\\csharp\\folder1\\timer", or can turn off escaping in C# by prefacing a string literal with an ampersand, @, like this: @"c:\csharp\folder1\timer".

FOR C++ PROGRAMMERS

In C#, the prefix @ in front of a string turns off escaping.

You can see another example using string methods in ch02_24.cs, Listing 2.24; in this example, we're using the string Insert method to insert "not " into the string "Now is the time.", giving us "Now is not the time.".

LISTING 2.24   Using the Insert Method (ch02_24.cs)

```
class ch02_24
{
  static void Main(string[] args)
  {
    string now = "Now is the time.";
    now = now.Insert(7, "not ");
    System.Console.WriteLine(now);
  }
}
```

Here's the result of ch02_24:

```
C:\>ch02_24
Now is not the time.
```

Besides the methods you see in Table 2.2, C# strings also enable you to work with *regular expressions*, which C++ does not.

Working with Regular Expressions

Regular expressions give you the ability to manipulate and search strings using a special syntax, and there is a great deal of support for regular expressions in C#. A regular expression can be applied to text, and can search and modify that text. Regular expressions are a language all their own, and it's not the easiest language to work with. Despite that, regular expressions are gaining popularity, and we'll see why as we work with them here.

A full treatment on creating regular expressions is beyond the scope of this book (this topic alone would take a complete chapter), but you can find many useful regular expressions already built into the Regular Expression Editor in the C# IDE. Here are some of the pre-built regular expressions you'll find there:

- Internet Email Address:
  `\w+([-+.]\w+)*@\w+([-.]\w+)*\.\w+([-.]\w+)*`

- Internet URL: `http://([\w-]+\.)+[\w-]+(/[\w- ./?%&=]*)?`

- US Phone number: `((\(\d{3}\) ?)|(\d{3}-))?\d{3}-\d{4}`

- German Phone Number: `((\(0\d\d\) |(\(0\d{3}\) )?\d )?\d?\d\d \d\d \d\d|\(0\d{4}\) \d \d\d-\d\d?)`

- US Social Security Number: `\d{3}-\d{2}-\d{4}`

As you can see, regular expressions are terse and pretty tightly packed. In the previous regular expressions, `\w` stands for a "word character" such as a letter or underscore, `\d` stands for a decimal digit, . matches any character (unless it's escaped as `\.`, in which case it simply stands for a dot), + stands for "one or more of," * stands for "zero or more of," and so on.

Let's take a look at an example. Say, for example, that you wanted to pick all the lowercase words out of a string.

Using Regular Expression Matches

Say that we had some sample text, `"Here is the text!"`, and we wanted to pull all words that only had lowercase letters out of it. To match words with lowercase letters only, you start with the regular expression `\b` token, which stands for a *word boundary*. That is, the transition in a string from a word character (like *a* or *d*) to a non-word character (like a space or punctuation mark), or vice versa. You can also create a *character class*, which lets you match a character from a set of characters using square brackets. For example, the character class `[a-z]` matches any lowercase letter, from a to z.

CREATING REGULAR EXPRESSIONS

For more on regular expressions and how to create them, search for "Regular Expression Syntax" in the C# documentation in the IDE, or take a look at `http://www.perldoc.com/perl5.8.0/pod/perlre.html`. (C#'s regular expression handling is based on the Perl language's regular expression specification.)

USING THE IDE'S PRE-BUILT REGULAR EXPRESSIONS

How do you open the IDE's Regular Expression Editor? You can do that by creating a Web application (see Chapter 8, "Creating C# Web Applications"). Then, add a Web regular expression validation control from the toolbox to a Web form, and click the control's Validation property in the Properties window, which opens the Regular Expression Editor. This editor displays many pre-built regular expressions, including the ones discussed here, ready and available for use.

So to match lowercase words, we can use the regular expression \b[a-z]+\b. The + operator means "one or more of," so this is a word boundary, followed by one or more lowercase letters, followed by a word boundary.

Now we have the regular expression—how do we use it? Using the System.Text. RegularExpressions.Regex class, we can create a new RegEx object, which holds your regular expression:

```
using System.Text.RegularExpressions;

class ch02_25
{
  static void Main()
  {
    string text = "Here is the text!";

    Regex regularExpression = new Regex(@"\b[a-z]+\b");
      .
      .
      .
```

Next, we can pass the regular expression object's Matches method the text we want to search, and this method will return an object of the MatchCollection class, holding the text that matched our regular expression:

```
  static void Main()
  {
    string text = "Here is the text!";

    Regex regularExpression = new Regex(@"\b[a-z]+\b");

    MatchCollection matches = regularExpression.Matches(text);
      .
      .
      .
```

This MatchCollection object contains the matches in text to our regular expression. All we have to do now is to loop over that object with a foreach loop to display those matches, as you see in ch02_25.cs, Listing 2.25.

LISTING 2.25   Using Regular Expressions (ch02_25.cs)

```
using System.Text.RegularExpressions;

class ch02_25
{
  static void Main()
  {
    string text = "Here is the text!";

    Regex regularExpression = new Regex(@"\b[a-z]+\b");

    MatchCollection matches = regularExpression.Matches(text);

    foreach (Match match in matches)
    {
      if (match.Length != 0)
      {
        System.Console.WriteLine(match);
      }
    }
  }
}
```

Here's what you see when you run this code:

```
C:>ch02_25
is
the
text
```

As you can see, the code found and displayed the lowercase words in the test string.

Using Regular Expression Groups

Regular expressions can also use *groups* to perform multiple matches in the same text string. For example, take a look at this string:

```
"Order number: 1234 Customer number: 5678"
```

Say that you wanted to pick out the order number (1234) and customer number (5678) from this text. You can match a digit with \d, so to match a four-digit number, you use \d\d\d\d.

Here's a regular expression that will match the string (note that in regular expressions, characters match themselves, so "Order number" in the regular expression will match "Order number" in the text string, and so on):

```
"Order number: (\d\d\d\d) Customer number: (\d\d\d\d)"
```

Note the parentheses around the four-digit numbers; these create match groups. The first group match will hold the order number and the second group match will hold the customer number. In the Perl language, there are various ways of accessing the text that a group matches; in C#, you *name* the group. For example, including the directive ?<order> names a group order, so we can name our two groups order and customer like this:

```
"Order number: (?<order>\d\d\d\d) "Customer number: (?<customer>\d\d\d\d)"
```

After we apply this regular expression to the sample text, we need to recover the text that matched each group to get the order and customer numbers. You do that with a Match object's Groups property—for example, *match*.Groups["order"] will return the match to the order group. You can see this at work in ch02_26.cs, Listing 2.26, where we're recovering matches to the order and customer groups.

LISTING 2.26   Using Regular Expression Groups (ch02_26.cs)

```csharp
using System.Text.RegularExpressions;

class ch02_26
{
  static void Main()
  {
    string text = "Order number: 1234 Customer number: 5678";

    Regex regularExpression =
      new Regex(@"Order number: (?<order>\d\d\d\d) " +
      @"Customer number: (?<customer>\d\d\d\d)");

    MatchCollection matches = regularExpression.Matches(text);

    foreach (Match match in matches)
    {
      if (match.Length != 0)
      {
        System.Console.WriteLine("Order number: {0}",
          match.Groups["order"]);
        System.Console.WriteLine("Customer number: {0}",
          match.Groups["customer"]);
```

LISTING 2.26   Continued

```
        }
      }
    }
}
```

Here's what you see when you run this code. As you can see, the code picked out the order and customer numbers:

```
C:\>ch02_26
Order number: 1234
Customer number: 5678
```

Using Capture Collections

You can even use the same group name multiple times in the same regular expression. For example, take a look at this text:

```
"Order, customer numbers: 1234, 5678";
```

Say that you wanted to get the two four-digit numbers here. In this case, you could use this regular expression with two named groups—both of which are named number:

```
"(?<number>\d\d\d\d), (?<number>\d\d\d\d)"
```

Now when you try to display the matches to the number group, you might use this code:

```
Regex regularExpression =
  new Regex(@"(?<number>\d\d\d\d), (?<number>\d\d\d\d)");

MatchCollection matches = regularExpression.Matches(text);

foreach (Match match in matches)
{
  if (match.Length != 0)
  {
    System.Console.WriteLine(match.Groups["number"]);
  }
}
```

The problem here is that when you run this code, you'll only see this result, which is the second number we're looking for:

```
5678
```

The second number group match overwrote the first group match. To find the matches to both groups even though they have the same name, you can use the Captures collection, which contains all the matches to groups with a particular name. In this case, `match.Groups["number"].Captures` will return a Captures collection of Capture objects holding all the matches to the number group. And all we have to do is to loop over that collection and display the matches we've found. You can see how this works in ch02_27.cs, Listing 2.27, which uses two groups named number in the same regular expression and displays the matches to both groups.

LISTING 2.27   Using Regular Expression Capture Groups (ch02_27.cs)

```
using System.Text.RegularExpressions;

class ch02_27
{
  static void Main()
  {
    string text = "Order, customer numbers: 1234, 5678";

    Regex regularExpression =
      new Regex(@"(?<number>\d\d\d\d), (?<number>\d\d\d\d)");

    MatchCollection matches = regularExpression.Matches(text);

    foreach (Match match in matches)
    {
      if (match.Length != 0)
      {
        foreach (Capture capture in
          match.Groups["number"].Captures)
        {
          System.Console.WriteLine(capture);
        }
      }
    }
  }
}
```

Here are the results of this code, which picked up both matches:

```
C:\>ch02_27
1234
5678
```

And that's it—now you're working with regular expressions in C#. We have some basic C# programming under our belts at this point; the next step, starting in Chapter 3, is where C# really starts to come into its own—in object-oriented programming.

In Brief

In this chapter, we took a look at some basic C# programming. Here's an overview of the topics we covered:

- C# includes several iterative statements: `for`, `while`, `do...while`, and `foreach`. The first three loops—`for`, `while`, `do...while`—are the old standards that appear in many programming languages, but the `foreach` loop is something new for C++ programmers coming to C#.

- The `foreach` loop is designed to loop over a collection, which includes arrays. This loop is useful when you want to loop over the elements in a collection, because it loops over them all automatically, without using a loop index. Loop indices, as you use with a `for` loop, are prone to off-by-one errors (as when you use < instead of <= in the termination expression of the loop), so `foreach` is a very popular addition to the language.

- The process of creating methods in C# is very similar to creating methods in C++. We took a look at how to create a method, call it, pass data to a method, and return data from a method. We also saw how to write methods that can accept variable numbers of arguments and make use of recursion.

- To avoid the use of pointers, C# has to get a little innovative when it comes to passing value types by reference. Passing variables by reference is good when you want to return multiple values from a method, and C# supports passing value types by reference with the `ref` and `out` keywords. You use the `ref` keyword to pass a value type by reference, and the `out` keyword when you want to do the same thing but also avoid having to initialize the variable before passing it to a method.

- You can handle runtime exceptions with `try-catch-finally` statements. You saw how to enclose sensitive code in a `try` block, catch exceptions in a `catch` block, filter exceptions, and rethrow them as needed. You even took a look at creating custom exceptions and throwing them.

- C# also has a large number of string methods available, as well as some that support the use of regular expressions.

C# Object-Oriented Programming

Creating Classes

This chapter discusses object-oriented programming in C#. OOP is what C# is all about; in this chapter, we're going to specialize on this topic. You may well be an accomplished OOP programmer already, in which case it's still a good idea to scan this chapter. OOP in C# has several differences from all other object-oriented languages.

If you're an OOP programmer, you know that object-oriented programming centers on creating types. The simple type int lets you declare integer variables, and in the same way, you can create your own classes, which contain not only data like the simple types, but methods as well. Just as you create integer variables with the int type, so you create objects from classes. An integer variable is an instance of the int type, just like an object is an instance of a class.

Classes are types, but are far more powerful than the simple types like int and float. Not only can you customize your data storage using classes, but you can also add methods to classes. That kind of compartmentalization—where data and methods are rolled up into a single class—is the entire reason that OOP was introduced in the first place. It enables the programmers to deal with larger programs. The process of wrapping related data and methods into a class (and so preventing them from cluttering up the rest of the program) to create a single entity is called *encapsulation*.

You create classes in C# with the class statement:

```
[attributes] [modifiers] class identifier [:base-list] { class-body }[;]
```

Here are the parts of this statement:

- *attributes* (Optional)—Attributes hold additional declarative information, as we'll see in Chapter 14, "Using Attributes and Reflection."

- *modifiers* (Optional)—The allowed modifiers are new, static, virtual, abstract, override, and a valid combination of the four access modifiers we'll see in this chapter.

- *identifier*—The class name.

- *base-list* (Optional)—A list that contains the base class and any implemented interfaces, separated by commas.

- *class-body*—Declarations of the class members.

FOR C++ PROGRAMMERS

The semicolon after a class declaration is optional in C#, unlike C++.

We've been using classes since the first page of this book, as in example ch01_01.cs:

```
class ch01_01
{
    static void Main()
    {
        System.Console.WriteLine("Hello from C#.");
    }
}
```

Here, the code is all contained in one class, the ch01_01 class. But there's nothing to stop you from creating other classes in the same file. For example, here, we've added another class, Calculator, with one method, Addem, which adds two integers and returns their sum:

```
class ch03_01
{
    static void Main()
    {
        .
        .
        .
    }
}
```

```
class Calculator
{
  public long Addem(int value1, int value2)
  {
    return value1 + value2;
  }
}
```

We've created a new class now—the `Calculator` class. To put that class to use, we simply have to create an object of that class.

Creating Objects

To create an object, also called an *instance*, of a class, you use the new keyword. We've seen how this process works; you can see how we create a new object of the `Calculator` class in ch03_01.cs, Listing 3.1, and use that object's `Addem` method to add 2 and 3. Note the parentheses after `Calculator` in the statement `Calculator obj = new Calculator();`. These parentheses are necessary when you use the new keyword. They let you pass data to a class's *constructor*, the special method that lets you initialize the data in a class. We'll go into depth about constructors later in this chapter.

LISTING 3.1   Creating a New Class (ch03_01.cs)

```
class ch03_01
{
  static void Main()
  {
    Calculator obj = new Calculator();
    System.Console.WriteLine("2 + 3 = {0}", obj.Addem(2, 3));
  }
}

class Calculator
{
  public long Addem(int value1, int value2)
  {
    return value1 + value2;
  }
}
```

Here's what you see when you run this example, ch03_01:

```
C:\>ch03_01
2 + 3 = 5
```

In C#, all objects are based on the System.Object class, which means that they already support the methods built into that class. You can see those methods in Table 3.1. Note in particular the ToString method, which returns a string representation of an object. You can customize this method to return a string for your own classes by overriding this method, as we'll see in the next chapter.

TABLE 3.1

Public Methods of System.Object Objects

METHOD	MEANS
Equals	Indicates whether two Object instances are equal.
GetHashCode	Serves as a hash function for a particular type.
GetType	Returns the Type of the current instance.
ReferenceEquals	Determines whether the specified Object instances are the same instance.
ToString	Returns a String that represents the current Object.

It's worth mentioning that you can also create simple variables using new as well, because even those simple types are based on the System.Object class and have their own constructors. Here's an example:

```
int int1 = new int();
int int2 = new int(5);   //Initialize int2 to 5
```

The first statement here creates a new int variable named int1. Remember that you can't use initialized variables in C#; in this case, int1 is automatically initialized to 0. In other words, the first statement above is logically identical to:

```
int int1 = 0;
```

You can see the default values of the various value types created when you use the new operator in Table 3.2. Note that, although you can't set reference types to a default value of 0 as you see for value types in Table 3.2, their default value is null (which means they do not reference an object on the heap).

TABLE 3.2

Default Values of Value Types

VALUE TYPE	DEFAULT VALUE
bool	false
byte	0
char	'\0'
decimal	0.0M
double	0.0D
enum	The value of the expression (E)0 (where E is the enum identifier)
float	0.0F
int	0
long	0L
sbyte	0
short	0
struct	The value produced by setting all value-type fields to their default values and all reference-type fields to null
uint	0
ulong	0
ushort	0

Using Access Modifiers

As mentioned at the beginning of the chapter, *encapsulation*, the capability to hide data and methods to stop them from cluttering up the rest of your code, is one of the biggest advantages of OOP. Encapsulating data and methods not only ensures that they don't clutter up the rest of your code, it also ensures that the rest of your code doesn't interfere with them. You can use access modifiers to set the allowed access to not only classes, but also to all members of those classes. Here are the available access modifiers:

- The public keyword gives a type or type member public access, the most permissive access level. There are no restrictions on accessing public members.

- The protected keyword gives a type or type member protected access, which means it's accessible from within the class in which it is declared, and from within any class derived from the class that declared this member. As discussed in the next chapter, a protected member of a base class is accessible in a derived class only if the access takes place through the derived class type.

- The internal keyword gives a type or type member internal access, which is accessible only within files in the same assembly. It is an error to reference a member with internal access outside the assembly within which it was defined. The C++ analog is friend.

■ The private keyword gives a type or type member private access, which is the least permissive access level. Private members are accessible only within the body of the class or the struct in which they are declared. It is a compile-time error to reference a private member outside the class or the struct in which it is declared.

FOR C++ PROGRAMMERS

The C++ counterpart for the C# internal access modifier, which restricts members to access within the same assembly, is friend.

The following five accessibility levels can be specified using the access modifiers: public, protected, internal, internal protected, and private.

Note that if you don't specify an access modifier for a type or type member, the default access modifier is private. For example, you might have noticed that we explicitly declared the Addem method public in the Calculator class (see Listing 3.1). We did that so we could access Addem using an object of the Calculator class in the program's main class, ch03_01. If we had another method, Subtractem, that we declared private in the Calculator class, Subtractem would be private to the Calculator class, which means that we can't access it using objects of that class. For example, this code won't compile:

```
class ch03_01
{
  static void Main()
  {
    Calculator obj = new Calculator();
    System.Console.WriteLine("2 + 3 = {0}", obj.Addem(2, 3));
    //This won't work!!
    System.Console.WriteLine("3 - 2 = {0}", obj.Subtractem(3, 2));
  }
}


class Calculator
{
  public long Addem(int value1, int value2)
  {
    return value1 + value2;
  }

  private long Subtractem(int value1, int value2)
  {
    return value1 - value2;
  }
}
```

Here's the error you'd see if you tried to compile this code:

```
ch03_01.cs(7,49): error CS0122: 'Calculator.Subtractem(int, int)'
is inaccessible due to its protection level
```

We'll see the protected keyword, which you use primarily with class inheritance, in the next chapter, and discuss the internal keyword in more depth in Chapter 13, "Understanding C# Assemblies and Security," when we discuss assemblies.

It's now time to get into some in-depth OOP as we create class members, including fields, methods, and properties.

Creating Fields and Using Initializers

The first type of class member we'll take a look at is the *field*, also called a *data member*. A field is just a class-level variable, outside any method. If you make your field public, it's accessible using an object of your class; for example, take a look at the Messager class here, which has a field named Message that holds the message that a method named DisplayMessage will display:

```
class Messager
{
  public string message;

  public void DisplayMessage()
  {
    System.Console.WriteLine(message);
  }
}
```

FOR C++ PROGRAMMERS

C# doesn't support this kind of C++ class definition, where you can use one access modifier for multiple members:

```
class Customer
{
  private:
    string firstName;
    string lastName;

  public:
    string GetName() {}
    void SetName(string firstName,
string lastName) {}
    .
    .
    .
}
```

DON'T MAKE FIELDS PUBLIC

Although this example shows how to make a field public, it's usually not good programming practice to give external code direct access to the data in your objects. Instead, it's better to use accessor methods or properties, coming up in the next two topics.

Because the message field is public, you can access it using objects of this class. For example, you can assign a string to the message field of a messager object and then call its DisplayMessage method to display that message, as you see in ch03_02.cs, Listing 3.2.

LISTING 3.2   Creating Fields (ch03_02.cs)

```
class ch03_02
{
  static void Main()
  {
    Messager obj = new Messager();
    obj.message = "Hello from C#.";
    obj.DisplayMessage();
  }
}

class Messager
{
  public string message = "Default message.";

  public void DisplayMessage()
  {
    System.Console.WriteLine(message);
  }
}
```

Here are the results when you run this example. As you can see, we can store data in our new object's public field message, which the DisplayMessage method of that object can use:

```
C:\>ch03_02
Hello from C#.
```

You can also initialize fields with *intializers*, which are just like the initial values you assign to variables. For example, you can use an initializer to assign the string "Default message." to the Message field like this:

```
class Messager
{
  public string message = "Default message.";

  public void DisplayMessage()
  {
    System.Console.WriteLine(message);
  }
}
```

If you don't use an initializer, fields are automatically initialized to the values in Table 3.2 for simple values, and to `null` for reference types.

You can also make fields read-only using the `readonly` keyword:

```
public readonly string message = "Default message.";
```

When a field declaration includes a `readonly` keyword, assignments to that field can occur only as part of the declaration, with an initializer, or in a constructor in the same class.

Creating Methods

We were introduced to creating methods in Chapter 2, "Basic C# Programming," but there are a few more considerations to add. First, as we saw in ch03_01.cs, Listing 3.1, methods can be declared with access modifiers, and that's important when you're creating objects. Declaring a method `public` makes it accessible outside an object, for example, whereas declaring it `private` locks it away inside the object.

Now that we're thinking in terms of objects and methods, it's also important to discuss the `this` keyword. This keyword works the same in C# as it does in C++, and it refers to the current object in which your code is executing. For example, say you're writing code to set up a button that appears in a window and you want to pass the whole button to a method named `ColorMe`. You can do that by passing the `this` keyword to that method:

```
public class Button
{
  public void SetUp()
  {
    ColorMe(this);
  }
}
```

Another use for the `this` keyword is to refer to a field in the current object. In this example, the method `SetMessage` is passed a parameter named `message`, which it is supposed to store in the field of the same name in the current object. To avoid confusion, you can refer to the field named `message` in the current object as `this.message`, like this:

```
private string message;

public SetMessage(string message)
{
  this.message = message;
}
```

This example also illustrates another use for methods in classes: creating *accessor methods*. In this case, access to the private message field is restricted. From outside the current object, you have to call the SetMessage method to assign data to this field. Restricting access to an object's internal data is usually a wise thing to do, so much so that accessor methods have been formalized in C# into *properties*.

Creating Properties

Properties are much like fields as far as code outside your object is concerned, but internally, they use accessor methods to get and set their data, giving you the chance to add code that restricts what data is written to and read from a property.

FOR C++ PROGRAMMERS

Properties do not formally exist in C++.

For example, we have a class named Customer in which we want to support a property called Name, which holds the customer's name. To store that name, we'll use a private field called name:

```
class Customer
{
  private string name;
        .
        .
        .
}
```

To implement a property, you set up get and set accessor methods; the get method returns the property's value, and the set method sets it. Here's how to implement the get accessor method for this property, which simply returns the customer's name:

```
class Customer
{
  private string name;

  public string Name
  {
    get
    {
      return name;
    }
        .
        .
```

```
        .
    }
}
```

This example just returns the customer's name, but you can place whatever code you wanted here to process data as needed before returning that data (such as converting Fahrenheit temperatures into Centigrade), and that's what makes properties so powerful. In the set accessor method, you're passed the new value of the property in a parameter named value, which we'll store like this:

```
class Customer
{
  private string name;

  public string Name
  {
   get
   {
     return name;
   }
   set
   {
     name = value;
   }
  }
}
```

Now we can create objects of the Customer class, as well as set and get values using the Name property. You can see that at work in ch03_03.cs, Listing 3.3.

LISTING 3.3   Creating a Property (ch03_03.cs)

```
class ch03_03
{
  static void Main()
  {
    Customer customer = new Customer();
    customer.Name = "Nancy";
    System.Console.WriteLine("The customer's name is {0}",
      customer.Name);
  }
}
```

LISTING 3.3   Continued

```
class Customer
{
  private string name;

  public string Name
  {
   get
   {
     return name;
   }
   set
   {
     name = value;
   }
  }
}
```

Here's what you see when you run ch03_03.cs. We have been able to set and retrieve a value with the new property:

```
C:\>ch03_03
The customer's name is Nancy
```

Property declarations take one of the following forms:

```
[attributes] [modifiers] type identifier {accessor-declaration}
[attributes] [modifiers] type interface-type.identifier {accessor-declaration}
```

Here are the parts of this statement:

- *attributes* (Optional)—Hold additional declarative information, as we'll see in Chapter 14.

- *modifiers* (Optional)—The allowed modifiers are new, static, virtual, abstract, override, and a valid combination of the four access modifiers.

- *type*—The property type, which must be at least as accessible as the property itself.

- *identifier*—The property name.

- *accessor-declaration*—Declaration of the property accessors, which are used to read and write the property.

- *interface-type*—The interface in a fully qualified property name.

Note that unlike a class's fields, properties are not considered variables, which means it's not possible to pass a property as a `ref` or `out` parameter.

Read-only Properties

You can also create read-only properties if you omit the `set` accessor method. For example, to make the `Name` property a read-only property, you use this code:

```
class Customer
{
  private string name;

  public string Name
  {
    get
    {
      return name;
    }
  }
}
```

Creating Constructors

We've created objects using new like this: `Customer customer = new Customer();`. If you're an OOP programmer, you know those parentheses after `Customer` are there for a reason, because when you create an object from a class, you're using the class's *constructor*. A constructor is a special method that has the same name as the class and returns no value. It is used to initialize the data in the object you're creating. In C#, constructors are declared this way:

```
[attributes] [modifiers] identifier([formal-parameter-list])
[initializer] { constructor-body }
```

Here are the parts of this statement:

- *attributes* (Optional)—Hold additional declarative information, as we'll see in Chapter 14.

- *modifiers* (Optional)—The allowed modifiers are new, static, virtual, abstract, override, and a valid combination of the four access modifiers.

- *identifier*—The same as the class name.

- *formal-parameter-list* (Optional)—The optional parameters passed to the constructor. The parameters must be as accessible as the constructor itself.

- *initializer* (Optional)—Invoked before the execution of the constructor body. The *initializer* can be one of the following with an optional *argument-list*:

  : base (*argument-list*)
  : this (*argument-list*)

- *constructor-body*—The block that contains the statements that initialize the object.

For example, we can add a constructor to the Customer class so that you can initialize the customer's name when you create an object of that class. Listing 3.4 shows what that looks like. Note that the constructor has the same name as the class itself, and that we pass the constructor the name "Paul".

LISTING 3.4   Creating a Constructor (ch03_04.cs)

```csharp
class ch03_04
{
  static void Main()
  {
    Customer customer = new Customer("Paul");
    System.Console.WriteLine("The customer's name is {0}",
      customer.Name);
  }
}

class Customer
{
  private string name;

  public Customer(string name)
  {
    this.name = name;
  }

  public string Name
  {
   get
   {
     return name;
   }
  }
}
```

Here's what you see when you run this code. Note that the name we passed to the constructor was indeed stored in the Customer object and was used:

```
C:\>ch03_04
The customer's name is Paul
```

If you don't declare a constructor, a default version without parameters is created automatically. (Note that if you do create *any* kind of a constructor, even a private one—which won't allow objects to be made from a class—C# will not create a default constructor.) In this default constructor, all the fields in your class are set to their default values (see Table 3.2).

> **FOR C++ PROGRAMMERS**
>
> C# doesn't support member initialization lists in constructors that follow a colon like this: `Customer (string name) : internalName(name){}`. Note also that there is no C++ counterpart for calling other constructors with the `this` keyword.

You can also have one constructor call another using the `this` keyword, as here, where a parameterless constructor is calling the constructor we just created and passing it the name `"George"`:

```
public Customer() : this("George"){}
```

Creating Copy Constructors

There's another kind of constructor—the *copy constructor*. When you copy one object to another, C# will copy the reference to the first object to the new object, which means that you now have two references to the *same* object. To make an actual copy, you can use a copy constructor, which is just a standard constructor that takes an object of the current class as its single parameter. For example, here's what a copy constructor for the Customer class might look like. Note that we're copying the name field to the new object:

```
public Customer(Customer customer)
{
  this.name = customer.name;
}
```

Now you can use this constructor to create copies. The copy will be a separate object, not just a reference to the original object. You can see this at work in ch03_05.cs, Listing 3.5. In that code, we create an object named customer with the name "Paul", and then copy it over to an object named customerCopy. Next, we change the name in customer to "Sam", and, to make sure customerCopy doesn't refer to the same data as customer, display the name in customerCopy—which is still "Paul".

LISTING 3.5   Creating a Copy Constructor (ch03_05.cs)

```
class ch03_05
{
  static void Main()
  {
    Customer customer = new Customer("Paul");
    Customer customerCopy = new Customer(customer);
    customer.Name = "Sam";
    System.Console.WriteLine("The new customer's name is {0}",
      customerCopy.Name);
  }
}

class Customer
{
  private string name;

  public Customer(string name)
  {
    this.name = name;
  }

  public Customer(Customer customer)
  {
    this.name = customer.name;
  }

  public string Name
  {
   get
   {
     return name;
   }
   set
   {
     name = value;
   }
  }
}
```

Here's what you see when you run ch03_05.cs. As you can see, `customerCopy` does not refer to the same object as `customer`:

```
C:\>ch03_05
The new customer's name is Paul
```

Creating Structs

C# also supports *structs*, which you create with the `struct` keyword. Structs in C# are like lightweight versions of classes. They're not reference types; they're value types, so when you pass them to methods, they're passed by value. They're like classes in many ways—they support constructors, for example (but not inheritance). They take up fewer resources in memory, so when you've got a small, frequently used class, give some thought to using a struct instead. Here's how you declare a `struct`:

```
[attributes] [modifiers] struct identifier [:interfaces] body [;]
```

Here are the parts of this statement:

- *attributes* (Optional)—Hold additional declarative information, as we'll see in Chapter 14.

- *modifiers* (Optional)—The allowed modifiers are `new`, `static`, `virtual`, `abstract`, `override`, and a valid combination of the four access modifiers.

- *identifier*—The struct name.

- *interfaces* (Optional)—A list that contains the interfaces implemented by the struct, all separated by commas.

- *body*—The struct body that contains member declarations.

Because structs are value types, you can create them without using `new` (although you can also use new and pass arguments to a struct's constructor).

Consider the `Complex` struct, which holds complex numbers. Complex numbers have both real and imaginary parts (the

> **FOR C++ PROGRAMMERS**
>
> In C++, structures are like classes, with only a few minor differences. In C#, structs are value types, not reference types, and cannot support inheritance, initializers, or destructors.

imaginary part is multiplied by the square root of 1). For example, in the complex number 1 + 2i, the real part is 1 and the imaginary part is 2. In this struct, we'll implement the public fields `real` and `imaginary`, as well as a constructor and a method named `Magnitude`, to return the magnitude of this complex number (which will use the `System.Math.Sqrt` method to calculate a square root):

```
struct Complex
{
  public int real, imaginary;

  public Complex(int real, int imaginary)
  {
    this.real = real;
    this.imaginary = imaginary;
  }

  public double Magnitude()
  {
    return System.Math.Sqrt(real * real +
      imaginary * imaginary);
  }
}
```

Now you can create new complex numbers without using new, just as you would for any value type. You can see an example in ch03_06.cs, Listing 3.6, where we create the complex number 3 + 4i (where i is the square root of -1), and display this number's magnitude.

LISTING 3.6   Creating a struct (ch03_06.cs)

```
class ch03_06
{
  static void Main()
  {
    Complex complexNumber;
    complexNumber.real = 3;
    complexNumber.imaginary = 4;
    System.Console.WriteLine("Maginitude: {0}",
      complexNumber.Magnitude());
  }
}

struct Complex
{
  public int real, imaginary;

  public Complex(int real, int imaginary)
  {
    this.real = real;
    this.imaginary = imaginary;
```

LISTING 3.6   Continued

```
  }

  public double Magnitude()
  {
    return System.Math.Sqrt(real * real +
      imaginary * imaginary);
  }
}
```

When you run this example, this is what you see:

```
C:\>ch03_06
Maginitude: 5
```

Creating Static Members

So far, the fields, methods, and properties we've been creating have all been members of objects. You can also create fields, methods, and properties that you use with classes directly, not with objects. These members are called *static members*, also called *class members* (not object members), and you use them with the class name, not the name of an object.

As you know, Main is declared static so that C# itself can call it without creating an object from your main class. That's the way it works with all static members— they're intended to be used with the class, not with an object. We'll take a look at creating static members now, starting with static fields.

FOR C++ PROGRAMMERS

Here's a big difference between C# and C++: in C#, you cannot access static members of a class using an object of that class, as you can in C++. You must use the class name to access static members, not an object.

Creating Static Fields

A static field is a class field, which means that its data is stored in one location in memory, no matter how many objects are created from its class. In fact, you can use a static field to keep track of how many objects have been created from a particular class. To do that, you might declare a static field, which we'll name numberOfObjects in the example, and increment that field each time the class's constructor is called (an explicit initializer is required for static fields, so we've assigned numberOfObjects the value 0 here):

```
public class CountedClass
{
  public static int numberOfObjects = 0;

  public CountedClass()
  {
    numberOfObjects++;
  }
}
```

Now each time a new object of this class is created, numberOfObjects is incremented. You can see how this works in ch03_07.cs, Listing 3.7, where we create three new objects and display the value of the class's numberOfObjects field each time.

LISTING 3.7   Creating a Static Field (ch03_07.cs)

```
class ch03_07
{
  static void Main()
  {
    System.Console.WriteLine("Number of objects: {0}",
      CountedClass.numberOfObjects);
    CountedClass object1 = new CountedClass();
    System.Console.WriteLine("Number of objects: {0}",
      CountedClass.numberOfObjects);
    CountedClass object2 = new CountedClass();
    System.Console.WriteLine("Number of objects: {0}",
      CountedClass.numberOfObjects);
    CountedClass object3 = new CountedClass();
    System.Console.WriteLine("Number of objects: {0}",
      CountedClass.numberOfObjects);
  }
}

public class CountedClass
{
  public static int numberOfObjects = 0;

  public CountedClass()
  {
    numberOfObjects++;
  }
}
```

Here's what you see when you run ch03_07.cs. As you can see, the class field numberOfObjects was incremented each time we created a new object:

```
C:\>ch03_07
Number of objects: 0
Number of objects: 1
Number of objects: 2
Number of objects: 3
```

Although for the sake of brevity in this example, we made numberOfObjects a public static field, it's usually not a good idea to make class fields public. Instead, you can use an accessor method, but if you do, make sure that it's declared static, as are the methods we'll see next.

Creating Static Methods

As we've discussed, when you have a static method, you don't need an object to call that method; you use the class name directly. You may have noticed, for example, that we used the System.Math.Sqrt method to find square roots and calculate the value of a complex number's magnitude in Listing 3.6; this is a static method of the System.Math class, and it's made static so you don't have to go to the trouble of creating a System.Math object before calling that method.

Let's see an example in which we can create our own static method. Although the System.Math class has a handy Sqrt method for calculating square roots, it doesn't have a method for calculating quad roots (fourth roots—the square root of a value's square root). We can correct that glaring omission by creating a new class, Math2, with a static method named QuadRt, which returns quad roots like this:

```
public class Math2
{
    public static double QuadRt(double value)
    {
        return System.Math.Sqrt(System.Math.Sqrt(value));
    }
}
```

Now you can use the QuadRt method with the Math2 class directly, no object needed, as you see in ch03_08.cs, Listing 3.8.

LISTING 3.8   Creating a Static Method (ch03_08.cs)

```
class ch03_08
{
  static void Main()
  {
    System.Console.WriteLine("The quad root of 81 is {0}",
      Math2.QuadRt(81));
  }
}

public class Math2
{
  public static double QuadRt(double value)
  {
    return System.Math.Sqrt(System.Math.Sqrt(value));
  }
}
```

Here's what you see when you run ch03_08.cs:

```
C:\>ch03_08
The quad root of 81 is 3
```

Note that because static methods are not part of an object, you cannot use the `this` keyword in such methods. It's important to know that static methods cannot directly access non-static members (which means, for example, that you cannot call a non-static method from a static method). Instead, they must instantiate an object and use the members of that object to access non-static members (as we saw when creating methods called from `Main` in Chapter 2).

SHOP TALK

CLASSES WITH ONLY STATIC MEMBERS

As part of programming teams, I've sometimes had to create utility classes, like the `System.Math` class, which only have static members. In that case, it's best not to allow objects to be created from that class (for one thing, in C#, none of your static members could be called such an object anyway). In these cases, I gave the utility classes a `private` constructor, which stops the creation of a default constructor, making sure no objects can be created from the class. When you're creating code for general distribution, it's always wise to think of worst-case scenarios. If your code can be used the wrong way, someone will do it.

Creating Static Constructors

You can also make constructors static, like this:

```
public class CountedClass
{
  public static CountedClass()
  {
    .
    .
    .
  }
}
```

Static constructors are called before any objects are created from your class, so you can use them to initialize the data in standard constructors, if you like. C# makes no promise when a static constructor is called. All you know is that it'll be called sometime between the beginning of the program and before an object is created from your class.

Static constructors are also called before any static members in your class are referenced, so you can use them to initialize a class (not just an object). Note that static constructors do not take access modifiers or have parameters.

Creating Static Properties

Like fields, properties can also be static, which means you don't need an object to use them. As an example, we'll convert the static field numberOfObjects in the static fields example (see Listing 3.7) into a property of the same name. That's easy enough—all we have to do is to implement the new property like this (note that the value of the property is stored in a private field, which must be static so we can access it from the static property):

```
public class CountedClass
{
  private static int number = 0;

  public CountedClass()
  {
    number++;
  }

  public static int NumberOfObjects
  {
    get
    {
```

```
    return number;
  }
  set
  {
    number = value;
  }
 }
}
```

Now we can use this new static property as we used the static field earlier, as you see in ch03_09.cs, Listing 3.9.

LISTING 3.9 Creating a Static Property (ch03_09.cs)

```
class ch03_09
{
  static void Main()
  {
    System.Console.WriteLine("Number of objects: {0}",
      CountedClass.NumberOfObjects);
    CountedClass object1 = new CountedClass();
    System.Console.WriteLine("Number of objects: {0}",
      CountedClass.NumberOfObjects);
    CountedClass object2 = new CountedClass();
    System.Console.WriteLine("Number of objects: {0}",
      CountedClass.NumberOfObjects);
    CountedClass object3 = new CountedClass();
    System.Console.WriteLine("Number of objects: {0}",
      CountedClass.NumberOfObjects);
  }
}

public class CountedClass
{
  private static int number = 0;

  public CountedClass()
  {
    number++;
  }

  public static int NumberOfObjects
  {
```

LISTING 3.9   Continued

```
    get
    {
      return number;
    }
    set
    {
      number = value;
    }
  }
}
```

Creating Destructors and Handling Garbage Collection

The flip side of constructors are *destructors*, which are called when it's time to get rid of an object and perform cleanup, such as disconnecting from the Internet or closing files. Getting rid of no-longer-needed objects involves the C# *garbage collector*, which calls your destructor. The C# garbage collector is far more sophisticated than the ones available in most C++ implementations, as we'll see soon. Let's start with destructors first.

Creating a Destructor

You place the code you want to use to clean up an object when it's being deleted, if any, in a destructor. Destructors cannot be static, cannot be inherited, do not take parameters, and do not use access modifiers. They're declared much like constructors, except that their name is prefaced with a tilda (~). You can see an example in ch03_10.cs, which appears in Listing 3.10, and includes a destructor for the Customer class. When there are no more references to objects of this class in your code, the garbage collector is notified and will call the object's destructor (sooner or later—you can't predict when it will happen).

LISTING 3.10   Creating a Destructor (ch03_10.cs)

```
class ch03_10
{
  static void Main()
  {
    Customer customer = new Customer();
  }
}
```

LISTING 3.10   Continued

```
public class Customer
{
  public Customer()
  {
    System.Console.WriteLine("In Customer's constructor.");
  }

  ~Customer()
  {
    System.Console.WriteLine("In Customer's destructor.");
  }
}
```

Here's what you see when you run ch03_10.cs:

```
C:\>ch03_10
In Customer's constructor.
In Customer's destructor.
```

In C#, destructors are converted into a call to the System.Object class's Finalize method (which you cannot call directly in C#). In other words, this destructor:

```
~Customer()
{
  // Your code
}
```

is actually translated into this code by C# (the call to base.Finalize calls the Finalize method in the class the current class is based on; more on the base keyword in the next chapter):

```
protected override void Finalize()
{
  try
  {
    // Your code
  }
  finally
  {
   base.Finalize();
  }
}
```

However, in C#, you must use the standard destructor syntax as we've done in Listing 3.10, and not call or use the Finalize method directly.

Understanding Garbage Collection

Destructors are actually called by the C# *garbage collector*, which manages memory for you in C# code. When you create new objects with the new keyword in C++, you should also later use the delete keyword to delete those objects and free up their allocated memory. That's no longer necessary in C#—the garbage collector deletes objects no longer referenced in your code automatically (at a time of its choosing).

What that means in practical terms is that you don't have to worry about standard objects in your code as far as memory usage goes. On the other hand, when you use "unmanaged" resources like windows, files, or network connections, you should write a destructor that can be called by the garbage collector, and put the code you

> **FOR C++ PROGRAMMERS**
>
> In C#, you no longer have to use delete to explicitly delete objects after allocating them with new. The garbage collector will delete objects for you by itself. In fact, delete is not even a keyword in C#.

want to use to close or deallocate those resources in the destructor (because the garbage collector won't know how to do that itself).

Implementing a Dispose Method

On some occasions, you might want to do more than simply put code in a destructor to clean up resources. You might want to disconnect from the Internet or close a file as soon as you no longer need those resources. For such cases, C# recommends that you create a Dispose method. Because that method is public, your code can call it directly to dispose of the object that works with important resources you want to close.

In a Dispose method, you clean up after an object yourself, without C#'s help. Dispose can be called both explicitly, and/or by the code in your destructor. Note that if you call the Dispose method yourself, you should suppress garbage

> **FOR C++ PROGRAMMERS**
>
> In C#, you can implement a Dispose method to explicitly deallocate resources.

collection on the object once it's gone, as we'll do here.

Let's take a look at an example to see how this works. The Dispose method is formalized in C# as part of the IDisposable interface (we'll discuss interfaces in the next chapter). That has no real meaning for our code, except that we will indicate we're implementing the IDisposable interface. In our example, the Dispose method will clean up an object of a class we'll call Worker.

Note that if you call Dispose explicitly, you can access other objects from inside that method; however, you can't do so if Dispose is called from the destructor, because those objects might already have been destroyed. For that reason, we'll track whether Dispose is being called explicitly or by the destructor by passing Dispose a bool variable (set to true if we call Dispose, and false if the destructor calls Dispose). If that bool is true, we can access other objects in Dispose—otherwise, we can't.

Also, if the object is disposed of by calling the Dispose method, we don't want the garbage collector to try to dispose of it as well, which means we'll call the System.GC. SuppressFinalize method to make sure the garbage collector suppresses garbage collection for the object. You can see what this code looks like in ch03.11.cs, Listing 3.11.

LISTING 3.11   Implementing the Dispose Method (ch03_11.cs)

```
class ch03_11
{
  static void Main()
  {
    Worker worker = new Worker();
    worker.Dispose();
  }
}

public class Worker: System.IDisposable
{
  private bool alreadyDisposed = false;

  public Worker()
  {
   System.Console.WriteLine("In the constructor.");
  }

  public void Dispose(bool explicitCall)
  {
   if(!this.alreadyDisposed)
   {
     if(explicitCall)
     {
     System.Console.WriteLine("Not in the destructor, " +
       "so cleaning up other objects.");
     // Not in the destructor, so we can reference other objects.
     //OtherObject1.Dispose();
     //OtherObject2.Dispose();
```

LISTING 3.11 Continued

```
      }
      // Perform standard cleanup here...
      System.Console.WriteLine("Cleaning up.");
    }
    alreadyDisposed = true;
  }

  public void Dispose()
  {
   Dispose(true);
   System.GC.SuppressFinalize(this);
  }

  ~Worker()
  {
   System.Console.WriteLine("In the destructor now.");
   Dispose(false);
  }
}
```

Here's what you see when you run ch03_11.cs. Note that the object was only disposed of once, when we called Dispose ourselves, and not by the destructor, because the object had already been disposed of:

```
C:\>ch03_11
In the constructor.
Not in the destructor, so cleaning up other objects.
Cleaning up.
```

Here's another thing to know if you're going to use Dispose—you don't have to call this method explicitly if you don't want to. You can let C# call it for you if you add the using keyword (this is not the same as the using directive, which imports a namespace). After control leaves the code in the curly braces following the using keyword, Dispose will be called automatically. Here's how this keyword works:

RENAMING DISPOSE

Sometimes, calling the Dispose method Dispose isn't appropriate. On some occasions, for example, Close or Deallocate might be a better name. C# still recommends you stick with the standard Dispose name, however, so if you do write a Close or Deallocate method, you can have it call Dispose.

```
using (expression | type identifier = initializer){}
```

Here are the parts of this statement:

- *expression*—An expression you want to call Dispose on when control leaves the using statement.

- *type*—The type of identifier.

- *identifier*—The name, or identifier, of the type *type*.

- *initializer*—An expression that creates an object.

Here's an example, where Dispose will be called on the Worker object when control leaves the using statement:

```
class usingExample
{
  public static void Main()
  {
    using (Worker worker = new Worker())
    {
     // Use worker object in code here.
    }
    // C# will call Dispose on worker here.
  {
}
```

Forcing a Garbage Collection

Here's one last thing to know about C# garbage collection—although the C# documentation (and many C# books) says you can't know when garbage collection will take place, that's not actually true. In fact, you can force garbage collection to occur simply by calling the System.GC.Collect method.

This method is safe to call, but if you do, you should know that execution speed of your code might be somewhat compromised.

Overloading Methods

A major topic in OOP is overloading methods, which lets you define the same method multiple times so that you can call them with different argument lists (a method's argument list is called its *signature*). C# not only supports method overloading, but revels in it. Most of the methods you'll find built into C# have several overloaded forms to make life easier for you—for example, you can call System.Console.WriteLine with a string, a float, an int, and so on, all because it's been overloaded to handle those types of arguments (it has 18 overloaded forms in all).

It's easy to overload a method; just define it multiple times, each time with a unique signature. You can see an example in ch03_12.cs, Listing 3.12, where we're working with our Math2 class again, adding an overloaded method named Area that can return the area of both squares and rectangles.

You can call Area with either one or two arguments. If you call this method with one argument, a, it'll assume you want the area of a square whose sides are a long. If you call this method with two arguments, a and b, the method will assume you want the area of a rectangle which is a long and b high. In other words, the code can determine what method to call based on the methods' signatures.

LISTING 3.12 Overloading a Method (ch03_12.cs)

```
class ch03_12
{
  static void Main()
  {
    System.Console.WriteLine("Here's the area of the square: {0}",
      Math2.Area(10));
    System.Console.WriteLine("Here's the area of the rectangle: {0}",
      Math2.Area(10, 5));
  }
}


public class Math2
{
  // This one's for squares
  public static double Area(double side)
  {
    return side * side;
  }

  // This one's for rectangles
  public static double Area(double length, double height)
  {
    return length * height;
  }
}
```

Here's what you see when you run ch03_12.cs. As you can see, we've overloaded the method successfully:

```
C:\>ch03_12
Here's the area of the square: 100
Here's the area of the rectangle: 50
```

Overloading Constructors

You can overload constructors just like any other method. For example, we could give the `Messager` class two constructors. (The `Messager` class appears in Listing 3.2.) One of these will take a string argument which holds the text the `Messager` object's `DisplayMessage` method should display, and the other constructor takes no arguments and simply stores a default string for use with `DisplayMessage`. Here's what it looks like:

```
public Messager()
{
  this.message = "Hello from C#.";
}

public Messager(string message)
{
  this.message = message;
}
```

You can see these two constructors at work in ch03_13.cs, Listing 3.13. In that code, we create `Messager` objects using both constructors, and then display the messages in those objects.

LISTING 3.13   Overloading a Constructor (ch03_13.cs)

```
class ch03_13
{
  static void Main()
  {
    Messager obj1 = new Messager();
    obj1.DisplayMessage();
    Messager obj2 = new Messager("No worries.");
    obj2.DisplayMessage();
  }
}
```

LISTING 3.13   Continued

```
class Messager
{
  public string message = "Default message.";

  public Messager()
  {
    this.message = "Hello from C#.";
  }

  public Messager(string message)
  {
    this.message = message;
  }

  public void DisplayMessage()
  {
    System.Console.WriteLine(message);
  }
}
```

Here's what you see when you run ch03_13.cs. As you can see, we've used both constructors, the one that takes no parameters, and the one that takes a single string parameter:

```
C:\>ch03_13
Hello from C#.
No worries.
```

Overloading Operators

If you're an OOP programmer, you know that you can also overload operators, not just methods. You do that by defining static methods using the operator keyword. Being able to overload operators like +, -, * and so on for your own classes and structs lets you use those classes and structs with those operators, just as if they were types built into C#. C# doesn't allow as many operators to be overloaded as C++ does. You can see the possibilities for C# in Table 3.3. Note the division into *unary* operators and *binary* operators—unary operators take one operand (like the negation operator, -x), and binary operators take two operands (like the addition operator, x + y).

TABLE 3.3

Overloading Possibilities for C# Operators

OPERATORS	OVERLOADING POSSIBILITIES
`+, -, !, ~, ++, --, true, false`	These unary operators can be overloaded.
`+, -, *, /, %, &, |, ^, <<, >>`	These binary operators can be overloaded.
`==, !=, <, >, <=, >=`	The comparison operators can be overloaded.
`&&, ||`	The conditional logical operators cannot be overloaded, but they are computed with & and |, which can be overloaded.
`[]`	The array indexing operator cannot be overloaded, but you can define indexers in C# (see Chapter 6, "Understanding Collections and Indexers").
`()`	The cast operator cannot be overloaded directly, but you can define your own conversion operators, as you'll do in this chapter.
`+=, -=, *=, /=, %=, &=, |=, ^=, <<=, >>=`	Assignment operators cannot be overloaded, but if you overload a binary operator, such as +, += is also overloaded.
`=, ., ?:, ->, new, is, sizeof, typeof`	These operators cannot be overloaded.

Note also that, unlike C++, the = assignment operator cannot be overloaded in C#. An assignment always performs a simple bit-by-bit copy of a value into a variable. On the other hand, when you overload a binary operator like +, the corresponding compound assignment operator, +=, is automatically overloaded. Cast operations are overloaded by providing conversion methods, as we'll see in a page or two.

FOR C++ PROGRAMMERS

Unlike C++, you cannot overload the =, (), [], &&, ||, and `new` operators in C#.

You can overload operators for either classes or structs. To see how this works, we'll overload the `Complex` struct we built earlier in the chapter (see Listing 3.6). This struct holds complex numbers like 1 + 2i, where i is the square root of -1, and we'll see how to overload operators like + so that we can add two `Complex` objects, or the unary negation operator so that if complex holds 1 + 2i, `-complex` will yield -1 - 2i. All this takes place in ch03_14.cs, which appears in Listing 3.14. We'll take this code apart in the next few sections.

LISTING 3.14   Overloading Operators (ch03_14.cs)

```
class ch03_14
{
  public static void Main()
  {
    Complex complex1 = new Complex(1, 2);
    Complex complex2 = new Complex(3, 4);
```

LISTING 3.14   Continued

```
      System.Console.WriteLine("complex1 = {0}", complex1);
      System.Console.WriteLine("complex2 = {0}", complex2);

      Complex complex3 = -complex1;
      System.Console.WriteLine("-complex1 = {0}", complex3);

      System.Console.WriteLine("complex1 + complex2 = {0}",
        complex1 + complex2);

      if(complex1 == complex2){
        System.Console.WriteLine("complex1 equals complex2");
      } else {
        System.Console.WriteLine("complex1 does not equal complex2");
      }
    }
  }

public struct Complex
{
  public int real;
  public int imaginary;

  public Complex(int real, int imaginary)
  {
    this.real = real;
    this.imaginary = imaginary;
  }

  public override string ToString()
  {
    if (imaginary >= 0){
      return(System.String.Format("{0} + {1}i", real, imaginary));
    } else {
      return(System.String.Format("{0} - {1}i", real,
      System.Math.Abs(imaginary)));
    }
  }

  public static Complex operator-(Complex complex)
  {
```

LISTING 3.14   Continued

```csharp
      return new Complex(-complex.real, -complex.imaginary);
  }

  public static Complex operator+(Complex complex1, Complex complex2)
  {
    return new Complex(complex1.real + complex2.real,
      complex1.imaginary + complex2.imaginary);
  }

  public static implicit operator Complex(int theInt)
  {
    return new Complex(theInt, 0);
  }

  public static explicit operator int(Complex complex)
  {
    return complex.real;
  }

  public static bool operator==(Complex complex1, Complex complex2)
  {
    if (complex1.real == complex2.real &&
      complex1.imaginary == complex2.imaginary)
    {
      return true;
    }
    return false;
  }

  public static bool operator!=(Complex complex1, Complex complex2)
  {
    return !(complex1 == complex2);
  }

  public override bool Equals(object obj)
  {
    if (!(obj is Complex))
    {
      return false;
    }
    return this == (Complex) obj;
  }
```

LISTING 3.14 Continued

```
public override int GetHashCode()
{
    return (int) System.Math.Sqrt(real * real +
      imaginary * imaginary);
}
}
```

Creating the Complex Struct

We start ch03_14.cs by using the Complex struct we saw earlier in this chapter, which has a constructor you pass the real and imaginary parts to, and we'll add the ToString method. Any time C# needs a string representation of a complex number (as when you pass it to System.Console.WriteLine), it'll call the number's ToString method:

```
public struct Complex
{
  public int real;
  public int imaginary;

  public Complex(int real, int imaginary)
  {
   this.real = real;
   this.imaginary = imaginary;
  }

  public override string ToString()
  {
  if (imaginary >= 0){
    return(System.String.Format("{0} + {1}i", real, imaginary));
  } else {
    return(System.String.Format("{0} - {1}i", real,
    System.Math.Abs(imaginary)));
  }
  }
   .
   .
   .
}
```

USING SYSTEM.STRING.FORMAT

Note the use of `System.String.Format` in the previous code. This method works just like `System.Console.WriteLine`, except that it returns a string instead of displaying text to the console. That means we can use it to embed the real and imaginary parts of the complex number into a string.

Overloading a Unary Operator

The next step is to start overloading operators for `Complex` numbers. We'll start by overloading the unary negation operator, `-`. To do that, you add this method to the `Complex` struct, which uses the `operator` keyword and is passed a `Complex` number to negate:

```
public static Complex operator-(Complex complex)
{
  return new Complex(-complex.real, -complex.imaginary);
}
```

All we have to do here is to negate the real and imaginary parts of the complex number and return the result, as you see in this code. Now if you created a complex number, 1 + 2i, and negated it like this:

```
Complex complex1 = new Complex(1, 2);
System.Console.WriteLine(-complex1;
```

You'd see this result:

```
-1 - 2i
```

Overloading a Binary Operator

We've been able to overload the - unary operator for complex numbers by adding a static method to the `Complex` struct that uses the `operator` keyword and is passed the operand to negate. When you're overloading a binary operator, like the + addition operator, you are passed two operands; in the case of the + operator, those are the complex numbers you're supposed to add. Here's the method you'd add to the `Complex` struct to overload the + operator for complex numbers:

```
public static Complex operator+(Complex complex1, Complex complex2)
{
  return new Complex(complex1.real + complex2.real,
    complex1.imaginary + complex2.imaginary);
}
```

Now if you were to use this code to add 1 + 2i and 3 + 4i:

```
Complex complex1 = new Complex(1, 2);
Complex complex2 = new Complex(3, 4);

System.Console.WriteLine("complex1 + complex2 = {0}",
  complex1 + complex2);
```

you would see this result:

```
complex1 + complex2 = 4 + 6i
```

Overloading Conversion Operations

You can also overload conversion operations. Conversions can be either implicit or explicit, and you use the implicit or explicit keywords in those cases. The name of the operator in this case is the target type you're converting to, and the parameter you're passed is of the type

FOR C++ PROGRAMMERS

It's not possible to create nonstatic operators overloads in C#, so binary operators must take two operands.

you're converting from. For example, here's how to convert from an integer value to a Complex number—note that we'll just assign the integer value to the real part of the resulting complex number. Because data will be lost, we'll make this an implicit conversion:

```
public static implicit operator Complex(int intValue)
{
  return new Complex(intValue, 0);
}
```

On the other hand, converting from a complex number to an int does imply some data loss, so we'll make this an explicit conversion:

```
public static explicit operator int(Complex complex)
{
  return complex.real;
}
```

Now when you cast from Complex to int explicitly, this method will be called.

Overloading Equality Operators

Overloading the == equality operator is like overloading any binary operator, with a few differences. For one, if you overload ==, C# will insist that you overload != as well, so we'll do both operators here.

FOR C++ PROGRAMMERS

If you overload ==, C# will insist that you also overload !=.

When you overload the == operator, you're passed two `Complex` objects to compare; you return `true` if they're equal and `false` otherwise. `Complex` numbers are equal if their real and imaginary parts are equal, so here's how to overload the == operator for complex numbers:

```
public static bool operator==(Complex complex1, Complex complex2)
{
  if (complex1.real == complex2.real &&
    complex1.imaginary == complex2.imaginary)
  {
    return true;
  }
   return false;
}
```

And here's how to overload !=:

```
public static bool operator!=(Complex complex1, Complex complex2)
{
    return !(complex1 == complex2);
}
```

If you only overload == and !=, C# will give you a warning when you compile your code that you haven't overridden the `Object.Equals(object o)` method. This method is sometimes used by code instead of the == operator to check for equality (in Visual Basic .NET, for example, you can't overload operators, so code would use the `Equals` method). For example, to check if complex1 equals complex2, you could call `complex1.Equals(complex2)`. C# wants us to *override* this method, replacing the default version in the `Object` class, not overload it, and we'll discuss overriding methods in the next chapter. All that means in this case is that we use the `override` keyword here. After using the `is` operator to ensure that the object passed to us is a `Complex` object, we just compare the current object to the one passed, and return the result of that comparison, like this:

```
public override bool Equals(object obj)
{
  if (!(obj is Complex))
  {
    return false;
  }
  return this == (Complex) obj;
}
```

But there's still more to do. If you've overloaded ==,!=, and Equals, C# will still give you another warning. You haven't overridden the Object.GetHashCode method. A hash method is used to quickly generate a hash code, which is an int that corresponds to the value of an object. Hash codes allow C# to store objects more efficiently in collections, as we'll discuss in Chapter 6. You don't have to override GetHashCode—you can simply ignore the warning. In this case, we'll return the magnitude of the complex number as its hash code:

```
public override int GetHashCode()
{
  return (int) System.Math.Sqrt(real * real +
    imaginary * imaginary);
}
```

Now, at last, you can compare two complex numbers using the == operator, like this, which compares 1 + 2i and 3 + 4i:

```
Complex complex1 = new Complex(1, 2);
Complex complex2 = new Complex(3, 4);

if(complex1 == complex2){
  System.Console.WriteLine("complex1 equals complex2");
} else {
  System.Console.WriteLine("complex1 does not equal complex2");
}
```

Here's what this code produces:

```
complex1 does not equal complex2
```

For the full story on operator overloading, run ch03_14.cs; this example implements all the operator overloads we've discussed and puts them to work using the code we've developed. Here's what you see when you run this example:

```
C:\>ch03_14
complex1 = 1 + 2i
complex2 = 3 + 4i
-complex1 = -1 - 2i
complex1 + complex2 = 4 + 6i
complex1 does not equal complex2
```

Creating Namespaces

The last OOP topic we'll look at in this chapter is how to create your own namespaces. As you know, namespaces let you divide programs up to avoid clashes between identifiers (even if you don't declare your own namespace, your code is given its own default namespace, the global namespace). To create your own namespace, you use the namespace keyword:

```
namespace name[.name1] ...] {
  type-declarations
}
```

Here are the parts of this statement:

- *name*, *name1*—A namespace name can be any legal identifier, and it can include periods.

- *type-declarations*—Within a namespace, you can declare one or more of the following types: another namespace, a class, interface, struct, enum, or delegate.

You can create as many namespaces in a file as you want; just enclose the code for each namespace in the code block following the namespace keyword. For example, here's how we can put the Messager class into the namespace Output:

```csharp
namespace Output
{
  class Messager
  {
    public string message = "Default message.";

    public void DisplayMessage()
    {
      System.Console.WriteLine(message);
    }
  }
}
```

NAMING NAMESPACES

Microsoft's suggestion is to name namespaces this way: CompanyName.ProjectName.Component. SubComponent.

To access Messager outside the Output namespace, you qualify its name as Output.Messsager, just as you can qualify Console.Writeline as System. Console.WriteLine. (Alternatively, you can use a using Output directive, just as you use a using System directive.) You can see this at work in ch03_15.cs, Listing 3.15.

LISTING 3.15   Namespace Example (ch03_15.cs)

```
class ch03_15
{
  public static void Main()
  {
    Output.Messager obj = new Output.Messager();
    obj.message = "Hello from C#.";
    obj.DisplayMessage();
  }
}

namespace Output
{
  class Messager
  {
    public string message = "Default message.";

    public void DisplayMessage()
    {
      System.Console.WriteLine(message);
    }
  }
}
```

Here's what you see when you run ch03_15.cs:

```
C:\>ch03_15
Hello from C#.
```

Namespaces can also extend over multiple files—more on how that works when we discuss
assemblies. We took a look at overloading in this chapter—how about overriding? As OOP
programmers know, overriding is one of the most important aspects of class inheritance, and
it's covered in the next chapter.

In Brief

This chapter covered the essentials of C# OOP, starting with creating classes and objects. We
saw that access modifiers let you restrict access to the members of classes and structs, encapsulating your data and methods as needed. Here's an overview of the topics we covered:

- We can add fields, methods, and properties to classes, and we can initialize fields with initializers. We can use the `this` keyword in methods, and create not only standard properties, but also read-only and static properties. And we can create constructors and copy constructors to initialize the data in objects.

- Static members are declared with the `static` keyword, and are associated with the class itself, not with objects created from that class. Static fields can store data for the class, and static methods and properties can be called without first instantiating an object.

- Method overloading is implemented by providing alternative definitions of the same method with different signatures. Operator overloading uses the `operator` keyword to let you specify which operator to overload.

- When we overloaded the `==` operator, C# will issue a warning unless we also override the `Object.Equals` and `Object.GetHashCode` methods.

Handling Inheritance and Delegates

4

Working with Inheritance

Inheritance is the process of deriving one type from another, which promotes code reuse and makes it possible to use the huge selection of classes already written for you in the FCL. For example, the class `System.Windows.Forms.Form`, which you can base your own windows on, is a huge class. When you derive your own classes from that class, you're free to customize that class as you like, adding buttons, list boxes, check boxes, menus, and so on. (If you're already familiar with inheritance in a language like C++, you might just want to skim this discussion for the "For C++ Programmers" sidebars to see how C# differs from C++ here.)

A major part of inheritance involves *polymorphism*. Polymorphism means that you can provide different implementations of a method in different classes, but can call them as members of the same object variable. For example, you have a class named `Animal` that you derive two classes from—`Mammal` and `Fish`. These two classes can both implement a method named `Breathe`, which will be quite different because fish and mammals breathe differently. Nonetheless, with a little preparation, you can assign objects of both the `Mammal` and `Fish` classes to `Animal` variables, and when you call the `Breathe` method of those variables, the method of the correct class, `Fish` or `Mammal`, will be called.

Here's a simple inheritance example. We'll create a class (structs don't support inheritance) named Window that can serve as the base class for all kinds of other user interface elements, such as buttons, menus, list boxes, radio buttons, and so on. The Window class has one method, Open, which displays the message "Opening...":

```
public class Window
{
  private string openingMessage = "Opening...";

  public void Open()
  {
   System.Console.WriteLine(openingMessage);
  }
}
```

If you wanted to create a new class, Menu, which displays drop-down menus, you could base that class on the Window class to take advantage of the screen-handling power already built into the Window class. To derive the Menu class from the Window class, you use this syntax:

```
public class Menu : Window
{

    .

    .

    .

}
```

Deriving a new class this way means that the new class inherits all the non-private members of the base class, so Menu inherits the Open method of the base class Window. However, opening a menu works differently from opening a window, so we might also want to change how the Open method of the Menu class works. In this case, we'll create a new method named Open in the Menu class, which displays the message "Displaying items...". Note that we use the new keyword (not the same as the new operator) to indicate that we want to redefine this method from the base class's version:

```
public class Menu : Window
{
  private string openingMessage = "Displaying items...";

  public new void Open()
  {
  System.Console.WriteLine(openingMessage);
  }
}
```

The new keyword hides an inherited member with the same signature; you use it to tell C# that you're intending to *redefine* a method from the base class, and that defining your new method with the same name and signature as a base class method is not a mistake.

Now when you create an object of the Window class and call the Open method, you'll see "Opening..." but when you create an object of the Menu class and call the Open method, you'll see "Displaying items...". You can see the code in ch04_01.cs, Listing 4.1.

FOR C++ PROGRAMMERS

You don't have to use the new keyword in C++ when redefining a method in a derived class this way. In C++, you simply override the base class method, but C# makes a distinction between redefining a method totally, which you do with new, and overriding it (that is, customizing it for the current class), which you do with the override keyword. (See the topic "Overriding Virtual Methods" later in this chapter for more information.)

LISTING 4.1   Using Inheritance (ch04_01.cs)

```
public class ch04_01
{
  public static void Main()
  {
    Window window = new Window();
    window.Open();

    Menu menu = new Menu();
    menu.Open();
  }
}

public class Window
{
  private string openingMessage = "Opening...";

  public void Open()
  {
    System.Console.WriteLine(openingMessage);
  }
}

public class Menu : Window
{
  private string openingMessage = "Displaying items...";
```

LISTING 4.1 Continued

```
public new void Open()
{
    System.Console.WriteLine(openingMessage);
}
}
```

Here's what you see when you run ch04_01.cs, create new objects of the Window and Menu classes, and call their Open methods:

```
C:\>ch04_01
Opening...
Displaying items...
```

If we hadn't redefined the Open method in the Menu class (using new or the virtual methods coming up in a few pages), calling Menu.Open would have called the Open method inherited from Window—that is, Window.Open—and this code would simply have displayed "Opening..." twice.

Using the Access Modifiers

When you derive classes, you have some options that will set the accessibility of members inherited from the base class. These are the access modifiers we saw in Chapter 3, "C# Object-Oriented Programming;" for example, because the Window class's Open method was declared as public, it automatically becomes a member of any class derived from Window, and can be called from objects of the derived class.

If Open was declared private, on the other hand, it's restricted to the Window class. You can't access it in classes derived from Window, or from Window objects—it's locked up tight in the Window class, for internal class use only.

Members declared protected, on the other hand, are available in the class where they're declared, and in classes derived from that class, but not outside those classes. For example, if we declared Open protected:

```
public class Window
{
    private string openingMessage = "Opening...";

    protected void Open()
    {
        System.Console.WriteLine(openingMessage);
    }
}
```

you could call it in code in the Window class, and code in classes derived from Window like Menu, but not outside those classes. For example, if you created an object of this version of the Window class in the Main method, you could not call its Open method.

In C#, you can also declare members internal, which restricts them to the access in the same assembly. Or you can declare members internal protected, which limits access to the current assembly, or types derived from the current class.

Calling Base Class Methods

We defined a new version of Open in the Menu class, which hides the Open method in the base Window class. But what if you wanted to reach the now-hidden Open method of the base class? That base class method is still available in the Menu class as base.Open. The base keyword refers to the base class you've inherited from, and gives you access to the base class members, which can be redefined in the derived class. For example, you can see how to call Window.Open from Menu.Open in ch04_02.cs, Listing 4.2.

LISTING 4.2   Calling a Base Class (ch04_02.cs)

```
public class ch04_02
{
  public static void Main()
  {
    Window window = new Window();
    window.Open();

    Menu menu = new Menu();
    menu.Open();
  }
}

public class Window
{
  private string openingMessage = "Opening...";

  public void Open()
  {
    System.Console.WriteLine(openingMessage);
  }
}

public class Menu : Window
{
```

LISTING 4.2 Continued

```
public new void Open()
{
  base.Open();
}
}
```

FOR C++ PROGRAMMERS

Note that the C# way of accessing base class members differs from the C++ way. In C++, you use the scope resolution operator (::) and the base class name, for example: `Window::Open()`.

Here's what you see when you run ch04_02.cs:

```
C:\>ch04_02
Opening...
Opening...
```

Calling Base Class Constructors

Classes can inherit members from their base classes, but they cannot inherit constructors, which means that it's up to you to define your own constructors in derived classes. On the other hand, you can pass data back to a base class constructor; to do that, you use the `base` keyword, passing this keyword the argument(s) your constructor was passed which you want passed to the base class's constructor. Here's what that looks like:

```
public Menu(string message) : base(message)
{
}
```

In this case, the `message` argument is passed to the base class's constructor (assuming the base class has a constructor that takes one string argument). You can see a full example in ch04_03.cs, Listing 4.3, where we're passing the argument named `message` back to the `Window` class's constructor.

LISTING 4.3 Calling Base Class Constructors (ch04_03.cs)

```
public class ch04_03
{
  public static void Main()
  {
    Menu menu = new Menu("Opening the menu...");
    menu.Open();
  }
}
```

LISTING 4.3 Continued

```
public class Window
{
  protected string openingMessage = "Opening...";

  public Window(string message)
  {
    openingMessage = message;
  }

  public void Open()
  {
    System.Console.WriteLine(openingMessage);
  }
}

public class Menu : Window
{
  public Menu(string message) : base(message){}

  public new void Open()
  {
    System.Console.WriteLine(openingMessage);
  }
}
```

When you pass the argument message back to the Window class's constructor, C# will look for a constructor that takes a single string argument and call it. Here's what you see when you run ch04_03.cs. Note that the text the Menu object was created with was passed back to the Window class's constructor, storing it in the protected openingMessage field, which is displayed in the Menu object's Open method:

```
C:\>ch04_03
Opening the menu...
```

FOR C++ PROGRAMMERS

When you pass arguments to a base class constructor in C++, you don't have to use the keyword base.

MULTIPLE-ARGUMENT CONSTRUCTORS

If you pass multiple arguments to a constructor, you don't have to pass them all back to a base class constructor; you can pass only the ones you want to, like this: public Menu(string message, int t, float f) : base(message, t){}.

Overriding Virtual Methods

In this chapter's first example, we defined the `Open` method in the derived `Menu` class with the new keyword:

```
public new void Open()
{
    System.Console.WriteLine(openingMessage);
}
```

The new keyword *hides* an inherited member with the same signature, and you use it when you are redefining a base class method into something entirely new. But here, `Open` isn't entirely new. In this case, we're just customizing it for the `Menu` class. Logically, this method does the same thing for the `Menu` class as it did for the `Window` class. For that reason, we should really be *overriding* the `Open` method, not specifying that we're redefining it entirely. Overriding it replaces it much as new does, but if you override a method, you're indicating that you're really just customizing it for the current class.

To override a method in a base class with the same signature, that base class method must be declared *virtual* or *abstract*. We'll take a look at virtual methods here and abstract methods in the next section. To make a method virtual, you just use the `virtual` keyword, as we can do with the `Open` method in the `Window` base class:

```
public class Window
{
    private string openingMessage = "Opening...";

    public virtual void Open()
    {
        System.Console.WriteLine(openingMessage);
    }
}
```

Methods are declared `virtual` so that they can be overridden with the `override` keyword, and you can see how to override the `Open` method with the new version in ch04_04.cs, Listing 4.4.

LISTING 4.4   Overriding Virtual Methods (ch04_04.cs)

```
public class ch04_04
{
    public static void Main()
    {
        Window window = new Window();
```

LISTING 4.4 Continued

```
    window.Open();

    Menu menu = new Menu();
    menu.Open();
  }
}

public class Window
{
  private string openingMessage = "Opening...";

  public virtual void Open()
  {
    System.Console.WriteLine(openingMessage);
  }
}

public class Menu : Window
{
  private string openingMessage = "Displaying items...";

  public override void Open()
  {
    System.Console.WriteLine(openingMessage);
  }
}
```

Here's what you see when you run this code—just what you saw when we used the new keyword, but here we're using the virtual and override keywords to override a virtual method:

```
C:\>ch04_04
Opening...
Displaying items...
```

So what's the difference between new and override? You use new when you're replacing a base class method with the same signature, and you use override when you're customizing it in the current class.

Note that you cannot override a non-virtual or static method—the method you're overriding in C# must be virtual, abstract, or itself be an overriding version of a base class's method (technically there actually are some exceptions to this rule; sometimes you can override methods in other cases if you're working directly in MSIL, for example). In Java, all methods are virtual, but in C++ and C#, they're not virtual unless you use the `virtual` keyword. (What happens if a base class and a derived class both have the same method marked as virtual? C# will use the version in the base class, and warn you about the version in the derived class.)

Creating Abstract Classes

Say that you decided to sell the `Window` class commercially. In that case, note that there's no guarantee that programmers would implement their own `Open` methods; they might leave the default `Open` method in place. If you consider that inappropriate—if you want to force those programmers to implement their own `Open` method if they derive classes from your `Window` class—you can declare the `Open` method *abstract*.

You declare a method abstract simply by using the `abstract` keyword, as you see in ch04_05.cs, Listing 4.5. Don't give the method any body; just end the declaration of the method with a semicolon, as you see in Listing 4.5. When you give a class an abstract method, that method must be overridden in any derived classes, and in addition, the class must be declared with the `abstract` keyword (even if it includes non-abstract methods in addition to the abstract methods), as you can also see in ch04_05.cs.

LISTING 4.5   Overriding Abstract Methods (ch04_05.cs)

```
public class ch04_05
{
  public static void Main()
  {
   Menu menu = new Menu();
   menu.Open();
  }
}

abstract public class Window
{
```

LISTING 4.5   Continued

```
abstract public void Open();
}

public class Menu : Window
{
  private string openingMessage = "Displaying items...";

  public override void Open()
  {
    System.Console.WriteLine(openingMessage);
  }
}
```

Here are the results of ch04_05.cs:

```
C:\>ch04_05
Displaying items...
```

SHOP TALK

USING ABSTRACT METHODS

In commercial development environments, abstract methods are only a half-way solution. For example, you might create an abstract class with abstract methods and publish it in your development environment, only to find months later classes derived from your class that don't implement your abstract methods. The problem is that although the first class, class A, derived from your class was constrained to implement your abstract methods, nothing constrained any classes derived from class A to implement those methods.

Although abstract classes are fine for very simple environments where there's only one level of derivation (as is often the case with the classes programmers derive from FCL classes), in commercial development environments—in which classes are derived from classes that are derived from classes—they aren't enough. As yet, there's no effective technique that will constrain the grandchildren of an abstract class to implement its abstract methods.

Sealed Classes

Abstract classes are designed to be inherited—but there's an opposite option available too. C# has *sealed* classes, which are designed not to be inherited. If you mark a class as sealed with the sealed keyword, that class cannot be inherited:

```
sealed public class Window
{
  private string openingMessage = "Opening...";

  public void Open()
  {
   System.Console.WriteLine(openingMessage);
  }
}
```

FOR C++ PROGRAMMERS

There is no `sealed` keyword in C++.

If you try to derive the Menu class from this version of Window, you'll see a message like this:

```
ch04_01.cs(23,14): error CS0509: 'Menu' :
  cannot inherit from sealed class 'Window'
```

Working with Polymorphism

Using virtual methods and the override keyword, you can implement *polymorphism*, the capability to determine at runtime which type of object is stored in a variable and to call that object's methods correctly. For example, if you derived Menu from a base class named Window and each of these classes had a different virtual version of the Open method, you could put off until runtime which type of object, Window or Menu, to place in a Window variable. If you put a Window object into a Window variable and called its Open method, Window.Open would be called, but if you placed a Menu object into a Window variable (which is legal since Menu is derived from Window) and called its Open method, Menu.Open would be called.

In other words, you don't have to specify until runtime which type of object you want to work with, which allows you to use the same code to handle objects of many different types. For example, you might have code in a procedure that you can pass Window objects to. Because of runtime polymorphism, you can also pass Menu objects to that procedure and the same code will work fine (as long as you don't use those objects to call methods defined only in Menu and not in Window).

For example, say you have the following version of the Window class. Note that the Open method is declared virtual:

```
public class Window
{
  private string openingMessage = "Opening...";
```

```
public virtual void Open()
{
  System.Console.WriteLine(openingMessage);
}
}
```

The Menu class is derived from Window, and it specifically overrides Open to display a different message than Window.Open:

```
public class Menu : Window
{
  private string openingMessage = "Displaying items...";

  public override void Open()
  {
    System.Console.WriteLine(openingMessage);
  }
}
```

Now you can place objects of either the Window or Menu classes into a Window variable, windowVariable. When you load a Window object into this variable and call windowVariable.Open, the Window version of Open will be called, but when you load a Menu object into this variable and call windowVariable.Open, the Menu version of Open will be called. In other words, you can use the same code with different types of objects. You can see this at work in ch04_06.cs, Listing 4.6. (Note that if you hadn't declared Open virtual in Window and overridden it in Menu, windowVariable.Open would call Window.Open no matter whether you had a Window or Menu object in windowVariable.)

LISTING 4.6 Using Polymorphism (ch04_06.cs)

```
public class ch04_06
{
  static void Main()
  {
    Window windowVariable;

    windowVariable = new Window();
    windowVariable.Open();

    windowVariable = new Menu();
    windowVariable.Open();
  }
}
```

LISTING 4.6   Continued

```
public class Window
{
  private string openingMessage = "Opening...";

  public virtual void Open()
  {
    System.Console.WriteLine(openingMessage);
  }
}

public class Menu : Window
{
  private string openingMessage = "Displaying items...";

  public override void Open()
  {
    System.Console.WriteLine(openingMessage);
  }
}
```

Here's what you see when you run ch04_06.cs. Note that although we made the same call, `windowVariable.Open`, the first time `Window.Open` was called and the second time `Menu.Open` was called:

```
C:\>ch04_06
Opening...
Displaying items...
```

Boxing and Unboxing Types

Even the simple value types like `int` in C# can be thought of as objects. In fact, there are formal terms for the conversion of value types into reference types (that is, objects) and back again—*boxing* and *unboxing*.

Boxing a value type is the conversion of that value type into the type `object`. Boxing is implicit, which means the compiler will do it for you. For example, say you pass an integer to `WriteLine` in this code, where `temperature` is an `int` variable:

```
System.Console.WriteLine("The temperature is {0}", temperature);
```

In the case where you use a format string with WriteLine, WriteLine is actually expecting you to pass an object after the format string. When you pass an int, C# will box it into an object, and call that object's ToString method.

Whereas boxing is implicit, *unboxing*—the process of converting from an object back to a simple type—must be explicit, using a type cast. You can see an example of both boxing (implicit) and unboxing (explicit) in ch04_07.cs, Listing 4.7.

LISTING 4.7   Boxing and Unboxing (ch04_07.cs)

```
public class ch04_07
{
  static void Main()
  {
    int int1 = 1;

    object obj1 = int1;    //Boxing

    int int2 = (int) obj1;  //Unboxing
  }
}
```

You can see the boxing and unboxing taking place in the MSIL for the Main method in ch04_07.cs:

```
.entrypoint
// Code size    18 (0x12)
.maxstack 1
.locals init (int32 V_0,
     object V_1,
     int32 V_2)
IL_0000: ldc.i4.1
IL_0001: stloc.0
IL_0002: ldloc.0
IL_0003: box     [mscorlib]System.Int32
IL_0008: stloc.1
IL_0009: ldloc.1
IL_000a: unbox   [mscorlib]System.Int32
IL_000f: ldind.i4
IL_0010: stloc.2
IL_0011: ret
```

Protecting Nested Classes

You can nest classes inside other classes in C#, and nested classes can access members of the host class, even private members. Nested classes work much like any other class member when it comes to inheritance; for example, say that that the Window class has a nested Point class, which keeps track of the upper-left point of the window. We might make the Point class protected like this:

```
public class Window
{
  private Point location;

  public Window(int x, int y)
  {
    this.location = new Point(x, y);
  }

  public Window()
  {
    this.location = new Point(100, 100);
  }

  public virtual void Open()
  {
    System.Console.WriteLine("Opening window at [{0}, {1}]",
    location.x, location.y);
  }

  protected class Point
  {
    public int x, y;

    public Point(int x, int y)
    {
      this.x = x;
      this.y = y;
    }
  }
}
```

Now say that you derive the Menu class from Window; because the nested Point class was declared protected, Menu can use that class also (if Point had been declared private, Menu couldn't use it):

```
public class Menu : Window
{
  private Point location;

  public Menu(int x, int y)
  {
    location = new Point(x, y);
  }

  public override void Open()
  {
    System.Console.WriteLine("Opening menu at [{0}, {1}]",
    location.x, location.y);
  }
}
```

You can see all this at work in ch04_08.cs (as shown in Listing 4.8), where we create Window and Menu objects, both of which use the Point class. Point is a nested protected class in the Window class, so when you derive the Menu class from Window, Menu also has access to the Point class.

LISTING 4.8 Using Nested Classes (ch04_08.cs)

```
public class ch04_08
{
  static void Main()
  {
    Window window = new Window(100, 200);
    window.Open();

    Menu menu = new Menu(100, 300);
    menu.Open();
  }
}

public class Window
{
  private Point location;

  public Window(int x, int y)
  {
    this.location = new Point(x, y);
  }
```

LISTING 4.8   Continued

```csharp
  public Window()
  {
    this.location = new Point(100, 100);
  }

  public virtual void Open()
  {
    System.Console.WriteLine("Opening window at [{0}, {1}]",
    location.x, location.y);
  }

  protected class Point
  {
    public int x, y;

    public Point(int x, int y)
    {
      this.x = x;
      this.y = y;
    }
  }
}

public class Menu : Window
{
  private Point location;

  public Menu(int x, int y)
  {
    location = new Point(x, y);
  }

  public override void Open()
  {
    System.Console.WriteLine("Opening menu at [{0}, {1}]",
    location.x, location.y);
  }
}
```

Here's what you see when you run ch04_08.cs. Note that both the Window and Menu class can use the nested Point class:

```
C:\>ch04_08
Opening window at [100, 200]
Opening menu at [100, 300]
```

It's often better for the sake of information hiding to make nested classes like `Point` private and inaccessible in derived classes. In this case, `Menu` wouldn't have direct access to the `Point` class, and you'd have to provide accessor methods like `GetPoint` and `SetPoint` to set the location of the upper-left side of the menu.

Using Interfaces

In C#, you can't inherit from multiple base classes at the same time. For example, if `Window` and `Graphics` are classes, deriving a class named `Menu` from them like this is illegal:

```
public class Menu : Window, Graphics    // Illegal
```

However, like Java, C# supports Java-style *interfaces*, which C# treats as a contract, indicating that a class will implement a certain set of properties, methods, events, and/or indexers. Unlike base classes, interfaces don't implement any of their members by providing the actual code for properties, methods, and so on. Interfaces are just specifications for those members, and if your class *implements* an interface, it must provide code for all the members of that interface. A single class can implement as many interfaces as it likes at the same time (as long as there isn't an unhandled name clash among members), so interfaces are as close as C# comes to implementing multiple inheritance.

To create an interface, you use the `interface` statement:

FOR C++ PROGRAMMERS

Unlike C++, C# supports Java-style interfaces, so this entire topic is C#-only.

MULTIPLE INHERITANCE VERSUS ABSTRACT CLASSES

Although interfaces are traditionally thought of in terms of a simplified version of multiple inheritance, it might be better to think of them as an extension of abstract classes. They're similar to abstract classes, whose members must be specifically implemented, except that you can implement multiple interfaces at once, whereas you can inherit from only one abstract class at a time.

```
[attributes] [modifiers] interface identifier [:base-list] {interface-body}[;]
```

Here are the parts of this statement:

- *attributes* (Optional)—Hold additional declarative information, as we'll see in Chapter 14, "Using Attributes and Reflection."

- *modifiers* (Optional)—The allowed modifiers are new and a valid combination of the four access modifiers.

- *identifier*—The interface name.

- *base-list* (Optional)—A list that contains one or more explicit base interfaces separated by commas.

- *interface-body*—Declarations of the interface members.

Implementing Interfaces

Say, for example, that you wanted to make sure that the Window class implemented both an Open and a Close method. To do that, you could make that class implement two interfaces, IOpenable, which has an Open method, and ICloseable, which has a Close method (you can add as many members to an interface as you like, of course, not just one):

```
interface IOpenable
{
  void Open();
}

interface ICloseable
{
  void Close();
}
```

Now you can indicate that your Window class will implement both IOpenable and ICloseable like this (both classes and structs can implement interfaces):

```
public class Window : IOpenable, ICloseable
{
      .
      .
      .
  }
}
```

You have to implement the members of these interfaces as well:

```csharp
public class Window : IOpenable, ICloseable
{
    public void Open()
    {
        System.Console.WriteLine("Opening...");
    }

    public void Close()
    {
        System.Console.WriteLine("Closing...");
    }
}
```

Now you can create new objects of the Window class and call that object's Open and Close methods, as you see in ch04_09.cs, Listing 4.9.

LISTING 4.9   Implementing Interfaces (ch04_09.cs)

```csharp
public class ch04_09
{

    static void Main()
    {
        Window window = new Window();
        window.Open();
        window.Close();
    }
}

interface IOpenable
{
    void Open();
}

interface ICloseable
{
    void Close();
}

public class Window : IOpenable, ICloseable
{
```

LISTING 4.9   Continued

```
  public void Open()
  {
   System.Console.WriteLine("Opening...");
  }

  public void Close()
  {
   System.Console.WriteLine("Closing...");
  }
}
```

Here's what you see when you run ch04_09.cs. Note that both Open and Close work as we've implemented them:

```
C:\>ch04_09
Opening...
Closing...
```

Deriving New Interfaces from Current Interfaces

You can derive new interfaces just as you do with classes; for example, you can base the IOpenable interface on an interface named IComponent:

```
interface IOpenable : IComponent
{
  void Open();
}
```

Now a class or struct that implements IOpenable has to implement all the members of the IOpenable and IComponent interfaces. You can also combine interfaces by having an interface implement multiple interfaces like this, where IOpenable implements both the IComponent and IBase interfaces:

```
interface IOpenable : IComponent, IBase
{
}
```

As you'd expect, however, you cannot create an object from an interface directly. Because an interface only specifies members and doesn't implement them, all the code you need for those members would be missing. However, you can use a cast to create an *instance* of an interface in C#. For example, you can cast the window object in ch04_09.cs to an instance of IOpenable using the cast (IOpenable). Because you've created this instance by casting the window object, you can then call its Open method (which is implemented in the Window class):

```
static void Main()
{
  Window window = new Window();
  window.Open();
  window.Close();
  IOpenable iwindow = (IOpenable) window;
  iwindow.Open();
}
```

If you added the highlighted code here to
ch04_09.cs, you'd see this new result:

```
C:\>ch04_09
Opening...
Closing...
Opening...
```

Checking Interface Types

It can be a good idea to determine
whether an object supports a particular
interface before trying to call that interface's methods. There are several ways of determining
which interfaces an object supports at runtime.

For example, you have an interface named IOpenable and the Window class implements that
interface:

```
interface IOpenable
{
  void Open();
}

public class Window : IOpenable
{
  public void Open()
  {
   System.Console.WriteLine("Opening...");
  }
}
```

You now create a Window object named window and want to determine whether it supports
the IOpenable interface. One way to do that is with the is keyword, which lets you know

> **USING INTERFACE INSTANCES WITH VALUE TYPES**
>
> Assume for example that you implement an interface in a struct—that is, a value type. When you create an interface instance using a variable of that struct type, there's an implicit boxing that goes on, creating an object. If you modify the data in the object, bear in mind that you *won't* be modifying the data in the original variable.

whether an object *is* a certain type. This keyword returns a `bool` value, `true` or `false`, so we can use it like this to determine whether `window` implements the `IOpenable` interface. Note that if `window` does implement the interface, we call its `Open` method, but not otherwise:

```
if (window is IOpenable){
  window.Open();
}
```

Alternatively, you can try to cast the window object to an instance of the `IOpenable` interface, and if there's no cast exception (`System.InvalidCastException`), you can call the `Open` method as before:

```
IOpenable iwindow;

try
{
  iwindow = window as IOpenable;
  iwindow.Open();
}
catch(System.InvalidCastException)
{
  System.Console.WriteLine("Casting exception.");
}
```

In fact, there's an easier way to try a cast to `IOpenable` without having to handle cast exceptions. You can use the as keyword to cast `window` to the `IOpenable` interface instance `iwindow`; if `iwindow` ends up being null, the cast wasn't successful, but no illegal cast exception occurs. You can see this and the other two methods of checking interface implementations in ch04_10.cs, Listing 4.10.

LISTING 4.10   Checking Interface Types (ch04_10.cs)

```
public class ch04_10
{
  static void Main()
  {
   Window window = new Window();
   IOpenable iwindow;

   if (window is IOpenable){
     window.Open();
   }

   try
```

LISTING 4.10 Continued

```
  {
    iwindow = window as IOpenable;
    iwindow.Open();
  }
  catch(System.InvalidCastException)
  {
    System.Console.WriteLine("Casting exception.");
  }

  iwindow = window as IOpenable;

  if(iwindow != null){
    window.Open();
  }
  }
}

interface IOpenable
{
  void Open();
}

public class Window : IOpenable
{
  public void Open()
  {
   System.Console.WriteLine("Opening...");
  }
}
```

Overriding Implemented Members

You can also make your implementation of an interface method virtual, meaning you can override it later. You can see an example in ch04_11.cs (Listing 4.11); there, the Window class implements the IOpenable interface's Open method as a virtual method. The Menu class is based on the Window class, and overrides the Open method with its own version.

IS VERSUS AS

It turns out that the is operator is not efficiently implemented internally; as is slightly more efficient, thus saving your code a little time.

LISTING 4.11   Overriding Implemented Members (ch04_11.cs)

```
public class ch04_11
{
  static void Main()
  {
    Window window = new Window();
    window.Open();

    Menu menu = new Menu();
    menu.Open();
  }
}

interface IOpenable
{
  void Open();
}

public class Window : IOpenable
{
  public virtual void Open()
  {
    System.Console.WriteLine("Opening...");
  }
}

public class Menu : Window
{
  public override void Open()
  {
    System.Console.WriteLine("Displaying items...");
  }
}
```

Here's what you see when you run ch04_11.cs:

```
C:\>ch04_11
Opening...
Displaying items...
```

Note that you don't have to use a virtual/override pair as was done in ch04_11.cs. You can simply use new to create a new version of Open if you prefer.

Resolving Member Conflicts

What if you're implementing interfaces and two members clash by having the same name? For example, say you have two interfaces like these, both with an Open method:

```
interface IOpenable
{
  void Open();
}

interface IComponent
{
  void Open();
}
```

How can you implement both interfaces and resolve the conflict here? You can do that with *explicit implementation,* where you indicate that you're explicitly implementing an interface's method. For example, to explicitly implement the IComponent.Open method, you can use code like this (explicitly implemented methods can't be declared with the abstract, new, virtual, or override keywords):

```
public class Window : IOpenable, IComponent
{
  void IComponent.Open()
  {
    System.Console.WriteLine("IComponent.Open opening...");
  }
    .
    .
    .
}
```

Now you can implement the IOpenable interface's Open method without needing to qualify it as IOpenable.Open. You can just define it as Open:

```
public class Window : IOpenable, IComponent
{
  void IComponent.Open()
  {
    System.Console.WriteLine("IComponent.Open opening...");
  }
```

```
    public void Open()
    {
      System.Console.WriteLine("IOpenable.Open opening...");
    }
}
```

This makes IOpenable's version of Open the implicit version that will be called when you use objects of the Window class:

```
Window window = new Window();
window.Open();  //Calls IOpenable.Open
```

On the other hand, you can also call IComponent's version of Open using an object of the Window class, but it takes a little more work. In this case, you have to create an instance of the IComponent class, which we'll call iwindow, and call iwindow.Open, as you see in ch04_12.cs, Listing 4.12. That's how you reach an explicitly implemented method.

LISTING 4.12   Resolving Member Conflicts (ch04_12.cs)

```
public class ch04_12
{
  static void Main()
  {
    Window window = new Window();
    window.Open();

    IComponent iwindow = window as IComponent;
    if (iwindow != null)
    {
      iwindow.Open();
    }
  }
}

interface IOpenable
{
  void Open();
}

interface IComponent
{
  void Open();
}
```

LISTING 4.12   Continued

```
public class Window : IOpenable, IComponent
{
  void IComponent.Open()
  {
    System.Console.WriteLine("IComponent.Open opening...");
  }

  public void Open()
  {
    System.Console.WriteLine("IOpenable.Open opening...");
  }
}
```

Here's what you see when you run ch04_12.cs. Note that we were able to reach both the implicit and explicit Open method:

```
C:\>ch04_12
IOpenable.Open opening...
IComponent.Open opening...
```

You can also have conflicts if you base one interface on another. For example, take a look at this code, where IOpenable inherits IComponent, and both have an Open method:

```
interface IComponent
{
  void Open();
}

interface IOpenable : IComponent
{
  void new Open();
}
```

In this case, to avoid conflicts, you have to implement one Open method or the other—or both—explicitly. Here are your options in a class that implements the IOpenable class:

```
public class Window : IOpenable
{
  void IComponent.Open(){}
  public void Open(){}
}
```

```
public class Window : IOpenable
{
  void Open(){}
  public void IOpenable.Open(){}
}
```

```
public class Window : IOpenable
{
  void IComponent.Open(){}
  public void IOpenable.Open(){}
}
```

Working with Delegates

Delegates let you pass methods as parameters. They provide you with another form of polymorphism, because you can assign methods to delegates at runtime, leaving the rest of your code unchanged but calling the methods you specify at runtime. You declare a delegate like this:

```
[attributes] [modifiers] delegate result-type identifier ([formal-parameters]);
```

Here are the parts of this statement:

- *attributes* (Optional)—Hold additional declarative information, as we'll see in Chapter 14.

- *modifiers* (Optional)—The allowed modifiers are new and a valid combination of the four access modifiers.

- *result-type*—The result type, which matches the return type of the method.

- *identifier*—The delegate name.

- *formal-parameters* (Optional)—The parameter list. If a parameter is a pointer, the delegate must be declared with the unsafe modifier.

FOR C++ PROGRAMMERS

In C++, the counterpart to delegates is the function pointer, but delegates are objects, and are safe in ways that pointers can't be. Delegates don't exist in C++, making all the material from this point to the end of the chapter related to C# only.

Here's an example. Say that you had a method, Caller, to which you wanted to pass other methods in order to call those methods. For example, if you had a method named Display that you wanted to have Caller call, you could pass a delegate to Caller, and Caller could use that delegate to call Display.

Here's how it works in code; you start by declaring a new delegate like this:

```
delegate void CallerDelegate(string text);
```

Now you can set up Caller to accept a delegate of the type we've just created:

```
delegate void CallerDelegate(string text);

public static void Caller(CallerDelegate SomeMethod)
{
    .
    .
    .
}
```

Inside Caller, we can use the delegate as we would any method, so to call Display with the text "No worries.", we use this code:

```
public static void Caller(CallerDelegate SomeMethod)
{
    SomeMethod("No worries.");
}
```

All that's left is to create the Display method and pass it as a delegate to Caller. This method must have the same signature as the delegate declaration itself, which means the Display method that displays the text you pass to it, looks like this:

```
public static void Display(string text)
{
    System.Console.WriteLine(text);
}
```

Now we just have to pass the Display method to Caller using a delegate. You can see how that works in ch04_13.cs, Listing 4.13.

LISTING 4.13   Using a Delegate (ch04_13.cs)

```
delegate void CallerDelegate(string text);

class ch04_13
{
    public static void Main()
    {
        Caller(new CallerDelegate(Display));
    }
```

LISTING 4.13   Continued

```
    public static void Caller(CallerDelegate SomeMethod)
    {
     SomeMethod("No worries.");
    }

    public static void Display(string text)
    {
     System.Console.WriteLine(text);
    }
}
```

Here's what you see when you run ch04_13.cs. Note that this example passes the `Display` method to `Caller` using a delegate, and that `Caller` calls `Display` using that delegate:

```
C:\>ch04_13
No worries.
```

In ch04_13.cs, we used a delegate with the static method `Display`, but delegates aren't restricted to static methods, of course. Say you have a class with a static member, `DisplayStatic`, and an instance method, `DisplayInstance`, both of which display a message:

```
public class Messager
{
  public void DisplayInstance()
  {
   System.Console.WriteLine("Hello from the instance method!");
  }

  static public void DisplayStatic()
  {
   System.Console.WriteLine("Hello from the static method!");
  }
}
```

You can use delegates to call both methods. When you pass the instance method to the delegate constructor, you just qualify the name of the method with the name of the object you want to use. You can see this in ch04_14.cs, Listing 4.14, where we pass `obj.DisplayInstance` to the delegate constructor.

LISTING 4.14   Using a Delegate with Static and Non-Static Methods (ch04_14.cs)

```
delegate void Delegate();

public class ch04_14
{
  static public void Main()
  {
    Messager obj = new Messager();

    Delegate delegate1 = new Delegate(obj.DisplayInstance);
    delegate1();

    delegate1 = new Delegate(Messager.DisplayStatic);
    delegate1();
  }
}

public class Messager
{
  public void DisplayInstance()
  {
   System.Console.WriteLine("Hello from the instance method!");
  }

  static public void DisplayStatic()
  {
   System.Console.WriteLine("Hello from the static method!");
  }
}
```

Here's what you see when you run ch04_14.cs:

```
C:\>ch04_14
Hello from the instance method!
Hello from the static method!
```

Delegate-Based Polymorphism

Delegates give you a new form of polymorphism, because you can assign a delegate variable different delegates at runtime. Your code stays the same, but different methods are called depending on which delegates you assign to the delegate variable. You can see an example of this in ch04_15.cs, Listing 4.15, where a single delegate variable, delegateVariable, is assigned two delegates and is used to call the corresponding methods at runtime.

LISTING 4.15   Delegate-Based Polymorphism (ch04_15.cs)

```
public class ch04_15
{
  static public void Main()
  {
   Delegate delegateVariable;
   Messager obj = new Messager();

    delegateVariable = new Delegate(obj.Display1);
    delegateVariable();

    delegateVariable = new Delegate(obj.Display2);
    delegateVariable();
  }
}

public class Messager
{
  public void Display1()
  {
   System.Console.WriteLine("No worries.");
  }

  public void Display2()
  {
   System.Console.WriteLine("No worries again.");
  }
}
```

Here's what you see when you run ch04_15.cs. As you can see, we've used the same delegate variable to call two methods at runtime:

```
C:\>ch04_16
No worries.
No worries again.
```

Creating Static Delegates

So far, the delegates we've created were created in the calling code. You can also create static delegates that are built into a class, so the calling code doesn't need to create its own delegate from scratch. For example, say that you had a class named Messager that has a Display method, and that you wanted to add a static delegate to Messager that corresponded to Display. To do that, you first declare a delegate type:

```
public class Messager
{
  public delegate void delegate1();

  static public void Display()
  {
   System.Console.WriteLine("No worries.");
  }
}
```

Then you create a static delegate for Display, which we'll name DisplayAlias, like this:

```
public class Messager
{
  public delegate void delegate1();

  public static readonly delegate1 DisplayAlias = new delegate1(Display);

  static public void Display()
  {
   System.Console.WriteLine("No worries.");
  }
}
```

Now DisplayAlias is a static member of the Messager class, and a delegate for the Display method. The calling code no longer has to go to the trouble of creating its own delegate; it can simply use the Messager class's built-in DisplayAlias static delegate, as you see in ch04_16.cs, Listing 4.16.

LISTING 4.16   Creating a Static Delegate (ch04_16.cs)

```
public class ch04_15
{
  static public void Main()
  {
  Messager.DisplayAlias();
  }
```

LISTING 4.16   Continued

```
}

public class Messager
{
  public delegate void delegate1();

  public static readonly delegate1 DisplayAlias = new delegate1(Display);

  static public void Display()
  {
   System.Console.WriteLine("No worries.");
  }
}
```

Here's what you see when you run ch04_16.cs, showing that `DisplayAlias` is indeed a delegate for the `Display` method:

```
C:\>ch04_16
No worries.
```

Delegate Multicasting

You can also use a single delegate to call multiple methods, a process called *multicasting*. In fact, operators like +, -, +=, and -= are overridden so you can add and remove delegates to other delegates. Let's take a look at an example. You want to send a message to three devices—the display, the debug log, and the system log. We'll use these three methods, `DisplayMethod`, `DebuggerMethod`, and `SystemLogMethod`, to do so:

```
public static void DisplayMethod(string text)
{
  System.Console.WriteLine("Sending to display: {0}", text);
}

public static void DebuggerMethod(string text)
{
  System.Console.WriteLine("Sending to debug log: {0}", text);
}

public static void SystemLogMethod(string text)
{
  System.Console.WriteLine("Sending to system log: {0}", text);
}
```

We can create a delegate for each one of these methods, `Display`, `Debugger`, and `SystemLog`, as well as a delegate for multicasting—`multiCaster`:

```
delegate void DisplayDelegate(string text);

DisplayDelegate Display, Debugger, SystemLog, multiCaster;

Display = new DisplayDelegate(DisplayMethod);
Debugger = new DisplayDelegate(DebuggerMethod);
SystemLog = new DisplayDelegate(SystemLogMethod);
```

Now we can use +, -, +=, and -= operators to combine delegates as we want in the `multiCaster` delegate. For example, to send the text `"No worries."` to the display and the debugger log at the same time, you can do this:

```
multiCaster = Display + Debugger;
System.Console.WriteLine("multiCaster = Display + Debugger");
multiCaster("No worries.");
```

Here's what you see in this case. Note that both `DisplayMethod` and `DebuggerMethod` were called by using a single delegate:

```
multiCaster = Display + Debugger
Sending to display: No worries.
Sending to debug log: No worries.
```

We'll put `multiCaster` to work in ch04_17.cs, Listing 4.17, adding and removing delegates from this multicast delegate.

LISTING 4.17 Multicasting Delegates (ch04_17.cs)

```
delegate void DisplayDelegate(string text);

public class ch04_17
{
  public static void Main()
  {
    DisplayDelegate Display, Debugger, SystemLog, multiCaster;

    Display = new DisplayDelegate(DisplayMethod);
    Debugger = new DisplayDelegate(DebuggerMethod);
    SystemLog = new DisplayDelegate(SystemLogMethod);
```

LISTING 4.17   Continued

```
    multiCaster = Display + Debugger;
    System.Console.WriteLine("multiCaster = Display + Debugger");
    multiCaster("No worries.");
    System.Console.WriteLine();

    multiCaster += SystemLog;
    System.Console.WriteLine("multiCaster += SystemLog");
    multiCaster("No worries.");
    System.Console.WriteLine();

    multiCaster -= Display;
    System.Console.WriteLine("multiCaster -= Display");
    multiCaster("No worries.");
  }

  public static void DisplayMethod(string text)
  {
    System.Console.WriteLine("Sending to display: {0}", text);
  }

  public static void DebuggerMethod(string text)
  {
    System.Console.WriteLine("Sending to debug log: {0}", text);
  }

  public static void SystemLogMethod(string text)
  {
    System.Console.WriteLine("Sending to system log: {0}", text);
  }
}
```

Here are the results of ch04_17.cs, where you can see the +, +=, and -= operators at work, adding and removing delegates as detailed in the text this example displays:

```
C:\c#\ch04>ch04_17
multiCaster = Display + Debugger
Sending to display: No worries.
Sending to debug log: No worries.

multiCaster += SystemLog
Sending to display: No worries.
```

```
Sending to debug log: No worries.
Sending to system log: No worries.

multiCaster -= Display
Sending to debug log: No worries.
Sending to system log: No worries.
```

Handling Events with Delegates

Objects in C# can also support *events*. Events were created for graphical user interfaces (GUIs) like Windows so the user can direct program execution. When something happens in a GUI—the user clicks a button, moves a scroll bar, or closes a window—an event occurs. GUI code is written to respond to events, rather than simply to execute huge monolithic code blocks without user interaction. When code responds to events, the user directs the action and the program responds.

We're going to work with events in detail when creating Windows and Web applications, because events are designed for GUI environments. However, because you can handle events in C# with delegates, we'll get an introduction to the topic here. In C#, an object can *publish* an event and other objects can *subscribe* to that event so they'll be notified when the event has occurred.

When you subscribe to an event, you use a delegate to indicate which method you want to call when the event occurs. Here's an example; say you create a `Button` class that will display a button, giving this class a `name` field to hold the name of the button:

```
public class Button
{
  public string name = "Button 1";
  .
  .
  .
}
```

You can give this class an event named `OnClick` that will occur when the button is clicked, and a delegate that will be in charge of calling all code that subscribes to the `OnClick` event:

```
public class Button
{
  public string name = "Button 1";

  public delegate void ButtonClickDelegate(object button, string text);
```

```
public event ButtonClickDelegate OnClick;
    .
    .
    .
}
```

You declare an event like `OnClick` with the event statement:

```
[attributes] [modifiers] event type declarator;
[attributes] [modifiers] event type member-name {accessor-declarations};
```

Here are the parts of this statement:

- *attributes* (Optional)—Hold additional declarative information, as we'll see in Chapter 14.

- *modifiers* (Optional)—Optional modifiers include `abstract`, `new`, `override`, `static`, `virtual`, `extern`, or one of the four access modifiers.

- *type*—The delegate of this event.

- *declarator*—The name of the event.

- *member-name*—The name of the event.

- *accessor-declarations* (Optional)—Declaration of the accessors, which are used to add and remove event handlers in client code (although we're not going to use accessors in this example). The accessors are `add` and `remove`.

We'll also add a method named `Click` to the `Button` class, which will *fire* the `OnClick` event (that is, make the `OnClick` event occur), giving you some way of making the `OnClick` event happen:

```
public class Button
{
  public string name = "Button 1";

  public delegate void ButtonClickDelegate(object button, string text);

  public event ButtonClickDelegate OnClick;

  public void Click()
  {
    OnClick(this, "Clicked");
  }
}
```

Other code can use this delegate to subscribe to this event and so be called when the event occurs. To see how that works, take a look at the ButtonHandlerClass class. This class subscribes to button events when you pass a Button object to its Subscribe method. To subscribe to an event, you just add your own delegate to the delegate in the Button class, like this:

```
public class ButtonHandlerClass
{
  public void Subscribe(Button button)
  {
    button.OnClick += new Button.ButtonClickDelegate(ButtonHandler);
  }
  .
  .
  .
}
```

The delegate we've added to the delegate in the Button class is for the ButtonHandler method, which means that method will be called when the button's OnClick event occurs. We can display a message in the ButtonHandler method indicating that it was notified of the event:

```
public class ButtonHandlerClass
{
  public void Subscribe(Button button)
  {
    button.OnClick += new Button.ButtonClickDelegate(ButtonHandler);
  }

  public void ButtonHandler(object button, string text)
  {
    System.Console.WriteLine("{0} reports: {1}",
      ((Button) button).name, text);
  }
}
```

At this point, the code is ready to go. To subscribe to a button's OnClick event, you just pass the Button object to a ButtonHandlerClass object's Subscribe method:

```
Button button = new Button();
ButtonHandlerClass buttonHandler1 = new ButtonHandlerClass();

buttonHandler1.Subscribe(button);
```

This subscribes buttonHandler1 to the button's OnClick event. When you call the button's Click method (which is how we fire the OnClick event in this example), the buttonHandler1 object's Buttonhandler method is called.

You can subscribe as many objects to the button's OnClick event as you want, as you see in ch04_18.cs, Listing 4.18, where two objects subscribe to that event. When the button's OnClick event fires, the event handlers that have subscribed to that event will be called, making them display a message.

LISTING 4.18   Events and Delegates (ch04_18.cs)

```
public class ch04_18
{
  public static void Main()
  {
    Button button = new Button();

    ButtonHandlerClass buttonHandler1 = new ButtonHandlerClass ();
    buttonHandler1.Subscribe(button);

    ButtonHandlerClass buttonHandler2 = new ButtonHandlerClass ();
    buttonHandler2.Subscribe(button);

    button.Click();
  }
}

public class Button
{
  public string name = "Button 1";
  public delegate void ButtonClickDelegate(object button, string text);

  public event ButtonClickDelegate OnClick;

  public void Click()
  {
    OnClick(this, "Clicked");
  }
}

public class ButtonHandlerClass
{
  public void Subscribe(Button button)
```

LISTING 4.18 Continued

```
  {
    button.OnClick += new Button.ButtonClickDelegate(ButtonHandler);
  }

  public void ButtonHandler(object button, string text)
  {
    System.Console.WriteLine("{0} reports: {1}",
      ((Button) button).name, text);
  }
}
```

Here's what you see when you run ch04_18.cs, shown in Listing 4.18. As you can see, both subscribed objects were notified of the OnClick event:

```
C:\>ch04_18
Button 1 reports: Clicked
Button 1 reports: Clicked
```

That's it for this chapter. In Chapter 5, "Working with C# Streams," we're going to work with I/O in C# when we take a look at data streams.

In Brief

This chapter looked at the important OOP topic of inheritance, the process of deriving one class from another. Although inheritance is familiar to OOP programmers, C# has its own takes on it. For example, structs are value types in C#, so they don't support inheritance. Here is an overview of the topics we discussed:

- There are various access modifiers available for protecting the members of a class or struct; the default access is private. We can create new members with the new keyword, hiding the members with the same signature in the base class. We can also reach the hidden members using the base keyword. And we can use virtual methods designed to be overridden with the override keyword.

- C# lets you create both abstract classes, whereby you need to derive new classes before you can create objects, and sealed classes, which you can't derive anything from.

- C# supports polymorphism using virtual methods, and using polymorphism, you can load derived class objects into base class variables and call the methods of the derived class using that variable. With polymorphism, you can decide at runtime which object's method you want to call, without having to rewrite your code.

- C# also supports boxing, unboxing, and nested classes. Boxing is the process of wrapping a value type in an object, whereas unboxing is the process of converting an object to a value type.

- Interfaces let you specify a set of members that classes or structs that implement those interfaces must define. Interfaces act like contracts—if you implement an interface, you agree to implement all the members of that interface.

- C# also supports delegates, which work like function pointers in C++, giving you a form of polymorphism much like inheritance-based polymorphism. In C#, delegates are objects, not pointers, and are far safer.

Working with Streams in C#

5

Working with Directories

This chapter covers file handling, so we'll start with the File and Directory classes, which enable you to work on files without opening them (you can copy a file to another directory, for example). After using the File and Directory classes to manipulate files and directories, we'll turn to the use of streams to handle the contents of files and other data streams directly.

There's a lot of support for working directly with directories in C#. For example, you can use the static members of the Environment class to get the current directory, the system directory, and so on. Here are some of the more useful members of the Environment class:

- System.Environment.CurrentDirectory—Returns or sets the (fully qualified) path of the current directory.

- System.Environment.SystemDirectory—Returns the (fully qualified) path of the system directory.

- System.Environment.CommandLine—Returns the command line used to start this application.

- System.Environment.GetEnvironmentVariable ("SystemRoot")—Returns the (fully qualified) path of the system root directory.

- System.Environment.GetEnvironmentVariable ("windir")—Returns the (fully qualified) path of the Windows directory.

FOR C++ PROGRAMMERS

Although stream handling in C# is similar to what you see in C++ in theory, in practice you use different classes and methods in C#. C# does not support the standard C# streams such as `cin`, `cout`, `istream`, `ostream`, and so on, so this chapter is new material for the C++ programmer.

QUOTING PATHNAMES

The directory separator character in Windows pathnames, \, can cause a lot of trouble in quoted strings because it's also the character you use for character escapes. If you want to avoid accidental escapes, use an ampersand, @, to indicate those strings are literals, as in @"c:\c#\example5.cs".

Working with directories in C# revolves around the `Directory` and `DirectoryInfo` classes. The `Directory` class is a static class, and you can find its significant methods in Table 5.1, allowing you to delete, move, navigate, and determine whether a directory exists.

TABLE 5.1

Significant Static Public Directory Methods

METHOD	PURPOSE
CreateDirectory	Creates directories.
Delete	Deletes a directory (and its contents).
Exists	Determines whether the given path refers to an existing directory.
GetCreationTime	Returns the creation date and time of a directory.
GetCurrentDirectory	Returns the current working directory of the application.
GetDirectories	Returns the names of subdirectories in the given directory.
GetDirectoryRoot	Returns the volume and root information for a given path.
GetFiles	Returns the names of files in the given directory.
GetLastAccessTime	Returns the date and time the given file or directory was last accessed.
GetLastWriteTime	Returns the date and time the given file or directory was last written to.
GetLogicalDrives	Returns the names of the logical drives on this machine in the form "*<drive letter>*:\".
GetParent	Returns the parent directory of the given path, including absolute and relative paths.
Move	Moves a file or a directory and its contents to a new location.
SetCreationTime	Sets the creation date and time for the given file or directory.
SetCurrentDirectory	Sets the application's current working directory to the given directory.
SetLastAccessTime	Sets the date and time the given file or directory was last accessed.
SetLastWriteTime	Sets the date and time a directory was last written to.

The `DirectoryInfo` class gives you more information about a particular directory; you create objects of this class for a specific directory, and that object will hold information about that directory. You can see its significant public properties in Table 5.2 and its significant public methods in Table 5.3.

TABLE 5.2

Significant Public DirectoryInfo Properties

PROPERTY	PURPOSE
Exists	Returns a value indicating whether the directory exists.
FullName	Returns the full path of the directory or file.
LastAccessTime	Returns or sets the time the current file or directory was last accessed.
LastWriteTime	Returns or sets the time the current file or directory was last written to.
Name	Returns the name of this `DirectoryInfo` instance.
Parent	Returns the parent directory of a given subdirectory.
Root	Returns the root portion of a path.

TABLE 5.3

Significant Public DirectoryInfo Methods

METHOD	PURPOSE
Create	Creates a directory.
CreateSubdirectory	Creates a subdirectory or subdirectories using the given path.
Delete	Deletes a `DirectoryInfo` object and its contents from a path.
GetDirectories	Returns the subdirectories of the current directory.
GetFiles	Returns a list of the files in the current directory.
MoveTo	Moves a `DirectoryInfo` object and its contents to a new path.

Here's an example that will display the names of all the subdirectories in the current directory. To do that, we need a `DirectoryInfo` object for the current directory, and you can pass the current directory's path to the `DirectoryInfo` class's constructor to create that `DirectoryInfo` object. Then you can determine the subdirectories of the current directory with the `GetDirectories` method, which returns an array of `DirectoryInfo` objects:

```
using System.IO;

string currentDirectory = System.Environment.CurrentDirectory;

DirectoryInfo dir = new DirectoryInfo(currentDirectory);
DirectoryInfo[] directories = dir.GetDirectories();
```

Now you can loop over the `DirectoryInfo` objects we got as you see in ch05_01.cs, Listing 5.1, displaying the name of each subdirectory in the current directory and when it was last accessed.

LISTING 5.1   Getting Subdirectory Information (ch05_01.cs)

```
using System.IO;

class ch05_01
{
  public static void Main()
  {
    string currentDirectory = System.Environment.CurrentDirectory;

    DirectoryInfo dir = new DirectoryInfo(currentDirectory);

    DirectoryInfo[] directories = dir.GetDirectories();

    foreach (DirectoryInfo directory in directories)
    {
      System.Console.WriteLine("{0} was last accessed on {1}",
      directory.Name, directory.LastAccessTime);
    }
  }
}
```

When you run ch05_01.cs, you'll see something like this (the subdirectories in the current directory are named ch01–ch05 here):

```
C:\>ch05_01
ch01 was last accessed on 2/11
ch02 was last accessed on 2/4
ch03 was last accessed on 2/7
ch04 was last accessed on 2/13
ch05 was last accessed on 2/17
```

Working with Files

There's a parallel set of classes to `Directory` and `DirectoryInfo` that enables you to work with files—`File` and `FileInfo`. The `File` class works with files in general, and the `FileInfo` class works with a specific file. Like `Directory`, `File` is a static class, and you can see the significant public methods of this class in Table 5.4, which let you create files, delete them, move them, and more.

TABLE 5.4

Significant Static Public File Methods

METHOD	PURPOSE
AppendText	Appends Unicode text to a file.
Copy	Copies a file to a new file.
Create	Creates a file using the given path.
CreateText	Creates or opens a file for writing.
Delete	Deletes the given file. (No exception is thrown if the given file does not exist.)
Exists	Determines whether the given file exists.
GetCreationTime	Returns the creation date and time of the given file or directory.
GetLastAccessTime	Returns the date and time the given file or directory was last accessed.
GetLastWriteTime	Returns the date and time the given file or directory was written to last.
Move	Moves a given file to a new location.
Open	Opens a file stream for a file.
OpenRead	Opens an existing file for reading.
OpenText	Opens an existing text file for reading.
OpenWrite	Opens an existing file for writing.
SetCreationTime	Sets the date and time the file was created.
SetLastAccessTime	Sets the date and time the given file was last accessed.
SetLastWriteTime	Sets the date and time that the given file was last written to.

You can see the significant public properties of the FileInfo class in Table 5.5 and its significant public methods in Table 5.6.

TABLE 5.5

Significant Public FileInfo Properties

PROPERTY	PURPOSE
CreationTime	Returns or sets the creation time of the current FileSystemInfo object.
Exists	Returns true if a file exists, false otherwise.
Extension	Returns the string representing the extension part of the file.
FullName	Returns the full path of the directory or file.
LastAccessTime	Returns or sets the time the current file or directory was last accessed.
LastWriteTime	Returns or sets the time when the current file or directory was written to last.
Length	Returns the size of a file.
Name	Returns the name of the file.

TABLE 5.6
Significant Public FileInfo Methods

METHOD	PURPOSE
AppendText	Appends text to the file.
CopyTo	Copies an existing file to a new one.
Create	Creates a file.
CreateText	Creates a StreamWriter object that writes a new text file.
Delete	Deletes a file.
MoveTo	Moves a given file to a new location.
Open	Opens a file.
OpenRead	Creates a read-only FileStream object.
OpenText	Creates a StreamReader that reads from an existing text file.
OpenWrite	Creates a write-only FileStream object.
Refresh	Refreshes the state of the object.

Here's an example using the FileInfo class to determine the name, length, and last modified date of all the files in the current directory. You can use the GetFiles method of a DirectoryInfo object to get an array of FileInfo objects. We loop over that array in ch05_02.cs, Listing 5.2, displaying the filenames and last-modified times.

LISTING 5.2   Getting File Information (ch05_02.cs)

```csharp
using System.IO;

class ch05_02
{
  public static void Main()
  {
    string currentDirectory =
      System.Environment.CurrentDirectory;

    DirectoryInfo dir = new DirectoryInfo(currentDirectory);

    FileInfo[] files = dir.GetFiles();

    foreach (FileInfo file in files)
    {
      System.Console.WriteLine(
        "{0} is {1} bytes long, last modified {2}.",
        file.Name, file.Length, file.LastWriteTime);
    }
  }
}
```

Here's the kind of display you see when you run ch05_02.cs:

```
C:\>ch05_02
ch05_02.cs is 518 bytes long, last modified 2/17 2:00:04 PM.
ch05_02.exe is 3584 bytes long, last modified 2/17 2:00:06 PM.
```

Here's another example, using the DirectoryInfo method CreateSubdirectory to create a new subdirectory named backup, and the FileInfo CopyTo method to copy all files in the current directory to the backup directory. You can see how this code works in ch05_03.cs, Listing 5.3.

LISTING 5.3 Copying Files (ch05_03.cs)

```csharp
using System.IO;

class ch05_03
{
  public static void Main()
  {
    string currentDirectory =
      System.Environment.CurrentDirectory;

    DirectoryInfo dir = new DirectoryInfo(currentDirectory);

    DirectoryInfo backupDirectory =
      dir.CreateSubdirectory("backup");

    FileInfo[] files = dir.GetFiles();

    foreach (FileInfo file in files)
    {
      string newName = backupDirectory.FullName +
        @"\" + file.Name;
      file.CopyTo(newName);
    }
  }
}
```

As you can see, the Directory, DirectoryInfo, File, and FileInfo classes enable you to work with directories and files without actually handing the data inside a file. As such, they provide only external services when handling your data; to open files and access their contents directly, you use streams.

Working with Streams

Streams are classes that specialize in data transfer. You use them to read and write data to and from files, networks, memory, strings, and the Internet. Here's an overview of the common stream classes in C#:

- `Stream`—Abstract class for working with bytes in streams; the base class for streams.

- `BinaryReader/BinaryWriter`—Reads and writes data in binary format.

- `BufferedStream`—Adds buffering to another stream.

- `MemoryStream`—Works with data in memory directly.

- `FileStream`—Reads and writes files. Supports synchronous and asynchronous random access to files.

- `TextReader/TextWriter`—Abstract text reader and writer classes that use Unicode.

- `StringReader/StringWriter`—Reads from and writes to text strings using streams.

- `NetworkStream`—Stream that works with a network connection.

You can determine the capability of a stream using the `CanRead`, `CanWrite`, and `CanSeek` properties. For streams that support seeking, use the `Seek` method and the `Position` property to get or set your current position in the stream, and the `Length` property to get the length of a stream. To write data to a stream, you use the `Write` method; to read data from a stream, you use the `Read` method.

You open a stream with the stream class's constructor; calling `Close` closes the stream. Some streams perform buffering of the underlying data to improve performance. For those streams, you can use the `Flush` method to clear any internal buffers and make sure that all data has been written out; the `Close` method also flushes internal data buffers. Usually, you're responsible for setting up your own data buffers, but the `BufferedStream` class provides the capability of wrapping a buffered stream around another stream in order to improve read and write performance.

Let's get to some examples. The basic, low-level stream for working with files is `FileStream`, so we'll start with that.

Reading and Writing Binary Files

The `FileStream` class lets you treat files in binary format, as simple bytes. Using the `Read` and `Write` methods of this class, you can read bytes from a file and write a set number of bytes out to a file. This class treats its data as a simple byte stream, without interpreting that data, as the text streams we'll see in a few pages do. You can see the significant public properties of `FileStream` in Table 5.7, and the significant public methods of that class in Table 5.8.

TABLE 5.7

Significant Public FileStream Properties

PROPERTY	PURPOSE
CanRead	Returns true if the current stream supports reading.
CanSeek	Returns true if the current stream supports seeking.
CanWrite	Returns true if the current stream supports writing.
Length	Returns the length in bytes of the stream.
Name	Returns the name of the file stream that was passed to the constructor.
Position	Returns or sets the current position of this stream.

TABLE 5.8

Significant Public FileStream Methods

METHOD	PURPOSE
BeginRead	Begins an asynchronous read.
BeginWrite	Begins an asynchronous write.
Close	Closes the file.
EndRead	Waits for the pending asynchronous read to finish.
EndWrite	Ends an asynchronous write, blocking (that is, not returning) until the I/O operation has completed.
Flush	Clears all buffers for this stream and causes any buffered data to be written out.
Lock	Stops other processes from changing the file stream (but permits read access).
Read	Reads a block of bytes and writes the data into a given buffer.
ReadByte	Reads a byte and advances the read position one byte.
Seek	Sets the current position of this stream to the given location.
SetLength	Sets the length of this stream to the given value.
Unlock	Allows access by other processes to a file that had been locked.
Write	Writes a block of bytes to this stream from a buffer.
WriteByte	Writes a byte to the current position in the file stream.

The best way to understand streams is to see them in action. Here's an example, ch05_04.cs, which treats its own source code as a binary file, reads it into a buffer, and writes that buffer out to a file named ch05_04.bak, providing you with a backup copy of this application's source code. This example uses the FileStream class's constructor to open files for reading and writing. As with other streams, there are various overloaded forms of this stream's constructor; here's the one we'll use:

```
FileStream(string, FileMode, FileAccess, FileShare);
```

Here are the members of the FileMode enumeration, indicating how you want to open the file:

- `FileMode.Append`

- `FileMode.Create`

- `FileMode.CreateNew`

- `FileMode.Open`

- `FileMode.OpenOrCreate`

- `FileMode.Truncate`

Here are the members of the `FileAccess` enumeration, indicating what you want to do with the file:

- `FileAccess.Read`

- `FileAccess.ReadWrite`

- `FileAccess.Write`

And here are the members of the `FileShare` enumeration, indicating how you want other processes to be able to work with the file at the same time:

- `FileShare.Inheritable`

- `FileShare.None`

- `FileShare.Read`

- `FileShare.ReadWrite`

- `FileShare.Write`

Here's how we use the `FileStream` constructor to open ch05_04.cs for reading, and ch05_04.bak for writing (this code will create ch05_04.bak if necessary, or if that file exists, open it and truncate it to zero length):

```
FileStream input = new FileStream("ch05_04.cs",
  FileMode.Open, FileAccess.Read, FileShare.None);
FileStream output = new FileStream("ch05_04.bak",
  FileMode.OpenOrCreate, FileAccess.Write, FileShare.None);
FileStream output = File.OpenWrite("ch05_04.bak");
```

We'll use the `FileStream` `Read` method to read data from the source file into a byte array buffer and the `Write` method to write that data to the target file. You pass the `Read` method the buffer to use for data, the offset in that buffer to store data at, and the length of the buffer. This method returns the number of bytes it's read, so we can keep looping until it runs out of data to read. The `Write` method writes data to the backup file; you pass it the data buffer, the offset in the buffer where your data starts, and the number of bytes to write. You can see this at work in ch05_04.cs, Listing 5.4.

LISTING 5.4   Opening and Writing Binary Files (ch05_04.cs)

```
using System.IO;

class ch05_04
{
  public static void Main()
  {
    int numberBytes;
    byte[] dataBuffer = new System.Byte[4096];

    FileStream input = new FileStream("ch05_04.cs",
      FileMode.Open, FileAccess.Read, FileShare.None);
    FileStream output = new FileStream("ch05_04.bak",
      FileMode.OpenOrCreate, FileAccess.Write, FileShare.None);

    while ((numberBytes = input.Read(dataBuffer, 0, 4096)) > 0)
    {
      output.Write(dataBuffer, 0, numberBytes);
    }

    input.Close();
    output.Close();
  }
}
```

USING FILE OR FILESTREAM METHODS

As with many stream techniques, there are many ways to open these files. Not only can you use other (and simpler) `FileStream` constructors, but you can also use the `File` class's `OpenRead` and `OpenWrite` methods to get `FileStream` objects. That is, the previous code performs the same action as this code:

```
FileStream input = File.OpenRead("ch05_04.cs");
FileStream output = File.OpenWrite("ch05_04.bak");.
```

When you run ch05_04, it opens its own source code, ch05_04.cs, and copies that code over, byte-by-byte, to ch05_04.bak.

Note that file handling is one of the most exception-prone things you can do in programming, so in general you should enclose your file-handling operations in a `try/catch` block like this:

```
using System.IO;

class ch05_04
```

```
{
  public static void Main()
  {
    int numberBytes;
    byte[] dataBuffer = new System.Byte[4096];

    try
    {
      FileStream input = new FileStream("ch05_04.cs",
        FileMode.Open, FileAccess.Read, FileShare.None);
      FileStream output = new FileStream("ch05_04.bak",
        FileMode.OpenOrCreate, FileAccess.Write, FileShare.None);

      while ((numberBytes = input.Read(dataBuffer, 0, 4096)) > 0)
      {
        output.Write(dataBuffer, 0, numberBytes);
      }

      input.Close();
      output.Close();
    }
    catch(System.Exception e)
    {
      System.Console.WriteLine(e.Message);
    }
  }
}
```

You can find which exceptions file-handling operations throw in the C# documentation; for example, the FileStream constructor can throw ArgumentException, ArgumentNullException, FileNotFoundException, IOException, and DirectoryNotFoundException exceptions. Although we're going to omit try/catch handling in this chapter for the sake of brevity, bear in mind that you should use it in general when working with files in a production environment.

Creating Buffered Streams

In the previous example, we created our own buffer to read and write data with. On the other hand, it turns out that sometimes, larger or smaller buffer sizes can improve file-handling performance. For that reason, you can wrap a FileStream object in a BufferedStream object, which will use its own internal buffer to maximize performance. All you have to do is to pass the FileStream object to the BufferedStream constructor and then use the returned BufferedStream object from then on. You can see this in action in ch05_05.cs, Listing 5.5.

LISTING 5.5   Buffered File I/O (ch05_05.cs)

```
using System.IO;

class ch05_05
{
  public static void Main()
  {
    int numberBytes;
    byte[] dataBuffer = new System.Byte[4096];

    FileStream input = new FileStream("ch05_05.cs",
      FileMode.Open, FileAccess.Read, FileShare.None);
    FileStream output = new FileStream("ch05_05.bak",
      FileMode.OpenOrCreate, FileAccess.Write, FileShare.None);

    BufferedStream bufferedInput = new BufferedStream(input);
    BufferedStream bufferedOutput = new BufferedStream(output);

    while ((numberBytes = bufferedInput.Read(dataBuffer, 0, 4096)) > 0)
    {
      bufferedOutput.Write(dataBuffer, 0, numberBytes);
    }

    bufferedOutput.Flush();
    bufferedInput.Close();
    bufferedOutput.Close();
  }
}
```

Reading and Writing Text Files

C# also supports the `StreamReader` and `StreamWriter` classes for working with text files. Text files are binary files like any other, but their data is Unicode text arranged into lines (in C#, a line is a sequence of characters followed by a line feed ["\n"] *or* a carriage return immediately followed by a line feed ["\r\n"]). What's special about the `StreamReader` and `StreamWriter` classes is that they offer the `ReadLine` and `WriteLine` methods that let you handle your data in a line-oriented way. You can see the significant public methods of the `StreamWriter` class in Table 5.9, and the significant public methods of the `StreamReader` class in Table 5.10.

TABLE 5.9

Significant Public StreamWriter Methods

METHOD	PURPOSE
BeginRead	Begins an asynchronous read.
Close	Closes the stream.
Flush	Clears all buffers for the current writer.
Write	Writes to the stream.
WriteLine	Writes data followed by a line terminator.

TABLE 5.10

Significant Public StreamReader Methods

METHOD	PURPOSE
Close	Closes the stream.
Peek	Returns the next available character but does not treat it as having been read.
Read	Reads the next character or next set of characters from the input stream.
ReadBlock	Reads a given maximum number of characters from the current stream.
ReadLine	Reads a line of characters from the current stream, returning them as a string.
ReadToEnd	Reads the stream from the current position to the end of the stream.

Here's an example, ch05_06.cs, which uses `StreamReader` to read a text file from disk and `StreamWriter` to write a copy of the file. This example opens its own source file, ch05_06.cs, and copies it to ch05_06.bak using text stream methods. In particular, this example uses the `WriteLine` and `ReadLine` methods to write and read whole lines of text at a time, as you'll see in ch05_06.cs, Listing 5.6. (Note that the `ReadLine` method returns `null` if there's no more data to read, letting us know when the program is finished reading the available data.)

LISTING 5.6   Working with Text Files (ch05_06.cs)

```
using System.IO;

class ch05_06
{
  public static void Main()
  {
    StreamReader input = new StreamReader("ch05_06.cs");
    StreamWriter output = new StreamWriter("ch05_06.bak");
    string inputString;

    while ((inputString = input.ReadLine())!= null)
    {
```

LISTING 5.6 Continued

```
      output.WriteLine(inputString);
   }

   input.Close();
   output.Close();
  }
}
```

When you run ch05_06.cs, it copies itself over into ch05_06.bak, line by line, using `ReadLine` and `WriteLine`, treating its data as text in a line-oriented way (as opposed to the `FileStream` class's `Read` and `Write` methods we saw earlier, which treat their data as binary). Note that an alternative to reading line by line in a loop is to use `ReadToEnd`, which reads all the text from your current position in the file, returning a single string.

Working with Asynchronous I/O

Up to this point, we've simply read data from a file and waited for the read operation to finish before doing anything. As we start working with network I/O, where things can be a lot slower, it won't be as easy to wait for reading and writing operations to complete. For that reason, the .NET Framework supports asynchronous I/O through the `BeginRead` and `BeginWrite` methods of the `Stream` class. You can call `BeginRead` to read a bufferfull of data, or `BeginWrite` to write a bufferfull of data, and then go on to do other work (we'll use a `for` loop for that purpose). You'll be called back when the read or write operation is complete.

Here's how it might work if you wanted to read a large file while doing other work at the same time. In this example, we'll create a method named `StartReading` to start the reading operation and then go on with other work. This method opens this example's source code file and calls the `BeginRead` method to read from the source code file into a buffer. To call `BeginRead`, you pass it the data buffer (`dataBuffer` here), the offset in the buffer at which to start reading (0), the number of bytes to read (`dataBuffer.Length`, using the `Length` array property), the delegate (`asyncDelegate`) to a callback method (`OnBufferFull`) which will be called when the buffer is full, and a state variable in which `BeginRead` can record the state of the current read operation (`null`). After the call to `BeginRead`, we'll turn to some other work—executing a `for` loop one million times:

```
FileStream input;
byte[] dataBuffer;
System.AsyncCallback asyncDelegate;

void StartReading()
{
  input = new FileStream("ch05_07.cs",
```

```
        FileMode.Open, FileAccess.Read, FileShare.None);
    dataBuffer = new byte[512];
    asyncDelegate = new System.AsyncCallback(this.OnBufferFull);

    input.BeginRead(dataBuffer, 0, dataBuffer.Length, asyncDelegate, null);

    for (int loopIndex = 0; loopIndex < 1000000; loopIndex++){}
}
```

While the loop executes, `BeginRead` fills the buffer with data. After a bufferfull of data has been read, the method `OnBufferFull` is called with an `IAsyncResult` argument, temporarily interrupting the `for` loop. You can pass the `IAsyncResult` argument to the stream's `EndRead` or `EndWrite` methods to get the number of bytes actually read or written, and we'll display that number here. If the number of bytes read is greater than 0, we'll go back to read more data into the buffer with another call to `BeginRead`:

```
void OnBufferFull(System.IAsyncResult asyncResult)
{
    int numberBytes = input.EndRead(asyncResult);
    System.Console.WriteLine(numberBytes);

    if (numberBytes > 0)
    {
        input.BeginRead(dataBuffer, 0, dataBuffer.Length, asyncDelegate, null);
    }
}
```

You can see the whole code in Listing 5.7, where we create an object of the `ch05_07` class so we can call non-static methods from `Main`, and call the `StartReading` method to start the asynchronous read process. (Note that to justify asynchronous reading here, you should use this kind of code to read in a huge file instead of just the sample's own source code.)

LISTING 5.7   Asynchronous File Reading (ch05_07.cs)

```
using System.IO;

public class ch05_07
{
    FileStream input;
    byte[] dataBuffer;
    System.AsyncCallback asyncDelegate;

    public static void Main()
```

LISTING 5.7   Continued

```csharp
    {
        ch05_07 appObj = new ch05_07();
        appObj.StartReading();
    }

    void StartReading()
    {
        input = new FileStream("ch05_07.cs",
            FileMode.Open, FileAccess.Read, FileShare.None);
        dataBuffer = new byte[512];
        asyncDelegate = new System.AsyncCallback(this.OnBufferFull);

        input.BeginRead(dataBuffer, 0, dataBuffer.Length, asyncDelegate, null);

        for (int loopIndex = 0; loopIndex < 1000000; loopIndex++){}
    }

    void OnBufferFull(System.IAsyncResult asyncResult)
    {
        int numberBytes = input.EndRead(asyncResult);
        System.Console.WriteLine(numberBytes);

        if (numberBytes > 0)
        {
            input.BeginRead(dataBuffer, 0, dataBuffer.Length, asyncDelegate, null);
        }
    }
}
```

The ch05_07.cs example is 1006 bytes long, and this is what you see when you run it. Note that it took two asynchronous buffered reads (512 + 494 = 1006) to read the file:

```
C:\>ch05_07
512
494
0
```

Working with Network I/O

In C#, you can read and write data using streams on the Internet much as we've already been doing with files. Network I/O is based on *sockets,* and a socket represents a connection to another socket somewhere on the network for the purposes of communication. You can use UDP or TCP/IP protocols with sockets, and we'll use the more common TCP/IP protocol here.

The type of applications we're going to build here are client/server applications. You build the client with the `TcpClient` class, and you build the server using the `TcpListener` class. Typically, the server *listens* for client connections, and when a client connects, a new `Socket` object is created. Using that socket, you can create a `NetWorkStream` object to send data to the client.

Creating a Network Server

Let's see how this works by creating a client/server TCP/IP application now. We'll start by building a server first, which will send its own source code to any client that connects to it, using an Internet socket. The server is based on the `TcpListener` class, and we'll use the `Socket` and `NetworkStream` classes to build it. You can see the significant public methods of the `TcpListener` class in Table 5.11, the significant public methods of the `Socket` class in Table 5.12, and the significant public methods of the `NetworkStream` class in Table 5.13.

TABLE 5.11

Significant Public TcpListener Methods

METHOD	PURPOSE
AcceptSocket	Accepts a connection request.
AcceptTcpClient	Accepts a TCP connection request.
Pending	Determines whether there are pending connection requests.
Start	Starts listening for connection requests.
Stop	Closes the listener.

TABLE 5.12

Significant Public Socket Methods

METHOD	PURPOSE
Accept	Creates a new socket for a new connection.
BeginAccept	Begins an asynchronous operation to accept an incoming connection.
BeginConnect	Begins an asynchronous request for a remote host connection.
BeginReceive	Begins to asynchronously receive data from a connected socket.
BeginReceiveFrom	Begins to asynchronously receive data from a given network device.
BeginSend	Sends data asynchronously to a connected socket.
BeginSendTo	Sends data asynchronously to a specific remote host.
Close	Closes the socket connection.
Connect	Establishes a connection to a remote host.
EndConnect	Ends a pending asynchronous connection request.
Listen	Places a socket in a listening state.

TABLE 5.12

Continued

METHOD	PURPOSE
Receive	Receives data from a bound socket.
ReceiveFrom	Receives a datagram and stores the source endpoint.
Send	Sends data to a connected socket.
Shutdown	Disables, sends, and receives using a socket.

TABLE 5.13

Significant Public NetworkStream Methods

METHOD	PURPOSE
BeginRead	Begins an asynchronous read from the network stream.
BeginWrite	Begins an asynchronous write to a stream.
Close	Closes the network stream.
EndRead	Handles the end of an asynchronous read.
EndWrite	Handles the end of an asynchronous write.
Flush	Flushes data from the stream.
Read	Reads data from the network stream.
ReadByte	Reads a byte from the stream and advances the position within the stream by one byte.
Seek	Sets the current position of the stream to the given value.
SetLength	Sets the length of the stream.
Write	Writes data to the network stream.
WriteByte	Writes a byte to the current position in the stream and advances the position in the stream by one byte.

Servers listen for connections to a client, and you can pass the TcpListener class an IP address (an Internet address of the form *xxx.xxx.xxx.xxx*; for example, microsoft.com's IP address is 207.46.134.222) and a port to listen on (ports range from 0 to 65,535). In this example, we'll use the constant IPAddress.Any to indicate that we want to listen for connections on any network interface, and the port number 65512. After you've created a TcpListener object in a method we'll call Listen, you start listening for connections from the client with the Start method:

```
private void Listen()
{
    TcpListener tcpListener = new TcpListener(IPAddress.Any, 65512);
    tcpListener.Start();
    .
```

.
.

IP ADDRESSES AND PORTS

To find an IP address, use the Windows `ping` utility like this: `ping microsoft.com`. Not all ports are available for programmer use; choosing a value above 65,000 is a good idea to avoid conflicts. To get a list of standard ports and their assigned uses, look at `http://www.iana.org/assignments/port-numbers`.

We'll do the actual listening with an endless while loop, calling the TCP/IP listener's `AcceptSocket` method to create a new socket; if that socket's `Connected` property is true, we've connected to the client. In that case, we use the `Socket` object to create a new `NetworkStream` object, and use the `NetworkStream` object to create a new `StreamWriter` object so we can use the `WriteLine` method to write to the client.

We'll also create a `StreamReader` object so we can read in this example's own source code. Here's how we read in that source code and send it to the client in the while loop:

```
private void Listen()
{
  TcpListener tcpListener = new TcpListener(IPAddress.Any, 65512);
  tcpListener.Start();

  System.Console.WriteLine("Listening...");

  while(true)
  {
    Socket socket = tcpListener.AcceptSocket();

    if (socket.Connected)
    {
      System.Console.WriteLine("Connected...");

      NetworkStream networkStream = new NetworkStream(socket);
      StreamWriter output = new StreamWriter(networkStream);
      StreamReader input = new StreamReader("ch05_08.cs");
      string inputString;

      System.Console.WriteLine("Sending...");

      while((inputString = input.ReadLine()) != null)
      {
        output.WriteLine(inputString);
        output.Flush();
      }
```

```
              .
              .
              .
          }
      System.Console.WriteLine("Quitting...");
  }
}
```

Note that after each WriteLine operation we call the Flush method to make sure all data was sent to the client and not cached. This is always a good idea with sockets.

All that's left is to call Listen from Main, close the streams when we're done, and break out of the while loop to finish the server's code. You can see how that works in the entire code in Listing 5.8.

LISTING 5.8   A Network Server (ch05_08.cs)

```
using System.IO;
using System.Net;
using System.Net.Sockets;

public class ch05_08
{
  public static void Main()
  {
    ch05_08 appObject = new ch05_08();
    appObject.Listen();
  }

  private void Listen()
  {
    TcpListener tcpListener = new TcpListener(IPAddress.Any, 65512);
    tcpListener.Start();

    System.Console.WriteLine("Listening...");

    while(true)
    {
      Socket socket = tcpListener.AcceptSocket();

      if (socket.Connected)
      {
        System.Console.WriteLine("Connected...");
```

LISTING 5.8   Continued

```
            NetworkStream networkStream = new NetworkStream(socket);
            StreamWriter output = new StreamWriter(networkStream);
            StreamReader input = new StreamReader("ch05_08.cs");
            string inputString;

            System.Console.WriteLine("Sending...");

            while((inputString = input.ReadLine()) != null)
            {
              output.WriteLine(inputString);
              output.Flush();
            }

            networkStream.Close();
            input.Close();
            output.Close();
            socket.Close();

            System.Console.WriteLine("Disconnected...");

            break;
          }
        System.Console.WriteLine("Quitting...");
      }
    }
}
```

Creating a Network Client

The next step is to create the client using the TcpClient class. You can see the significant public methods of the TcpClient class in Table 5.14.

TABLE 5.14

Significant Public TcpClient Methods

METHOD	PURPOSE
Close	Closes the TCP connection.
Connect	Connects the client to a remote TCP host using the given hostname and port number.
GetStream	Returns the network stream used to send and receive data.

We'll need a `TcpClient` object to create the client application for this example. You can pass the `TcpClient` constructor the name of a remote host and a port number to connect on, like this: (`"www.microsoft.com"`, `80`), where port 80 is the one used for HTTP communication. In this example, we'll run both the client and the server on the same machine, using port 65512, so the name of the host will be `"localHost"`. To use the `StreamReader ReadLine` method to read text from the server, we'll use the `TcpClient` object's `GetStream` method to get its underlying `NetWorkStream` stream, and pass that stream to the `StreamReader` constructor like this:

```
TcpClient client = new TcpClient("localHost", 65512);

NetworkStream network = client.GetStream();
System.IO.StreamReader input = new System.IO.StreamReader(network);
```

All that's left is to use `ReadLine` to keep reading text from the server, and then to close the connection, as you see in Listing 5.9.

LISTING 5.9 A Network Client (ch05_09.cs)

```
using System.Net.Sockets;

public class ch05_09
{
  static public void Main()
  {
    TcpClient client = new TcpClient("localHost", 65512);

    NetworkStream network = client.GetStream();
    System.IO.StreamReader input = new System.IO.StreamReader(network);

    string outputString;

    while((outputString = input.ReadLine()) != null)
    {
      System.Console.WriteLine(outputString);
    }
    input.Close();
    network.Close();
  }
}
```

That's all you need. Now start the server, ch05_08.exe, in one DOS window, and then the client, ch05_09.exe, in a second DOS window. The two will connect on port 65512; the server will send its own source code, ch05_08.cs, to the client, which will display it. Here's what you see when you run the server:

```
C:\>ch05_08
Listening...
Connected...
Sending...
Disconnected...
```

Here's what you see when you run the client. As you can see, we've connected using Internet sockets and ports:

```
C:\>ch05_09
using System.IO;
using System.Net;
using System.Net.Sockets;

public class ch05_08
{
    .
    .
    .
```

Supporting Asynchronous Network I/O

The previous example used synchronous network I/O, but if you have a number of clients all trying to connect to your server at once, it's a better idea to use asynchronous I/O. To handle multiple clients, for example, you might create a new class, Client, and create a new object of that class to handle each new client as requests come in. To perform the actual asynchronous reads and writes in that object, you can use BeginRead and BeginWrite, as we did earlier in this chapter.

You can see an example of this in ch05_10.cs, which is an asynchronous network I/O server, and ch05_11.cs, which is an asynchronous client. In this case, the server will be set up for both asynchronous reads and writes. The client will send it some text (in this example, that's the text message "Network Streaming!"), and the server will read that text asynchronously and write it back asynchronously, giving the server the time it needs to handle other clients.

In order to handle multiple clients, you can pass the connected socket to the Client class's constructor when a new client connects, thus creating a new Client object that will handle the new client. This enables you to accept as many incoming connections as you want to:

```
public static void Main()
{
  TcpListener tcpListener = new TcpListener(IPAddress.Any, 65512);
  tcpListener.Start();

  System.Console.WriteLine("Waiting for connection...");

  while (true)
  {
    Socket socket = tcpListener.AcceptSocket();
    if (socket.Connected)
    {
      Client client = new Client(socket);
    }
  }
}
```

You can see how the Client class works in Listing 5.10; when you create an object of this class, its constructor starts reading from the client with BeginRead. When text has been read, BeginWrite is called to write the received text back to the client, and the code tries to read more from the client. If there's no more to read, the code closes the connection.

CONVERTING BYTE ARRAYS INTO STRINGS

Note the handy utility method we call to convert the text in the data buffer into a string object in Listing 5.10—System.Text.Encoding.ASCII.GetString. You can pass char arrays to the String class's constructor, but not byte arrays of the kind we must use here (and C# won't let you cast from a byte array to a char array), so System.Text.Encoding.ASCII.GetString is a good method to use.

LISTING 5.10   An Asynchronous Network Server (ch05_10.cs)

```
using System.Net;
using System.Net.Sockets;

public class ch05_10
{
  public static void Main()
  {
    TcpListener tcpListener = new TcpListener(IPAddress.Any, 65512);
    tcpListener.Start();

    System.Console.WriteLine("Waiting for connection...");

    while (true)
    {
```

LISTING 5.10   Continued

```csharp
      Socket socket = tcpListener.AcceptSocket();
      if (socket.Connected)
      {
        Client client = new Client(socket);
      }
    }
  }
}

class Client
{
  byte[] dataBuffer;
  Socket socket;
  NetworkStream networkStream;
  System.AsyncCallback readDelegate;
  System.AsyncCallback writeDelegate;

  public Client(Socket socket)
  {
    this.socket = socket;
    dataBuffer = new byte[512];
    networkStream = new NetworkStream(socket);

    System.Console.WriteLine("Connected to a client...");

    readDelegate = new System.AsyncCallback(this.OnRead);
    writeDelegate = new System.AsyncCallback(this.OnWrite);
    networkStream.BeginRead(dataBuffer, 0,
      dataBuffer.Length, readDelegate, null);
  }

  private void OnRead(System.IAsyncResult asyncResult)
  {
    int numberBytes = networkStream.EndRead(asyncResult);

    if (numberBytes > 0)
    {
      string outputString = System.Text.Encoding.ASCII.GetString(
        dataBuffer, 0, numberBytes - 2);
      System.Console.WriteLine("Read this text: \"{0}\".", outputString);
      networkStream.BeginWrite(dataBuffer, 0, numberBytes,
```

LISTING 5.10   Continued

```
          writeDelegate, null);
    }
    else
    {
      System.Console.WriteLine(
        "Read operation with this client finished...");
      networkStream.Close();
      networkStream = null;
      socket.Close();
      socket = null;
    }
}


private void OnWrite(System.IAsyncResult asyncResult)
{
  networkStream.EndWrite(asyncResult);
  System.Console.WriteLine("Sent text back to client...");
  networkStream.BeginRead(dataBuffer, 0, dataBuffer.Length,
    readDelegate, null);
}
}
```

The client in this case needs to connect to the server with a `NetworkStream` object, create a `StreamWriter` object to write to the server, and create a `StreamReader` object to read from the server. You can see how that works in the client's code, ch05_11.cs, Listing 5.11.

LISTING 5.11   An Asynchronous Network Client (ch05_11.cs)

```
using System.Net.Sockets;

public class ch05_11
{
  static public void Main()
  {
   ch05_11 appObject = new ch05_11();
  }

  ch05_11()
  {
   NetworkStream networkStream;
```

LISTING 5.11   Continued

```
    System.Console.WriteLine("Connecting to server...");

    TcpClient tcpSocket = new TcpClient("localHost", 65512);
    networkStream = tcpSocket.GetStream();

    string outputString = "Network streaming!";
    System.Console.WriteLine("Sending this message to server: \"{0}\".",
      outputString);

    System.IO.StreamWriter output = new System.IO.StreamWriter(networkStream);
    output.WriteLine(outputString);
    output.Flush();

    System.IO.StreamReader input = new System.IO.StreamReader(networkStream);
    string inputString = input.ReadLine();
    System.Console.WriteLine("Got this message from server: \"{0}\".",
      inputString);

    System.Console.WriteLine("Disconnecting from server...");
    networkStream.Close();
  }
}
```

When you start the server, ch05_10.exe, you'll see this:

```
C:\>ch05_10
Waiting for connection...
```

Starting a client, ch05_11.exe, in a new DOS window shows how the client can send the message, "Network Streaming!" to the server, and how the server sends it back:

```
C:\c#\ch05>ch05_11
Connecting to server...
Sending this message to server: "Network streaming!".
Got this message from server: "Network streaming!".
Disconnecting from server...
```

Here's what the server displays after the connection is made:

```
C:\>ch05_10
Waiting for connection...
Connected to a client...
Read this text: "Network streaming!".
Sent text back to client...
Read operation with this client finished...
```

You can make multiple connections to this server, running the client application in multiple DOS windows. Each time you do, a new Client object will be created to handle the new connection, and read/write operations with the new client will be handled asynchronously. That means that one client doesn't have to wait until the server is done with all other clients before it gets any attention, which is how it's done in the real world.

Working with Internet Streams

The FCL also includes the HttpWebRequest and HttpWebResponse classes to let you work directly with HTTP streams on the Web. We'll take a look at how to send a request to a Web server, requesting the Web page at www.microsoft.com, and reading the Web server's response when it comes in. You can see the significant public properties of the HttpWebRequest class, which enable you to send commands to Web servers just as browsers do, in Table 5.15, and its significant public methods in Table 5.16.

TABLE 5.15

Significant Public HttpWebRequest Properties

PROPERTY	PURPOSE
Accept	Returns or sets the value of the Accept HTTP header.
Address	Returns the URI of the Internet resource that responds to the request.
Connection	Returns or sets the value of the Connection HTTP header.
ContentLength	Returns or sets the Content-length HTTP header.
ContentType	Returns or sets the value of the Content-type HTTP header.
CookieContainer	Returns or sets the cookies associated with the request.
Headers	Returns a collection of the name/value pairs that make up the HTTP headers.
KeepAlive	Returns or sets whether to connect to the Internet resource in a persistent way.
MediaType	Returns or sets the media type of the request.
Method	Returns or sets the method for the request.
Timeout	Returns or sets the time-out value for a request.
UserAgent	Returns or sets the value of the User-agent HTTP header.

TABLE 5.16

Significant Public HttpWebRequest Methods

METHOD	PURPOSE
Accept	Returns or sets the value of the Accept HTTP header.
Abort	Cancels a request.
BeginGetResponse	Begins an asynchronous request to an Internet resource.
EndGetResponse	Ends an asynchronous request to an Internet resource.
GetRequestStream	Returns a stream object to use to write request data.
GetResponse	Returns a response from an Internet resource.

The `HttpWebResponse` class lets you handle what the Web server sends back to you. You'll find the significant public properties of the `HttpWebResponse` class in Table 5.17, and its significant public methods in Table 5.18.

TABLE 5.17

Significant Public HttpWebResponse Properties

PROPERTY	PURPOSE
Accept	Returns or sets the value of the Accept HTTP header.
CharacterSet	Returns the character set of the response.
ContentLength	Returns the length of the content.
ContentType	Returns the content type of the response.
Cookies	Returns or sets cookies.
Headers	Returns the headers for this response from the server.
LastModified	Returns the last date and time that the response contents were modified.
Method	Returns the method used to return the response.
ProtocolVersion	Returns the version of the HTTP protocol used for the response.
ResponseUri	Returns the URI of the Internet resource that responded to the request.
Server	Returns the name of the server that sent the response.
StatusCode	Returns the status of the response.
StatusDescription	Returns the status description of the response.

TABLE 5.18

Significant Public HttpWebResponse Methods

METHOD	PURPOSE
Close	Closes the response stream.
GetResponseHeader	Returns the contents of a header returned with the response.
GetResponseStream	Returns a stream object used to read the body of the response.

Browsers work by sending the kinds of requests to Web servers that we'll send here, and by receiving the kinds of responses we'll get in return. In this next example, the application will act much like a browser when we use HttpWebRequest to send a request for the HTML of the page www.microsoft.com, and HttpWebResponse to create a StreamReader object so we can read that page. To create the request for that page, you don't use the HttpWebRequest constructor directly; you use the Create method of its base class, WebRequest. To get the response from the Web site, you use the GetResponse method of the WebRequest class. And to get a StreamReader stream corresponding to the Web page itself, you use the WebResponse class's GetResponseStream method, which returns a Stream object that you can pass on to the StreamReader constructor:

```
HttpWebRequest webRequest = (HttpWebRequest)
  WebRequest.Create("http://www.microsoft.com");
HttpWebResponse webResponse = (HttpWebResponse) webRequest.GetResponse();
StreamReader input = new StreamReader(webResponse.GetResponseStream());
```

Now that we have a StreamReader object, all we have to do is to read the Web page using the ReadLine method, as you see in ch05_12.cs, Listing 5.12.

LISTING 5.12   An Asynchronous Network Client (ch05_12.cs)

```
using System.IO;
using System.Net;

public class ch05_12
{
  static public void Main( string[] Args )
  {
    HttpWebRequest webRequest = (HttpWebRequest)
      WebRequest.Create("http://www.microsoft.com");
    HttpWebResponse webResponse = (HttpWebResponse) webRequest.GetResponse();
    StreamReader input = new StreamReader(webResponse.GetResponseStream());

    string inputString;

    while ((inputString = input.ReadLine()) != null)
    {
      System.Console.WriteLine(inputString);
    }
    input.Close();
  }
}
```

When you run ch05_12, it downloads the HTML of the Web page at www.microsoft.com and displays it. That's all there is to it.

Serializing Objects

C# enables you to save an entire object, including all its data (called an *object-graph*) through a process called *serialization*. Serialization lets you write entire objects out to disk and read them back in later. Objects that pass between assembly boundaries (through a process called *marshalling*) are also serialized.

You use the BinaryFormatter class to serialize and deserialize objects; the significant public methods of this class appear in Table 5.19.

TABLE 5.19

Significant Public BinaryFormatter Methods

METHOD	DOES THIS
Deserialize	Deserializes a stream into an object-graph.
Serialize	Serializes an object to the given stream.

Here's an example, ch05_13.cs, which will serialize and deserialize an object. The ch05_13 class contains some internal values in an array named data, which are initialized in the constructor with the values 1, 2, and 3. When you create an object of this class, it'll serialize itself to disk automatically with a call to a method we'll name Serialize in the constructor. Here's how we start the ch05_13 class. Note the [Serializable] attribute at the beginning— to make a class serializable, you must use this attribute:

```
[Serializable]
class ch05_13
{
  private int[] data;

  public ch05_13()
  {
    data = new int[3];
    data[0] = 1;
    data[1] = 2;
    data[2] = 3;
    Serialize();
  }
  .
  .
  .
```

In this class's `Serialize` method, we will serialize the current object to a file named ch05_13.out. To do that, we'll use a `FileStream` object, using a `BinaryFormatter` object to do the actual serialization:

```
private void Serialize()
{
  System.Console.WriteLine("Serializing it...");
  FileStream output = new FileStream("ch05_13.out", FileMode.Create);
  BinaryFormatter formatter = new BinaryFormatter();
  formatter.Serialize(output, this);
  output.Close();
}
```

To deserialize the object, we read it back from the ch05_13.out file—we'll add a method named `Deserialize`. In this method, we use another `FileStream` object to read the object from disk, passing the `FileStream` object to a `BinaryFormatter` object's `Deserialization` method and returning the deserialized object:

```
public ch05_13 Deserialize()
{
  System.Console.WriteLine("Deserializing it...");
  FileStream input = new FileStream("ch05_13.out", FileMode.Open);
  BinaryFormatter formatter = new BinaryFormatter();
  return (ch05_13) formatter.Deserialize(input);
}
```

That's all we need. To see this in action, we start by creating a `ch05_13` object. This object automatically serializes itself to ch05_13.out in the constructor; we can deserialize that object and store it in a new object variable named `deserializedObject`, displaying the data in `deserializedObject` with the code you see in ch05_13.cs, Listing 5.13.

LISTING 5.13   *Serializing an Object (ch05_13.cs)*

```
using System;
using System.IO;
using System.Runtime.Serialization;
using System.Runtime.Serialization.Formatters.Binary;

[Serializable]
class ch05_13
{
  private int[] data;
```

LISTING 5.13   Continued

```csharp
public static void Main()
{
  System.Console.WriteLine("Creating an object...");
  ch05_13 obj = new ch05_13();

  ch05_13 deserializedObject = obj.Deserialize();
  deserializedObject.DisplayItems();
}

public ch05_13()
{
  data = new int[3];
  data[0] = 1;
  data[1] = 2;
  data[2] = 3;
  Serialize();
}

private void DisplayItems()
{
  System.Console.WriteLine("Displaying the object's items...");
  foreach (int value in data)
  {
    System.Console.WriteLine(value);
  }
}

private void Serialize()
{
  System.Console.WriteLine("Serializing it...");
  FileStream output = new FileStream("ch05_13.out", FileMode.Create);
  BinaryFormatter formatter = new BinaryFormatter();
  formatter.Serialize(output, this);
  output.Close();
}

public ch05_13 Deserialize()
{
  System.Console.WriteLine("Deserializing it...");
  FileStream input = new FileStream("ch05_13.out", FileMode.Open);
```

LISTING 5.13 Continued

```
    BinaryFormatter formatter = new BinaryFormatter();
    return (ch05_13) formatter.Deserialize(input);
  }
}
```

Here are the results you see when you run ch05_13. As you see, the code creates an object, serializes it to disk, and reads it back in successfully:

```
C:\>ch05_13
Creating an object...
Serializing it...
Deserializing it...
Displaying the object's items...
1
2
3
```

Working with Non-Serialized Data

You don't have to serialize all the members of an object; for example, if you have a huge array filled with sequential numbers that's easy to re-create, there's no benefit to taking up a great deal of disk space by storing that array to memory. To mark members that you don't want serialized, you use the [NonSerialized] attribute.

For example, if you didn't want to serialize the data array in ch05_13.cs, you could mark it with [NonSerialized]; note that when you use this attribute, you should implement the IDeserializationCallback interface, which we do here as well:

```
[Serializable]
class ch05_14 : IDeserializationCallback
{
  [NonSerialized] int[] data;
    .
    .
    .
```

To use the IDeserializationCallback interface, you must implement the OnDeserialization method, which is called during the deserialization process to allow you to re-create the data that wasn't serialized. For this example, that looks like this, where we re-create the data array in the OnDeserialization method:

```
public virtual void OnDeserialization(Object obj)
{
  System.Console.WriteLine("Recreating data...");
  data = new int[3];
  data[0] = 1;
  data[1] = 2;
  data[2] = 3;
}
```

Now we can create an object of this new class, ch05_14, serialize it, deserialize it, and check to make sure its data was correctly re-created. You can see the code in ch05_14.cs, Listing 5.14.

LISTING 5.14   Handling Non-Serialized Data (ch05_14.cs)

```
using System;
using System.IO;
using System.Runtime.Serialization;
using System.Runtime.Serialization.Formatters.Binary;

[Serializable]
class ch05_14 : IDeserializationCallback
{
  [NonSerialized] int[] data;

  public static void Main()
  {
    System.Console.WriteLine("Creating an object...");
    ch05_14 obj = new ch05_14();

    ch05_14 deserializedObject = obj.Deserialize();
    deserializedObject.DisplayItems();
  }

  public ch05_14()
  {
    data = new int[3];
    data[0] = 1;
    data[1] = 2;
    data[2] = 3;
    Serialize();
  }
```

LISTING 5.14   Continued

```
private void DisplayItems()
{
  System.Console.WriteLine("Displaying the object's items...");
  foreach (int value in data)
  {
    System.Console.WriteLine(value);
  }
}

private void Serialize()
{
  System.Console.WriteLine("Serializing it...");
  FileStream output = new FileStream("ch05_14.out", FileMode.Create);
  BinaryFormatter formatter = new BinaryFormatter();
  formatter.Serialize(output, this);
  output.Close();
}

public ch05_14 Deserialize()
{
  System.Console.WriteLine("Deserializing it...");
  FileStream input = new FileStream("ch05_14.out", FileMode.Open);
  BinaryFormatter formatter = new BinaryFormatter();
  return (ch05_14) formatter.Deserialize(input);
}

public virtual void OnDeserialization(Object obj)
{
  System.Console.WriteLine("Recreating data...");
  data = new int[3];
  data[0] = 1;
  data[1] = 2;
  data[2] = 3;
}
}
```

When you run it, you see the same results for ch05_14.cs as we just saw for ch05_13.cs. The new object is serialized and deserialized correctly. There is a difference, however; because we did not serialize the data array in ch05_14, we saved some disk space. ch05_13.out is 141 bytes long, but ch05_14.out is only 107 bytes. The difference here is small in bytes but large in significance. Imagine the savings if we had avoided serializing a 100,000-by-100,000 element array.

Using Isolated Storage

You can also use streams to save configuration data for applications, using *isolated storage*. Isolated storage saves data for your application that you might have stored in the Registry before; for example, you might want to save the location of your application window's upper-left point, the background color as set by the user, window size as resized by the user, or other configuration data.

SHOP TALK

ISOLATED STORAGE OR THE REGISTRY

In isolated storage, you can see Microsoft's exploration of alternatives to the Windows Registry for holding application data. When first introduced, the Registry was of limited size. Microsoft hadn't anticipated the massive use that applications would make of the Registry when dumping their data under keys like HKEY_CURRENT_USER, and users soon started seeing Registry overflow messages regularly. Microsoft responded by allowing the Registry to reach arbitrary lengths in succeeding versions of Windows, but now it's not uncommon to see 15MB or longer registries. Because the Registry is read into memory when you boot, that can give you quite a performance hit. Such heavy use of the Registry makes unrecoverable corruption of the Registry ever more probable. Isolated storage is an attempt to address this problem by letting applications store their own configuration data in assembly-specific files in randomly named subdirectories of C:\Documents and Settings*username*\Local Settings\Application Data\IsolatedStorage (this path will vary with your version of Windows). In this way, they're a partial throwback to the early days of .INI files that the Registry was meant to supplant, but configuration files are handled by Windows instead in a well-defined way, and represent a significant improvement—at least potentially—to the huge amount of data some applications dump in the Registry.

To store data in isolated storage, you use the IsolatedStorageFileStream class; you can see the significant public properties of this class in Table 5.20, and its significant methods in Table 5.21.

TABLE 5.20

Significant Public IsolatedStorageFileStream Properties

PROPERTY	PURPOSE
CanRead	Returns true if the file can be read.
CanSeek	Returns true if seek operations are supported.
CanWrite	Returns true if you can write to the file.

TABLE 5.20

Continued

PROPERTY	PURPOSE
IsAsync	Returns true if the stream was opened asynchronously.
Length	Returns the length of the stream.
Name	Returns the name of the file stream that was passed to the constructor.
Position	Returns or sets the current position in the stream.

TABLE 5.21

Significant Public IsolatedStorageFileStream Methods

METHOD	PURPOSE
BeginRead	Begins an asynchronous read.
BeginWrite	Begins an asynchronous write.
Close	Closes the stream.
EndRead	Ends an asynchronous read request.
EndWrite	Ends an asynchronous write.
Flush	Flushes the stream.
Lock	Prevents other processes from modifying the stream (while permitting read access).
Read	Reads bytes from the stream.
ReadByte	Reads a single byte from isolated storage.
Seek	Sets the current position in this stream.
SetLength	Sets the length of this stream.
Unlock	Allows access by other processes to a file that had been locked.
Write	Writes a block of bytes to the stream from a byte array.
WriteByte	Writes a single byte to the stream.

Here's an example; in this case, we'll write out the configuration string "Color = blue" to the configuration file ch05_15.cfg and then read that string back in. We do that by creating an IsolatedStorageFileStream object, passing that object to a StreamWriter object's constructor, and writing the configuration data to isolated storage like this:

```
public class ch05_15
{
  public static void Main()
  {
    IsolatedStorageFileStream storage =
        new IsolatedStorageFileStream("ch05_15.cfg", FileMode.Create);

    StreamWriter output = new StreamWriter(storage);

    output.WriteLine("Color = blue");
```

```
output.Close();
storage.Close();
    .
    .
    .
```

That stores the data for the next time the application runs and wants to check that data. (Note that configuration data is stored by assembly. Don't try to read this data from a different assembly.) In this example, we'll read the configuration data back using an IsolatedStorageFileStream object and a StreamReader object, as you see in ch05_15.cs, Listing 5.15.

LISTING 5.15   Working with Isolated Storage (ch05_15.cs)

```
using System;
using System.IO;
using System.IO.IsolatedStorage;

public class ch05_15
{
  public static void Main()
  {
    IsolatedStorageFileStream storage =
        new IsolatedStorageFileStream("ch05_15.cfg", FileMode.Create);

    StreamWriter output = new StreamWriter(storage);

    output.WriteLine("Color = blue");
    output.Close();
    storage.Close();

    storage = new IsolatedStorageFileStream("ch05_15.cfg", FileMode.Open);
    StreamReader input = new StreamReader(storage);
    string item;

    while((item = input.ReadLine()) != null)
    {
      Console.WriteLine(item);
    }

    input.Close();
    storage.Close();
  }
}
```

Here's what you see when you run this example. As you can see, we've been able to store and retrieve configuration data:

```
C:\>ch05_15
Color = blue
```

In Brief

This chapter discussed how to work with streams in C#, including these topics:

- Streams are objects designed to let you handle data transfer. There are many stream classes available, such as FileStream, StreamWriter and StreamReader, NetworkStream, and others.

- Buffered streams can be created with the BufferedStream class. (If you use a stream like FileStream, you're responsible for setting up your own data buffers.)

- Binary files can be handled with the FileStream class's Read and Write methods.

- Text files can be handled with the StreamReader and StreamWriter classes, which support the WriteLine and ReadLine methods, respectively. Unlike the standard Write and Read methods, WriteLine and ReadLine are line-oriented.

- The .NET Framework supports asynchronous streaming I/O with the BeginRead and BeginWrite methods of the Stream class. You can call BeginRead to read a bufferfull of data, or BeginWrite to write a bufferfull of data, and then continue other work. Your code will be called back when the read or write operation is complete.

- Network I/O is based on the TcpListener and TcpClient classes, which let you create streams that use the TCP/IP protocol.

- The HttpWebRequest and HttpWebResponse classes enable you to work directly with HTTP streams on the Internet, sending requests from Web servers and reading their responses.

- When you serialize an object, you store that object, whether to disk or across assembly boundaries. You can pass a BinaryFormatter object a stream to serialize objects.

- Isolated storage enables you to store application data in a configuration file, so you can avoid using the Registry. You use the IsolatedStorageFileStream class to support isolated storage.

Understanding Collections and Indexers

Using Collections

This chapter is about the rich support in C# for handling collections such as arrays, bit arrays, queues, stacks, hash tables, and others. Collections are groupings of objects that support properties such as Count to hold the number of objects in the collection, and methods such as Add to add a new object to the collection. You can access members of the collection with various methods, such as using [ ] with arrays, Push and Pop methods with stacks, and so on.

As you become experienced in C#, you'll find yourself using collections more and more frequently as your code scales to larger applications. We've already worked with arrays throughout the book—now we'll see what they're capable of as we take a more in-depth look. After arrays, we'll continue with queues, stacks, hash tables and other collections, including how to create your own indexers to create your own collections.

Using Arrays

We're already familiar with arrays; they're those indexed collections of objects that must be the same type. Arrays are based on the System.Array class, but you don't use this class directly to create arrays (System.Array is an abstract class); as we've seen, you use C# language syntax like this to create an array:

FOR C++ PROGRAMMERS

C++ uses the Standard Template Library (STL) to support collection classes such as queues and stacks, but C# does not support the STL. That means nearly all the material in this chapter is new for programmers coming to C# from C++.

USING THE SYSTEM.ARRAY CLASS TO CREATE ARRAYS

The Array class is an abstract class in C#, but it turns out that you can create an object from this class using its CreateInstance method: System.Array array = System.Array.CreateInstance(typeof(System.String), 4);. However, you can't use the [] operator on this array, you have to use the GetValue and SetValue methods instead, like this: string value = array.GetValue(*index*) or array.SetValue("No worries.", *index*). Overall, you're better off with the standard array syntax.

```
int[] intArray = new int[4] {1, 2, 3, 4};
```

We have already discussed the fundamentals of handling arrays—they're zero-based collections that are reference types. We've seen the default value of array elements in Chapter 3, "C# Object-Oriented Programming," (Table 3.2). However, we haven't learned about the power that the Array class, which arrays are based on, gives us. You can find the significant public properties of Array objects in Table 6.1. The most commonly used is the Length property, which holds the total number of items in the array. You can likewise find the significant public methods of the Array class—some of which are static—in Table 6.2.

TABLE 6.1

Significant Public Properties of Array Objects

PROPERTY	PURPOSE
IsFixedSize	Returns true if the array has a fixed size.
IsReadOnly	Returns true if the array is read-only.
IsSynchronized	Returns true if access to the array is thread-safe.
Length	Returns a 32-bit integer holding the total number of elements in all the dimensions of the array.
LongLength	Returns a 64-bit integer holding the total number of elements in all the dimensions of the array.
Rank	Returns the number of dimensions of the array.

TABLE 6.2

Significant Public Methods of Array Objects

PROPERTY	PURPOSE
IsFixedSize	Returns true if the array has a fixed size.
static BinarySearch	Searches a one-dimensional sorted array for a value.
static Clear	Clears a range of elements, setting them to zero, to false, or to a null reference, depending on the element type.
static Copy	Copies a section of one array to another.
CopyTo	Copies all the elements of the current one-dimensional array to the given one-dimensional array.
static CreateInstance	Creates a new object of the Array class.
GetEnumerator	Returns an IEnumerator object for the array.
GetLength	Returns a 32-bit integer holding the number of elements in the given dimension of the array.
GetLongLength	Returns a 64-bit integer holding the number of elements in the given dimension of the array.
GetLowerBound	Returns the lower bound of the given dimension.
GetUpperBound	Returns the upper bound of the given dimension.
GetValue	Returns the value of the given element in the current array.
static IndexOf	Returns the index of the first occurrence of a value.
Initialize	Initializes every element of the value-type array.
static LastIndexOf	Returns the index of the last occurrence of a value.
static Reverse	Reverses the order of the elements in a one-dimensional Array.
SetValue	Sets the given element in the current Array to the given value.
static Sort	Sorts the elements in a one-dimensional array.

The elements you store in arrays are always objects in C#. Even simple data types are objects in C#, of course. Here's an example where we explicitly create our own objects and store them in an array; in this case, we'll store Customer objects in an array, where the Customer class stores the customer's name and has cast operators to and from strings:

```
public class Customer
{
  private string name;

  public Customer(string name)
  {
    this.name = name;
  }
}
```

```
public static implicit operator string(Customer customer)
{
  return customer.name;
}

public static implicit operator Customer(string name)
{
  return new Customer(name);
}
}
```

Because the Customer class has a cast operator from strings to Customer objects, you can initialize a set of Customer objects in an array with a set of strings in curly braces, just as you can for a standard string[] array. You can see the code in ch06_01.cs, where we're filling an array with Customer objects and then looping over the array to display the name of each customer.

LISTING 6.1   Storing Objects in Arrays (ch06_01.cs)

```
public class ch06_01
{
  static void Main()
  {
    Customer[] customerArray = new Customer[4] {"Bob", "Tom", "Mary", "Sue"};

    System.Console.WriteLine("Here are the customers:");
    foreach (Customer customer in customerArray)
    {
      System.Console.WriteLine(customer);
    }
  }
}

public class Customer
{
  private string name;

  public Customer(string name)
  {
    this.name = name;
  }
```

LISTING 6.1 Continued

```
public static implicit operator string(Customer customer)
{
  return customer.name;
}

public static implicit operator Customer(string name)
{
  return new Customer(name);
}
}
```

Here's what you see when you run ch06_01:

```
C:\>ch06_01
Here are the customers:
Bob
Tom
Mary
Sue
```

Creating Multidimensional Arrays

Up to now we've used only single-dimension arrays, but C# supports multidimensional arrays as well. You can indicate how many dimensions a multidimensional array has using commas in the brackets following the array type in its declaration. For example, here's how you might create a two-dimensional array of numberRows rows and numberColumns columns:

```
int[ , ] array = new int[numberRows, numberColumns];
```

Now you can address the elements in this array as array[*row*, *column*]. You can see an example in ch06_02.cs, Listing 6.2, where we create a two-dimensional array with two rows and three columns, fill it with random numbers using an object of the System.Random class (the Next method of this class returns an integer with the maximum value you pass to it; in this case, 10), and display those values.

LISTING 6.2 Creating a Multidimensional Array (ch06_02.cs)

```
public class ch06_02
{
  static void Main()
  {
```

LISTING 6.2   Continued

```
const int numberRows = 2;
const int numberColumns = 3;
System.Random random = new System.Random();

int[ , ] array = new int[numberRows, numberColumns];

for (int row = 0; row < numberRows; row++)
{
    for (int column = 0; column < numberColumns; column++)
    {
        array[row, column] = random.Next(10);
    }
}

for (int row = 0; row < numberRows; row++)
{
    for (int column = 0; column < numberColumns; column++)
    {
        System.Console.Write("array[{0}, {1}] = {2} ",
            row, column, array[row, column]);
    }
    System.Console.WriteLine();
}
}
}
```

Here's what you might see when you run ch06_02, where each array element has been filled with a random integer up to a value of 10:

```
C:\>ch06_02
array[0, 0] = 3 array[0, 1] = 6 array[0, 2] = 6
array[1, 0] = 3 array[1, 1] = 4 array[1, 2] = 8
```

You can also initialize multidimensional arrays in much the same way as you can with a single-dimensional array. For example, to store the integers we've just seen in the previous example in array, you can use code like the following. You just enclose the multiple dimensions of the initializers in successive levels of curly braces:

```
public class ch06_02
{
  static void Main()
  {
```

```
const int numberRows = 2;
const int numberColumns = 3;
System.Random random = new System.Random();

int[ , ] array =
{
    {3, 6, 6},
    {3, 4, 8}
};

for (int row = 0; row < numberRows; row++)
{
    for (int column = 0; column < numberColumns; column++)
    {
        System.Console.Write("array[{0}, {1}] = {2} ",
            row, column, array[row, column]);
    }
    System.Console.WriteLine();
}
}
}
```

This code gives you the same results as ch06_01.cs.

Creating Arrays of Arrays: Jagged Arrays

You can also create arrays of arrays, called *jagged arrays* because they need not be rectangular. Here's the syntax you use to create an array of arrays. Note the syntax in this case, int[][]:

```
int[][] array = new int[4][];
```

This creates an array of four single-dimensional arrays, each of which can be a different length. To create the jagged array, you assign those single-dimensional arrays to the various elements of the jagged array like this:

```
int[][] array = new int[4][];

array[0] = new int[5];
array[1] = new int[3];
array[2] = new int[5];
array[3] = new int[3];
```

Now you can use this new jagged array as you can any rectangular array; just remember how many elements are in each row and don't try to access elements outside the bounds of the array. You can see how this works in code in ch06_03.cs, Listing 6.3, where we use two foreach loops to loop over each array in array and display every value in the entire jagged array.

LISTING 6.3   Creating a Jagged Array (ch06_03.cs)

```
public class ch06_03
{
  static void Main()
  {
    int[][] array = new int[4][];

    array[0] = new int[5];
    array[1] = new int[3];
    array[2] = new int[5];
    array[3] = new int[3];

    array[0][2] = 1;
    array[0][4] = 3;

    array[1][1] = 5;
    array[1][2] = 3;

    array[2][1] = 9;
    array[2][2] = 2;
    array[2][4] = 1;

    array[3][0] = 7;
    array[3][1] = 4;
    array[3][2] = 9;

    foreach(int[] a in array)
    {
      foreach(int i in a)
      {
        System.Console.Write("{0} ", i);
      }
      System.Console.WriteLine();
    }
  }
}
```

Here's what the jagged array looks like when you display its elements:

```
C:\>ch06_03
0 0 1 0 3
0 5 3
0 9 2 0 1
7 4 9
```

Sorting and Reversing Arrays

The System.Array class comes with a number of good utility methods built into it; for example, the Reverse method reverses the order of the elements in an array, and the Sort method sorts those elements. You can see both methods at work in ch06_04.cs, where we reverse and sort an array with the elements "Now", "is", "the", and "time".

LISTING 6.4   Sorting and Reversing an Array (ch06_04.cs)

```
public class ch06_04
{
  static void Main()
  {
    string[] array = {"Now", "is", "the", "time"};

    System.Console.WriteLine("The array:");
    foreach (string element in array)
    {
      System.Console.Write("{0} ", element);
    }

    System.Array.Reverse(array);

    System.Console.WriteLine();
    System.Console.WriteLine("The reversed array:");
    foreach (string element in array)
    {
      System.Console.Write("{0} ", element);
    }

    System.Array.Sort(array);

    System.Console.WriteLine();
    System.Console.WriteLine("The sorted array:");
    foreach (string element in array)
```

LISTING 6.4   Continued

```
    {
        System.Console.Write("{0} ", element);
    }
  }
}
```

Here's what you see when you run ch06_04. As you can see, the array was indeed reversed and sorted as desired:

```
C:\>ch06_04
The array:
Now is the time
The reversed array:
time the is Now
The sorted array:
is Now the time
```

Using Bit Arrays

Bit arrays are a special kind of array, supported by the BitArray class. The elements in these arrays are treated as bit values and you can use logical methods like And and Or on them. Bit arrays can be useful when you need to perform operations on the individual bits in a value. For example, if you need to set the seventeenth bit in the octal value 777356, what would the new value be? You can pass integer values to the BitArray constructor and use the Set and Get methods to set and get the values of individual bits. You can also access the individual bits in a bit array as you can any element in an array, like this: bitArray[5] = true. You can see the significant public properties of BitArray objects in Table 6.3 and the significant public methods in Table 6.4.

TABLE 6.3

Significant Public Properties of BitArray Objects

PROPERTY	PURPOSE
Count	Holds the number of elements.
IsReadOnly	true if the bit array is read-only.
Item	Returns or sets the value of the bit at a specific position.
Length	Returns or sets the number of elements.

TABLE 6.4

Significant Public Methods of BitArray Objects

METHOD	PURPOSE
And	Performs the bitwise AND operation on the elements in the current bit array with the corresponding elements in the given bit array.
CopyTo	Copies the entire bit array to a compatible one-dimensional array.
Get	Returns the value of the bit at a specific position.
GetEnumerator	Returns an enumerator that can iterate through the bit array.
Not	Inverts all the bit values (true values are changed to false, and false values are changed to true).
Or	Performs the bitwise OR operation on the elements in the current bit array with the corresponding elements in the given bit array.
Set	Sets the bit at a specific position to the given value.
SetAll	Sets all bits to the given value.
Xor	Performs the bitwise eXclusive OR operation on the elements in the current bit array with the corresponding elements in the given bit array.

For example, we'll create two bit arrays, initializing the bits in them with bool values, and then And them together and display the result. You can see the code in ch06_05.cs, Listing 6.5. Note that BitArray, like the other collections we'll see in this chapter, is in the System.Collections namespace (excluding Array, which is in the System namespace).

LISTING 6.5   Creating a Bit Array (ch06_05.cs)

```
using System.Collections;

public class ch06_05
{
  public static void Main()
  {
    bool[] boolArray = new bool[5] {true, false, true, true, false};
    BitArray bitArray1 = new BitArray(boolArray);
    boolArray = new bool[5] {true, true, false, true, false};
    BitArray bitArray2 = new BitArray(boolArray);
    BitArray bitArray3;

    System.Console.WriteLine("bitArray1:" );
    foreach(bool element in bitArray1)
    {
      System.Console.Write("{0} ", element);
    }
```

LISTING 6.5   Continued

```
    System.Console.WriteLine();
    System.Console.WriteLine("bitArray2:");
    foreach(bool element in bitArray2)
    {
      System.Console.Write("{0} ", element);
    }

    bitArray3 = bitArray1.And(bitArray2);

    System.Console.WriteLine();
    System.Console.WriteLine("bitArray1.And(bitArray2):");
    foreach(bool element in bitArray3)
    {
      System.Console.Write("{0} ", element);
    }
  }
}
```

When you run ch06_05, you see our two bit arrays expressed as arrays of Boolean values, followed by the result of Anding them together:

```
C:\>ch06_05
bitArray1:
True False True True False
bitArray2:
True True False True False
bitArray1.And(bitArray2):
True False False True False
```

Using Array Lists

Unlike Visual Basic .NET, where you can use the ReDim statement to re-dimension an array, arrays are of a fixed size in C#. There are times when you might want to use variable-length arrays in your code, however, as when the user specifies at runtime how many items an array should have, or when you're opening various unknown databases full of records. The ArrayList class lets you add or remove elements to an array at runtime, thus creating dynamic-length arrays. You can see the significant public properties of ArrayList objects in Table 6.5, and the significant public methods of these objects in Table 6.6.

TABLE 6.5

Significant Public Properties of ArrayList Objects

PROPERTY	PURPOSE
Capacity	Returns or sets the number of elements that the array list can contain.
Count	Returns the number of elements in the array list.
IsFixedSize	Returns true if the array list has a fixed size.
IsReadOnly	Returns true if the array list is read-only.
IsSynchronized	Returns true if access to the array list is thread-safe.
Item	Returns or sets the element at the given index.

TABLE 6.6

Significant Public Methods of ArrayList Objects

METHOD	PURPOSE
Add	Adds an object to the end of the array list.
AddRange	Adds the elements of a collection to the end of the array list.
BinarySearch	Uses a binary search algorithm to locate a specific element in the sorted array list.
Clear	Removes all elements.
Contains	Determines whether an element is in the array list.
CopyTo	Copies the array list to a one-dimensional array.
GetEnumerator	Returns an enumerator that can iterate through the array list.
GetRange	Returns an array list that represents a subset of the elements in the source array list.
IndexOf	Returns the zero-based index of the first occurrence of a value.
Insert	Inserts an element into the array list.
InsertRange	Inserts the elements of a collection into the array list at the given index.
LastIndexOf	Returns the zero-based index of the last occurrence of a value.
Remove	Removes the first occurrence of a specific object.
RemoveAt	Removes the element at the given index of the array list.
RemoveRange	Removes a range of elements from the array list.
Reverse	Reverses the order of the elements.
SetRange	Copies the elements of a collection over a range of elements in the array list.
Sort	Sorts the elements in the array list.
ToArray	Copies the elements of the array list to a new array.
TrimToSize	Sets the capacity to the actual number of elements.

Using array lists, you can use the Add method to add new elements, and the Remove and RemoveAt methods to remove elements. You can access elements with the [] operator as you can with standard arrays. As an example, we'll create a new array list and add a few elements to it, and then loop over it with a `for` loop (using the `Count` property to determine how many elements are in the array list). The elements are displayed this way:

```
ArrayList arrayList = new ArrayList();
arrayList.Add("Now");
arrayList.Add("is");
arrayList.Add("the");
arrayList.Add("time");

for (int loopIndex = 0; loopIndex < arrayList.Count; loopIndex++)
{
  System.Console.Write("{0} ", arrayList[loopIndex]);
}
```

You can also loop over the elements in an array list with `foreach`, as you see in ch06_06.cs, Listing 6.6.

LISTING 6.6   Creating an Array List (ch06_06.cs)

```
using System.Collections;
public class ch06_06
{
  public static void Main()
  {
    ArrayList arrayList = new ArrayList();
    arrayList.Add("Now");
    arrayList.Add("is");
    arrayList.Add("the");
    arrayList.Add("time");

    for (int loopIndex = 0; loopIndex < arrayList.Count; loopIndex++)
    {
      System.Console.Write("{0} ", arrayList[loopIndex]);
    }

    System.Console.WriteLine();
    foreach(object text in arrayList)
    {
      System.Console.Write("{0} ", text);
    }
  }
}
```

Here's what you see when you run ch06_06:

```
C:\>ch06_06
Now is the time
Now is the time
```

Note also that, unlike standard arrays, array lists can store data of different types:

```
arrayList.Add("No worries.");
arrayList.Add(5);
```

Using Queues

Queues work much as they sound—they are first-in, first-out (FIFO) collections, like when you stand in line for tickets. These collections are good when you have a group of objects you want to process as they come in, such as when you receive client requests to connect to a Web service. Queues are supported with the Queue class. You can see the significant public properties of Queue objects in Table 6.7, and their significant public methods in Table 6.8. You use the Enqueue method to add items to the end of a queue and Dequeue to remove the first item from the front of the queue.

TABLE 6.7

Significant Public Properties of Queue Objects

PROPERTY	PURPOSE
Count	Returns the number of elements contained in the queue.
IsSynchronized	Returns true if access to the queue is thread-safe.

TABLE 6.8

Significant Public Methods of Queue Objects

METHOD	PURPOSE
Clear	Removes all objects from the queue.
Contains	Determines whether an element is in the queue.
CopyTo	Copies the queue elements to an existing one-dimensional array.
Dequeue	Removes and returns the object at the beginning of the queue.
Enqueue	Adds an object to the end of the queue.
GetEnumerator	Returns an enumerator that can iterate through the queue.
Peek	Returns the object at the beginning of the queue without removing it.
ToArray	Copies the queue's elements to a new array.
TrimToSize	Sets the capacity to the actual number of elements.

You can see an example in ch06_07.cs, Listing 6.7, where we're adding items to a queue:

```
Queue queue = new Queue();
```

```
queue.Enqueue(0);
queue.Enqueue(1);
queue.Enqueue(2);
queue.Enqueue(3);
queue.Enqueue(4);
```

We then de-queue one or two items to confirm that they come off the front of the queue:

```
System.Console.WriteLine("Dequeued {0}", queue.Dequeue());
```

You can see the code in Listing 6.7. Note that as with the other C# collections, you can iterate over the members of a queue using `foreach`. This is done in ch06_07.cs to display everything that's in the queue.

LISTING 6.7   Creating a Queue (ch06_07.cs)

```
using System.Collections;

public class ch06_07
{
  static void Main()
  {
    Queue queue = new Queue();
    System.Console.WriteLine("Queuing 0 1 2 3 4");

    queue.Enqueue(0);
    queue.Enqueue(1);
    queue.Enqueue(2);
    queue.Enqueue(3);
    queue.Enqueue(4);

    System.Console.Write("The queue: ");
    foreach(object obj in queue)
    {
      System.Console.Write("{0} ", obj);
    }
    System.Console.WriteLine();

    System.Console.WriteLine("Dequeued {0}", queue.Dequeue());
```

LISTING 6.7 Continued

```
    System.Console.Write("The queue: ");
    foreach(object obj in queue)
    {
        System.Console.Write("{0} ", obj);
    }
    System.Console.WriteLine();

    System.Console.WriteLine("Dequeued {0}", queue.Dequeue());

    System.Console.Write("The queue: ");
    foreach(object obj in queue)
    {
        System.Console.Write("{0} ", obj);
    }
    System.Console.WriteLine();
}
}
```

Here's what you see when you run ch06_07:

```
C:\>ch06_07
Queuing 0 1 2 3 4
The queue: 0 1 2 3 4
Dequeued 0
The queue: 1 2 3 4
Dequeued 1
The queue: 2 3 4
```

Here, we've queued 0, 1, 2, 3, and 4; when we de-queue a value, 0 comes off the front of the stack. When we de-queue another value, 1 comes off. Note that you can also check the next value about to come off the queue with the Peek method, which returns that value without actually removing it from the queue.

Using Stacks

Queues are first-in, first-out—FIFO—constructs, which is often what you need to handle time-consuming tasks that you want to handle in a first-come, first-served manner. But there are occasions when you want to reverse the order of retrieval with first-in, last-out—FILO—constructs, and in that case you use *stacks*. The usual example here is a spring-loaded stack of plates in cafeterias, where the first plate in the stack is the last plate taken off. You've probably heard of stacks in programming; local variables in methods are *pushed* onto the top of the application's internal stack to store them and *popped* from the top of the stack to retrieve them in reverse order. You can see the significant public properties of Stack objects in Table 6.9 and their significant public methods in Table 6.10.

TABLE 6.9

Significant Public Properties of Stack Objects

PROPERTY	PURPOSE
Count	Returns the number of elements contained in the stack.
IsSynchronized	Returns true if access to the stack is thread-safe.

TABLE 6.10

Significant Public Methods of Stack Objects

METHOD	PURPOSE
Clear	Removes all objects from the stack.
Contains	Determines whether an element is in the stack.
CopyTo	Copies the stack to an existing one-dimensional array, starting at the given array index.
GetEnumerator	Returns an IEnumerator for the stack.
Peek	Returns the object at the top of the stack without removing it.
Pop	Removes and returns the object at the top of the stack.
Push	Inserts an object at the top of the stack.
ToArray	Copies the stack to a new array.

The following parallels the queue example, except that, as you'll see, values come off the stack in reverse order. We first push a few values onto the stack:

```
Stack stack = new Stack();

stack.Push(0);
stack.Push(1);
stack.Push(2);
stack.Push(3);
stack.Push(4);
```

Then we pop a value and display both it and the current values on the stack:

```
System.Console.WriteLine("Popped {0}", stack.Pop());

System.Console.Write("The stack: ");
foreach(object obj in stack)
```

```
{
  System.Console.Write("{0} ", obj);
}
System.Console.WriteLine();
```

After popping a few values, we also use the stack's ToArray method to copy the stack into an array and display the values in the array:

```
object[] array = stack.ToArray();

System.Console.Write("The stack in an array: ");
foreach(object obj in array)
{
  System.Console.Write("{0} ", obj);
}
System.Console.WriteLine();
```

You can see the full code in ch06_08.cs, Listing 6.8.

LISTING 6.8   Creating a Queue (ch06_08.cs)

```
using System.Collections;

public class ch06_08
{
  static void Main()
  {
    Stack stack = new Stack();

    System.Console.WriteLine("Pushing 0 1 2 3 4");
    stack.Push(0);
    stack.Push(1);
    stack.Push(2);
    stack.Push(3);
    stack.Push(4);

    System.Console.Write("The stack: ");
    foreach(object obj in stack)
    {
      System.Console.Write("{0} ", obj);
    }
    System.Console.WriteLine();
```

LISTING 6.8   Continued

```
  System.Console.WriteLine("Popped {0}", stack.Pop());

  System.Console.Write("The stack: ");
  foreach(object obj in stack)
  {
    System.Console.Write("{0} ", obj);
  }
  System.Console.WriteLine();

   System.Console.WriteLine("Popped {0}", stack.Pop());

  System.Console.Write("The stack: ");
  foreach(object obj in stack)
  {
    System.Console.Write("{0} ", obj);
  }
  System.Console.WriteLine();

  object[] array = stack.ToArray();

  System.Console.Write("The stack in an array: ");
  foreach(object obj in array)
  {
    System.Console.Write("{0} ", obj);
  }
  System.Console.WriteLine();
  }
}
```

Here's what you see when you run ch06_08:

```
C:\>ch06_08
Pushing 0 1 2 3 4
The stack: 4 3 2 1 0
Popped 4
The stack: 3 2 1 0
Popped 3
The stack: 2 1 0
The stack in an array: 2 1 0
```

As you see, the items on the stack come off in reverse order; compare that to queues, where they come off in the same order that they went on.

Using Hash Tables

Dictionaries are collections that let you store *values* that are indexed by *keys*, not index numbers. For example, say you wanted to create a data record for each of your customers. You could store each customer's record using an array of values, but then you have to remember that index 0 in the array holds the customer's name, index 2 holds the address, index 3 the phone number, and so on. It is easier to index those values with text string keys like "Name", "Address", "Phone", and so on, and that's what dictionaries let you do. In fact, in .NET, you can use any kind of key—an integer, object, float, string, and so on—with any kind of value—an integer, object, float, string, and so on.

Hash tables are dictionaries that are highly optimized for fast data retrieval. You can see the significant public properties of Hashtable objects in Table 6.11, and their significant methods in Table 6.12.

TABLE 6.11

Significant Public Properties of Hashtable Objects

PROPERTY	PURPOSE
Count	Returns the number of key/value pairs.
IsFixedSize	Returns true if the hash table has a fixed size.
IsReadOnly	Returns true if the hash table is read-only.
IsSynchronized	Returns true if access to the hash table is thread-safe.
Item	Returns or sets the value associated with the given key.
Keys	Returns an ICollection object containing the keys.
Values	Returns an ICollection object containing the values.

TABLE 6.12

Significant Public Methods of Hashtable Objects

METHOD	PURPOSE
Add	Adds an element with the given key and value into the hash table.
Clear	Removes all elements from the hash table.
Contains	Determines whether the hash table contains a specific key. (This method is just like ContainsKey.)
ContainsKey	Determines whether the hash table contains a specific key.
ContainsValue	Determines whether the hash table contains a specific value.
CopyTo	Copies the hash table elements to a one-dimensional array instance at the given index.
GetEnumerator	Returns an IDictionaryEnumerator that can iterate through the hash table.
Remove	Removes the element with the given key.

Like other dictionary objects, hash tables implement the IDictionary interface, which supports the public property Item to access values; you can also reach this property with the [] operator. That means you can access a value in a hash table like this: *value = hashtable[key];*.

Here's an example, ch06_09.cs, in Listing 6.9. This code starts by creating a new hash table named customer and adds the value "Cary Grant" under the key "Name", the value "1313 Mockingbird Lane" under the key "Address", and so on. Then we access the customer's name using the "Name" key like so:

```
Hashtable customer = new Hashtable();
customer.Add("Name", "Cary Grant");
customer.Add("Address", "1313 Mockingbird Lane");
customer.Add("Phone", "555.1212");
customer.Add("ID", "12345");

System.Console.WriteLine("customer[\"Name\"] = {0}", customer["Name"]);
```

You can also get a collection of the keys from a hash table using the Keys property, which returns an ICollection object containing the keys in the hash table. You can also get the values from a hash table using the Values property, which returns an ICollection containing the values in the hash table. Here's how you can loop over the keys and values from the hash table:

```
ICollection keys = customer.Keys;
ICollection values = customer.Values;

System.Console.WriteLine();
System.Console.WriteLine("Keys");
foreach(string key in keys)
{
  System.Console.WriteLine("{0} ", key);
}

System.Console.WriteLine();
System.Console.WriteLine("Values:");
foreach (string value in values)
{
  System.Console.WriteLine("{0} ", value);
}
```

You can see the entire example, ch06_09.cs, in Listing 6.9, where we store values in a hash table, retrieve values, and loop over both the keys and values.

LISTING 6.9   Creating a Hash Table (ch06_09.cs)

```
using System.Collections;

public class ch06_09
{
  static void Main()
  {
    Hashtable customer = new Hashtable();
    customer.Add("Name", "Cary Grant");
    customer.Add("Address", "1313 Mockingbird Lane");
    customer.Add("Phone", "555.1212");
    customer.Add("ID", "12345");

    System.Console.WriteLine("customer[\"Name\"] = {0}", customer["Name"]);

    ICollection keys = customer.Keys;
    ICollection values = customer.Values;

    System.Console.WriteLine();
    System.Console.WriteLine("Keys:");
    foreach(string key in keys)
    {
      System.Console.WriteLine("{0} ", key);
    }

    System.Console.WriteLine();
    System.Console.WriteLine("Values:");
    foreach (string value in values)
    {
      System.Console.WriteLine("{0} ", value);
    }
  }
}
```

Here's what you see when you run ch06_09:

```
C:\>ch06_09
customer["Name"] = Cary Grant

Keys:
ID
Name
```

```
Address
Phone

Values:
12345
Cary Grant
1313 Mockingbird Lane
555.1212
```

Creating Your Own Collections

We've thus far looked at some of the most popular collection classes in this chapter. However, you can also build your own collections, and we'll see how to do that in the rest of this chapter.

SHOP TALK

ADDING A COLLECTION CLASS

In a production or team environment, it's often not enough to simply release a new and useful class for others to use. You'll also normally have to add documentation, as well as register versioning and tracking data in a central data store. In C#, it's also common to release a collection class for objects of your new class—if you don't, it's one of the things people are sure to ask for. There are a number of interfaces to implement in order to build C# collections, and we'll take a look at them in this chapter.

Creating Indexers

The most common way to access the elements in a collection is using the [ ] operator, and in C#, you can support [ ] in your own collections by using an *indexer*.

FOR C++ PROGRAMMERS

You cannot overload the [ ] operator in C# as you can in C++; you use indexers instead.

For example, say we wanted to create a collection named CustomerList (technically speaking, it's not a true list collection because it won't implement all the properties and methods of the IList interface, which we'll see at the end of the chapter). We'll store a name for each customer in the list, allowing programmers to pass a list of strings to the CustomerList constructor. After we implement the indexer, you can access customer names like this: *customerlist[index]*. Here's what the constructor looks like. Note that we've allowed for a variable number of names passed to the constructor:

```csharp
public class CustomerList
{
  private string[] customers;
  private int number = 0;

  public CustomerList(params string[] customerNames)
  {
    customers = new string[100];

    foreach (string name in customerNames)
    {
      customers[number++] = name;
    }
  }
  .
  .
  .
```

To write an indexer, you use the `this` keyword as the indexer's name. You also use square brackets for the single parameter passed to the indexer, which is the index value that the calling code wants to access. The rest of the indexer's code is similar to a property's code. You use get and set methods to get and set the value at the given index, using the `value` keyword as you do when writing a property:

```csharp
public string this[int index]
{
  get
  {
    return customers[index];
  }
  set
  {
    customers[index] = value;
  }
}
```

That's all it takes to implement an indexer. You can see this code at work in ch06_10.cs, Listing 6.10. In this example, we're creating a `CustomerList` object, storing four customers in it, and then looping over them with a `for` loop that retrieves those names with the [ ] operator.

LISTING 6.10   Creating a Collection Class (ch06_10.cs)

```
public class ch06_10
{
  static void Main()
  {
    CustomerList customerList = new CustomerList("Ralph", "Ed",
      "Alice", "Trixie");

    for (int loopIndex = 0; loopIndex < 4; loopIndex++)
    {
      System.Console.WriteLine("customerList[{0}] = {1}",
        loopIndex, customerList[loopIndex]);
    }
  }
}

public class CustomerList
{
  private string[] customers;
  private int number = 0;

  public CustomerList(params string[] customerNames)
  {
    customers = new string[100];

    foreach (string name in customerNames)
    {
      customers[number++] = name;
    }
  }

  public string this[int index]
  {
    get
    {
      return customers[index];
    }
    set
    {
      customers[index] = value;
    }
  }
}
```

Here's what you see when you run ch06_10:

```
C:\>ch06_10
customerList[0] = Ralph
customerList[1] = Ed
customerList[2] = Alice
customerList[3] = Trixie
```

You don't need to index with integers; as with other collections, you can index on any data type, or even multiple types, if you overload an indexer. For example, ch06_11.cs (as presented in Listing 6.11) shows how to overload the indexer in the previous example for strings as well as integers, allowing you to access customers as *customerlist*["zero"], *customerlist*["one"], and so on.

WATCH THE VALUES PASSED TO INDEXERS

Example ch06_10.cs demonstrates how to write an indexer, but note that you should implement code in an indexer as carefully as you would for a property, making sure values you consider illegal are not stored. Even more important is making sure that the index value isn't outside the bounds of the array you're using to store data for the collection; if it is, C# will stop your application.

LISTING 6.11   Indexing with Strings (ch06_11.cs)

```
public class ch06_11
{
  static void Main()
  {
    CustomerList customerList = new CustomerList("Ralph",
      "Ed", "Alice", "Trixie");

    System.Console.WriteLine("customerList[\"{0}\"] = {1}",
      "zero", customerList["zero"]);
    System.Console.WriteLine("customerList[\"{0}\"] = {1}",
      "one", customerList["one"]);
    System.Console.WriteLine("customerList[\"{0}\"] = {1}",
      "two", customerList["two"]);
    System.Console.WriteLine("customerList[\"{0}\"] = {1}",
      "three", customerList["three"]);
  }
}

public class CustomerList
{
  private string[] customers;
  private int number = 0;
```

LISTING 6.11   Continued

```
public CustomerList(params string[] customerNames)
{
  customers = new string[100];

  foreach (string name in customerNames)
  {
    customers[number++] = name;
  }
}

public string this[int index]
{
  get
  {
    return customers[index];
  }
  set
  {
    customers[index] = value;
  }
}

public string this[string index]
{
  get
  {
    switch (index)
    {
      case "zero":
        return customers[0];
      case "one":
        return customers[1];
      case "two":
        return customers[2];
      case "three":
        return customers[3];
      default:
        return "Out of bounds.";
    }
  }
  set
```

LISTING 6.11 Continued

```
    {
        switch (index)
        {
            case "zero":
                customers[0] = value;
                break;
            case "one":
                customers[1] = value;
                break;
            case "two":
                customers[2] = value;
                break;
            case "three":
                customers[3] = value;
                break;
        }
    }
}
```

Here's what you see when you run ch06_11, where we've indexed with strings:

```
C:\>ch06_11
customerList["zero"] = Ralph
customerList["one"] = Ed
customerList["two"] = Alice
customerList["three"] = Trixie
```

Creating Enumerators

We've used a for loop to iterate over the members of our CustomerList collection. How about working with the foreach loop as other collections do? To do that, you must implement the IEnumerable interface (as other collections like arrays, array lists, queues, stacks do).

The IEnumerable interface is made up of a MoveNext method that moves to the next element in the collection, returning false if there are no more elements and true if there are. This interface also has a Current property that returns the current element in the collection, and a Reset method to make the first object in the collection the current object again. To add enumerator support to the CustomerList collection, you have to add a method named GetEnumerator, which will return an enumerator object that implements the IEnumerable interface.

That enumerator object will be of a new class we'll call `CustomerListEnumerator`, a private class nested in the `CustomerList` class. The `MoveNext` method of this object will return `true` if it can move to the next element in the customer list, and `false` otherwise. The `Current` property returns the current object, and the `Reset` method sets the index back to -1:

```
private class CustomerListEnumerator : IEnumerator
{
  private CustomerList customerList;
  private int index;

  public CustomerListEnumerator(CustomerList customerList)
  {
    this.customerList = customerList;
    index = -1;
  }

  public bool MoveNext()
  {
    if (index < customerList.number - 1){
      index++;
      return true;
    }
    else {
      return false;
    }
  }

  public object Current
  {
    get
    {
      return(customerList[index]);
    }
  }

  public void Reset()
  {
    index = -1;
  }
}
```

That's all you need to create an enumerator. To let the `CustomerList` class return an enumerator object, we need to add a method named `GetEnumerator` to `CustomerList`:

```
public IEnumerator GetEnumerator()
{
  return (IEnumerator) new CustomerListEnumerator(this);
}
```

Now code can loop over the elements in a `CustomerList` collection using a `foreach` loop, as you see in ch06_12.cs, Listing 6.12.

LISTING 6.12   Implementing IEnumerable (ch06_12.cs)

```
using System.Collections;

public class ch06_12
{
  static void Main()
  {
    CustomerList customerList = new CustomerList("Ralph", "Ed",
      "Alice", "Trixie");

    foreach (string customer in customerList)
    {
      System.Console.WriteLine(customer);
    }
  }
}

public class CustomerList: IEnumerable
{
  private string[] customers;
  private int number = 0;

  public CustomerList(params string[] customerNames)
  {
    customers = new string[100];

    foreach (string name in customerNames)
    {
      customers[number++] = name;
    }
  }

  public string this[int index]
  {
```

LISTING 6.12   Continued

```
      get
      {
        return customers[index];
      }
      set
      {
        customers[index] = value;
      }
    }

  public IEnumerator GetEnumerator()
  {
    return (IEnumerator) new CustomerListEnumerator(this);
  }

  private class CustomerListEnumerator : IEnumerator
  {
    private CustomerList customerList;
    private int index;

    public CustomerListEnumerator(CustomerList customerList)
    {
      this.customerList = customerList;
      index = -1;
    }

    public bool MoveNext()
    {
      if (index < customerList.number - 1){
        index++;
        return true;
      }
      else {
        return false;
      }
    }

    public object Current
    {
      get
```

LISTING 6.12   Continued

```
        {
            return(customerList[index]);
        }
    }

    public void Reset()
    {
        index = -1;
    }
}
```

Here's what you see when you run ch06_12:

```
C:\>ch06_12
Ralph
Ed
Alice
Trixie
```

Note that you don't need a foreach loop to work with an enumerator; you can handle the enumerator yourself, directly. For example, here's how you might use an enumerator to perform the same work as the foreach loop in ch06_12.cs:

```
System.Collections.IEnumerator enumerator = customerList.GetEnumerator();
while (enumerator.MoveNext())
{
  System.Console.WriteLine(enumerator.Current);
}
```

You can also handle dictionary-based collections with IDictionaryEnumerator objects, which support both Key and Value properties. Here's an example:

```
IDictionaryEnumerator enumerator = hashTable.GetEnumerator();
while (enumerator.MoveNext())
{
  System.Console.WriteLine("key: {0} value:{1}",
    enumerator.Key, enumerator.Value );
}
```

Supporting Sorts and Comparisons

You can set up your collection to support comparisons and sorts by implementing the
IComparable and IComparer interfaces. The IComparable interface lets you compare objects
on an object-by-object basis, and the IComparer interface lets you customize how comparisons are performed between all objects in your collection. We'll take a look at the
IComparable interface first.

Implementing IComparable

The IComparable interface supports the CompareTo method, which is built into every object
in your collection. This method compares the current object to another object you pass to it,
which lets you use this method for object-by-object comparisons. If you implement the
IComparable interface and then use C# collections like arrays or array lists to build a collection of your objects, the collection's sorting routines, like Array.Sort, will know how to sort
your objects. The IComparable interface's CompareTo method returns a value that is:

- *Less than zero* if the current object is less than the passed object.

- *Zero* if the current object is equal to the passed object.

- *Greater than zero* if the current object is greater than the passed object.

Here's an example where we implement the IComparer interface in the Customer class. When
we build a collection of these objects using an array and then sort that array, each object's
CompareTo method will be called by Array.Sort. In this case, we'll just use the standard
String class's CompareTo to implement our own CompareTo method, sorting on the customer's
name:

```
public class Customer : System.IComparable
{
  private string name;

  public Customer(string name)
  {
    this.name = name;
  }

  public override string ToString()
  {
    return name;
  }

  public int CompareTo(object obj)
  {
    Customer customer = (Customer) obj;
```

```
        return this.name.CompareTo(customer.name);
    }
}
```

Now the `Sort` methods built into C# collections like `Array` and `ArrayList` will know how to sort `Customer` objects. You can see how this works in ch06_13.cs, Listing 6.13, where we create an array of `Customer` objects, each with their own built-in `CompareTo` method, and sort that array using `Array.Sort`.

LISTING 6.13 Implementing `IComparable` (ch06_13.cs)

```csharp
using System.Collections;

public class ch06_13
{
  static void Main()
  {
    Customer[] customerArray = new Customer[4];

    customerArray[0] = new Customer("Ralph");
    customerArray[1] = new Customer("Ed");
    customerArray[2] = new Customer("Alice");
    customerArray[3] = new Customer("Trixie");

    System.Console.WriteLine("The customers:");
    for (int loopIndex = 0; loopIndex < customerArray.Length; loopIndex++)
    {
      System.Console.Write("{0} ", customerArray[loopIndex]);
    }
    System.Console.WriteLine();
    System.Console.WriteLine();

    System.Array.Sort(customerArray);

    System.Console.WriteLine("The sorted customers:");
    for (int loopIndex = 0; loopIndex < customerArray.Length; loopIndex++)
    {
      System.Console.Write("{0} ", customerArray[loopIndex]);
    }
    System.Console.WriteLine();
  }
}
```

LISTING 6.13   Continued

```
public class Customer : System.IComparable
{
  private string name;

  public Customer(string name)
  {
    this.name = name;
  }

  public override string ToString()
  {
    return name;
  }

  public int CompareTo(object obj)
  {
    Customer customer = (Customer) obj;
    return this.name.CompareTo(customer.name);
  }
}
```

Here's what you see when you run ch06_13.cs. First you see the unsorted array of Customer objects, and then the sorted version:

```
C:\>ch06_13
The customers:
Ralph Ed Alice Trixie

The sorted customers:
Alice Ed Ralph Trixie
```

Implementing IComparer

You can gain more control over how your objects are sorted in a C# collection like an array or array list by implementing the IComparer interface. This interface has one method, Compare, which is passed two objects to compare. You use the interface we just saw, IComparable, to implement object-by-object comparisons, because that interface's CompareTo method only compares the current object to an object passed to that method. On the other hand, the IComparer interface's Compare method is passed both objects to compare, which means you can customize the way sorts are performed in general.

Let's take a look at an example to make this clearer. Say that you wanted to store both a first name and a last name for each customer in Customer objects, and that you wanted to let code sort on the first name or the last name. If you implemented the `IComparable` interface, you'd have to pass data to *each* object letting it know whether to sort on the first or last name in those objects' `CompareTo` methods. On the other hand, if you create an object of the `IComparer` interface, you only need to tell that *one* object whether you're comparing first or last names, because both `Customer` objects to compare will be passed to you in the `Compare` method, and you can customize the sort for first or last names yourself.

To implement this in code, we expand the `Customer` class to store first and last names for each customer:

```
public class Customer
{
  private string firstName;
  private string lastName;

  public Customer(string firstName, string lastName)
  {
    this.firstName = firstName;
    this.lastName = lastName;
  }
  .
  .
  .
```

Next, we add a new nested class to the `Customer` class named `CustomerComparer`, which implements the `IComparer` interface's `Compare` method. We'll add a new field named `useFirstName` to the `CustomerComparer` class; if this field is `true`, the sort will be on customers' first names, and on their last names otherwise. The `Compare` method is passed both `Customer` objects to compare, and we can perform the actual comparison with a new version of the `CompareTo` method in each `Customer` object. This new version will take not only the `Customer` object to compare the current object to, but also the `useFirstName` argument to determine whether it should compare first or last names:

```
public class CustomerComparer : IComparer
{
  public bool useFirstName = true;

  public int Compare(object object1, object object2)
  {
    Customer customer1 = (Customer) object1;
    Customer customer2 = (Customer) object2;
    return customer1.CompareTo(customer2, useFirstName);
  }
}
```

The old version of the Customer class's CompareTo method only took the object to compare the current object to, but this version also accepts the useFirstName argument, which indicates whether the sort should be on the first or last names:

```
public int CompareTo(object obj, bool useFirstName)
{
  Customer customer = (Customer) obj;
  if (useFirstName){
    return this.firstName.CompareTo(customer.firstName);
  } else {
    return this.lastName.CompareTo(customer.lastName);
  }
}
```

When you want to sort an array of Customer objects, you can pass the Array.Sort method the IComparer object to use. We use an object of the CustomerComparer class here. To get that object, we add a static method to the Customer class named GetComparer:

```
public static CustomerComparer GetComparer()
{
  return new Customer.CustomerComparer();
}
```

Now when you want to sort an array of Customer objects, you can call Customer.GetComparer to get a CustomerComparer object, customize that object's useFirstName field to true or false, and pass that object to the Array.Sort method, as you see in ch06_14.cs, Listing 6.14. In this way, you have to set only the useFirstName field of the single CustomerComparer object instead of customizing each Customer object for the type of sort you want to do.

LISTING 6.14   Implementing IComparer (ch06_14.cs)

```
using System.Collections;

public class ch06_14
{
  static void Main()
  {
    Customer[] customerArray = new Customer[4];

    customerArray[0] = new Customer("Ralph", "Smith");
    customerArray[1] = new Customer("Ed", "Franklin");
    customerArray[2] = new Customer("Alice", "Johnson");
    customerArray[3] = new Customer("Trixie", "Patterson");
```

LISTING 6.14 Continued

```
    System.Console.WriteLine("The customers:");
    for (int loopIndex = 0; loopIndex < customerArray.Length; loopIndex++)
    {
      System.Console.Write("{0} ", customerArray[loopIndex]);
    }
    System.Console.WriteLine();
    System.Console.WriteLine();

    Customer.CustomerComparer comparer = Customer.GetComparer();
    comparer.useFirstName = false;
    System.Array.Sort(customerArray, comparer);

    System.Console.WriteLine("The sorted customers:");
    for (int loopIndex = 0; loopIndex < customerArray.Length; loopIndex++)
    {
      System.Console.Write("{0} ", customerArray[loopIndex]);
    }
    System.Console.WriteLine();
  }
}

public class Customer
{
  private string firstName;
  private string lastName;

  public Customer(string firstName, string lastName)
  {
    this.firstName = firstName;
    this.lastName = lastName;
  }

  public override string ToString()
  {
    return firstName + " " + lastName;
  }

  public int CompareTo(object obj, bool useFirstName)
  {
    Customer customer = (Customer) obj;
    if (useFirstName){
```

LISTING 6.14   Continued

```
        return this.firstName.CompareTo(customer.firstName);
      } else {
        return this.lastName.CompareTo(customer.lastName);
      }
    }

    public static CustomerComparer GetComparer()
    {
      return new Customer.CustomerComparer();
    }

    public class CustomerComparer : IComparer
    {

      public bool useFirstName = true;

      public int Compare(object object1, object object2)
      {
        Customer customer1 = (Customer) object1;
        Customer customer2 = (Customer) object2;
        return customer1.CompareTo(customer2, useFirstName);
      }
    }
  }
}
```

Creating a True Collection

If you want to build an "official" C# collection, you should also implement the ICollection interface, which all built-in C# collections implement. This collection has the following properties and methods:

- The Count property returns the number of objects in the collection.

- The IsSynchronized property is true if the collection is thread-safe (which we'll discuss in Chapter 15, "Using Multithreading and Remoting").

- The SyncRoot property returns an object that threads can use to synchronize access to the collection (only when the collection is thread-safe). Thread synchronization is also discussed in Chapter 15.

- The CopyTo method copies the collection to an array.

For example, you can pass the CopyTo method an array to copy the collection into, along with the zero-based index in the array at which copying begins:

```
void CopyTo(Array array, int index);
```

Here's how you might implement that method in the CustomerList collection:

```
public class CustomerList
{
  private string[] customers;
  private int number = 0;
      .
      .
      .
  public void CopyTo(object[] array, int index)
  {
    if(index >= number){
      array = null;
      return;
    }
    for(int loopIndex = index; loopIndex < number; loopIndex++){
      array[loopIndex - index] = customers[loopIndex];
    }
  }
}
```

Now you can use the CopyTo method of the new CustomerList collection, which implements the ICollection interface, to copy the customer list into an array, as you see in ch06_15.cs, Listing 6.15.

LISTING 6.15   Implementing ICollection (ch06_15.cs)

```
public class ch06_15
{
  static void Main()
  {
    CustomerList customerList = new CustomerList("Ralph", "Ed",
      "Alice", "Trixie");
    string[] array = new string[4];
    customerList.CopyTo(array, 0);

    for (int loopIndex = 0; loopIndex < array.Length; loopIndex++)
    {
      System.Console.WriteLine("array[{0}] = {1}",
        loopIndex, array[loopIndex]);
```

LISTING 6.15   Continued

```
    }
  }
}

public class CustomerList
{
  private string[] customers;
  private int number = 0;

  public CustomerList(params string[] customerNames)
  {
    customers = new string[100];

    foreach (string name in customerNames)
    {
      customers[number++] = name;
    }
  }

  public void CopyTo(object[] array, int index)
  {
    if(index >= number){
      array = null;
      return;
    }
    for(int loopIndex = index; loopIndex < number; loopIndex++){
      array[loopIndex - index] = customers[loopIndex];
    }
  }

  public int Count
  {
    get
    {
      return number;
    }
  }

  public bool IsSynchronized
  {
    get
```

LISTING 6.15   Continued

```
        {
            return true;
        }
    }

    public object SyncRoot
    {
        get
        {
            return this;
        }
    }

    public string this[int index]
    {
        get
        {
            return customers[index];
        }
        set
        {
            customers[index] = value;
        }
    }
}
```

Here are the results of ch06_15.cs, where the `CustomerList` collection, which now implements the `ICollection` interface, was converted to an array and displayed:

```
C:\>ch06_15
array[0] = Ralph
array[1] = Ed
array[2] = Alice
array[3] = Trixie
```

Creating a List-Based Collection

The advantage of lists like `ArrayList` is that you can use the `Add` and `Remove` methods to add and remove elements at runtime. To create a list-based collection, you need to implement the `IList` interface, which has these properties:

- ■ IsFixedSize—When implemented by a class, returns true if the list has a fixed size.

- ■ IsReadOnly—When implemented by a class, returns true if the list is read-only.

- ■ Item—When implemented by a class, gets or sets the element at the given index.

The IList interface also has these methods:

- ■ Add adds an item to the list.

- ■ Clear removes all items from the IList.

- ■ Contains determines whether the list contains a specific value.

- ■ IndexOf determines the index of a specific item in the list.

- ■ Insert inserts an item to the list at the given position.

- ■ Remove removes the first occurrence of a specific object from the list.

- ■ RemoveAt removes the list item at the given index.

In Brief

This chapter discussed how to work with and create your own collections in C#. Here's an overview of the topics we've discussed:

- ■ Arrays, which are supported by the System.Array class. This is actually an abstract class; you're better off using the standard array syntax in C#. Arrays support the methods and properties of the System.Array class.

- ■ Bit arrays, based on the BitArray class, let you access the individual elements of an array as bits.

- ■ ArrayList collections work much like arrays, except that they're extensible. You can add and remove elements in array lists using the Add and Remove methods.

- ■ Hashtable collections are dictionary collections that let you store values using keys. Instead of an array index, you pass the key to the hash table to access the corresponding value.

- ■ Queue collections are first-in first-out, FIFO, collections, much like the queues in front of a theater. You add elements to the end of a queue with the Queue method and remove them from the front with the Dequeue method.

- ■ Stack collections are first-in last-out, FILO, collections, much like the stacks of plates in cafeterias. You add an element to a stack with the Push method and remove an element with the Pop method.

- You can create your own collections by implementing the appropriate interfaces. The `ICollection` interface is the official collection interface, with `Count`, `IsSynchronized`, and `SyncRoot` properties, as well as the `CopyTo` method.

- Indexers enable you to use the `[]` operator with your custom collections.

- The `IEnumerator` interface enables you to add an enumerator to your collection, which means that you can use `foreach` with your collection. You can also use an enumerator to iterate over your collection directly.

- You can also implement the `IComparable` and `IComparer` interfaces to support sorting in your custom collections.

Creating C# Windows Applications

7

Creating a Windows Application

For the next six chapters, we're going to get *visual*, working with Windows and Web applications. There is an immense amount of support for Windows and Web applications in the .NET FCL, and we're going to get a kick-start programming Windows applications here.

Because this is a programmer-to-programmer book, we're going to focus on the skills needed to work with Windows and Web applications instead of discussing every individual property and method in the FCL. Once you know how to work with Windows controls in general, you can easily switch between, say, handling labels, text boxes, and list boxes.

We'll be using the C# Integrated Development Environment (IDE) in the next few chapters. When it comes to writing Windows and Web applications, programmers almost invariably use the IDE, and we'll do so here. To introduce the IDE, we'll write your first Windows application by hand, and then let the IDE write it for us to get an idea of the IDE's advantages.

You can see the first Windows application in ch07_01.cs, Listing 7.1. It's not much different from what we've seen before. To display a window and the controls in it, we're going rely on the FCL classes available to us. In this

USING EARLIER VERSIONS OF THE IDE

The examples for this and the next few chapters in the downloadable code for this book were created using the current version of Visual Studio .NET, Visual Studio .NET 2003. However, the C# code itself is the same as you'd use in earlier versions of Visual Studio .NET. So if your version is earlier than version 2003, take a look at the readme.txt in the downloadable code. You can simply copy the C# code we'll create here and paste it into projects created with earlier versions of Visual Studio .NET.

example, we're creating a new window by deriving our main class, ch07_01, from the System.Windows.Forms.Form class (the windows you develop are called *forms* in C#), and adding a text box (class: System.Windows.Forms.TextBox) and a button (class: System.Windows.Forms.Button) to the form.

After customizing the text box and button by setting their Location properties (which you set to an object of the System.Drawing.Point class), Text properties (in this example, the text box will hold the text "Windowed Applications!" and the button will display the caption "Close"), and Size properties (which you set to an object of the System.Drawing.Size class), we add these two controls to the form's Controls collection, which you need to do if you want to display those controls in that form. In the Main method, we run the application by passing an object of our new form class to the Application.Run method like this: Application.Run(new ch07_01());. That's all it takes.

LISTING 7.1 A Windows Application (ch07_01.cs)

```
using System;
using System.Windows.Forms;

public class ch07_01 : Form
{
    private System.Windows.Forms.TextBox textBox1;
    private System.Windows.Forms.Button button1;

    public ch07_01()
    {
        this.textBox1 = new System.Windows.Forms.TextBox();
        this.button1 = new System.Windows.Forms.Button();
        this.Text = "Windowed Applications!";

        textBox1.Location = new System.Drawing.Point(25, 80);
        textBox1.Text = "Windowed Applications!";
        textBox1.Size = new System.Drawing.Size(220, 24);

        button1.Location = new System.Drawing.Point(90, 140);
        button1.Size = new System.Drawing.Size(120, 32);
```

LISTING 7.1 Continued

```
        button1.Text = "&Close";

        button1.Click += new System.EventHandler(this.button1_Click);

        this.ClientSize = new System.Drawing.Size(300, 300);
        this.Controls.Add(this.button1);
        this.Controls.Add(this.textBox1);
    }

    protected void button1_Click(object sender, System.EventArgs e)
    {
        Application.Exit();
    }

    public static void Main()
    {
        Application.Run(new ch07_01());
    }
}
```

In addition, we've created a method named button1_Click in ch07_01.cs which will handle Click events for the button we've labeled Close. In this case, it'll simply end the program with a call to Application.Exit. We connect the button's Click event to the button1_Click method using the standard delegate class System.EventHandler, similar to how we worked with delegates in Chapter 4:

```
button1.Click += new System.EventHandler(this.button1_Click);
```

Now when the application starts, you'll see a window with a text box with the text "Windowed Applications!" in it and a button with the caption Close in it, as shown in Figure 7.1. You can close the application with the Close button or with the X button in the upper-right corner of the window. That's our first real Windows application.

Now let's take a look at creating the same application in the IDE. IDE was introduced in Chapter 1, "Essential C#," (take a look at Figure 1.2, where the parts of the IDE are labeled). To create a new Windows application named ch07_02, select the File, New Project menu item in the IDE. Doing so opens the New Project dialog box you see in Figure 7.2.

To create a new C# Windows application, select the Visual C# folder in the Project Types box and the Windows Application icon in the Templates box, as you see in Figure 7.2. Give this new application the name ch07_02, specify the location you want to use, and then click the OK button.

This creates the new Windowed application you see under design in the IDE in Figure 7.3. The form of this application appears at the center of the IDE, in a *form designer*.

FIGURE 7.1   Creating a new Windows application.

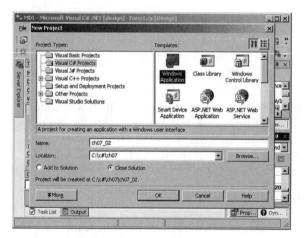

FIGURE 7.2   Creating a new Windows application in the IDE.

To create the example application we've already written by hand, drag a text box onto the form from the IDE's toolbox (the window just to the left of the form designer; refer to the labeled figure showing the IDE in Chapter 1, Figure 1.2), and then size the text box to match the one in Figure 7.3. The small boxes that appear around the perimeter of a control at design time are called *sizing handles*; just drag these with the mouse to size the control as you want it. This creates a new text box object that the IDE names textBox1 in your code (the IDE will name the objects it creates using the same naming conventions used throughout the book). The new text box will have the text "textBox1" already in it; you can change that to "Windowed Applications!" by selecting the text box and clicking its Text property in the properties window at lower-right in the IDE (as labeled in Figure 1.2). Just change the data for the Text property to "Windowed Applications!".

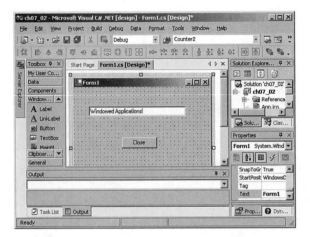

FIGURE 7.3 Designing a new Windows application in the IDE.

Similarly, you create a button by dragging one from the toolbox to the form as you see in Figure 7.3. Change its Text property to "Close" in the properties window. The next step is to add some code to the Close button's Click event that will end the application when the user clicks that button. To add code to a control's event, select that control in the IDE and click the lightning button you see in the properties window. This will display the control's events (the button to the left of the lightning button will make the properties window display the control's properties again).

> ## SELECTING THE DEFAULT EVENT
>
> There's also a shortcut process for opening the button's click event handler. The Click event is the default event for buttons, so if you simply double-click the button in the form designer, the IDE will open button1_Click in a code designer automatically. Double-clicking any control in a form designer will open the event handler for the control's default event in a code designer. Note also that you can use the tabs at the top of the central window in the IDE to switch between form and code designers.

Double-click the button's Click event in the properties window, which opens the *code designer* you see in Figure 7.4. The code designer displays a skeleton version of the click event handler method button1_Click.

The button1_Click method is called when the button is clicked, and it's passed two objects, sender and e (these are the same objects passed to every control event handler in C#). The sender object is a reference to the object that caused the event, which is the button in this case, and e is an object that holds event-dependent data, such as the location of the mouse in a mouse click event. In this case, we're simply going to end the application when the user clicks the Close button, so we add this code to the button1_Click method in the code designer:

```csharp
private void button1_Click(object sender, System.EventArgs e)
{
    Application.Exit();
}
```

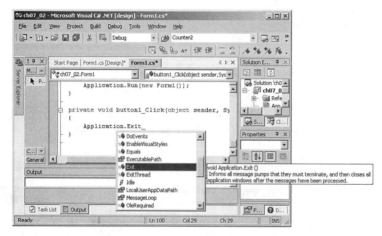

FIGURE 7.4   Adding code in a code designer.

As you type in this code, the IDE prompts you by displaying a list of members of the Application object you can select, as you see in Figure 7.4, and even describes the method it thinks you have selected. This is the IDE's *IntelliSense* facility, and it's a significant help in coding because you rarely have to remember all the arguments of every method. You just type the method's name followed by an open parenthesis, (, and IntelliSense will list the various arguments for the methods, even for overloaded methods.

DEBUG VERSUS RELEASE VERSIONS

By default, the IDE will include debugging information in the .EXE files you create. To avoid including such information, switch to release mode. To do that, select Release from the drop-down list box. This presently displays Debug at the top-center of the IDE, as you see in Figure 7.3.

That's completes the code; now you can run the application by selecting the Debug, Start menu item, which starts the application as shown in Figure 7.5. This displays the new Windows application with the IDE in the background. When you click the Close button, the application closes and the IDE comes to the foreground again. If there's a problem with your code, the IDE will reappear and let you debug your code, stepping line by line if you want, while your application is running.

You can also start an application from the IDE without the debugger running in the background with the Debug, Start Without Debugging menu item. And you can select the Build, Build Solution menu item to build ch07_02.exe, which can be run outside the IDE.

The IDE created this example Windows application, ch07_02, for us. In fact, the code it generates is much like the code we generated in ch07_01.cs. The code for the form in this project is in the file Form1.cs, which you can see in Listing 7.2. Note the similarity of this code to the hand-written version in Listing 7.1.

FIGURE 7.5 Running a Windows application.

LISTING 7.2 An IDE-Designed Windows Application (Form1.cs in the ch07_02 Project)

```
using System;
using System.Drawing;
using System.Collections;
using System.ComponentModel;
using System.Windows.Forms;
using System.Data;

namespace ch07_02
{
    /// <summary>
    /// Summary description for Form1.
    /// </summary>
    public class Form1 : System.Windows.Forms.Form
    {
        private System.Windows.Forms.TextBox textBox1;
        private System.Windows.Forms.Button button1;
        /// <summary>
        /// Required designer variable.
        /// </summary>
        private System.ComponentModel.Container components = null;

        public Form1()
        {
            //
            // Required for Windows Form Designer support
            //
```

LISTING 7.2   Continued

```
        InitializeComponent();

    //
    // TODO: Add any constructor code after InitializeComponent call
    //
}

/// <summary>
/// Clean up any resources being used.
/// </summary>
protected override void Dispose( bool disposing )
{
    if( disposing )
    {
        if (components != null)
        {
            components.Dispose();
        }
    }
    base.Dispose( disposing );
}

#region Windows Form Designer generated code
/// <summary>
/// Required method for Designer support - do not modify
/// the contents of this method with the code editor.
/// </summary>
private void InitializeComponent()
{
        this.textBox1 = new System.Windows.Forms.TextBox();
        this.button1 = new System.Windows.Forms.Button();
        this.SuspendLayout();
        //
        // textBox1
        //
        this.textBox1.Location = new System.Drawing.Point(32, 40);
        this.textBox1.Name = "textBox1";
        this.textBox1.Size = new System.Drawing.Size(208, 20);
        this.textBox1.TabIndex = 0;
        this.textBox1.Text = "Windowed Applications!";
        //
```

LISTING 7.2   Continued

```csharp
            // button1
            //
            this.button1.Location = new System.Drawing.Point(104, 104);
            this.button1.Name = "button1";
            this.button1.TabIndex = 1;
            this.button1.Text = "Close";
            this.button1.Click += new System.EventHandler(this.button1_Click);
            //
            // Form1
            //
            this.AutoScaleBaseSize = new System.Drawing.Size(5, 13);
            this.ClientSize = new System.Drawing.Size(292, 273);
            this.Controls.Add(this.button1);
            this.Controls.Add(this.textBox1);
            this.Name = "Form1";
            this.Text = "Form1";
            this.ResumeLayout(false);

        }
        #endregion

        /// <summary>
        /// The main entry point for the application.
        /// </summary>
        [STAThread]
        static void Main()
        {
            Application.Run(new Form1());
        }

        private void button1_Click(object sender, System.EventArgs e)
        {
            Application.Exit();
        }
    }
}
```

We now have a start in Windows programming. We'll take a look at the basic Windows programming skills next, followed by a look at the available Windows controls, and finally a look at multi-window applications later in the chapter to round off the Windows programming coverage.

Basic Windows Programming Skills

There are a number of essential Windows skills that are demonstrated in the ch07_03 project in the code for this book, which you can see at work in Figure 7.6. For example, clicking the See Message button in this application displays the message "No worries!" in the application's text box, as you see in Figure 7.6. Clicking the Maximize window button maximizes the window, and so on.

Besides the buttons and the text box you see in Figure 7.6, note that this application also uses a label control to display the message "Windows Applications". Labels are simple controls similar to text boxes, except that the user can't enter text in them directly. To create the label in Figure 7.6, drag a label control from the toolbox onto the form, set its Text property to "Windows Applications", and use its Font property to set the size of the displayed text to 24 points (a point is 1/72 of an inch).

FIGURE 7.6   Running the ch07_03 example.

Displaying Text in a Text Box

We've seen that you can set the text in a text box using its Text property at design time. You can also set the Text property of a text box at runtime, so to display the message "No worries!" in textBox1 when the user clicks button1, we simply have to add this code to button1_Click in this application:

```
private void button1_Click(object sender, System.EventArgs e)
{
    textBox1.Text = "No worries!";
}
```

SETTING WINDOW TITLE TEXT

Forms also have a Text property, which corresponds to the title of the form displayed in its title bar.

You can also read the text in a text box using the Text property at any time in your code:

```
string text = textBox1.Text;
```

Moving Controls

When you click the Move text box button in ch07_03, the code moves the text box down to the position you see in Figure 7.7.

FIGURE 7.7 Moving a text box.

You can move any control in a Windows form using the SetBounds method, which you can use like this:

object.SetBounds(*newX*, *newY*, *newWidth*, *newHeight*);

All measurements like *newX*, *newY*, *newWidth*, and *newHeight* are in pixels in Windows applications. The *newX* and *newY* arguments give the new X and Y coordinates of the control's upper-left corner. In a Windows application, the X coordinates are positive downwards and Y coordinates are positive to the right. The origin, (0, 0), is the upper-left pixel in the client area. (The client area is the area where you draw in a Windows application—it's the area below any title bars, menus and toolbars, and above any status bars at the bottom. It extends from the inside edge of the left border to the inside edge of the right border.) To move the text box to a new location, we can use code like this:

```
private void button2_Click(object sender, System.EventArgs e)
{
    textBox1.SetBounds(168, 148, 104, 23);
}
```

Moving Windows

You can also use the SetBounds method to move the whole window as easily as moving a control. However here, the coordinates you use are screen coordinates, not client coordinates, which means the origin, (0, 0), is at upper-left in the screen. To move the window when the user clicks the Move window button, we can use this code:

```
private void button3_Click(object sender, System.EventArgs e)
{
    this.SetBounds(this.Left + 100, this.Top + 100, 336, 300);
}
```

Here, we use the Left and Top properties of the form to determine the current location of its upper-left corner, and add 100 pixels to both those values to set its new location. The Left and Top properties are properties of all controls, which are derived from the System.Windows. Forms.Control class. Because forms are derived from the System.Windows.Forms. Control class, they also support the Top and Left properties.

RUNTIME VERSUS DESIGN-TIME PROPERTIES

To get or set dimensions, controls and forms support the Left, Right, Top, Bottom, Width, and Height properties, all of which are read/write. However, these properties, like other runtime properties, are only available at runtime. You won't find them in the properties window.

Displaying Message Boxes

You can display a message box to get input from the user using the `MessageBox.Show` method. Here's how we display a message box with the text `"No worries!"`, the caption `"Message Box"`, and an OK and Cancel button when the user clicks the See Message Box button:

```
private void button4_Click(object sender, System.EventArgs e)
{
    if(MessageBox.Show("No worries!", "Message Box",
        MessageBoxButtons.OKCancel) == DialogResult.OK){
        textBox1.Text = "You clicked OK.";
    }
}
```

You can see the message box in Figure 7.8.

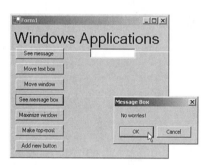

FIGURE 7.8   Displaying a message box.

You can pass a member of the `MessageBoxButtons` enumeration to the `MessageBox.Show` method to indicate which buttons to display in the message box; for example, `MessageBoxButtons.AbortRetryIgnore` displays Abort, Retry, and Ignore buttons:

- `MessageBoxButtons.AbortRetryIgnore`
- `MessageBoxButtons.OK`
- `MessageBoxButtons.OKCancel`
- `MessageBoxButtons.RetryCancel`
- `MessageBoxButtons.YesNo`
- `MessageBoxButtons.YesNoCancel`

The `MessageBox.Show` method returns a member of the `DialogResult` enumeration indicating which button the user clicked:

- `DialogResult.Abort`
- `DialogResult.Cancel`
- `DialogResult.Ignore`
- `DialogResult.No`
- `DialogResult.None`
- `DialogResult.OK`

- `DialogResult.Retry`

- `DialogResult.Yes`

In the code for the Show Message Box button in ch07_03, we check to make sure the user clicked the OK button, and if so, display the message `"You clicked OK."` in the application's text box.

```
if(MessageBox.Show("No worries!", "Message Box",
    MessageBoxButtons.OKCancel) == DialogResult.OK){
    textBox1.Text = "You clicked OK.";
}
```

Maximizing and Minimizing Windows

You can set a window's state—maximized, minimized, or normal—with its `WindowsState` property, which you set to a member of the `FormWindowState` enumeration. Here's how we maximize the ch07_03 window when the user clicks the Maximize window button:

```
private void button5_Click(object sender, System.EventArgs e)
{
    this.WindowState = FormWindowState.Maximized;
}
```

Here are the members of the `FormWindowState` enumeration:

- `FormWindowState.Maximized`

- `FormWindowState.Minimized`

- `FormWindowState.Normal`

Making a Window Top-Most

When the user clicks the Make top-most button, the code makes the application's window a *top-most* window, which means it will stay on top of any other standard window. Here's what the code looks like:

```
private void button6_Click(object sender, System.EventArgs e)
{
    this.TopMost = true;
}
```

Give this a try. When you make the window top-most, it'll ride over any other standard window, even when you click a standard window that the top-most window partially obscures. Top-most windows are great for displaying control panels in multi-window applications.

Adding Controls at Runtime

You can also add controls to a form at runtime, and even connect them to event handlers at the same time. For example, when the user clicks the button labeled Add Button in the ch07_03 application, a new button appears, as you see in Figure 7.9. When this new button is clicked, its caption will change from "Click Me" to "Clicked!".

FIGURE 7.9 Adding a new button at runtime.

When the user clicks the button labeled Add New Button, we can use code similar to the code in the hand-written example, ch07_01.cs. Here's the necessary code. Note that we also add an event handler, newButton_Click, to this new button:

```
private System.Windows.Forms.Button newButton;

private void button7_Click(object sender, System.EventArgs e)
{
    newButton = new System.Windows.Forms.Button();
    newButton.Location = new System.Drawing.Point(160, 240);
    newButton.Name = "newButton";
    newButton.Text = "Click Me";
    this.Controls.Add(this.newButton);
    newButton.Click += new System.EventHandler(this.newButton_Click);
}

private void newButton_Click(object sender, System.EventArgs e)
{
    newButton.Text = "Clicked!";
}
```

This code creates a new button, newButton, positions it, gives it a caption, and adds it to the form's Controls collection, which displays it in the form. It also adds the event handler newButton_Click to the new button's Click event. When the button is clicked, its Text property, which corresponds to its caption, is changed to "Clicked!".

Using Basic Windows Controls

With the basic Windows programming skills under our belts, we'll take a look at working with basic Windows controls next. There are many controls available, from buttons to tree views. To get a look at how the basic Windows controls work, take a look at the ch07_04 example, which appears in Figure 7.10. We'll take a look at handling the various controls in this example next.

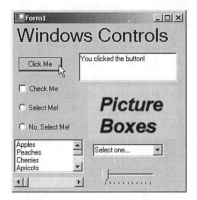

FIGURE 7.10 Running the ch07_04 example.

Labels

You use label controls to display text that the user isn't supposed to change at runtime, such as the result of some long calculation. The label in ch07_04 displays the text "Windows Controls", and its font has been set to 24 points using its Font property.

The main property here is the Text property, which holds the displayed text. The default event is the Click event, which responds to user clicks.

Buttons

We've already seen buttons at work. When you click the button in the ch07_04 example, the text "You clicked the button!" appears in the text box, as you see in Figure 7.10. Here's the code that made that happen:

```
private void button1_Click(object sender, System.EventArgs e)
{
    textBox1.Text = "You clicked the button!";
}
```

The main property of buttons is the Text property, which holds the button's caption. The default event is the Click event. Buttons have a Click method that you can call to click them. Prefacing a letter in a button's caption with an ampersand (&) makes that letter the button's *access key*. For example, if a button's

MAKING A LABEL LOOK LIKE A TEXT BOX

You can make a label look like a read-only text box by setting its BackColor property (which all controls and forms support) to white and its BorderStyle property to BorderStyle.Fixed3D. (At design time, you can select colors from the many displayed when you select the BackColor property in the properties window; at runtime, you can assign the value System.Drawing.Color.White to BackColor.)

caption is set to E&xit, the x appears underlined at runtime, and the user can click the button by pressing Alt+X. Other controls, such as menus, can also use access keys.

Text Boxes

The text box in ch07_04, Figure 7.10, is a *multiline* text box because it allows users to enter multiple lines of text. By default, you can only enter a single line of text in a text box, but if you set its Multiline property to true, it'll accept multiple lines of text, and you can resize it vertically (which you can't do for single-line text boxes). Multiline text boxes wrap words by default, but you can turn that off by setting the WordWrap property to false.

You can set the maximum number of characters a text box can accept with the MaxLength property, and if you set the PasswordChar property to a character such as "*", the text box becomes a password control, displaying * for every character the reader types (you can still read the underlying text with the text box's Text property). The default event for text boxes is the TextChanged event, which occurs when the text in a text box changes and the text box loses the focus (the *focus* is the target of keystrokes in a Windows application). Text boxes also support the Cut, Copy, and Paste methods so you can let users select text with the mouse and cut, copy, or paste it using the Windows Clipboard.

In addition to standard text boxes, C# also supports rich text boxes, which you can find in the toolbox. Rich text boxes support rich-text format (RTF) text, which includes all kinds of formatting like italics, underlining, different fonts, and so on. These controls act like word processors in a control. They can save and read .RTF files (use their SaveFile and LoadFile methods), which can then be read by other word processors such as Microsoft Word.

Check Boxes

The check box in the ch07_04 example appears under the Click Me button, and has the caption Check Me. When the user clicks this control, its CheckChanged event occurs. We can determine whether the check box is checked with its Checked property, and report its status in the application's text box:

```
private void checkBox1_CheckedChanged(object sender, System.EventArgs e)
{
    if(checkBox1.Checked == true)
    {
        textBox1.Text = "The check box is checked.";
    }
    else
    {
        textBox1.Text = "The check box is not checked.";
    }
}
```

Note that the `Checked` property is read/write. Not only can you determine whether a check box is checked using this property, you can also check or uncheck it by setting this property to `true` or `false` respectively. The `Text` property sets the check box's caption, and the default event for check boxes is the `CheckedChanged` event.

Radio Buttons

Radio buttons enable the users to make an exclusive selection from a set of options. Although you can select as many check boxes as you want from a set, you can select only one radio button from a set of radio buttons—the others are automatically cleared. As with check boxes, you can set the caption for radio buttons using the `Text` property, and set or get the checked status with the `Checked` property. The default event is the `CheckedChanged` event.

There are two radio buttons in the ch07_04 example, as you see in Figure 7.10. When you select one, the other is

> **CREATING RADIO BUTTON GROUPS: PANELS AND GROUP BOXES**
>
> All the radio buttons on a form act in concert, allowing you to select only one at a time. That might not be what you want however. For example, you might want to have two sets of radio buttons, one to allow users to select the day of the month, and the other to allow users to select the day of the week. To create independent radio button sets, you first drag a `Panel` or `GroupBox` control onto the form from the toolbox, and then add the radio buttons you want to act together into the `Panel` or `GroupBox`.

automatically unselected. That means we don't have to look at the `Checked` property in the `CheckedChanged` event handler. If a radio button was clicked, it's been selected. We can therefore display the status of the radio buttons in the application's text box like this:

```
private void radioButton1_CheckedChanged(object sender, System.EventArgs e)
{
    textBox1.Text = "Radio button 1 is selected.";
}

private void radioButton2_CheckedChanged(object sender, System.EventArgs e)
{
    textBox1.Text = "Radio button 2 is selected.";
}
```

List Boxes

Under the radio buttons in Figure 7.10, you can see a list box displaying the names of various fruits. When the user selects a fruit, the selection appears in the application's text box, as shown in Figure 7.11.

FIGURE 7.11   Making a selection in a list box.

When you add a list box to a form from the toolbox, that list box is empty. To add items to the list box at design time, select the list box's Items property, and click the ellipsis (...) button that appears next to the Items property to open the String Collection Editor, as you see in Figure 7.12. You can enter the strings you want to display in the list box, also shown in Figure 7.12.

The Items property is actually a list collection, so you can use methods like Add, Remove, RemoveAt, and so on to manipulate the contents of a list box. In this case, we're adding bananas to the list:

```
listBox1.Items.Add("Bananas");
```

The default event for list boxes is the SelectedIndexChanged event, which occurs when a new selection is made in a list box. You can get an object corresponding to the current selection using the list box's SelectedItem property, so we can display the currently selected item in the application's text box this way:

```
private void listBox1_SelectedIndexChanged(object sender, System.EventArgs e)
{
    textBox1.Text = "You selected " + listBox1.SelectedItem + ".";
}
```

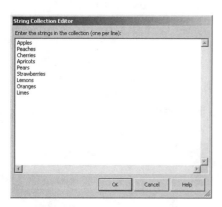

FIGURE 7.12   Using the String Collection Editor.

When the MultiColumn property is set to true, the list box displays items in multiple columns and a horizontal scroll bar appears. When ScrollAlwaysVisible is set to true, the scroll bar appears regardless of the number of items.

The SelectedIndex (not SelectedItem) property returns a 0-based integer value that corresponds to the first selected item in the list box. You can programmatically change the selected item by changing the SelectedIndex property in code; the corresponding item in the list will appear highlighted on the Windows Form. If no item is selected, the SelectedIndex value is –1. If the first item in the list is selected, the SelectedIndex value is 0. The Items.Count property reflects the number of items in the list.

List boxes can also support multiple selections; the SelectionMode property determines how many list items can be selected at a time. You can set this property to these values from the SelectionMode enumeration:

- SelectionMode.MultiExtended—Multiple items can be selected. The user can use the Shift, Ctrl, and the arrow keys to make multiple selections.

- SelectionMode.MultiSimple—Multiple items can be selected.

- SelectionMode.None—No items can be selected.

- SelectionMode.One—Only one item can be selected at a time.

You can access the items in a list box with the Items collection like this: In single-selection list boxes, you use the SelectedIndex and SelectedItem properties to determine which item has been selected. On the other hand, when you support multiple selections, you use the SelectedIndices property to get the selected indices (as an array) and the SelectedItems property to access the selected items themselves (as a collection of objects). For example, here's how you might use a foreach loop to loop over and display the selected items in a multiple selection list box:

```
foreach(int index in listBox1.SelectedIndices)
{
    textBox1.Text += listBox1.Items[index] + "  ";
}
```

You can also sort a list box's list if you set the Sorted property to true (the default is false).

Scroll Bars

Under the list box in the ch04_07 example, you can see a horizontal scroll bar; C# lets you use both horizontal and vertical scroll bars in forms. Scroll bars are usually tied to other controls, and they appear automatically in text boxes, list boxes, and other controls as needed. However, you can also use your own free-standing scroll bars in Windows applications.

The important properties for scroll bars are the Value, Maximum, and Minimum properties, which hold the current value of the scroll bar, the maximum possible value (default = 100), and the minimum possible value (default = 0). The default event for scroll bars is the Scroll event. Here's how we use it to report the new position of the scroll bar in the application's text box after the user has scrolled that scroll bar:

```
private void hScrollBar1_Scroll(object sender, System.Windows.Forms.ScrollEventArgs e)
{
    textBox1.Text = "New scroll position: " + hScrollBar1.Value + ".";
}
```

You can see this code at work in Figure 7.13, where the user has scrolled the scroll bar. Scroll bars like these are good when you want the user to be able to select visually from a numeric range, as when setting red, green, and blue values in colors. In this case, you can pass the three color values, 0-255, to the static method System.Drawing.Color.FromArgb(*red*, *green*, *blue*), which returns a System.Drawing.Color object that you can assign to the forms' and controls' ForeColor and BackColor properties.

FIGURE 7.13   Using a scroll bar.

Picture Boxes

As the name implies, picture boxes display images. You can see one under the multiline text box in the ch07_04 example application in Figure 7.10. Picture boxes can display images from files in many formats (.BMP, .GIF, .JPG, .PNG, and .ICO). To load an image into a picture box at design time, select its Image property in the properties window. Click the ellipsis button that appears to browse to the image you want to load into the picture box. In this example, we're displaying the image in a file named image.jpg, which is included with the code you can download for this book.

You can also load images into picture boxes at runtime using code like this:

```
pictureBox1.Image = Image.FromFile("image.jpg");
```

Clipping and positioning images is handled by the SizeMode property, which is set to values from the PictureBoxSizeMode enumeration. You can change the size of the display area at runtime with the ClientSize property. By default, picture boxes don't display any borders; you can display a standard or three-dimensional border using the BorderStyle property.

Picture boxes also support the Click event, which is their default event. Here's how we report when the picture box was clicked in the ch07_04 example:

```
private void pictureBox1_Click(object sender, System.EventArgs e)
{
    textBox1.Text = "You clicked the picture box.";
}
```

Combo Boxes

Combo boxes are similar to list boxes with an added text box into which the users can enter their own text. You use the DropDownStyle property to make a list a combo box. Here are the options:

- **ComboBoxStyle.Simple**—A simple drop-down combo box in which the list is always displayed.

- **ComboBoxStyle.DropDownList**—A drop-down list box in which the text box is not editable and you must select an arrow to view the drop-down list box.

- **ComboBoxStyle.DropDown**—The default drop-down list box style, in which the text box is editable and the user must press the arrow key to view the list.

You can see the combo box in the ch07_04 example, at work in Figure 7.14. This control displays various colors for the user to select from. After users make their selection, the example displays that selection in the application's text box.

True to the name, combo boxes combine aspects of both text boxes and list boxes. For example, you can access the text in a combo box using the `Text` property like a text box. And like list boxes, you can use the `SelectedIndex` and `SelectedItem` properties to access the selected item in a combo box. (Unlike list boxes, however, you can select at most one item in a combo box. You click the combo box's drop-down list, and when you click the list once, the list immediately closes.) The `Items.Count` property contains the number of items in the drop-down list.

FIGURE 7.14 Using a combo box.

To manage the drop-down list, you can use the `Items.Add`, `Items.Insert`, `Items.Clear`, `Items.AddRange`, and `Items.Remove` methods. You can also add items to and remove items from the list by using the `Items` property at design time. You can also sort a combo box's list if you set the `Sorted` property to `true` (the default is `false`).

Like list boxes, the default event for combo boxes is the `SelectedIndexChanged` event, and we can use that event to display the user's new selection like this:

```
private void comboBox1_SelectedIndexChanged(object sender, System.EventArgs e)
{
    textBox1.Text = "You selected: " + comboBox1.SelectedItem + ".";
}
```

Track Bars

Track bars are similar to scroll bars, except that they look more like the controls you find on stereos. You can see a track bar in the bottom-right corner of Figure 7.10, under the combo box.

Like scroll bars, track bars support the Minimum (default = 0), Maximum (default = 10), and Value properties, and the default event is the Scroll event. We can display the new value the user scrolls the track bar to like this in the ch07_04 example application:

```
private void trackBar1_Scroll(object sender, System.EventArgs e)
{
    textBox1.Text = "New track position: " + trackBar1.Value + ".";
}
```

That finishes the discussion of basic Windows controls. We'll take a look at some advanced controls next.

Using Advanced Controls

FIGURE 7.15 Running the ch07_05 example.

If you take a look at the ch07_05 example in Figure 7.15, you'll see a few advanced controls at work in C#. This example supports timers, tooltips, image lists, and tree views. It uses one of the built-in dialog box controls that comes with C#.

Built-in Dialog Boxes

C# comes with seven built-in controls corresponding to standard Windows dialog boxes:

- System.Windows.Forms.ColorDialog—A color selection dialog box that returns a System.Drawing.Color object in its Color property.

- System.Windows.Forms.OpenFileDialog—An Open File dialog box that returns the selected filename as a string in its FileName property.

- System.Windows.Forms.SaveFileDialog—A Save File dialog box that gets the name of a file to save data in and returns that name as a string in the FileName property.

- System.Windows.Forms.FolderBrowserDialog—A folder selection dialog box that lets the users select a folder, returned as a path string in its SelectedPath property.

- System.Windows.Forms.FontDialog—A font selection property that returns a System.Drawing.Font object in its Font property.

- System.Windows.Forms.PageSetupDialog—A page setup dialog box that lets the users customize pages to be printed.

- System.Windows.Forms.PrintDialog—A print dialog box that lets the users print to a specific device.

These dialog boxes look just like the standard Windows dialog boxes used for opening files, saving files, and so on. They allow your application to fit in other Windows applications. All of these dialog boxes correspond to controls that can be dragged from the toolbox onto a Windows form.

The ch07_05 example displays an Open File dialog box when you click its Open File button. To do that, it uses an OpenFileDialog control, openFileDialog1, which you can drag from the toolbox onto the main form in this example, form1. This dialog box doesn't have any visual appearance on the form, so instead of appearing on the form at design time, it appears in the *component tray* just below form1, as you see in Figure 7.16. The component tray displays controls that have no visual appearance in a form at runtime.

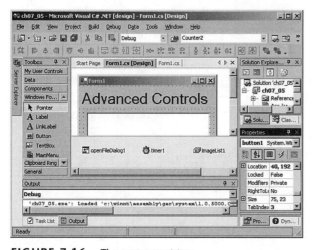

FIGURE 7.16   The component tray.

When the user clicks the Open File button, we can show this new dialog box. You show the dialog box with the dialog control's ShowDialog method, which returns a value from the DialogResult enumeration we've already seen. If the user clicks the Open button in our Open File dialog box, which will make ShowDialog return DialogResult.OK, we can display the name of the file they've selected in a text box like this:

```
private void button1_Click(object sender, System.EventArgs e)
{
    if(openFileDialog1.ShowDialog() == DialogResult.OK)
    {
        textBox1.Text = "You selected " + openFileDialog1.FileName;
    }
}
```

You can see the dialog box that appears when the user clicks the Open File button in Figure 7.17, where the user is selecting the file C:\c#\ch07\ch07_01.cs.

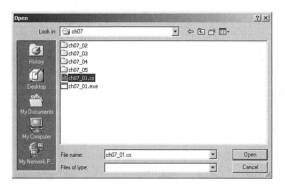

FIGURE 7.17   An Open File dialog box.

When the user clicks the Open button after selecting this file, they'll see this message in the application's text box: "You selected C:\c#\ch07\ch07_01.cs".

Timers

Timers let you create periodic events, called *timer ticks*. The associated code is executed every time the event occurs. These controls are helpful when you need to perform some task repeatedly, such as when you're polling a connection or displaying the time.

There's a Timer control in ch07_05, as you can see in the component tray in Figure 7.16. By default, the Enabled property for timers is set to false and their Interval property, which holds the interval between timer tick events, is set to 100 milliseconds (.1 seconds). To make the ch_07 example display the current time when the user clicks the Start Clock button, set the Interval property of timer1 to 1000 milliseconds, or one second. When the user clicks the Start Clock button, we can enable the timer like this:

```
private void button2_Click(object sender, System.EventArgs e)
{
    timer1.Enabled = true;
}
```

Enabling the time in this case means that timer1_Tick events will occur every second. You can add code to this event's handler just as you can to any event. In this case, we'll display the current time in the application's text box, using the System.DateTime.Now.ToShortTimeString method:

```
private void timer1_Tick(object sender, System.EventArgs e)
{
    textBox1.Text = System.DateTime.Now.ToShortTimeString();
}
```

This event handler is called once a second, so the time displayed in the application's text box is updated that often. You can see this at work in Figure 7.18. (Note that this example has no way to turn off the clock—if you want to do that, you need to add code to set the clock's Enabled property to false.)

FIGURE 7.18   Using a timer.

Image Lists

Image list controls are simply repositories for images; they don't appear in forms at runtime. Other controls, like the tree view control coming up next, use image lists to store the images they display. You can see an image list, imageList1, in the ch07_05 example in the component tray in Figure 7.16. When you click the ellipsis button that appears when you select the image list's Images property, the Image Collection Editor appears, as you see in Figure 7.19.

You can add images to the image list by clicking the Add button and browsing to the images you want. Each image in the list is given an index, starting with 0 for the first image. In this example, we're storing icons that display open and closed folders, as well as a generic document icon, for use with the tree view control, which we'll discuss next. You can see these icons in the tree view control in the middle of Figure 7.15. (Visual Studio comes with many icons, including the ones we're using here; you can find them in the Visual Studio Common7\Graphics directory.)

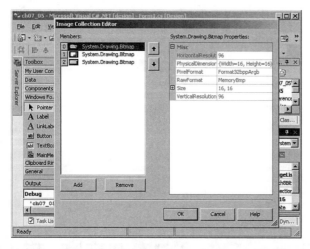

FIGURE 7.19 Managing images in an image list.

Tree Views

You can see a tree view control, treeView1, in Figure 7.15 in the ch05_07 example. As the name indicates, tree views display trees of nodes, much like the left pane of the Windows Explorer is used to display directory hierarchies. To add nodes to a tree view at design time, you can click the ellipsis button that appears when you select the tree view's Nodes property in the properties window. Doing so displays the TreeNode Editor, as you see in Figure 7.20.

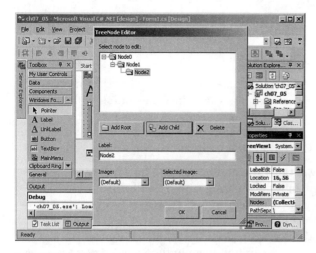

FIGURE 7.20 Managing images in an image list.

On the other hand, node trees are rarely built at design time; you usually build them at runtime, in code (as when you want to display the directory structure the user has browsed to). Each node in the tree is a TreeNode object, and each node has a Nodes collection that you can add nodes to with the Add method, remove with the Remove method, and so on (we saw this in action in the list collections in Chapter 6).

To create the node tree you see in Figure 7.15 when the form first appears, you can add code to the form's Form_Load event, which is the default event for forms, and which occurs when the form loads. We'll build our tree view in that event's handler method.

Each node has two properties that let you specify the normal image it will display and the image it will display when the node is selected, ImageIndex and SelectedImageIndex. These properties refer to the index of the images you want to use in an image list, so first assign our image list, imageList1, to the tree view's ImageList property in the properties window. In this example, we use a closed folder icon for nodes that have subnodes, and an open folder icon when those nodes are selected. We give the subnodes a simple document icon, as you can see in Figure 7.15. Here, then, is how we build our tree view display when the form loads:

```csharp
private void Form1_Load(object sender, System.EventArgs e)
{
    TreeNode node;
    node = new TreeNode("Node 1");
    node.ImageIndex = 2;
    node.SelectedImageIndex = 0;

    treeView1.Nodes.Add(node);

    for(int intLoopIndex = 2; intLoopIndex <= 3; intLoopIndex++)
    {
        node = new TreeNode("Node " + intLoopIndex);
        node.ImageIndex = 1;
        node.SelectedImageIndex = 1;
        treeView1.Nodes[0].Nodes.Add(node);
    }

    node = new TreeNode("Node 4");
    node.ImageIndex = 2;
    node.SelectedImageIndex = 0;

    treeView1.Nodes[0].Nodes.Add(node);

    for(int intLoopIndex = 5; intLoopIndex <= 6; intLoopIndex++)
```

```
    {
        node = new TreeNode("Node " + intLoopIndex);
        node.ImageIndex = 1;
        node.SelectedImageIndex = 1;
        treeView1.Nodes[0].Nodes[2].Nodes.Add(node);
    }
}
```

You can also handle tree view selections with the `AfterSelect` event, which is the default event for tree views. This event's handler is passed a `System.Windows.Forms.TreeViewEventArgs` object whose `Node` property holds the selected node, and the `Text` property of that node will give you the node's text, which we can display in a text box:

```
private void treeView1_AfterSelect(object sender,
    System.Windows.Forms.TreeViewEventArgs e)
{
    textBox1.Text = e.Node.Text + " was selected.";
}
```

FIGURE 7.21   Selecting a tree view node.

You can see the results in Figure 7.21. When the user selects a node in our tree view, that node is reported in the text box.

Tooltips

The ch07_05 example also supports tooltips, as you see in Figure 7.15. The mouse is resting over the Open file button, which makes the button display a tooltip with the explanatory text "Opens a file." To add tooltips to a form, drag a `ToolTip` control from the toolbox to the form, creating `toolTip1`. This adds a new property to every control in the form, as well as to the form itself—"Tooltip on `toolTip1`". When you supply text for that property for a particular control, that text becomes that control's tooltip.

Creating Multi-Window Applications

So far we've limited the Windows application to a single window, but there's no reason to limit yourself; you can use as many windows as you want in a Windows application. In this next example, ch07_06, which you can see at work in Figure 7.22, we'll take a look at

FIGURE 7.22 Running the ch07_06 example.

multi-window applications. This example illustrates how to support the Multiple Document Interface (MDI), multiple and owned windows, and custom dialog boxes. In particular, this example uses an MDI parent window to enclose MDI child windows, as you see in Figure 7.22 (each MDI child window displays a rich text box to let the users enter and edit text).

Menus

Example ch07_06 is also designed to show how to work with menus in Windows forms. It uses a menu system to enable users to select various options, as you see in Figure 7.22. Creating a menu system in a form is easy in the IDE; you simply add a new MainMenu control (which appears in the component tray) from the toolbox to the form. When you do, boxes with the text "Type Here" appear in the upper-left corner of the form, as you see in Figure 7.23. This is where the menu will appear at runtime.

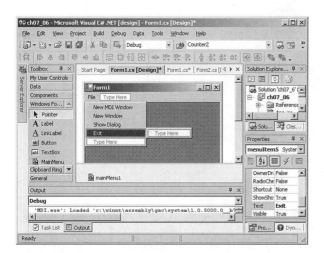

FIGURE 7.23 Creating a menu system.

To create menus and menu items—and even submenus—all you have to do is to enter text into the "Type Here" boxes. To add code to a menu item, you just double-click that item, opening its Click event handler in a code designer. For example, you can add this code to menuItem5, which is the Exit item you see in Figure 7.23, to end the application:

```
private void menuItem5_Click(object sender, System.EventArgs e)
{
```

```
    Application.Exit();
}
```

MDI Applications

The ch07_06 example displays an MDI parent window, and each time you select its File, New MDI Window menu item, a new MDI child window will appear inside the MDI parent, as you see in Figure 7.22. To convert the standard form that is created when you create a Windows application into an MDI parent window, you select that form and set its IsMdiContainer property to true in the properties window.

We'll also need some MDI children, so select the IDE's Project, Add Windows Form menu item to open the Add New Item dialog box you see in Figure 7.24. You can add all kinds of items to your application this way; in this case, select the Windows Form icon and click Open, creating a new form class, Form2, which is stored in Form2.cs.

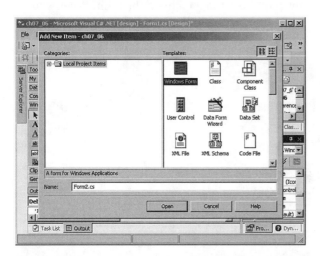

FIGURE 7.24   Adding a new form to a Windows application.

To display a rich text box in each MDI child, double-click the Form2.cs entry in the IDE's Solution Explorer (the Solution Explorer is the top-right window in the IDE, as labeled in Chapter 1, Figure 1.2). The Solution Explorer opens Form2 in a form designer (you can click the two icons in the Solution Explorer under the word "Solution" to switch between a form's code designer and form designer). Add a rich text box from the toolbox to Form2. To make the rich text box cover the entire client area of this new form, you *dock* it to the form. To do that, select the rich text box's Dock property in the properties window, and click the middle button in the button group that appears, as you see in Figure 7.25. You can dock a control to any edge of a form; in this case, we're docking the rich text to fill the form's entire client area.

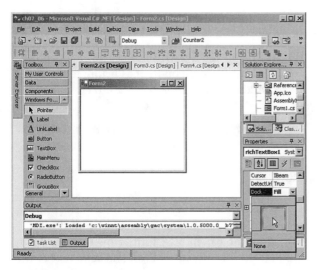

FIGURE 7.25 Docking a rich text box.

Now the Form2 class is ready to be used. When the user clicks the File, New MDI Window menu item in the MDI parent window, we create a new Form2 object, named form, make it an MDI child of the MDI parent by setting the form object's MdiParent property to the MDI parent, and show the new MDI child form by calling its Show method:

```
private void menuItem2_Click(object sender, System.EventArgs e)
{
    Form2 form = new Form2();
    form.MdiParent = this;
    form.Show();
}
```

This code creates a new MDI child and adds it to the client area of the MDI parent, as you see in Figure 7.22. Every time you select the File, New MDI Window menu item in this example, a new MDI child window, covered with a rich text box, will appear in the MDI parent.

DIFFERENT TYPES OF MDI CHILDREN

MDI children do not need to be all of the same class as they are in this example. MDI parents can display many kinds of MDI children at the same time. You can create your own form classes and make them MDI children of an MDI parent. All you have to do is to set their MdiParent properties to the MDI parent window.

Multiple Windows

You can also support multiple independent windows, not just MDI child windows, in a Windows application. For instance, when you select the File, New Window menu item in the ch07_06 example, a new window appears (see Figure 7.26). To show how communication between windows works, the MDI parent window has sent this new window the text "Multiple Windows!", which the new window displays in a text box.

To make this work, you add a new Windows form using the Project, Add Windows Form menu item as before to create the Form3 class. Add a Close button to Form3 to close the window:

```
private void button1_Click(object sender, System.EventArgs e)
{
    this.Close();
}
```

FIGURE 7.26   Displaying a new window.

Give the new form a multiline text box in which to display text sent to it from the parent MDI form. How does the MDI parent communicate with this new form and send text to the text box? Say, for example, that you create a new object of the Form3 class: Form3 form = new Form3();. In the code for the MDI parent, you can then refer to the new form as form, and show it with a call to the form.Show method. So how can you access the text in the text box in a Form3 object? Could you refer to it as form.textBox1.Text? No, because the text box in Form3 is private by default. You can change the text box's declaration to public, in which case you can refer directly to

CLOSING VERSUS DISPOSING OF WINDOWS

The Form.Close method closes a window, but doesn't dispose of it, so even after a window has been closed, you can still access its properties. To actually dispose of a Form object, you call its Dispose method.

form.textBox1.Text in the code in the MDI parent, but that's not good programming practice.

A better idea is to add a new public property to Form3, giving you control over which values are accepted or returned. In this example, we'll call that property DisplayText, so add this code to the Form3 class now:

```
public string DisplayText
{
    set
    {
        textBox1.Text = "The opening window sent this text: " + value;
    }
}
```

Now when you assign the `DisplayText` property some text, the text box in a `Form3` object will display that text. Here's how we might create a new `Form3` object, send it some text, and display it:

```
private void menuItem3_Click(object sender, System.EventArgs e)
{
    Form3 form = new Form3();
    form.DisplayText = "Multiple windows!";
    form.Show();
}
```

This gives you the results you see in Figure 7.26, where we've been able to communicate between windows using a custom property. That's how windows in the same application usually communicate with each other—using custom properties and methods.

Here's another multi-window topic. You can also make one form "own" another form. An owned form will close when you close its owner, and will be minimized and restored automatically when you minimize and restore its owner. To allow the MDI parent to own the `Form3` object form, you just pass form to the MDI parent's `AddOwnedForm` method:

```
private void menuItem3_Click(object sender, System.EventArgs e)
{
    Form3 form = new Form3();
    this.AddOwnedForm(form);
    form.DisplayText = "Multiple windows!";
    form.Show();
}
```

You can determine which forms a form owns by checking that form's `OwnedForms` property. That property returns an `Form[]` array or `null` if there are no owned forms.

FIGURE 7.27 Displaying a dialog box.

Dialog Boxes

You can retrieve text input from the user with dialog boxes. The ch07_06 sample application is an example; when you select the File, Show Dialog menu item in the MDI parent, a new dialog box appears, asking you to enter your comments as you see in Figure 7.27.

When you type some comments into the dialog box and click OK, those comments are retrieved by the MDI parent form and displayed in a message box, as you see in Figure 7.28.

FIGURE 7.28   Reading text from a dialog box.

To make this work, we've added a new form, `Form4`, to our example application. We'll customize this new form to act as a dialog box so when the user selects the File, Show Dialog menu item in the MDI parent, you can use the `ShowDialog` method to display this form. That method will return a result from the `DialogResult` enumeration. If the user clicks the OK button in the dialog box, we'll display their comments, retrieving those comments from the `Data` property, which we'll add to the dialog box:

```
private void menuItem4_Click(object sender, System.
EventArgs e)
    {
    Form4 dialog = new Form4();
    if(dialog.ShowDialog() == DialogResult.OK)
    {
        MessageBox.Show("Your comments were: " + dialog.Data);
    }
}
```

MODAL VERSUS NON-MODAL DIALOG BOXES

Dialog boxes can be *modal*, which means the user must dismiss them before working with the rest of the application, or *non-modal*, which means they can stay open while the user works with the other windows in the application. Using the `ShowDialog` method makes the dialog box modal; using the standard `Form` method `Show` (as you use with any other window you want to open from your code) makes the dialog box non-modal.

The next step is to set up the dialog box, `Form4`. To make this form as much like a dialog box as possible, you set its `FormBorderStyle` property to `FormBorderStyle.FixedDialog`, giving it a fixed (non-resizable) border. Although windows are usually represented by buttons in the Windows task bar, dialog boxes are not, so you set this form's `ShowInTaskBar` property to `false`. In addition, set the form's `ControlBox` property to `false` to remove the maximize, minimize, and close buttons in the title bar. As with any other form, you can set its title bar text with the `Text` property.

You can also add the controls you see in the dialog box in Figure 7.27—a multiline text box, as well as OK and Cancel buttons, button1 and button2. To make button1 into a true OK button, set the form's `AcceptButton` property to button1; similarly, to make button2 into a true Cancel button, set the form's `CancelButton` property to button2. Now, for example, if you use the `ShowDialog` method to display the dialog box and the user clicks the Cancel button, the `ShowDialog` method will return `DialogResult.Cancel`.

You can also set the dialog box's result value by assigning a value to the `DialogResult` keyword. For example, to return a value of `DialogResult.OK` when the user clicks the OK button, you can use this code:

```
private void button1_Click(object sender, System.EventArgs e)
{
    DialogResult = DialogResult.OK;
}
```

The calling code is set up to retrieve the text in the text box using a property named `Data`, so you add that property to the code for the `Form4` class:

```
public string Data
{
    get
    {
        return textBox1.Text;
    }
}
```

That's all the code we need. Now when the dialog box is displayed using the `ShowDialog` method, it'll return `DialogResult.OK` if the user clicked the OK button and `DialogResult.Cancel` if the user clicked the Cancel button. If the user clicked the OK button, you can read the text they've entered with the dialog box's `Data` property. That finishes the dialog box example.

The examples in this chapter are meant to give you a solid foundation in Windows programming. We haven't covered all the details here, of course. There are other types of windows you can work with, such as those targeted to PDAs and other smart devices, and even non-rectangular windows. And there are other controls as well—we haven't covered list views, toolbars, status bars, and some others. The objective here is to get a kick-start in the topic, and now we're up to speed. We're ready to press on to Web applications in the next chapter.

In Brief

This chapter looked at Windows programming in C#. Here's an overview of the topics we've discussed:

- Windows are based on the `System.Windows.Forms.Form` class, and programming with them is straightforward. To create your own form, you just derive from this class. In `Main`, you pass a new object of the startup form you want the application to display to the `Application.Run` method.

- Although you can write windowed applications by hand, you usually create them in the C# Integrated Development Environment (IDE). The IDE has a large set of tools available for rapid code development.

- Forms and controls have a number of properties, such as the Text property, which displays title bar text in a form and caption text in buttons, as well as methods such as the SetBounds method to move or resize the form or control.

- Message boxes are displayed with the MessageBox.Show method and enable you to display a message with a variety of buttons to the users. You can determine which button the user clicked with the return value from this method, which is a member of the DialogResult enumeration.

- Basic Windows controls include text boxes, labels, buttons, check boxes, radio buttons, list boxes, scroll bars, picture boxes, combo boxes, track bars, and others.

- Advanced Windows controls include the seven built-in dialog boxes (Open File, Save File, and so on), timers, image lists, tree views, and others.

- You can add controls at runtime by creating a new control object using classes such as System.Windows.Forms.TextBox, configuring the control as you like, and then adding it to a form's Controls collection. You can also connect an event handler to a control's event using code like this: newButton.Click += new System.EventHandler(this.newButton_Click).

- Communication between windows in multi-window applications is usually via custom properties and methods. Even when a window is closed, you can still access its properties and methods until its Dispose method is called.

- Multiple Document Interface (MDI) applications have an MDI parent and one or more MDI children that appear in the parent's client area. To make a window an MDI window, you set its IsMdiContainer property to true. To make a form an MDI child, assign the MDI parent form to its MdiParent property.

- Dialog boxes are normal forms that you customize, giving them a fixed border, removing the control box (which contains the maximize, minimize, and close buttons), as well as setting its ShowInTaskBar property to false. You can assign the buttons in a dialog box to its AcceptButton and CancelButton properties to create OK and Cancel buttons, as well as assign values from the DialogResult enumeration to the DialogResult return value. You can display a modal dialog box with the ShowDialog method and a non-modal dialog box with the Show method.

Creating C# Web Applications

8

Introducing Web Applications

C# Web applications are based on the ASP.NET protocol (ASP is Active Server Pages, Microsoft's software that runs on the server and lets you create HTML to send back to the browser). You don't have to know ASP in order to create Web applications, and that's the beauty here—C# and the IDE will handle the details for you. You might be creating an application on the Internet, but the development process feels just as though you're writing a Windows application. The IDE even uploads your code to the Web server. However, there are many differences between Windows and Web applications, and you'll get a good feel for those differences in this chapter as well.

In order to develop Web applications, you'll need access to a Web server that runs Microsoft Internet Information Services (IIS) version 5.0 or later. IIS must be running on a Windows machine with the .NET Framework installed so your C# code can run. You can also use IIS locally, on the same machine as Visual Studio.

As with Windows applications, Web applications center on forms, but this time they're not Windows forms, they're *Web forms*.

Creating Web Forms

Unlike Windows applications, the user interface in Web applications is designed to appear in Web browsers, not in a standard Windows window. In Web applications, you display Web forms, which are based on the

DO YOU ALREADY HAVE IIS?

IIS comes installed in some operating systems (like Windows 2000 Server), and it's on the CDs for some other systems (like Windows 2000 Professional). If you're going to use IIS locally, it should be installed before Visual Studio.

WHICH BROWSER TO USE?

The Web forms you create don't have to run in Microsoft's Internet Explorer. But if they don't, a number of features will be disabled.

`System.Web.UI.Page` class (unlike Windows forms, which are based on the `System.Windows.Forms.Form` class), which are specially designed to appear in Web browsers. As far as your C# development goes, however, Web forms look and act very much like Windows forms.

Developing a Web application is much like developing a Windows application. You can still make use of all that the C# IDE offers, such as drag-and-drop development, IntelliSense prompts, what-you-see-is-what-you-get visual interface, project management, and so on. When you create a new Web application, a default Web form is added to the project, just as a Windows form is added to new Windows projects. You can populate that Web form with Web controls, not Windows controls. You can add Web controls to Web forms just as you can with Windows controls—you just use the toolbox—but Web controls are different from Windows controls. To start, there are different types of Web controls—those that run on the server, and those that run in the client (the browser).

Web Server Controls

Web server controls are the controls we'll work with for the most part. These controls are designed to appear and act much like Windows controls. They don't run in the browser, but in the server. When an event occurs, the browser has to send the Web page back to the server so the event can be handled by your C# code. The reason things work this way is because Web browsers differ greatly in their capabilities. To give you a more controlled—and more powerful—programming environment for Web applications, you can run your code back on the server.

On the other hand, sending the Web page back to the server slows things down, so Microsoft has restricted the number of events that are available for Web server controls; some Web server controls can only handle `Click` events. Nor do Web forms handle mouse events such as `MouseMove`. There are no Web server scroll controls because the endless round-trips to the server would be too time consuming.

To add Web server controls to a Web form, you select the Web Forms tab in the toolbox. The advantage of Web server controls is that because their code runs on the server, you can use code with them. That means the C# programming we've already seen applies here too. To run in Web browsers, Web server controls are actually made up of standard HTML same kinds of controls you see in standard HTML pages—but because C# often functionality from a control than HTML controls can give, Web server controls are sometimes made up of a combination of standard HTML controls. Here are the Web server controls that ship with Visual Studio .NET:

- `AdRotator`—Displays ad banners.

- `Button`—Displays a button.

- `Calendar`—Displays a calendar for choosing dates.

- `CheckBox`—Displays a check box.

- `CheckBoxList`—Displays a group of check boxes.

- `DataGrid`—Displays data in a table of columns.

- `DataList`—Displays data with more formatting options than a repeater control.

- `DropDownList`—Allows users to select items from a list or enter text directly.

- `HyperLink`—Displays a hyperlink.

- `Image`—Displays an image.

- `ImageButton`—Displays a clickable image.

- `Label`—Displays non-editable text.

- `LinkButton`—Displays a button that looks like a hyperlink.

- `ListBox`—Displays a list box.

- `Panel`—Lets you group other controls.

- `RadioButton`—Displays a radio button.

- `RadioButtonList`—Supports a group of radio buttons.

- `Repeater`—Displays information from a dataset using HTML elements.

- `Table`—Displays an HTML table.

- `TableCell`—Displays a cell in an HTML table.

- `TableRow`—Displays a row in an HTML table.

- `TextBox`—Displays a text box.

Web server controls give you a lot of power in Web applications, but Microsoft also knows that users might expect to see the kind of standard HTML controls they normally see in Web pages. For that reason, C# also supports the standard HTML controls like HTML text fields (in HTML, text boxes are called text fields) and HTML buttons. When you want to add these controls to a Web form, you use the HTML tab in the toolbox. There are two kinds of HTML controls—*HTML server controls* and *HTML client controls*.

HTML Server Controls

You can turn standard HTML controls into *HTML server controls* whose events are handled back at the server. To do that, you right-click a control and select the Run As Server Control item. When you do, you can handle such HTML server controls in C# code in your program by connecting event-handling code to them just as you would in Windows forms. Here are the HTML server controls:

- HtmlAnchor—Creates a hyperlink <a> element for navigation.

- HtmlButton—Creates an HTML button using the <button> element.

- HtmlForm—Creates an HTML form.

- HtmlGenericControl—Creates a basic control for an HTML element.

- HtmlImage—Creates an HTML <img> element.

- HtmlInputButton—Creates an HTML button using the <input> element.

- HtmlInputCheckbox—Creates an HTML check box.

- HtmlInputFile—Creates an HTML file upload control.

- HtmlInputHidden—Creates an HTML hidden control.

- HtmlInputImage—Creates an HTML button that displays images.

- HtmlInputRadioButton—Creates an HTML radio button.

- HtmlInputText—Creates an HTML text field. (You can also use this control to create password fields.)

- HtmlSelect—Creates an HTML select control.

- HtmlTable—Creates an HTML table.

- HtmlTableCell—Creates an HTML cell in a table.

- HtmlTableRow—Creates an HTML row in a table.

- HtmlTextArea—Creates an HTML text area (a two-dimensional text field).

HTML Client Controls

By default, when you add an HTML control to a Web form from the HTML tab in the toolbox, that control is a standard HTML control, an *HTML client control* in C#. HTML client controls are handled in the browser, out of the reach of C# code. If you handle events in the Web client—the browser—the page doesn't have to make the round-trip to the server.

Because these controls run in the browser, you have to program them with a language the browser understands, such as JavaScript. We'll get to an example in a few pages.

There's another type of control available as well—the *validation control*.

Validation Controls

Before sending user input back to the server, a validation control lets you test that input. For example, you can make sure that the user has entered an email address into the Web page's email text box. You can perform many tests using these controls, such as comparing what's been entered against a pattern of characters or numbers. We'll work with several of the validation controls in this chapter.

That completes the overview you need on the controls you can use in Web pages; it's time to start coding your own Web applications.

Creating a Web Application

To create Web applications, you need access to an installation of Microsoft's Internet Information Server (IIS) running on a server that must have the .NET Framework installed. Visual Studio will create the files you need and upload them directly to the server when you create the Web application (usually in the IIS Web root directory named wwwroot).

USING IIS VIRTUAL DIRECTORIES

To avoid cluttering the Web root directory, you can create IIS virtual directories in which to store your Web applications. To support virtual directories, right-click a folder in the Windows Explorer and select Web Sharing.

To create a Web application, make sure IIS is running and, in the IDE, select the File, New, Project menu item to open the New Project dialog box you see in Figure 8.1. This time, select the ASP.NET Web Application icon in the Templates box, as you see in the figure. Enter the URL of your Web server in the Location box or browse to it by clicking the Browse button. If you're developing your Web applications with an installation of IIS on the same machine as Visual Studio, as in this example, the URL will be http://localhost. To create a Web application named ch08_01, we enter this location in the Location box: http://localhost/ch08_01.

OPENING AN EXISTING WEB APPLICATION PROJECT

To open a Web application that you've already created, use the File, Open, Project From Web menu item (not the File, Open, Project menu item). The IDE will ask for the URL of the server to use, and then will open the Open Project dialog box.

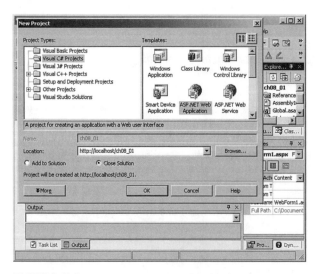

FIGURE 8.1   Creating a new Web application.

By default, a new Web form is automatically added to the new Web application, and that Web application opens in the IDE, as you see in Figure 8.2.

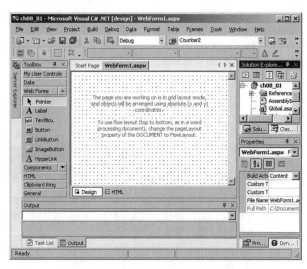

FIGURE 8.2   A Web application under design.

Working with Web Forms

You can see the new Web form, WebForm1, in the middle of Figure 8.2. What you're looking at is the visual representation of the Web form's file, WebForm1.aspx. Web forms like WebForm1 are based on the System.Web.UI.Page class, as you can see in the beginning of the actual code for WebForm1.aspx:

```
namespace ch08_01
{
  /// <summary>
  /// Summary description for WebForm1.
  /// </summary>
  public class WebForm1 : System.Web.UI.Page
  {
    .
    .
    .
```

The text in the Web form you see in Figure 8.2 indicates that the Web form is in *grid layout mode*, which means you can position controls where you want them in the Web form, just as you can in a Windows form.

You can set the Web form's layout yourself using the pageLayout property. Besides the grid layout mode, the other option is *flow layout*. Flow layout is the layout for controls that browsers usually use. With flow layout, the controls you add to a Web form "flow," much like the words in a word processor's page, changing position when the page changes size. To place your controls where you want them, use grid layout.

Now that you have the Web form open in the C# IDE, you can customize it much as you'd customize a Windows form. For example, you can set the Web form's background color using the properties window. This time, however, use the bgColor property, which corresponds in Web pages to the BackColor property of Windows forms. At design time, the properties window will display the HTML properties of the Web form you can work with. (In the IDE, HTML properties begin with a lowercase initial letter, such as bgColor and link.) You can set the foreground color (that is, the default color of text) used in Web forms and HTML pages with the text property, mirroring the attribute of the same name in HTML pages.

You can also set the text in the browser's title bar when the Web form is being displayed using the title property. And as in other Web pages, you can set the background image used in Web forms and HTML pages, using the background property. You can set this property to the URL of an image at runtime. Or, at design time, you can browse to an image file to assign to this property.

The Web form itself, WebForm1.aspx, is where the actual HTML that browsers will open is stored. You can see that HTML directly if you click the HTML button at the bottom of the Web form designer (next to the Design button), as you see in Figure 8.3.

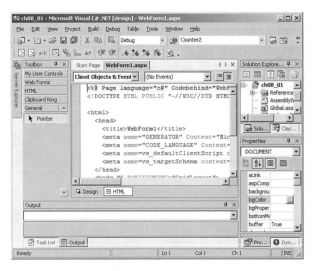

FIGURE 8.3   Using the HTML view.

This is the HTML that a Web browser will see, and you can edit this HTML directly, as we'll do later in this chapter. Note the ASP directives in this document, which begin here with `<%@` and `<asp:`. These ASP.NET directives will be executed by IIS, which will create HTML from them, and that's what is sent to the browser.

Let's add some Web server controls to this Web application. Click the Design button in the IDE to get back to the visual representation of the Web form, select the Web Forms tab in the toolbox, and then drag a button and a text box to the Web form. Give the button the caption Click Me using the properties window as you would in Windows applications. This adds a new `System.Web.UI.WebControls.Button` object and a new `System.Web.UI.WebControls.TextBox` object to WebForm1.aspx:

```
namespace ch08_01
{
  /// <summary>
  /// Summary description for WebForm1.
  /// </summary>
  public class WebForm1 : System.Web.UI.Page
  {
    protected System.Web.UI.WebControls.Button Button1;
    protected System.Web.UI.WebControls.TextBox TextBox1;
```

.
.
.
.

As you've done in Windows applications, double-click the button to open its `Click` event handler in the "code-behind" file, WebForm1.aspx.cs, which is where your C# code for the Web application goes:

```
private void Button1_Click(object sender, System.EventArgs e)
{

}
```

Except for the fact that `Button1` is capitalized here—all Web server names begin with an initial capital—this is exactly what you'd see in a Windows application. Add this code to display a message, `"Web Applications!"`, in the text box:

```
private void Button1_Click(object sender, System.EventArgs e)
{
  TextBox1.Text = "Web Applications!";
}
```

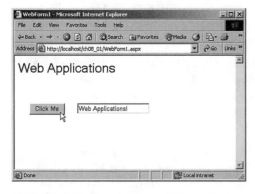

FIGURE 8.4   Running a new Web application.

Now run this new application just as you would any Windows application, by selecting the Debug, Start menu item. This makes Visual Studio upload your code to the Web server and launches Internet Explorer to display your Web application, as you see in Figure 8.4. When you click the Click Me button, the message `"Web Applications!"` appears in the text box, as you see in Figure 8.4.

Coding this application was remarkably like coding a Windows application. But there are still significant differences, as we'll see in the next section.

Basic Web Programming Skills

The major differences between programming Web applications and Windows applications appear in the ch08_02 example, which you can see at work in Figure 8.5.

FIGURE 8.5   The ch08_02 application.

We'll take a look at the various differences between Windows and Web applications in this example next.

Handling Events

When you click the See Message button in ch08_02, the message `"No worries."` appears in the text box, as you see in Figure 8.5. As we've seen, the code to handle a button click is identical to the code used in a Windows application, except that object names like `TextBox1` begin with an initial capital letter by default:

```
private void Button1_Click(object sender,
System.EventArgs e)
{
    TextBox1.Text = "No worries.";
}
```

However, there are huge differences behind the scenes. The most obvious difference is that ch08_02 appears in a Web browser while its code is handled on a remote Web server. Because Web server controls must work in a browser, they have fewer capabilities, and fewer properties and methods, than their Windows counterparts.

What's important to keep in mind is that each time you click a button, the entire Web form must be sent back to the server. In other words, if you're going to stick to C# code, you need a server round-trip every time something happens in the Web form. That introduces some complications—among other things, the Web server won't preserve the value of the variables across server round-trips unless we take some specific steps.

However, you don't need a server round-trip if you use a language that the browser understands, such as a scripting language like JavaScript. To use JavaScript, you use HTML client controls, not Web server controls. For example, to add an HTML button and text field (in HTML, text boxes are called text fields) to a Web form, click the HTML tab in the toolbox, and then add those controls to the form. HTML controls are not given names by default, so enter `"Button1"` for the button's (id) property in the properties window. Similarly, set the (id) property of the text field to `"TextField1"`. You can also give the button the caption "Show Message" by entering that text in the button's `value` property.

The next step is to add the JavaScript code. To do that, click the HTML button in the form designer so that you see the Web form's HTML. Next, select the button, `Button1`, in the left drop-down list box above the code designer, and the `onclick` event (which is the HTML version of the C# Click event) in the right drop-down list. Doing so adds a new JavaScript event handler to the HTML for the button in our Web form's <HEAD> section like this:

```
<HEAD>
   .
   .
   .
<!--
function Button1_onclick()
{

}
//-->
</HEAD>
```

When the button is clicked, the code in Button1_onclick will run. In JavaScript, you can refer to the text in the text field as document.Form1.TextField1.value. Therefore, to display the message "No worries." in the text field, you can use this JavaScript:

```
function Button1_onclick()
{
    document.Form1.TextField1.value = "No worries."
}
```

Moving Web Controls at Runtime

The second button in ch08_02 moves the text box when you click this button. But here too, things are different from how you'd code this in a Windows application. Web server controls don't have handy properties like Top or Right that let you position them at runtime. However, you can access properties like that as *CSS style properties*. Specifically, you can set the top and right location of a Web control by assigning values to the Style["Top"] and Style["Right"] properties, and the bottom and left locations with the Style["Bottom"] and Style["Left"] properties.

When you click the Move Text Box button, the code moves the text box down the page by assigning TextBox1.Style["Top"] the value 150px (that is, 150 pixels):

```
private void Button2_Click(object sender, System.EventArgs e)
{
    TextBox1.Style["Top"] = "150px";
}
```

You can see the result in Figure 8.6, where the text box has been moved downwards. Note that you must use grid layout for this to work, not flow layout. You can only position Web

FIGURE 8.6   Moving a text box at runtime.

elements in an absolute way when you're using grid layout, or when you set the control's `Style["Position"]` property to `"Absolute"`.

There are plenty of CSS styles available. You'll find the complete listing of CSS style properties like `Top` and `Bottom` at `http://www.w3.org/TR/REC-CSS1` for CSS level 1 (called CSS1) and `http://www.w3.org/TR/REC-CSS2/` for CSS level 2 (CSS2). These CSS specifications are maintained by the *World Wide Web Consortium, W3C,* a group responsible for standardizing HTML and XML. All of CSS1 and most of CSS2 is supported in Internet Explorer 6. If you want to learn about moving, coloring, and formatting your Web controls in a browser, these URLs are the place to do your research. For example, you can access the background color of a control like a text box this way: `TextBox1.Style["Background-Color"]`.

Posting Data Back to the Server

Take a look at the list box in ch08_02, Figure 8.6, which you see under the second button. When you add a list box to a Web form at design time, you can click the ellipsis button for its `Items` property in the properties window to open the ListItem Collection Editor that you see in Figure 8.7. Each item in a Web Server list box is a `ListItem` object, and you can configure those objects using that editor.

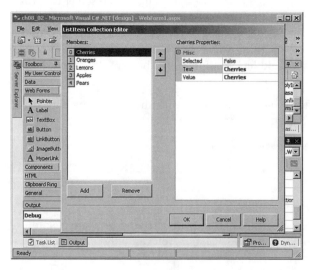

FIGURE 8.7   The ListItem Collection Editor.

As with Windows forms, the default event for list boxes is SelectedIndexChanged, and we can display the item the user selected in the ch08_02 application's text box this way:

```
private void ListBox1_SelectedIndexChanged(object sender, System.EventArgs e)
{
  TextBox1.Text = "You selected " + ListBox1.SelectedItem;
}
```

However, there's another difference here from Windows applications. If you run this application as we've created it and click a selection in the list box, nothing happens. The reason nothing happens is that the page wasn't sent back to the Web server.

Only the default event in a few controls, such as the Click event in buttons, automatically sends the page back to the server. Other events are stored and handled on the server when the whole page is sent back (as when a button is clicked). That's the standard way Web pages work—you make your selections and click a Submit button (which is what Web server buttons actually are) to send the page back to the server.

FIGURE 8.8   Using the AutoPostBack property.

However, you can *force* all of a control's events, such as the list box's SelectedIndexChanged event, to be sent back to the Web server if you set the control's AutoPostBack property to true (the default is false). When you set the list box's AutoPostBack property to true in the properties window and select an item in that list box at runtime, you'll see your selection in the text box, as you see in Figure 8.8.

Preserving a Web Application's Data Between Server Accesses

Another significant way in which Web applications differ from Windows applications is in saving the data in your application while the user works with that application. That's not an issue in Windows programming, because the program is running as the user works with it. But in a Web application, you're not directly connected to the server code. You're looking at a Web page in your browser on your own computer.

That means there are two places your application can store data—in the client (the browser) and on the server. This is an important issue because the data in your application's code on the server is *not*

> **IMPLEMENTING** AUTOPOSTBACK
>
> In HTML, the AutoPostBack property is handled by a JavaScript function named doPostBack (so AutoPostBack won't work in non-JavaScript browsers).

preserved by default between round-trips. They're reset to their default value each time the page is sent on a round-trip to the server, so making sure that the data in your variables is preserved is up to you.

For example, take a look at the Increment Counter button in the ch08_02 example. In Windows, you can program this button to use a variable named something like `counter` and increment it each time the button is clicked, displaying the new value in the text box:

```
int counter = 0;

private void Button3_Click(object sender, System.EventArgs e)
{
  counter++;
  textBox1.Text = "Counter value: " + counter;
}
```

That's not going to work here, because each time you click this button, the entire Web page is sent back to the server, and the page's code is reloaded. This means all values like `counter` are initialized back to their initial values. Each time you click the button, you'd see `"Counter value: 1"` in the text box, no matter how many times you clicked the button. To fix that, you have to preserve the value of your data across server round-trips, and we'll take a look at two ways to do that.

Preserving Data in the Client

By default, the data in the controls in a Web form is stored in an HTML hidden field (an HTML <input> element with the `type` attribute set to "hidden") when the page is sent back to the server, so you don't have to worry about it. When the page is sent to the server and then back, that data is automatically restored in the controls. You can store your own data in that hidden control using the form's `ViewState` property. You store data with this property under a key as you would in a hash table; in this case, we'll use the key `"counter"`. When the user clicks the Increment Counter button, we'll retrieve the counter value, increment it, display it, and store it again:

```
private void Button3_Click(object sender, System.EventArgs e)
{
  int counter = (int) this.ViewState["counter"];
  counter++;
  TextBox1.Text = "Counter value: " + counter;
  this.ViewState["counter"] = counter;
}
```

You still need to initialize `counter` to 0 the first time before trying to retrieve it from the `ViewState` property. You can do that in the `Page_Load` (not `Form_Load`) event, which occurs when the Web page first loads. To make sure counter is initialized only once, you can use the

Web form's `IsPostBack` property, which is true the first time the page loads, but false every time the page is posted back from the server:

```
private void Page_Load(object sender, System.EventArgs e)
{
  if(!IsPostBack)
  {
    this.ViewState["counter"] = 0;
  }
}
```

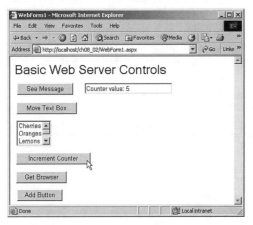

FIGURE 8.9 Preserving data in the client.

Now whenever you click the Increment Counter button, the counter is correctly incremented, as you see in Figure 8.9.

Preserving Data in the Server

You can also store data on the server using the ASP.NET `Session` object. When the user starts working with your Web application, a `Session` object is created for precisely the purpose we'll put it to—to store local data. Note, however, that `Session` objects, maintained on the server, can time out after a period of no client accesses (usually 30 minutes, although you can alter a session's time out with its `TimeOut` property, which is set in minutes).

You can store and retrieve values using the `Session` object in C# code; here's how that might look when the user clicks the button to increment counter:

```
private void Button3_Click(object sender, System.EventArgs e)
{
  int counter = (int) Session["counter"];
  counter++;
  TextBox1.Text = "Counter value: " + counter;
  Session["counter"] = counter;
}
```

Also we should initialize counter in the `Page_Load` event:

```
private void Page_Load(object sender, System.EventArgs e)
{
  if(!IsPostBack)
```

```
{
    Session["counter"] = 0;
}
}
```

Detecting Browser Capabilities

There's another issue that you don't have to confront in Windows applications—determining what browser the user has. Different browsers have different capabilities, which can make a big difference in the code you write if you are working with HTML directly. ASP.NET uses the Request object to handle the incoming data from the browser, and you can use it to learn about the user's browser. For example, to determine what kind of browser you're dealing with—and therefore how you can work with it—you can use the Request object's Browser property. This property returns an object which itself has various properties that tell you about the browser the user has. You can see these properties in Table 8.1. Each property contains text (such as the browser's name) or a Boolean value of true or false.

TABLE 8.1

Request.Browser Properties

TO DETERMINE	USE THIS
Browser name (example: IE)	Request.Browser.Browser
Browser type (example: IE6)	Request.Browser.Type
Is this a beta version?	Request.Browser.Beta
Is this an AOL browser?	Request.Browser.AOL
Is this Win16?	Request.Browser.Win16
Is this Win32?	Request.Browser.Win32
Major version (example: 6)	Request.Browser.MajorVersion
Minor version (example: 0)	Request.Browser.MinorVersion
Platform (example: WinNT)	Request.Browser.Platform
Supports ActiveX controls?	Request.Browser.ActiveXControls
Supports cookies?	Request.Browser.Cookies
Supports frames?	Request.Browser.Frames
Supports Java applets?	Request.Browser.JavaApplets
Supports JavaScript?	Request.Browser.JavaScript
Supports tables?	Request.Browser.Tables
Supports VBScript?	Request.Browser.VBScript
Version (example: 6.0b)	Request.Browser.Version

For example, if you click the Get Browser button in our ch08_02 example, the code will display the name and version of the user's browser in the application's text box:

```
private void Button4_Click(object sender, System.EventArgs e)
{
    TextBox1.Text = "Your browser is " + Request.Browser.Browser
        + " " + Request.Browser.Version;
}
```

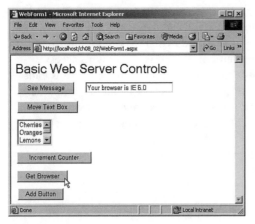

FIGURE 8.10 Getting browser information.

You can see how this works in Figure 8.10.

Besides the Request object, there's also a Response object. This object handles the data the server sends back to the browser. For example, to redirect users to another page, you can use the ASP.NET Response object's Redirect method. The Response object allows you to customize what you send back to the browser. For example, here's how the code might work in a Page_Load event handler if you wanted the user's browser to be immediately redirected to another page:

```
private void Page_Load(object sender,
System.EventArgs e)
{
    Response.Redirect("http://www.microsoft.com");
}
```

The Response object is useful in other ways. For example, this object has a method, Write, that lets you write HTML directly to Web pages. To write an <h1> header with the text "No worries" in a Web form at runtime, you can use this C# code in the Page_Load event handler:

```
private void Page_Load(object sender, System.EventArgs e)
{
    Response.Write("<h1>No worries</h1>");
}
```

Adding Controls at Runtime

If you click the button labeled Add Button in ch08_02, a new button will appear, and when you click that new button, the text "You clicked the new button." will appear in the application's text box, as you see in Figure 8.11.

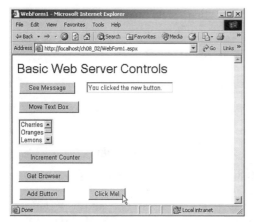

FIGURE 8.11   Adding a button at runtime.

Adding Web controls to a Web form at runtime takes a little more work than in Windows forms. Controls based on the `System.Web.UI.Control` class support a `Controls` collection that holds the controls contained in the control. You can use the `Add` method of that collection to add new controls to a container control.

It's easiest to add new controls to a Web form by adding them to a container control, not to the Web form itself (to add controls directly to a Web form, you must add them to the Web form's `<FORM>` element, which is not easy to access directly). One popular container control is `Panel` (based on the HTML `<div>` element), and we'll add our new button to a `Panel` control, `Panel1`, in the ch08_02 example. When the user clicks the button labeled Add Button, we create a new `System.Web.UI.WebControls.Button` object, set its caption to `"Click Me!"`, and add an event handler to it like this:

```
System.Web.UI.WebControls.Button newButton;

private void Button5_Click(object sender, System.EventArgs e)
{
  newButton = new System.Web.UI.WebControls.Button();
  newButton.Text = "Click Me!";
  Panel1.Controls.Add(newButton);
  this.newButton.Click += new System.EventHandler(this.newButton_Click);
}

private void newButton_Click(object sender, System.EventArgs e)
{
  TextBox1.Text = "You clicked the new button.";
}
```

So far, so good. There's a problem here, however. The new button isn't actually stored in the data for the page, so every time the Web page gets sent back to the server—including when the new button itself is clicked—this new button will disappear. You can solve this problem by creating a new `bool` value named `showButton` that will keep track of whether the button has been created, and if so, will create the button again in the `Page_Load` event. Here's the code:

```
System.Web.UI.WebControls.Button newButton;
bool showButton;
```

```
private void Button5_Click(object sender, System.EventArgs e)
{
  newButton = new System.Web.UI.WebControls.Button();
  newButton.Text = "Click Me!";
  Panel1.Controls.Add(newButton);
  this.newButton.Click += new System.EventHandler(this.newButton_Click);
  showButton = true;
  this.ViewState["button"] = showButton;
}

private void Page_Load(object sender, System.EventArgs e)
{
  if(!IsPostBack)
  {
    this.ViewState["counter"] = 0;
    this.ViewState["button"] = false;
  }
  showButton = (bool) this.ViewState["button"];
  if (showButton == true)
  {
    newButton = new System.Web.UI.WebControls.Button();
    newButton.Text = "Click Me!";
    Panel1.Controls.Add(newButton);
    this.newButton.Click += new System.EventHandler(this.newButton_Click);
  }
}
```

That completes the overview of Web server applications and how they differ from Windows applications. Now it's time to start taking a closer look at the available Web server controls.

Using Basic Web Server Controls

There are plenty of Web server controls available, although there are fewer than the available Windows controls. Because Web server controls operate in Web browsers, they're also much simpler than Windows controls, and support fewer properties, methods, and events. They're still much like programming Windows controls, however, and you can see an assortment of the basic Web server controls in Figure 8.12, in the ch08_03 example. Compare this figure to Figure 7.10 in Chapter 7. As you can see, the basic Windows controls are practically unchanged (at least in appearance) when you move to Web server programming.

FIGURE 8.12   Running the ch08_03 example.

Labels

You can see a label control in the ch08_03 example, Figure 8.12, displaying the text "Web Server Controls". When you're working with Web Server controls, you're working with HTML controls (even if a single Web server control is made up of a combination of HTML controls). In this case, that means that Web server labels are converted to HTML <SPAN> elements; here's the HTML used to create the label you see in Figure 8.12:

```
<span id="Label1" style="font-size:X-Large;
Z-INDEX: 101; LEFT: 12px;
POSITION: absolute; TOP: 14px">Web Server
Controls</span>
```

You can set the font in a control (in label controls or others like text boxes) to a standard HTML font with the Font property. The Font holds a FontInfo object, which has these properties (note that not all properties will be supported by all browsers):

- Bold—Returns or sets whether the font is bold. Set to True or False.

- Italic—Returns or sets whether the font is italic. Set to True or False.

- Name—Returns or sets the main font name.

- Names—Returns or sets an array of font names.

- Overline—Returns or sets whether the font is overlined. Set to True or False.

- Size—Returns or sets the font size.

- Strikeout—Returns or sets whether the font is struck out. Set to True or False.

- Underline—Returns or sets whether the font is underlined. Set to True or False.

You can set these properties at design time or at runtime. For example, at runtime, you can make the text in Label1 italic like this:

```
Label1.Font.Italic = true;
```

You set the Font.Size property to members of the FontUnit enumeration: FontUnit.Large, FontUnit.Larger, FontUnit.Medium, FontUnit.Small, FontUnit.Smaller, FontUnit.XLarge, FontUnit.XSmall, FontUnit.XXLarge, and FontUnit.XXSmall. Here's how you set the font to XXLarge:

```
Label1.Font.Size = FontUnit.XXLarge;
```

You can also use CSS styles to set the style of a label, because labels are really <SPAN> elements. For example, to underline text in a label, you can use code like this:

```
Label1.Style["Text-Decoration"] = "underline";
```

Buttons

Buttons are much like the buttons discussed in Chapter 7; when the user clicks the button labeled Click Me in Figure 8.12, the text "No worries." appears in the text box, as you see in the figure. Because the entire Web page has to be sent back to the server when the user clicks a button, they're really HTML Submit buttons. Here's the HTML for the button you see in Figure 8.12:

```
<input type="submit" name="Button1" value="Click Me" id="Button1"
style="Z-INDEX: 102; LEFT: 15px; POSITION: absolute; TOP: 66px" />
```

The Click event is the big (and default) event for buttons. Programming a Web server button's Click event works just as for a button in Windows, as in this code from WebForm1.aspx.cs:

```
private void Button1_Click(object sender, System.EventArgs e)
{
  TextBox1.Text = "No worries.";
}
```

As with Windows buttons, you can set the caption of a Web server button with its Text property.

You can also turn Web server buttons into *command buttons*. You turn a button into a command button simply by assigning text to its CommandName property. Besides CommandName, you can also assign an object, usually text, to a button's CommandArgument property. When you click a command button, the button's Click event fires as well as its Command event. The CommandEventArgs object passed to the Command event handler has both a CommandName and CommandArgument property, and you can recover the text in those properties using this object.

Text Boxes

You can see a text box in Figure 8.12, displaying the text "No worries." Text boxes are similar to text boxes in Windows programs; their default event is TextChanged (you need to set AutoPostBack to true if you want to handle this event as it occurs), and their text is accessed through the Text property. Here's the HTML for the text box in Figure 8.12:

```
<input name="TextBox1" type="text" id="TextBox1"
style="width:212px;Z-INDEX: 103; LEFT: 140px; POSITION: absolute; TOP: 69px" />
```

Web server text boxes do differ from Windows text boxes in a number of ways. For example, although you can create multiline and password controls using text boxes, you don't do so with `MultiLine` and `PasswordChar` properties. Instead, you use the `TextMode` property. By default, the `TextMode` property is set to `SingleLine` to create a single-line HTML text field, but it can also be set to `MultiLine` for a multiline text box, or set to `Password` to create a password control.

Password controls are turned into HTML `<input>` controls with the `type` attribute set to `"password"` like this:

```
<input name="TextBox1" type="password" id="TextBox1"
style="Z-INDEX: 104; LEFT: 182px; POSITION: absolute; TOP: 209px" />
```

A multiline text box is actually an HTML text area control. Here's what one looks like in the HTML that ASP.NET sends to the browser:

```
<textarea name="TextBox1" id="TextBox1"
style="height:74px;width:157px;Z-INDEX: 103; LEFT: 100px;
POSITION: absolute; TOP: 100px"></textarea>
```

Check Boxes

In Figure 8.12, you'll see a check box set up to handle the `CheckChanged` event in code. When you check or uncheck a check box, this event occurs, and you can use the check box's `Checked` property to determine its new setting. Here's what the HTML looks like for this check box:

```
<span style="Z-INDEX: 104; LEFT: 14px; POSITION: absolute; TOP: 110px">
<input id="CheckBox1" type="checkbox" name="CheckBox1"
  onclick="__doPostBack('CheckBox1','')"
language="javascript" /><label for="CheckBox1">Check Me</label></span>
```

When you check or uncheck the check box, the code indicates the check box's new setting, as you see in Figure 8.13.

To make this code work, all you have to do is to look at the `Checked` property to determine whether a check box is checked, and display that information in the text box. (Don't forget to set the check box's `AutoPostBack` property to `True` if you want the `CheckChanged` event to be handled immediately; otherwise, it'll be handled the next time the page is sent back to the server, such as when the user clicks a button.)

```
private void CheckBox1_CheckedChanged(object sender, System.EventArgs e)
{
    if(CheckBox1.Checked == true)
```

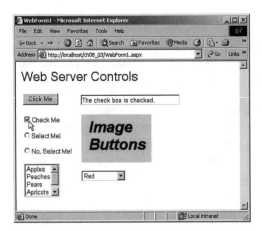

FIGURE 8.13 Checking or unchecking the check box.

```
{
    TextBox1.Text = "The check box is checked.";
}
else
{
    TextBox1.Text = "The check box is not
checked.";
}
}
```

If you wanted to check or uncheck a check box in code, you can set the check box's Checked property to true or false. You can also set a check box's Checked property to true at design time (the default is false), and if you do, the check box will appear checked when the application first starts.

Besides individual check boxes, C# also supports *check box lists*. A check box list is a single control that can display a number of check boxes at once—in other words, they create check box *groups*. This is useful in some circumstances, as when you want to loop over a set of check boxes that are part of a set, such as check boxes that let the user select items for a pizza. They're most useful when you want to vary the number of check boxes you display at runtime. For example, check box lists are often connected to the data in database records, because the number of check boxes can vary depending on the number of bool fields in a record, and true or false easily translate into checked and unchecked.

Check box lists have an Items collection, inherited from the ListControl class, with members corresponding to check boxes in the list. The main event here is the SelectedIndexChanged (not CheckChanged) event, which occurs when the user clicks a check box. Each item in the Items collection is an object of the ListItem class, and you can use the ListItem class's Value, Text, and Selected properties to work with the individual check boxes. To find out which check boxes are checked, you can loop through the list and test the Selected property of each item.

Check box lists also support SelectedItem or SelectedIndex properties, but these are less useful than you might think. Because check box lists can support multiple selections, the SelectedItem and SelectedIndex properties hold only the selected item with the lowest index value, and the index value of the selected item with the lowest index value. This tells you nothing about the other selected items. You will typically use the SelectedItem or SelectedIndex properties with radio button lists, which only support a single selected item.

Radio Buttons

Radio buttons usually operate in groups, in which only one radio button at a time can be checked. When you add radio buttons to a Windows form, they're automatically placed into a single group. That's not true in Web forms—in this case, you must set the `GroupName` property of every radio button you want to be in a group to the same name as the others in the group. If you want a radio button's events to be handled when they occur rather than waiting for the next server round-trip, you must set the radio button's `AutoPostback` property to `true`. Radio buttons are supported in the Web browser with the HTML `<input type="radio">` element like this for the two radio buttons you see at work in the ch08_03 example, Figure 8.14:

```
<span style="Z-INDEX: 105; LEFT: 13px; POSITION: absolute; TOP: 143px">
<input id="RadioButton1" type="radio" name="group1" value="RadioButton1"
onclick="__doPostBack('RadioButton1','')" language="javascript" />
<label for="RadioButton1">Select Me!</label></span>

<span style="Z-INDEX: 106; LEFT: 13px; POSITION: absolute; TOP: 175px">
<input id="RadioButton2" type="radio" name="group1" value="RadioButton2"
checked="checked" onclick="__doPostBack('RadioButton2','')" language="javascript" />
<label for="RadioButton2">No, Select Me!</label></span>
```

In C#, you can handle Web server radio buttons just as you can Windows radio buttons, using the default `CheckChanged` event. Here's the code that handles the two radio buttons in the ch08_03 example:

```
private void RadioButton1_CheckedChanged(object
sender, System.EventArgs e)
{
   TextBox1.Text = "Radio button 1 is selected.";
}

private void RadioButton2_CheckedChanged(object
sender, System.EventArgs e)
{
   TextBox1.Text = "Radio button 2 is selected.";
}
```

FIGURE 8.14 Selecting a radio button.

Besides individual radio buttons, you can also use radio button lists, which work like check box lists. The radio buttons in a radio button list control are automatically part of the same group, and at runtime, a radio button list looks just like a set of standard radio buttons.

Image Buttons

Web server controls include image controls, which are like picture boxes in Windows, except that they don't support a click event. Image controls are translated into HTML <IMG> controls like this:

```
<img id="Image1" border="0" src="file:///C:\inetpub\wwwroot\ch08_03\image.jpg"
style="Z-INDEX: 110; LEFT: 204px; POSITION: absolute; TOP: 269px" />
```

Image buttons do support Click events, and you can see an image button in the ch08_03 example, Figure 8.12. Here's the HTML for this control—an HTML <input type="image"> control:

```
<input type="image" name="ImageButton1" id="ImageButton1"
src="file:///C:\inetpub\wwwroot\ch08_03\image.jpg" border="0"
style="Z-INDEX: 110; LEFT: 141px; POSITION: absolute; TOP: 110px" />
```

You're passed an object of the System.Web.UI.ImageClickEventArgs class in the Click event handler, and this object's X and Y properties tell you where the user clicked. You can report that location in the application's text box like this:

```
private void ImageButton1_Click(object sender,
  System.Web.UI.ImageClickEventArgs e)
{
  TextBox1.Text = "You clicked at (" + e.X + ", " + e.Y + ").";
}
```

FIGURE 8.15   Clicking an image button.

You can see this at work in Figure 8.15, where the user has clicked the image button and the code for this application is telling the user where they clicked.

Image maps often let the user navigate to a new URL when you click a "hotspot" in them, and you can handle that with the Response object's Redirect method. Here's an example which makes the browser navigate to http://www.microsoft.com when the user clicks a region of the image—the rectangle stretching from (100, 50) to (300, 150)—which we'll treat as a hotspot:

```
private void ImageButton1_Click(object sender,
  System.Web.UI.ImageClickEventArgs e)
```

```
if (e.X >= 100 && e.X <= 300) && (e.Y >= 50 && e.Y <= 150) {
  Response.Redirect("http://www.microsoft.com");
}
}
```

You can also use the Command event handler to make an image button control work like a command button. In this case, you assign a command name to the image button with the CommandName property, and the CommandArgument property can also be used to pass additional information about the command.

As with image controls, you can also set the URL of the image to be used to the ImageUrl property. To set the ImageUrl property at design time, click this property in the properties window and browse to the image you want to use. You can also set the ImageUrl property at runtime; just assign it a string containing the URL of an image. And you can set the image's width and height with the Width and Height properties.

Using List Boxes

You can see a Web server list box in the ch08_03 example, Figure 8.12, displaying the names of various fruits like the list box we saw in Chapter 7 in the basic Windows controls example. You can add items to a list box at design time using the ListItem Collection Editor, which opens when you select the list box's Items property and click the ellipsis button that appears, as shown in Figure 8.7. In HTML, the list box is a <SELECT> control, and it looks like this in the browser:

```
<select name="ListBox1" size="4" onchange="__doPostBack('ListBox1','')"
language="javascript" id="ListBox1"
style="Z-INDEX: 107; LEFT: 17px; POSITION: absolute; TOP: 212px">
  <option value="Apples">Apples</option>
  <option value="Peaches">Peaches</option>
  <option value="Pears">Pears</option>
  <option value="Apricots">Apricots</option>
  <option value="Oranges">Oranges</option>
</select>
```

As in Windows list boxes, the default event here is the SelectedIndexChanged event, and we handle that event in the ch08_03 example by displaying the new selected item:

```
private void ListBox1_SelectedIndexChanged(object sender, System.EventArgs e)
{
  TextBox1.Text = "You selected " + ListBox1.SelectedItem + ".";
}
```

FIGURE 8.16   Making a selection in a list box.

You can see how this works in Figure 8.16. Note that if you want to handle a list box's events immediately, you must set its `AutoPostBack` property to `true`.

Multiple-Selection List Boxes

To allow the user to select multiple items, you set the `SelectionMode` property to `ListSelectionMode.Multiple`. You can determine the selected item in a single-selection list box using the `SelectedItem` and `SelectedIndex` properties. The `SelectedItem` property returns the selected item as a `ListItem` object, which supports `Text`, `Value`, and `Selected` properties. The `ListControl` class's `Items` property holds a collection of `ListItem` objects that you can use to access any item in a list box.

Standard Web server list boxes let the users select only one item at a time. However, if you set the list box's `SelectionMode` property to `Multiple`, the list box will support multiple selections. You can make multiple selections in list boxes the same way as in other Web controls. You can use the Shift key with the mouse to select a range of items, or the Ctrl key to select multiple items, clicking one after the other. The HTML for the multiple-selection list box is almost the same as for the single-selection list box we saw earlier, except for the addition of the `multiple` attribute.

When the user makes a selection in a multiple-selection list box, a `SelectedIndexChanged` event occurs. You don't usually send the page back to the server each time the user selects a new item in a multiple selection list box, however; you normally use a Submit button and read the list box selections in the button's `Click` event handler.

To determine which items are selected in a multiple selection list box, you can loop over the `Items` collection of `ListItem` objects, checking each item's `Selected` property to see whether that item is selected. Here's how that looks:

```
private void Button1_Click(object sender, System.EventArgs e)
{
    TextBox1.Text = "You selected: " + "\n";
    for (int loopIndex = 0; loopIndex < ListBox1.Items.Count - 1; loopIndex++)
    {
        if (ListBox1.Items[loopIndex].Selected ){
            TextBox1.Text += ListBox1.Items[loopIndex].Text + "\n";
        }
    }
}
```

That's all you need to handle multiple selections in Web server list boxes.

Adding Items to List Boxes at Runtime

When you use any Web server control based on the ListControl class, you can use the Items collection's Add method to add items to it, and that works for Web server list boxes as well. The Items collection is a collection of ListItem objects, and you can pass either a ListItem object to the Add method, or the text you want to give to the new item:

```
private void Button1_Click(object sender, System.EventArgs e)
{
    ListBox1.Items.Add("Item " + ListBox1.Items.Count);
}
```

Using Drop-Down Lists

The drop-down list you see under the image button in the ch08_03 example, Figure 8.12, allows the users to select from an assortment of colors, as you see in Figure 8.17. When the user selects a color, the selection appears in the text box, as you also see in Figure 8.17.

FIGURE 8.17 Making a selection in a drop-down list.

The items of a drop-down list aren't visible until the user clicks the control's down arrow button. Clicking that button makes the control display its drop-down list, and the user can select an item in that list. He can't select multiple items, because the list closes as soon as a selection is made. Like Web server list boxes, drop-down lists are supported with <SELECT> controls. In this case, the <SELECT> controls are created without a SIZE attribute, which means the browser will create a drop-down list instead of a list box (the SIZE attribute indicates how many items in the list to display at one time, and if you omit it, the browser displays a drop-down list). Here's what the drop-down list in the ch08_03 example looks like in HTML:

```
<select name="DropDownList1" onchange="__doPostBack('DropDownList1','')"
language="javascript" id="DropDownList1"
style="width:95px;Z-INDEX: 109; LEFT: 141px; POSITION: absolute; TOP: 227px">
  <option value="Red">Red</option>
  <option value="Green">Green</option>
  <option value="Blue">Blue</option>
</select>
```

As with standard list boxes, the default event in drop-down lists is the `SelectedIndexChanged` event, and you can get the selected item with the `SelectedItem` property this way:

```
private void DropDownList1_SelectedIndexChanged(object sender,
  System.EventArgs e)
{
    TextBox1.Text = "You selected " + DropDownList1.SelectedItem;
}
```

You can see the results of this code in Figure 8.17. As with list boxes, you need to set this control's `AutoPostBack` property to `true` if you want events handled on the server as soon as they happen. When the user has selected an item in a drop-down list, you use the control's `SelectedIndex` and `SelectedItem` properties in code to determine which selection was made. The `SelectedIndex` property gives you the index in the list of the selected item, and the `SelectedItem` property gives you the actual `ListItem` object that corresponds to the selected item. You can use the `ListItem` class's `Value`, `Text`, and `Selected` properties to get more information about the selection.

There's another property worth looking at both here and in standard list boxes—the `Value` property. Controls that hold `ListItem` objects, such as check box lists, radio button lists, list boxes, and drop-down list boxes, let you add text to each item using the `Value` property. That's useful if you want to store more text in each item than is displayed in the control itself.

For example, a drop-down list might display the names of various colors, red, green, blue, and so on as in our example. However, behind the scenes, each item in the list stores each color in HTML terms as `"#ff0000"`, `"#00ff00"`, `"#0000ff"`, and so on, in its `Value` property. That text can be retrieved and used in your code when the user makes a selection.

You can set a `ListItem` object's `Value` property at runtime in code, or at design time using the ListItem Collection Editor. To work with the current selection in list-oriented controls, you can use the `SelectedIndex`, `SelectedItem`, and `SelectedValue` properties. The `SelectedValue` property holds the value in the `Value` property of the currently selected item.

Using Advanced Web Server Controls

The basic Web server controls we've seen mirror the same controls in Windows applications—text boxes, buttons, list boxes, and so forth. However, more advanced Web server controls aren't similar to Windows controls, and we'll take a look at a set of these more advanced controls in the ch08_04 example. You can see this example at work in Figure 8.18. This example introduces ad rotators, hyperlinks, link buttons, literals, XML controls, and validators.

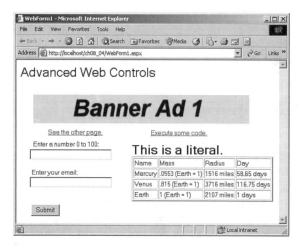

FIGURE 8.18   The ch08_04 example.

Ad Rotators

Ad rotators display banner ads of the kind you've seen on the Internet; these ads can be of any type a browser can display, including animated GIF files. Ad rotators "rotate" through a set of banner ads by selecting which one to display randomly; you can also weight ads to appear more frequently than others. In fact, you can write your own code to cycle through the ad banners.

You can see an ad rotator at work in Figure 8.18. If you reload this example, the page reloads and displays another randomly selected ad banner. When you click the ad banner, the browser will navigate to a URL you've associated with that banner.

Putting an ad rotator to work is not very difficult—you just add this control to a Web form and set up the banners you want to show. You can set up your ads in the AdCreated event, or, more commonly, with an XML file; we'll use an XML file here. Even though this file is written in XML, you won't need any special knowledge to adapt it for yourself.

The XML file in this example is called rotation.xml. For each ad, this file gives the URL of the banner ad image, the URL to navigate to if the user clicks the ad, the alternative text to display if the ad banner isn't available, a numeric value holding the relative probability of how often the ad should be shown (which lets you weight ad banner appearances as you like), and a keyword to use in selecting ads (you can use the ad rotator's KeyWordFilter property to filter ads for target audiences). You can see rotation.xml in Listing 8.1.

LISTING 8.1   rotation.xml (ch08_04 Project)

```
<Advertisements>
  <Ad>
    <ImageUrl>banner1.jpg</ImageUrl>
    <NavigateUrl>http://www.bigwhopperstore.com/product1.html</NavigateUrl>
    <AlternateText>Product 1 is the best!
    </AlternateText>
    <Impressions>90</Impressions>
    <Keyword>Food</Keyword>
  </Ad>

  <Ad>
    <ImageUrl>banner2.jpg</ImageUrl>
    <NavigateUrl>http://www.bigwhopperstore.com/product2.html</NavigateUrl>
    <AlternateText>Millions of Product 2 sold already!</AlternateText>
    <Impressions>90</Impressions>
    <Keyword>Electrical</Keyword>
  </Ad>

  <Ad>
    <ImageUrl>banner3.jpg</ImageUrl>
    <NavigateUrl>http://www.bigwhopperstore.com/product3.html</NavigateUrl>
    <AlternateText>Product 3 wins every time!</AlternateText>
    <Impressions>90</Impressions>
    <Keyword>Toys</Keyword>
  </Ad>
</Advertisements>
```

We'll put rotation.xml in the main IIS folder for this application, wwwroot\ch08_04. You assign the location of this XML document to the `AdvertisementFile` property of the ad rotator control, and the control reads it and uses the data in that document.

We'll also store the banner ads, which will be named banner1.jpg, banner2.jpg, and banner3.jpg here, in the main folder for the ch08_04 application. In this case, each banner ad is a JPG image, and by default banner ads are 468×60 pixels (although you can set their sizes in the ad rotator control's `Height` and `Width` properties).

As you'd expect, the HTML sent to the browser for this ad rotator appears as <a> hyperlink elements surrounding an <img> image element:

```
<a id="AdRotator1" href="http://www.starpowder.com/product1.html"
 target="_top" style="Z-INDEX: 104; LEFT: 36px; POSITION: absolute; TOP: 72px">
<img src="/ch08_04/banner1.jpg" alt="You can't get any better than Product 1!"
border="0" style="height:60px;width:468px;" /></a>
```

SHOP TALK

TRACKING BANNER HITS

If you've every actually tried to sell banner ads in commercial applications, you'll quickly see that the ad rotator control isn't powerful enough to be used in commercial environments. When you sell ads in your Web pages, your clients will demand to see click-through ratios at the very least, which ad rotators don't support. You'll also need to record the number of impressions displayed for each ad. It's somewhat surprising that Microsoft released this control without the capability to record this kind of data. Tracking support will likely be added to future versions of ad rotators. If you want to write the code, you can track ad banner statistics and click-through ratios yourself. You'll need to create a new page to record statistics and then redirect the browser to the ad target. To do this, add parameters to the `<NavigateUrl>` element in the usual way for URLs something like this: `<NavigateUrl>redirector.`
`aspx?ad=executivetoys&amp;target=http://microsoft.com</NavigateUrl>`. In the redirection page, you can retrieve the strings for the ad and target parameters with code like this: `String ad =`
`Request.QueryString["ad"];` and `String target = Request.QueryString["target"];`. Now you know both which ad was clicked and what its target is, so you can record a click-through for this ad and send it to the target.

Hyperlinks

Web pages can contain hyperlinks, and in C# .NET Web applications, you use the `HyperLink` control to create hyperlinks. You can see a hyperlink with the text `"See the other page"` in ch08_04, Figure 8.18. When the user clicks that hyperlink, we want to show a new page, so at design time, select the Project, Add Web Form menu item to open the Add New Item dialog box. This dialog box lets you add Web forms and HTML pages to an application just by selecting the appropriate file-type icon and clicking Open.

In this case, we add a new HTML page (not a new Web form) to our Web application. This new HTML page is just a standard HTML page, and is named HTMLPage1.htm by default. Because this is an HTML page, the C# IDE will only allow you to add HTML client controls to it; in this case, we'll add an HTML label with the text `"The Other Page"`. To place that text in the HTML label, edit the text directly in the label (because HTML client controls support no true C# properties, you'll find very few entries for them in the properties window).

To connect a hyperlink control in WebForm1 to this new HTML page, add a hyperlink control to WebForm1 and set its `Text` property to `"See the other page"` as you see in Figure 8.18. To set the hyperlink's URL target, select the its `NavigateUrl` property and click the ellipsis button that appears to open the Select URL dialog box that you see in Figure 8.19. Browse to the target of this hyperlink, HTMLPage1.htm, and click OK.

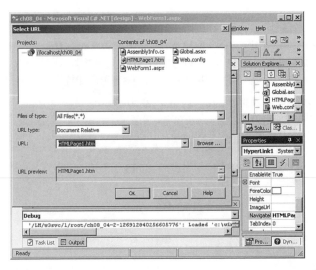

FIGURE 8.19   The Select URL dialog box.

When the user clicks this hyperlink at runtime, the browser will navigate to HTMLPage1.htm, as you see in Figure 8.20.

OPENING A URL IN ANOTHER WINDOW

If you want to open a URL in a new browser window, set the hyperlink's `Target` property to `_blank`.

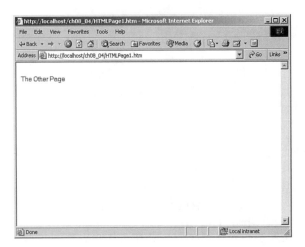

FIGURE 8.20   Navigating to a new URL.

Link Buttons

You have little control over what happens when the user clicks a hyperlink, because the browser takes over. But what if you need to set a hyperlink's target on the fly when it's clicked, or execute some C# code when a link is clicked? For that, you use link buttons.

Link buttons look just like hyperlinks, but act just like buttons, with both `Click` and `Command` events. When the corresponding hyperlink is clicked, you can take some action in code, not just let the browser automatically navigate to a new page. For example, in the ch08_04 example, Figure 8.18, there's a link button with the text `"Execute some code."`. When the user clicks this link button, we execute this code to set the text in the application's label control to `"You clicked the link button."`:

```
private void LinkButton1_Click(object sender, System.EventArgs e)
{
    Label1.Text = "You clicked the link button.";
}
```

You can see how this works in Figure 8.21; when the user clicks the link button, the application executes code instead of just navigating to a new URL.

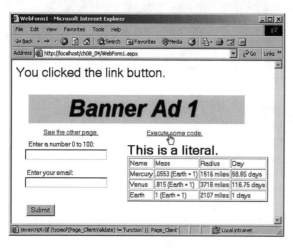

FIGURE 8.21   Clicking a link button.

As with hyperlink controls, link buttons are translated into HTML <a> elements, but the HTML for link buttons is really a JavaScript URL whose JavaScript calls __doPostBack to send the page back to the server for processing. Here's what the HTML for the link button you see in Figure 8.18 looks like:

```
<a id="LinkButton1" href="javascript:{if (typeof(Page_ClientValidate)
!= 'function' ¦¦ Page_ClientValidate()) __doPostBack('LinkButton1','')} "
style="Z-INDEX: 103; LEFT: 291px; POSITION: absolute; TOP: 143px">
Execute some code.</a>
```

Validators

Validator controls are some of the few Web server controls that execute in the client (using JavaScript), not the server. Validator controls let you check user-entered data before sending it back to the server, as is standard in many pages on the Internet. If there's a problem with that data, the validator will display an error message and block attempts to send the page back to the server. Each validator is like a label control (they're based on the System.Web.UI.WebControls.Label class) that's invisible until there's been an error, when they display their error message, as set with the ErrorMessage property. If the user corrects the error, the error message disappears. You can find the validation controls, and what they do, in Table 8.2.

TABLE 8.2

Validation Controls

VALIDATOR	PURPOSE
RequiredFieldValidator	Ensures the user enters data in a data-entry control you specify.
CompareValidator	Uses comparison operators to compare user-entered data to constant data or to the data in another data-entry control.
RangeValidator	Ensures that user-entered data is in a range between given lower and upper bounds.
RegularExpressionValidator	Ensures that user-entered data matches a regular-expression pattern successfully.
CustomValidator	Ensures user-entered data passes validation criteria that you implement in a script function.

We'll take a look at a few of the validator controls here—required field validators, range validators, and regular expression validators.

Required Field Validators

Required field validators make sure that the user has entered data into a specific control. If users haven't done so, the validators display an error message when the users try to send the page back to the server. These validators have a property called InitialValue (which holds an empty string, "", by default). If the data in the control has not changed from the value in InitialValue when the user tries to send the page back to the server, the required field validator will display its error message.

USE A REQUIRED FIELD VALIDATOR WITH OTHER VALIDATORS

You should know that if a data-entry control is empty, no validation is performed by any of the validation controls, *except* for required field validators. In other words, all validation operations will appear to succeed if a data-entry control is empty, except for required field validations. That means it's usually a good idea to use a required field validator *in addition* to any other validators you are using.

To use a required field validator, add one to a Web page, set the `ControlToValidate` property to the control whose data you want to validate, the `InitialValue` property to the initial value of that data, and the `ErrorMessage` property to the error message you want to display if there's a problem. By default, validators display their messages in red; to change to another color, set their `ForeColor` property. If the data in the control to validate is unchanged from the `InitialValue` value when the user tries to send the page back to the server, this validator will display its error message.

Range Validators

Range validators let you determine whether the data in a control is inside a specific range. This validator checks the data in a control when that control loses the focus (unlike required field validators, which check their data only just before the page is sent back to the server). The range validator properties you set are the `ControlToValidate` property, and the `MinimumValue` and `MaximumValue` properties to hold the minimum and maximum values of the range of data you want to accept. You should also set the `Type` property to the data type of the values to compare (the default value is `String`).

If the value in the control, which the validator validates is out of range, the validator will display its error message. You can see this at work in Figure 8.22, where we've asked the user to enter a value between 0 and 100, but received a value of 555. This causes the range validator in this example to display its error message, `"Must be between 0 and 100."`.

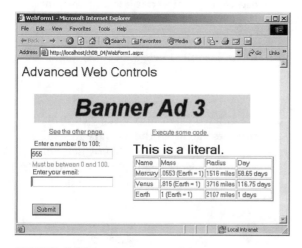

FIGURE 8.22   Using a range validator.

Regular Expression Validators

Regular expression validators let you check the text in a control against a regular expression of the kind we've seen in Chapter 2, "Basic C# Programming." As with range validators, these validators check their data when the control they're validating loses the focus. If you don't want to create your own regular expressions, the Regular Expression Editor lets you select from a number of pre-written regular expressions. To display that editor, select the validator's ValidationExpression property and click the ellipsis button that appears. For example, here's the regular expression C# uses to determine whether text matches a valid email address:

```
\w+([-+.]\w+)*@\w+([-.]\w+)*\.\w+([-.]\w+)*
```

You can see a regular expression at work in Figure 8.23, where it's checking the email address entered in a text box, as set with the ControlToValidate property. In this case, it's reporting that the text "no way!" is not a valid email address.

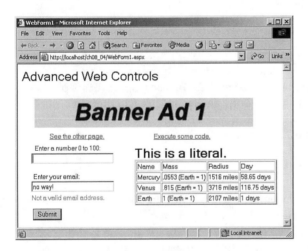

FIGURE 8.23   Using a regular expression validator.

Validation Summaries

The validator controls we've seen are tied to individual controls whose data they validate, but you can also use a *validation summary* to display all the errors in a page. Validation summaries display their error messages (in a list) only when the user tries to send the page back to the server, as when they click a Submit button.

You can see a validation summary at work in Figure 8.24. You just position this control where you want the list of errors to appear, and when the user tries to send the page back to the server, the validation summary control displays that list of errors (which it gets from the other validation controls in the page).

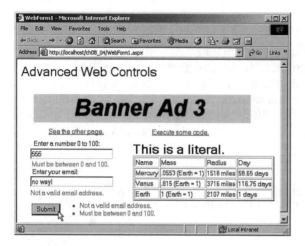

FIGURE 8.24 Using a validation summary.

The error list can be displayed as a simple list, as a bulleted list, or as a single paragraph. You select between these options with the `DisplayMode` property, which you can set to `ValidationSummaryDisplayMode.List`, `ValidationSummaryDisplayMode.BulletList`, or `ValidationSummaryDisplayMode.SingleParagraph`. You can also specify whether the summary should be displayed in the Web page itself or in a message box with the `ShowSummary` and `ShowMessageBox` properties, respectively.

Literals

So far, Web server controls have shielded us from the actual HTML in a Web page, but there are controls designed to be used directly with that HTML—*literal controls*. A literal control holds HTML that will go directly into your Web form, and you can assign that HTML to the literal's `Text` property. When you add a literal control to a Web page at design time, it appears at upper left, as you can see in Figure 8.25 (where it's hiding behind the ad rotator). There's no special position for a literal, and you can't position it on a Web page at design time—if you want the HTML you place in a literal to display an HTML element at a specific location, you can use CSS positioning as we'll do here.

For example, if you wanted to position an `<H1>` HTML header with the text `"This is a literal."` in it, you could use this code in the `Page_Load` event (or you could assign this text to a literal control at design time):

```
private void Page_Load(object sender, System.EventArgs e)
{
  Literal1.Text = "<div align='left' " +
  "style='POSITION: absolute; TOP: 170px; LEFT: 250px'>" +
  "<h1>This is a literal.</h1></div>";
}
```

FIGURE 8.25 Creating a literal control.

You can see the results of this code in Figure 8.18, where you see the text "This is a literal." at middle right.

XML Controls

The final Web server control we'll take a look at is the XML control. You can use this control to display XML in a Web page, and you can also format that XML document as you like. To format XML documents with this control, you use an XSLT (Extensible Stylesheet Language Transformations) stylesheet. XSLT can transform the data in an XML document into an XML document of another type, or into an HTML document, or plain text, or any other text-based format, including rich text, RTF, format.

Like literal controls, XML controls don't have any specific location in a Web page; they appear at upper left at design time, as you can see in Figure 8.25. You assign an XML control's DocumentSource property the name of a XML document, and assign the TransformSource property the name of a XSLT stylesheet (you can browse to these documents at design time).

> **MORE ON XML AND XSLT**
>
> For more on XML, see the XML specification at http://www.w3.org/TR/xml11. For more on XSLT, see the XSLT specification at http://www.w3.org/TR/xslt.

For example, in the ch08_04 example, the XML control formats the XML in a document named planets.xml (included in the downloadable code for this book), which holds data on several of the planets. This example uses the XSLT stylesheet planets.xsl (also included in the code for this book), which formats the planetary data into an HTML table and positions that table using CSS styles in the Web page, as you see in Figure 8.18.

And that's it—now you're transforming XML into HTML using XSLT and the XML control.

In Brief

This chapter looked at C# Web applications. Here's an overview of this chapter's discussion:

- Creating Web applications is analogous to creating Windows applications using the C# IDE. However, you do need an IIS installation on an accessible Web server that also has .NET installed.

- Web forms are similar to Windows forms, except that they're based on the `System.Web.UI.Page` class. Although you can perform many of the same operations with Web forms as you can with Windows forms, such as moving controls and adding new controls at runtime, these operations are not performed in the same ways as in Windows forms.

- Web applications are disconnected from the server, which means executing C# code requires a round-trip back to the server. That also means that your local data is not preserved across server round-trips by default. You can, however, preserve that data using the `ViewState` or `Session` properties.

- There are three types of controls for use in Web applications—Web server controls and HTML server controls, whose code is run back at the server, and HTML client controls, whose code is run in the browser.

Using ADO.NET and Databases

9

Connections, Data Adapters, and Datasets

This chapter begins our database work, a very big topic in C#. In fact, Microsoft says that most Visual Studio work involves databases. Database handling is an extensive subject in C# programming, so we'll spend this and the next chapter on it. As with the rest of the book, this will be a programmer-to-programmer discussion, so we're going to omit some of the basics; for example, we're going to assume you're familiar with what a database is and at least introductory SQL here.

There are two ways to work with databases in C#—using the IDE's visual tools, and in code. In this chapter, we're going to work with the visual tools, and in the next chapter, we'll handle databases exclusively in code.

When you work with databases in C#, you work with three objects: connection objects, data adapters, and dataset objects. To work with databases, you have to master all three of these objects.

Connection objects, data adapters, and dataset objects are the foundation of ADO.NET (ActiveX Data Objects .NET), the primary data access protocol in C#. We'll start this chapter with an overview of these objects, working through how to connect to a data source step by step. Say, for example, that you have a database you want to gain access to in your code. You start by getting a connection object for the database, and that's where we'll start in this chapter.

Using Connection Objects

To work with data, you first connect to a *data source* (such as a database made accessible by a data server, like Microsoft's SQL Server). To do that, you use a *connection object*. The type of connection object you use depends on which database provider you're working with. There are four types of connection objects in C#:

- SqlConnection objects are supported by the .NET Framework Data Provider for SQL Server and are recommended for applications using Microsoft SQL Server 7.0 or later.

- OleDbConnection objects are supported by the .NET Framework Data Provider for Object Linking and Embedding Database protocol (OLE DB) and are recommended for applications using Microsoft SQL Server 6.5 or earlier, or any OLE DB provider that supports the OLE DB interfaces.

- OdbcConnection objects are supported by the .NET Framework Data Provider for Open Database Connectivity (ODBC, which is a data protocol supported in earlier versions of Visual Studio). These objects are recommended for applications using ODBC data sources.

- OracleConnection objects are supported by the .NET Framework Data Provider for Oracle and are recommended for applications using Oracle data sources.

EARLIER VERSIONS OF .NET AND C#

Note that the Oracle classes like OracleConnection and the ODBC classes like OdbcConnection are built into .NET Framework 1.1 and Visual Studio .NET 2003. They're also available via free download from Microsoft for .NET Framework 1.0 and Visual Studio .NET 2002. In this book, we're not going to be using the Oracle or ODBC classes in any case.

By default, the data provider that Visual Studio works with is Microsoft's SQL Server, version 7.0 or later. We'll use SQL Server 2000 in this book, but C# can also work with any data provider that can support ODBC, OLE DB, or Oracle protocols. (Note that even if you don't have a high-end database system to work with, you can still connect to databases created with MS Access, which comes with MS Office.)

Using Data Adapters

When you have a connection object for a data source, you next create a *data adapter* to work with that data. You need a data adapter because datasets do not maintain an active connection to the database. They are *disconnected* from the database and connect only as needed (which enables you, for example, to work with databases on the Internet). The data adapter is in charge of managing your connection to the data source—you're not connected to the data source by default, and the data adapter connects you to the data source when you need to be connected.

The data adapter is where you store the SQL statements that will be executed on the data in the database; the data adapter applies your SQL to the database when you need to connect to that database, and it fills your datasets with data. To access the data in a database's table, you first create a connection to the database the table was stored in, and then create a data adapter with the appropriate SQL statement to retrieve that table. For example, if the table was named prices, that SQL might be SELECT * FROM prices, which retrieves all the records from the students table.

The type of data adapter you use depends on the type of your data source; the possibilities are SqlDataAdapter, OleDbDataAdapter, OdbcDataAdapter, and OracleDataAdapter.

Using Datasets

Now that you have a data adapter, you can generate a *dataset* using that data adapter. Datasets are local repositories for the data you get from the data source through the data adapter. They're what you actually work with in your code when you want to handle data from a database.

You can use a data adapter to fill a DataSet object. Then you can use the methods of the DataSet object to read the data from individual records. If you change the data in a dataset, you can call the data adapter's Update method to send those changes back to the data provider.

There are three essential objects you need to understand in order to work with databases using ADO.NET: connections to connect to the database, data adapters to connect when needed and execute SQL, and datasets to store the actual data which your code will actually work on. That's how the process works in overview. There are plenty of other objects available in ADO.NET, but these are the fundamental ones.

Creating a Data Application

It's time to use these objects now, putting them to work in an example to see how things fit together. The C# IDE lets you work with the objects we've seen in a way that's relatively easy, simply using visual tools. We'll see how they work in the first example for this chapter, named ch09_01 in the code for this book.

This example fetches the data in the authors table of the pubs example database that comes with SQL Server, and displays it in a C# data grid control. To start, create the Windows application named Ch09_01 now.

Creating a Data Connection

To work with the pubs example database in SQL Server, you first need a connection to that database. In the IDE, you use a tool called the Server Explorer to establish connections to databases.

ADDING SERVERS TO THE SERVER EXPLORER

As you install Visual Studio, it searches your computer for data providers and adds them to the Server Explorer automatically as it finds them. You can also add additional servers to the Server Explorer at any time. To do that, select Tools, Connect to Server (or right-click the Servers node that appears at the bottom of the Server Explorer, and select Add Server). This opens the Add Server dialog box, which lets you enter new data providers identified by computer name or Internet IP address.

You can see the Server Explorer at left in Figure 9.1 in the IDE. Usually, the Server Explorer is docked to the left edge of the IDE. You can open it by letting the mouse pointer move over the Server Explorer tab. To display the Server Explorer if it's not already visible, choose View, Server Explorer, or press Ctrl+Alt+S.

The Server Explorer lets you create and examine *data connections*, including connections to data providers in the Web. It's important to realize that a *data connection* is not the same as a *connection object*. A data connection is not specific to any C# application. You can use a data connection from the Server Explorer with any application; they're always available in the Server Explorer. To work with a data provider, you need a data connection, and in the IDE, those data connections are managed by the Server Explorer. Using a data connection, you can create a connection object in an application, and those connection objects *are* specific to one particular application (they appear in a form's component tray). Using that connection object, you can create a data adapter, and using that data adapter, you can create a dataset.

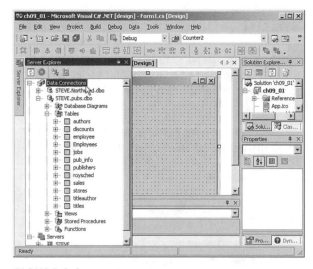

FIGURE 9.1   The Server Explorer.

In the Ch09_01 example, we're going to display the data from the authors table in the Microsoft SQL Server's pubs sample database, so we'll need a data connection to that database. To create that data connection, right-click the Data Connections icon in the Server Explorer and select the Add Connection item, or choose Tools, Connect to Database. Doing so opens the Data Link Properties dialog box you see in Figure 9.2.

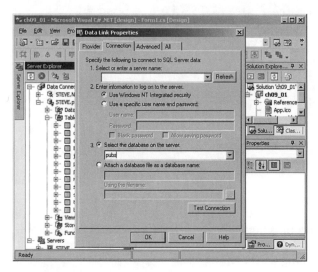

FIGURE 9.2   The Data Link Properties dialog box.

You use the Data Link Properties dialog box to create a new data connection. You can enter the name of the server you want to work with, as well as your login name and password, if they apply. We'll use Windows NT integrated security to connect to the database, because SQL Server is on the same machine as Visual Studio in this case, but you can choose a server name and enter a username and password in the Data Link Properties dialog box if you prefer.

In the Data Link Properties dialog box, you can choose a database on the server with the Select the Database on the Server option, or another database with the Attach a Database File as a Database Name option. In this case, we'll use the pubs example database that comes with SQL Server, so select the first option and choose the pubs database, as you see in Figure 9.2.

When you create a data connection, the default data provider is SQL Server, but you can specify a data provider other than SQL Server, of course. To do that, you click the Provider tab in the Data Link Properties dialog box, as you see in Figure 9.3, which displays a list of the data protocols supported. You select from the list data protocols that match the data provider you're working with, and then click the Connection tab and select the database you want to work with.

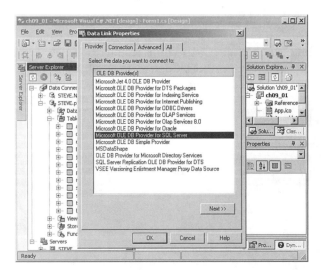

FIGURE 9.3   Selecting a data provider.

To test the new data connection, select the Connection tab and click the Test Connection button you see in Figure 9.2. If the data connection works, you'll see a message box with the message `Test connection succeeded` as you see in Figure 9.4. If the data connection isn't working, you'll see a message box explaining what's wrong.

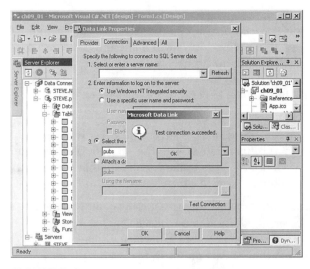

FIGURE 9.4   Testing a data connection.

If the data connection test was successful, click the OK button in the Data Link Properties dialog box to complete creating the new data connection. The SQL Server on the machine this example is on is named STEVE, so the connection to the pubs database is named STEVE.pubs.dbo, as you see in the Server Explorer in Figure 9.1. You can open the new connection using the + icon in front of the connection in the Server Explorer, which displays the tables in the pubs database, as you see in the figure. You can see that the table we plan to work with, the authors table, is visible in the figure. We can now access that table in our applications.

At this point, the data connection you've created is part of your programming environment; it's not part of any specific application. The next step is to put this new data connection to work, and we'll do that by creating connection and data adapter objects.

DELETING A DATA CONNECTION

You can also delete data connections; just right-click the connection in the Server Explorer and select Delete.

Creating Connection, Data Adapter, and Dataset Objects

The IDE lets you create a connection object and a data adapter at the same time—all you have to do is drag a data adapter object from the toolbox onto a form. The toolbox has its own tab for data objects, the Data tab. Click that tab now and drag a SqlDataAdapter object from the toolbox to Form1 in the Ch09_01 application.

When you drop the data adapter onto the form, the IDE opens the Data Adapter Configuration Wizard that you see in Figure 9.5. This is the Wizard that lets you customize your data adapter, and that usually means creating the SQL statement this adapter will use.

FIGURE 9.5   The Data Adapter Configuration Wizard.

Click the Next button in the Data Adapter Configuration Wizard to choose the data connection you want to use, as you see in Figure 9.6. Here, you can use an existing data connection, like the one we've already created, or click the New Connection button to create a new data connection (clicking the New Connection button opens the Data Link Properties dialog box which we've used to create a new data connection). In this example, we'll use the connection we've made to the pubs database, as you see in Figure 9.6.

FIGURE 9.6   Selecting a data connection.

Click Next to move to the next pane in the Data Adapter Configuration Wizard. In this pane, you choose a query type for the new data adapter, as you see in Figure 9.7. In this case, we're going to create a SQL statement, as you see in the figure, but notice that you can create new or use existing stored SQL procedures.

THE SQL SPECIFICATION

To work with databases in C# beyond the most basic, you have to be pretty familiar with SQL. You can get the International Organization for Standardization (ISO) documents that define SQL online. As of this writing, they're at http://www.iso.org/iso/en/CatalogueListPage.CatalogueList?ICS1=35&ICS2=60&ICS3=. This page lists the ISO's catalog for SQL documents (these documents are not free, however). In case this URL no longer works by the time you read this, go to www.iso.org, find the link for Information Technology, and then click the link for Languages Used in Information Technology.

Clicking Next again displays the dialog box you see in Figure 9.8. This is the dialog box used to create the SQL statement we'll use in this data adapter to get data from the data provider.

You can use a visual tool to make writing the SQL easier; just click the Query Builder button you see in Figure 9.8. This displays the Add Table dialog box that you see in Figure 9.9. In the Add Table dialog box, you select the table(s) you want to work with and click the Add button. When you've selected all the tables you want to work with in this way, click the Close button. In this example, we're just going to display a few fields from the authors table, so select that table and click Add in the Add Table dialog box, and then click Close to close the Add Table dialog box.

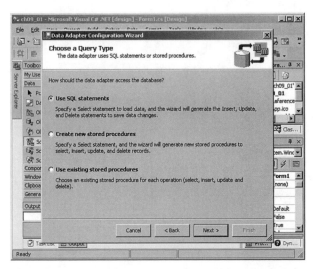

FIGURE 9.7 Choosing a query type.

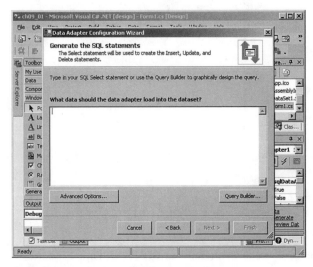

FIGURE 9.8 Generating a SQL statement.

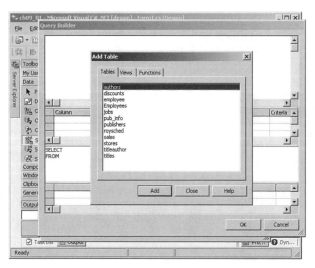

FIGURE 9.9   The Query Builder's opening dialog box.

Closing the Add Table dialog box opens the Query Builder tool, as you see in Figure 9.10.

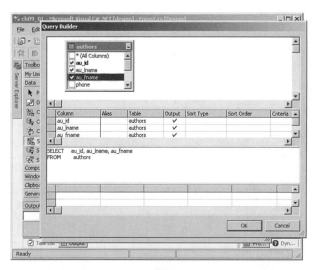

FIGURE 9.10   The Query Builder.

You can see a window displaying the fields in the authors table at the top of Figure 9.10. You add a field to the SQL statement you're creating by clicking the field's check box in a table's window. You must select at least one field when creating the SQL for a data adapter, or the Query Builder won't create working SQL for you. In Figure 9.10, for example, we've checked the au_id, au_lname, and au_fname fields, which means our SQL statement will fetch the data for those fields. You can select all fields in a table by checking the check box labeled with an asterisk (*).

Clicking OK in the Query Builder closes that tool and you see the resulting SQL in the Data Adapter Configuration Wizard in Figure 9.11.

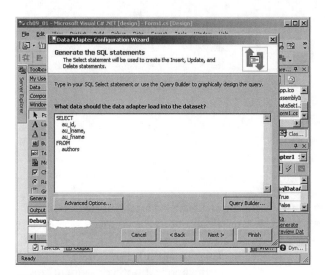

FIGURE 9.11   A created SQL statement.

Here's what that SQL statement looks like. Note that we're selecting the au_id, au_lname, and au_fname fields of records in the authors table:

```
SELECT
  au_id,
  au_lname,
  au_fname
FROM
  authors
```

In this way, you've been able to create the SQL this data adapter will use to retrieve data from the database. Clicking Next in the Data Adapter Configuration Wizard makes the wizard configure the data adapter and reports its results, as you see in Figure 9.12. In this case, the Data Adapter Configuration Wizard knows what data we want to work with, and has generated a SQL SELECT statement to fetch that data. It's also generated SQL INSERT, UPDATE, and DELETE statements to manipulate that data if needed. And that's it; click the Finish button to close the Data Adapter Configuration Wizard and complete the creation of the data adapter.

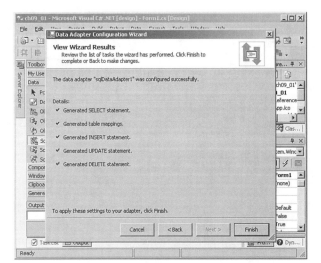

FIGURE 9.12   Configuring a data adapter.

RECONFIGURING A DATA ADAPTER

You can right-click a data adapter object at any time and select Configure Data Adapter to change an adapter's configuration, including its internal SQL.

Closing the Data Adapter Configuration Wizard creates both the connection object, sqlConnection1, and the data adapter we'll need, sqlDataAdapter1. Both these objects appear in the application's component tray, as you see in Figure 9.13. The connection object has been configured automatically with a *connection string*, which tells this object what to connect to; in this case, that connection string is "workstation id=STEVE;packet size=4096;integrated security=SSPI;initial catalog=pubs;persist security info=False". In the next chapter, we'll be connecting to databases in code, and it can be difficult to know how to write these connection strings for various data providers. One way to solve the problem is to let the visual tools we're using in this chapter write those strings for us.

The next step is to create a new dataset using this data adapter. You do that by selecting Data, Generate Dataset in the IDE, which opens the Generate Dataset dialog box you see in Figure 9.14.

This dialog box lists the data available in the various data adapters in your application, and will create a new dataset class, which will be named DataSet1 by default. In this case, the data available is only the authors table in the data adapter sqlDataAdapter1. Make sure that table is selected, and click OK to create the new dataset object, dataSet11 (that is, the first object of the DataSet1 class), which you can see in the component tray in Figure 9.15.

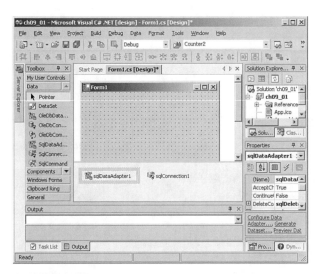

FIGURE 9.13 New connection and data adapter objects.

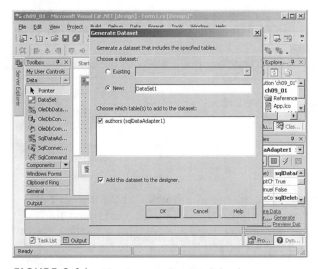

FIGURE 9.14 The Generate Dataset dialog box.

The next step is to display the data in the dataset. To do that, drag a new data grid control, which is designed to display entire data tables, to the Windows form in this application. To *bind* this data grid to the data in dataSet11, set the data grid's DataSource property to dataSet11, and its DataMember property to authors. Binding a control to a data source makes it display data from that source automatically.

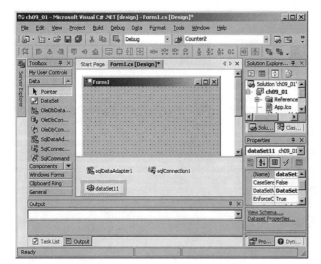

FIGURE 9.15   A new dataset object.

Because your application is disconnected from the data source, you'll also need to use the data adapter to connect to that data source and fetch the data. For that reason, let's add a Get Data button to this application, using this code to fill the dataset with data from the data adapter. (Note that if you prefer, you can put this code into the Form_Load event handler so the dataset is filled automatically when the form loads.)

```
private void button1_Click(object sender, System.EventArgs e)
{
  dataSet11.Clear();
  sqlDataAdapter1.Fill(dataSet11);
}
```

Now the users can load data into the data grid when they want to by clicking the Get Data button. The user can also edit the data in the data grid, thereby changing that data. To update the data stored in the database, you can call the data adapter's Update method. In this example, we'll do that with a new button called Save Data. Here's the code for this button:

```
private void button2_Click(object sender, System.EventArgs e)
{
  sqlDataAdapter1.Update(dataSet11);
}
```

The data grid and the dataset are bound, which means that when the user edits the data in the data grid control, that control automatically updates the dataset. To send the new data back to the database, you can use the data adapter's Update method, as we're doing here.

And that's it. Now we have two buttons in our application—Load Data and Save Data, as you see in Figure 9.16. They allow users to load and save data on demand. To implement these buttons, we've used the data adapter's `Fill` and `Update` methods. As you can see in Figure 9.16, each record displays the fields we configured the dataset to display.

In Web applications, the process is similar, but here you also have to explicitly call the `DataBind` method of any controls bound to the dataset to refresh the data binding each time the page is loaded. For example, here's how that might look when you've bound a data grid to `dataSet11` in a Web application, and refresh the data binding in the `Page_Load` event:

```
private void Page_Load(object sender, System.EventArgs e)
{
  dataSet11.Clear();
  sqlDataAdapter1.Fill(dataSet11);
  DataGrid1.DataBind();
}
```

FIGURE 9.16   Running a data application.

This refreshes the data in the bound control each time the page loads. You don't have to do this in Windows applications, because there that connection is "live". Otherwise, working with databases in Web applications is very similar to working with databases in Windows applications. You can see a data Web application displaying the `authors` table in a Web form data grid in Figure 9.17.

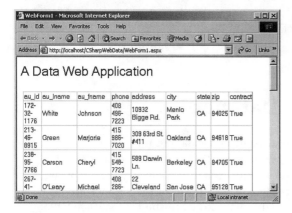

FIGURE 9.17   A data Web application.

SHOP TALK

WEB SECURITY

There's one more issue to consider when creating data-aware Web applications. Microsoft has been taking hits for its security handling for a long time, and it's been an especially acute problem on the Web. Almost every few days it seems one reads about a new security issue with Microsoft Internet software. Accordingly, somewhere between the original release of Visual Studio .NET and Visual Studio .NET 2003, Microsoft tightened up the way Web applications can access data sources like SQL Server. This decision is a controversial one, and it surely doesn't make life easier for the programmer. Microsoft now requires you to be a qualified user to log into SQL Server from a Web application, for example. You can log in with a name and password, but it's not a good idea to hard code those items into a Web application's code. The way I prefer to solve this problem is to treat the Web application itself as a qualified user. Web applications operate with the username "ASPNET" when they run, and if you can treat ASPNET as a qualified user and maintain your security, you've solved this problem. Treating ASPNET as a qualified user means creating an account for ASPNET in the data provider. If the data provider and IIS are on the same machine, you can use Windows integrated security to log ASPNET into the data provider. In SQL Server, you create a login name of *computername*\ASPNET, where *computername* is the name of your computer.

How you create a new SQL Server login depends on the version of SQL Server you're using. For example, in SQL Server 2000, you can open the SQL Enterprise Manager, open the Security folder, right-click the Logins node, and select the New Login item to open the SQL Server Login Properties dialog box. You enter the name of the new user (such as STEVE\ASPNET for the computer named STEVE we've been using), and click the Windows Authentication radio button to enable Windows integrated security. (You don't have to use Windows integrated security if you prefer not to; you can click the SQL Server Authentication radio button and enter a password to use a SQL Server login.) Make sure the Grant Access radio button is clicked, and then click the OK button to add this new user.

Working with Relational Databases

Relational databases are powerful databases that connect the data in multiple tables. For example, say that you are using the pubs sample database that we've already used in this chapter, and want to display all the books that the authors in the authors table have written. That's not a simple task, because in the pubs database, the names of the authors are stored in the authors table, but the books that they've written are stored in the titleauthor table (these books are actually stored by book ID, not by title). And the titleauthor table is a separate table.

How do you join the authors names from the authors table with the titles they've written from the titleauthor table into one dataset? You can use a SQL *inner join*, and we're going to see how this works in our next example, the Ch09_02 example.

To follow along, create an application named Ch09_02, and drag a data adapter onto the main form, opening the Data Adapter Configuration Wizard. To configure the adapter's SQL statement, click the Query Builder button, and use the Add Table dialog box to add *both* tables from the SQL Server pubs database: authors and titleauthor, as you see in Figure 9.18.

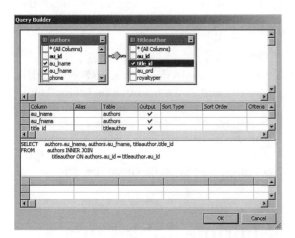

FIGURE 9.18 A relation between tables in the Query Builder.

These two tables share the author ID field, au_id, which is the key that relates the records of one table to the records of the other. The Query Builder realizes that this is a shared field and displays this relation graphically, as you see in Figure 9.18.

Select the au_lname and au_fname fields from the authors table, and the title_id field from the titleauthor table in the Query Builder as you see in Figure 9.18. Then click OK to close the Query Builder, creating this SQL (remember that you can edit the SQL generated by the Query Builder by hand):

```
SELECT
  authors.au_lname,
  authors.au_fname,
  titleauthor.title_id
FROM
  authors INNER
JOIN
  titleauthor ON
    authors.au_id = titleauthor.au_id
```

You can see the SQL JOIN statement here, which is what joins the tables we want. Because we're working with multiple tables, the Data Adapter Configuration Wizard won't be able to generate SQL statements for updating any data because that would involve updating parts of records in multiple tables. To avoid warnings in the Data Adapter Configuration Wizard, click the Advanced Options button now and deselect the Generate Insert, Update, and Delete Statements check box. Then click the Next button and follow through to the end of the process as before to finish configuring the data adapter.

DATA RELATION OBJECTS

In this example, we used SQL to join two related tables, but there's another way to work with related tables in C#. You can create an FCL data relation object to make the relationship explicit. Creating such an object encapsulates the relationship between data tables, while still leaving the two tables independent.

After you've configured the data adapter, generate a dataset as before, and connect it to data grid as we've also done before. You can see the results in Figure 9.19, where we've combined data from two tables that are related to each other. The authors and titleauthor tables have been *joined*, using their common field, au_id. Because some authors have written multiple books, you'll see multiple entries for them in the dataset. For example, you can see that Marjorie Green has two title_id entries, as do others.

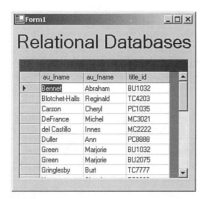

FIGURE 9.19   Running the Ch09_02 example.

Using Multiple Tables in a Single Dataset

So far, the datasets we've used only held a single table of data, but a dataset can contain several tables at once. To see how this works, take a look at the Ch09_03 example in the code for this book. This example uses two SqlDataAdapter controls, sqlDataAdapter1, connected to the authors table in the pubs database, and sqlDataAdapter2, connected to the titleauthor table in the pubs database (in this example, we'll select all fields of both these tables). When you create a dataset using these data adapters, you can add data from both adapters into a single dataset.

To see how this works, create these data adapter objects now and select Data, Generate Dataset. You can add both data tables to a single dataset if you select them both in the Generate Dataset dialog box, as you see in Figure 9.20.

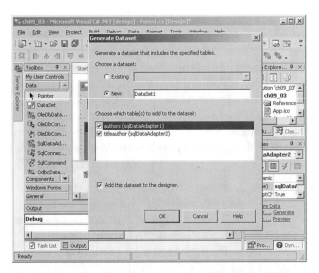

FIGURE 9.20 Adding multiple tables to a dataset.

When you close the Generate Dataset dialog box, you've added both tables to the same dataset. To see the data in these tables, add two data grids to the main form, and set the `DataSource` property of both to the new dataset object, `DataSet11`. Set the `DataMember` property of the first data grid to `authors` and the `DataMember` property of the second data grid to `titleauthor`. All that's left is to use the adapters to fill `DataSet11` like this, which we can do when the form loads:

```
private void Form1_Load(object sender, System.EventArgs e)
{
  sqlDataAdapter1.Fill(dataSet11);
  sqlDataAdapter2.Fill(dataSet11);
}
```

And that's it; you've stored two tables in one dataset. You can see the result in Figure 9.21, where both data grids are bound to the same dataset, but are displaying data from different tables.

C# keeps track of the multiple tables in a dataset with the `Tables` collection, which we're going to take a look at more closely in Chapter 10. Each element in a `Tables` collection is a `Table` object, which corresponds to a data table. Each `Table` object has a `Rows` collection that holds the data in the rows of that table as `Row` objects. To access the data in an individual field, you use the `Item` property, and you can pass the field's name or number to the `Item` property. For example, field 0 in the `authors` table is the `au_id` field, so these statements both retrieve the author ID of author number 5 in the `authors` table (more on handling databases in code in Chapter 10):

```
string ID = dataSet11.Tables[0].Rows[5].Item[0];
string ID = dataSet11.Tables[0].Rows[5].Item["au_id"];
```

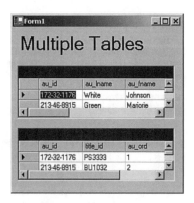

FIGURE 9.21   Retrieving multiple tables from a dataset.

Here's another useful visual tool you can use when you have a data adapter object. You can take a look at the data in that object by choosing Data, Preview Data in the IDE, and then clicking the Fill Dataset button in the Data Adapter Preview dialog box that opens. You can see this dialog box at work in Figure 9.22. This dialog box is useful when you want to look at the data a data adapter provides you at design time.

Although datasets don't hold any data at design time, you can get a look at a dataset's *properties* by selecting Data, Dataset Properties, or by right-clicking a dataset and selecting Dataset Properties. Doing so opens the Dataset Properties dialog box you see in Figure 9.23; the properties you see there include, among other things, the format of each field in each table in the dataset.

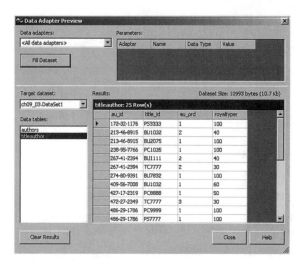

FIGURE 9.22   Previewing dataset data.

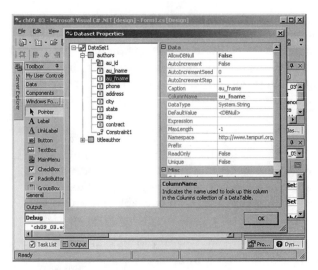

FIGURE 9.23 Previewing dataset properties.

Working with Data Views

There's another handy kind of object that's much like a dataset—a data view object. You normally use datasets to hold local copies of data from a data source, but data views are also available as alternative data containers. They're much like read-only datasets—snapshots of your data (as the term data view suggests)—and can give you faster access to your data than datasets can. Their chief advantage is that they let you filter data from a dataset according to criteria you set, without having to retrieve that data from the data source again.

You can use SQL-like expressions in a data view's `RowFilter` property to filter the records you want to take a look at. For example, say that you want to look at only those authors whose last name is White from the `authors` table. You could loop over all the records in a dataset, choosing only those `au_lname` field holds "White", or you could simply bind a data view to the dataset and set the data view's `RowFilter` property to `au_lname = 'White'`. (Note the single quotes here; C# won't accept `au_lname = "White"` as the value of this property, because it will surround the text with double quotation marks before passing it on to SQL Server, and the string `"au_lname = "White""` isn't going to work with SQL Server.) In other words, data views let you manipulate and even sort the data from a dataset as you want. They give you the ability to execute SQL-like expressions on the data in a dataset without having to connect to and retrieve data from the data store. And, like datasets, you can also bind data views to controls.

You can see a data view in action in the ch09_04 example in the code for this book. To follow along, create a Windows application named ch09_04. Use a data adapter to connect to the authors table in the pubs database and generate a dataset, dataSet11, to hold the authors table from that data adapter (select all fields in the authors table). Next, drag a new data view object from the Data tab in the toolbox onto the application's main form. As with other data objects, this new data view, dataView1, will appear in the component tray at design time.

You bind a data view to a specific data table using its Table property, so set that property to the authors table from dataSet11 now (when you select the Table property in the properties window, a list will appear displaying the available tables to work with). Next, add a data grid to the main form, and set its DataSource property to dataView1. You don't need to set the data grid's DataMember property, because we're only working with one table in the data view. By doing this, you've connected the data grid to the authors table through the data view.

This is where the data view's RowFilter property comes in. We want to look only at records in which the author's last name is White, so set the data view's RowFilter property to au_lname = 'White'. To finish the code, make sure you populate the dataset from the data adapter, as usual:

```
private void Form1_Load(object sender, System.EventArgs e)
{
    sqlDataAdapter1.Fill(dataSet11);
}
```

And that's it; you can see the results in Figure 9.24, where the single author whose last name is White is displayed. Using a data view, you've been able to create a filtered snapshot of your data and bound it to a data grid, pointing out one of the uses of data views—searching data for a record matching a specific criterion.

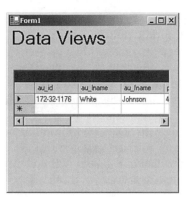

FIGURE 9.24   Using a data view.

Besides filtering rows, you can also use a data view's RowStateFilter property to filter rows depending on their *state*. For example, you can examine the rows of a table that have been marked as deleted (before you've called your data adapter's Update method to actually delete them back in the database) or are new in a data view using this property. Here are the possible states you can specify, and the types of rows they match, from the DataRowState enumeration:

■ DataRowState.Added—Identifies added rows.

■ DataRowState.CurrentRows—Identifies current rows (including all unchanged, new, and modified rows).

■ DataRowState.Deleted—Identifies deleted rows.

- `DataRowState.ModifiedCurrent` — Identifies current rows (even if they have been modified from the original data).

- `DataRowState.ModifiedOriginal` — Identifies original rows before they have been modified.

- `DataRowState.None` — Identifies no rows.

- `DataRowState.OriginalRows` — Identifies original rows, including unchanged and deleted rows.

- `DataRowState.Unchanged` — Identifies the unchanged rows.

For example, here's how you might take a look at the rows that have been marked as deleted in a data view:

```
private void Form1_Load(object sender, System.EventArgs e)
{
  sqlDataAdapter1.Fill(dataSet11);
  dataView1.RowStateFilter = DataViewRowState.Deleted;
}
```

You can also use data views to navigate through a dataset. For example, if you store the position of the record you want in a variable named `position`, you can use code like this to load the corresponding record into a data view, which will also update any controls bound to the data view:

```
string id = dataSet11.Tables[0].Rows[position].Item["au_id"];
dataView1.RowFilter = "au_id = '" + id + "'";
```

In fact, navigating through the data in a dataset is such a common thing to do that there's a great deal of support for it in the FCL. In particular, you can use the `BindingContext` property of Windows forms to set your position in datasets that your controls are bound to. And that brings up our next topic—data binding.

Handling Data Binding

Binding data to controls in Windows and Web forms is a big topic in .NET programming. So big that Microsoft has made all Windows controls data-aware, which means you can bind them to data sources. For example, you might bind the `au_lname` field from the `authors` table to a text box. At runtime, the current author's last name will appear in that text box. Or you might bind the `au_id` field to a list box, which will make all the author IDs appear in the list box. Or you might bind the whole `authors` table to a data grid.

You can bind any property of any control to a data source, and we're going to see how that works here. After binding a dataset or data view to controls in a form, you can navigate through the data in that dataset or data view, and the data that appears in the bound controls will be updated automatically as you move from record to record. You'll often see bound controls used in data-entry forms, forms that let the users navigate through a dataset, master/detail forms (in which, for example, the users can use one control to specify the state they want to find authors from, making the other controls automatically display the authors from that state), and so on.

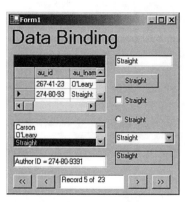

To understand data binding in concrete terms, take a look at the Ch09_05 example, which you can see at work in Figure 9.25. This example binds various controls to the last name of authors in the authors table in the SQL Server pubs example database. You can use the buttons at the bottom to navigate through the authors table, and as you do, each bound control will display the last name of the current author. We're going to dissect this example piece by piece next.

FIGURE 9.25   The Ch09_05 example.

There are actually two types of binding—simple binding and complex binding. We'll start by addressing the difference between these two.

Implementing Simple Data Binding

Some controls, like text boxes and labels, are simple-bound controls, and some, like data grids and list boxes, are complex-bound controls. Simple binding binds one, and only one, data field to a simple-bound control. For example, you can see a text box at upper right in the ch09_05 example, Figure 9.25, which is simple bound to the au_lname field in the authors table. Actually, it's bound to the au_lname field of the *current record*, as set by the binding context in the form. When you click a navigation button at the bottom of the ch09_05 example, the current record in the binding context changes, and the text box will display the au_lname field of the new current record.

Let's put this example together. To access the data in the authors table, this example uses a dataset object, dataSet11, which is connected through a data adapter to the authors table in the pubs database. So the first issue becomes how to actually bind a text box to a dataSet11. In particular, how do you bind a text box's Text property to the au_lname field?

When you open a text box's DataBindings property in the properties window, you'll see the most common data-bindings properties listed, such as the Text properties for a text box, as shown in Figure 9.26. You can select a field in a dataset to bind to just by clicking a property and selecting a field from a table from the drop-down menu that appears, as you see in the figure.

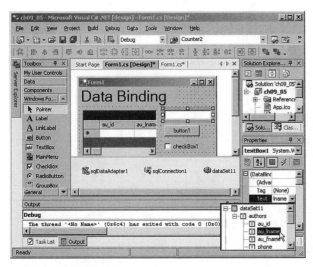

FIGURE 9.26   Binding a text box.

That's how you bind the Text property of a text box to the data in a dataset object. You expand the text box's DataBindings property in the properties window and use the drop-down menu to select the field in a data source you want to bind the Text property to. In this way, you can bind the most commonly bound properties of various controls to a field in a dataset, as long as that property is of the same data type as that field.

You can actually bind any property of a control like a text box to fields in a dataset. Only the most commonly bound properties of a control are listed in the DataBindings property in the properties window, but you can access any property for data binding. To do that, click the ellipsis button that appears when you click the Advanced entry in the DataBindings property, which opens the Advanced Data Binding dialog box you see in Figure 9.27.

In the Advanced Data Binding dialog box, you can bind any property of a control to a data source. As you can see in Figure 9.27, you can even tie such unlikely text box properties such as PasswordChar, ScrollBars, and MultiLine to a data source. (However, note that although the PasswordChar property can be bound to a text field in a data source, ScrollBars and MultiLine have to be bound to a bool field—for example, to the contract field in the authors table, which holds bool values.)

Because simple-bound controls can only show data from the current record, it's common to include some sort of navigation controls, like the buttons in the Ch09_05 example, to let the users move from record to record. You can see several simple-bound controls displaying data from a single field from the data source in Figure 9.25, and we'll take a look at those controls in a little more depth now.

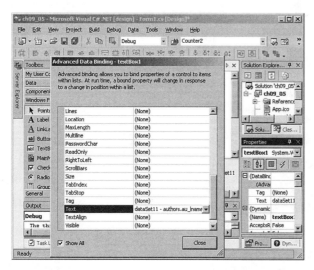

FIGURE 9.27   The Advanced Data Binding dialog box.

Binding Text Boxes

The text box in Figure 9.25 binds to the author's last name in the current record. Text boxes are simple data-bound controls. Here are the commonly-bound properties displayed when you expand the DataBindings property of a text box (the Tag property of a control lets you store text for the control that is accessible in code, as when you might want to store a description of the control's function):

- Tag
- Text

When you select either of these properties, you can connect them to a database field by selecting from the choices offered in a drop-down menu.

As with any control, you're not limited to the bindable properties displayed in the DataBindings property, of course. You can bind any property to any data source field of the same data type—just click the Advanced entry in the DataBindings property to open the Advanced Data Binding dialog box you see in Figure 9.27.

Binding Buttons

You can see a data-bound button in Figure 9.25, where the caption is bound to the author's last name in the current record for the form's binding context. Like text boxes, buttons are simple data-binding controls. Here are the commonly-bound properties displayed when you expand the `DataBindings` property—the same as those for text boxes:

- Tag
- Text

Binding Check Boxes

The caption of the check box in Figure 9.25 is bound to the last name in the current record in the `authors` table. Check boxes are also simple data-binding controls, and here are the commonly-bound properties displayed when you expand the `DataBindings` property (the `CheckAlign` property sets the horizontal and vertical alignment of the check box in the control):

- CheckAlign
- Checked
- CheckState
- Tag
- Text

You must make sure that the data type of the field you bind properties like these to matches the data type of the property. For example, the `Checked` property of the check box must be bound to a `bool` field, such as the `contract` field in the `authors` table.

Binding Radio Buttons

You can see a data-bound radio button in Figure 9.25. Radio buttons are also simple data-binding controls; here are the commonly-bound properties displayed when you expand the `DataBindings` property:

- CheckAlign
- Tag
- Text

Binding Labels

The last of the simple-bound controls in Figure 9.25 is a label. Like the others we've discussed, labels are also simple data-binding controls. Here are the commonly-bound properties displayed when you expand the `DataBindings` property:

- Tag
- Text

Performing Simple Binding in Code

As you'd expect, you don't have to create data bindings at design time. You can create them at runtime as well, working with various bindings objects. If you're going to connect to different data sources as requested by the user on the fly, you'll have to set up your data bindings on the fly.

You can implement simple binding using a control's `DataBindings` property, which holds a collection of `Binding` objects corresponding to the bindings for that control. For example, here's how you can bind a text box to the `au_lname` field of the current record in `dataSet11`. In code, you use the `DataBindings` collection's `Add` method to add a data binding, passing this method the property to bind, the data source to use, and the specific field you want to bind in the table you want to use. Here we can bind the `au_lname` field of the `authors` property to the `Text` property of a text box like this:

```
textBox1.DataBindings.Add("Text", dataSet11, "authors.au_lname");
```

BINDING PROPERTIES TO PROPERTIES

You might be interested to learn that data binding has become so advanced that you can bind a property of one control to a property of another control, which is not well known among C# programmers. For example, you can bind the `Text` property of `textBox1` to the `Text` property of `textBox2`, and when you change the text in `textBox2`, the text in `textBox1` will change automatically to match. Here's how you create this binding in code:

```
textBox1.DataBindings.Add("Text", textBox2, "Text");
```

The `Add` method is overloaded, and another form of this method lets you pass a `Binding` object to it directly. Here's what that looks like. This code binds the same text box to the `au_lname` field in the same `dataSet11` object:

```
textBox1.DataBindings.Add(new Binding("Text", dataSet11, "authors.au_lname"));
```

That completes the discussion on simple binding for the moment (we'll come back to it later when we discuss navigating through a dataset). We'll take a look at complex data binding next.

Implementing Complex Binding

Simple data binding binds a simple-bound control to one field in the current record. You use simple binding with those controls that can display only one data item at a time, like text boxes or labels. Some controls, such as list boxes and data grids, however, can display multiple items at the same time, and you use complex data binding with those controls.

In fact, we've already seen complex binding at work when we started working with data grids. To bind a data grid to a table, you set the `DataSource` property of the data grid to an object like a dataset or data view, and its `DataMember` property to a table in that dataset or data view. The data grid will automatically display that entire table. As with data grids, complex binding centers on properties like `DataSource` and `DataMember`; here are the properties you use:

- `DataSource`—Set to the data source, usually a dataset object, like `dataSet11`.

- `DataMember`—Set to the data member you want to work with in the data source, usually a table in a dataset like the `authors` table in the `pubs` database.

- `DisplayMember`—Set to the field whose data you want to display, such as the author's first name, au_fname. This property specifies the user-friendly data you want to display in the control. (Combo boxes and list boxes use the `DisplayMember` and `ValueMember` properties instead of a `DataMember` property.)

- `ValueMember`—Set to the field you want the control to return, such as the au_id field for the author's ID number, in the `SelectedValue` property. This property often specifies the code-friendly data you want to read from the control after a selection is made. (Combo boxes and list boxes use the `DisplayMember` and `ValueMember` properties instead of a `DataMember` property.)

We're familiar with the `DataSource` and `DataMember` properties already, but what about the `DisplayMember` and `ValueMember` properties? These properties let some controls, like list boxes, display data from one field, but return data from another field. For example, say that you want to work with the ID of `authors` the user selects in a list box in your code. You could display the ID of those authors directly in the list box, but values such as `"141-89-2133"` won't mean much to the users when displayed in a list box.

Instead, you can set the `DisplayMember` property of the list box to the au_lname property so the list box will display authors' last names, and the `ValueMember` property to au_id, which means that the `SelectedValue` property of the list box will return the same author's ID value. In this way, a list box can display user-friendly data from one data field, while sending code-friendly data from another field on to your code.

You can see how this works with the list box in Figure 9.25. When an author is selected in the list box, or you navigate to a new author using the navigation buttons, that author's ID is displayed in the text box under the list box using this code:

```
private void listBox1_SelectedIndexChanged(object sender, System.EventArgs e)
{
    textBox2.Text = "Author ID = " + listBox1.SelectedValue;
}
```

You can see some of the controls that support complex binding (note that most controls in C# only support simple binding) at work in Figure 9.25. In particular, the combo box, list box, and data grid in that example are complex-bound controls. We'll take a look at complex-binding these controls next.

Binding List Boxes

The list box you see in Figure 9.25 is a complex data-bound control. Here are the properties you use to bind this control to a data source, all of which we've seen before:

- `DataSource`
- `DisplayMember`
- `ValueMember`

The list box in the Ch09_05 example is bound to the au_lname property in the authors table using the `DataSource` and `DisplayMember` properties. And as already mentioned, there's more going on here—the list box's `ValueMember` property is set to au_id, so when you select an author's name in the list box, you'll see the author's ID value appear in the text box under that list box, as in Figure 9.25.

Binding Combo Boxes

List boxes and combo boxes are complex-bound controls, and you can see one in the ch09_05 example. Here are the properties you use to bind this control to a data source:

- `DataSource`
- `DisplayMember`
- `ValueMember`

The combo box you see in the Ch09_05 example, which you see in Figure 9.25, has its `DataSource` property set to dataSet11, which is connected to the authors table, and its `DisplayMember` property set to the au_lname field. This makes the combo box display the current record's au_lname value, as you see in Figure 9.25.

Binding Data Grids

Data grids, which can display an entire data table at once, are a favorite control among C# programmers. We've seen this control at work early in this chapter, and you can see one in the Ch09_05 example in Figure 9.25 at upper left. In this case, the data grid is showing the `authors` table from the `pubs` database.

Here are the properties you use to bind data grids to a data source:

- `DataSource`
- `DisplayMember`

To bind a data grid to a table, you can set the data grid's `DataSource` property (to an object like `dataSet11`) and `DataMember` property (usually to a table such as `authors`). You can bind these data objects with the data grid's `DataSource` property:

- `DataSet` objects
- `DataTable` objects
- `DataView` objects
- `DataViewManager` objects
- Single dimension arrays

In data grids, you can also use the `CurrentCellChanged` event to be informed when the user gives the focus to a new cell. And when the user moves around in a data grid using the keyboard, the `Navigate` event occurs. You can always determine which cell has the focus in a

BINDING ARRAYS TO DATA GRIDS

Note that you can actually bind a data grid to an array of numbers to quickly display the data in that array.

data grid with the `CurrentCell` property. And you can access and change the value of any cell using this kind of code:

```
dataGrid1[row, column] = "Lincoln";
```

Data grids are one of the more enjoyable controls to work with, because you have to set only a few properties, and the control does all the work behind the scenes.

Performing Complex Binding in Code

Despite the name, it's easier to handle complex binding in code than simple binding, because complex binding is based on the four properties—`DataSource`, `DataMember`, `DisplayMember`, and `ValueMember`. For example, here's how you can bind a data grid to a dataset in code:

```
dataGrid1.DataSource = dataSet11;
dataGrid1.DataMember = "authors";
```

You can also use the data grid method SetDataBinding (supported only by data grids) to bind to a table like this:

```
dataGrid1.SetDataBinding(dataSet11, "authors");
```

Here's how you can bind other complex-bound controls to a dataset at runtime. This example binds a list box:

```
listBox1.DataSource = dataSet11;
listBox1.DisplayMember = "authors.au_lname"
listBox1.ValueMember = "authors.au_id"
```

In other words, complex binding is simple; you just assign values to the complex binding properties the control you're working with normally uses.

That completes the discussion on complex binding. But we're not done with the topic of data binding yet. In fact, when it comes to simple-bound controls (which means most C# controls), we've seen only half the story. When you use simple binding, as when you bind a text box to a data source, you'll see data only from the current record in the form's binding context. And if that was the end of the story, all you'd ever see in simple-bound controls would be the data in the first record in the form's binding context. So how do you move to other record? You do that with the form's binding context, and that's what we're going to take a look at next—navigating through a dataset using bound controls.

Navigating Through Datasets Using Bound Controls

Because simple-bound controls display data only from a single record at a time, it's common to add navigation controls like the buttons you see in the ch09_05 example, Figure 9.25, to enable users to move from record to record. When the users click the << button, they move to the first record; when they click the >> button, they move to the last record; the > button moves to the next record, and the < button moves back one record.

Note also that the user's current position is indicated in a label (customized to look like a text box) between the navigation buttons in Figure 9.25. And as you can see in that figure, the complex-bound controls, such as the data grid and the list box, also automatically indicate the current record as you move through the data in the dataset they're bound to.

The controls you see in the ch09_05 example are bound to the current record in the form's binding context. In early versions of Visual Studio programming (pre .NET), the current record was maintained by the data store using data *cursors* (which are supported in most data providers), but because you now work with data in disconnected datasets, that's no longer possible, which is why binding contexts, which can maintain the current record locally, were introduced. In particular, you use a Windows form's `BindingContext` property (this property is part of the `Control` class, which the `Form` class is based on), which holds a collection of `BindingManagerBase` objects, to set the current record for all controls in the form.

The properties of the `BindingManagerBase` class that we'll be using are the `Position` property—which returns or sets the position of the current record in the binding context— and `Count`, which returns the number of records in the binding context. Let's start getting to some code. Our first job is to report the user's current location in the label you see between the navigation buttons.

Displaying the Current Record

If you take a look at Figure 9.25, you'll see that the label between the navigation buttons displays the current location in the binding context with the text "Record 5 of 23", indicating that the user is currently looking at record number 5 of 23 total records. To get both the current position and the total number of records, we'll use a `BindingManagerBase` object, which we get by specifying the data object we're working with (`dataSet11` in this case), and the table in that data object (`authors` in this example) in the collection of `BindingManagerBase` objects returned by the form's `BindingContext` property. When we get our `BindingManagerBase` object, we can use its `Position` and `Count` properties to determine where we are in the binding context. Here's how to convert that data into a string and display it in the label:

```
private void Form1_Load(object sender, System.EventArgs e)
{
    sqlDataAdapter1.Fill(dataSet11);
    label3.Text = "Record " +
        (((this.BindingContext[dataSet11, "authors"].Position + 1).ToString() +
        " of ") + this.BindingContext[dataSet11, "authors"].Count.ToString());
}
```

That's how you display the current position and the total number of records in the binding context for controls bound to the `authors` table in `dataSet11`. So far, so good. Now what about moving to the next record?

Moving to the Next Record

When the user clicks the > button, the next record in the dataset (if there is a next record) becomes the current record. We can do that easily enough—all we have to do is to increment the Position property in the `BindingManagerBase` object and then display the new location in the label between the buttons:

```
private void button4_Click(object sender, System.EventArgs e)
{
  this.BindingContext[dataSet11, "authors"].Position =
    (this.BindingContext[dataSet11, "authors"].Position + 1);
  label3.Text = "Record " +
    (((this.BindingContext[dataSet11, "authors"].Position + 1).ToString() +
    " of ") + this.BindingContext[dataSet11, "authors"].Count.ToString());
}
```

You might think it necessary to check whether there's a next record before attempting to increment the Position property, but in fact the `BindingManagerBase` object takes care of that for you. If you try to move beyond the end of the data in the dataset, the Position property will not be incremented. Now when the user moves to the new record in the dataset, all the controls that are simple-bound to that dataset will display the new current record, and the complex-bound controls will highlight the new current record.

Moving to the Previous Record

It's just as easy to move to the previous record as it is to move to the next record. Here's the code we can use to move to the previous record in the binding context when the user clicks the < button:

```
private void button3_Click(object sender, System.EventArgs e)
{
  this.BindingContext[dataSet11, "authors"].Position =
    (this.BindingContext[dataSet11, "authors"].Position - 1);
  label3.Text = "Record " +
    (((this.BindingContext[dataSet11, "authors"].Position + 1).ToString() +
    " of ") + this.BindingContext[dataSet11, "authors"].Count.ToString());
}
```

Note that, just as when we incremented the Position property, if we attempt to decrement the Position property to a location before the beginning of the data in a dataset, the Position property will not be changed.

Moving to the First Record

Click the << button in the ch09_05 example moves the users back to the first record in the bound dataset. This one's easy to implement—just set the Position property to 0 and then display the new position in the dataset like this:

```
private void button2_Click(object sender, System.EventArgs e)
{
    this.BindingContext[dataSet11, "authors"].Position = 0;
    label3.Text = "Record " +
        (((this.BindingContext[dataSet11, "authors"].Position + 1).ToString() +
        " of ") + this.BindingContext[dataSet11, "authors"].Count.ToString());
}
```

Moving to the Last Record

And you can also let the users move to the last record in the dataset when they click the >> button. In this case, you just set the Position property to Count - 1, subtracting 1 because Position is 0-based, and then display the new location this way:

```
private void button5_Click(object sender, System.EventArgs e)
{
    this.BindingContext[dataSet11, "authors"].Position =
        this.BindingContext[dataSet11, "authors"].Count - 1;
    label3.Text = "Record " +
        (((this.BindingContext[dataSet11, "authors"].Position + 1).ToString() +
        " of ") + this.BindingContext[dataSet11, "authors"].Count.ToString());
}
```

To sum up, you can use the BindingContext property to access the BindingManagerBase object for the binding you're interested in from the collection of such objects returned by the property. You use the BindingManagerBase object's Position and Location properties to navigate through the records in a dataset, automatically updating any controls bound to that dataset to match.

USING THE DATA FORM WIZARD

In this chapter, we've written our own navigation code from scratch, but there is another visual tool that will write this kind of code for you, the Data Form Wizard. You use this wizard to create a new data form. To start this wizard, choose Project, Add New Item, and then select the Data Form Wizard icon in the Templates box and click OK. Using this wizard, you can create data forms that will bind controls to all the fields in a dataset, as well as display navigation buttons, Add, Update, and Cancel buttons.

Working with SQL Parameters

NAVIGATING THROUGH DATASETS IN WEB APPLICATIONS

Before leaving the topic of data navigation, it's important to note that, unlike Windows forms, there is no BindingContext property in Web forms, which means that there is no Position subproperty to use. If you want to navigate through the records in a dataset in a Web form, you must do it yourself. One good trick is to use data views for this purpose. For example, this code shows how you can move to the next record in the authors table using a data view bound to various controls in a Web form:

```
int position = this.ViewState["position"];
if(position <
dataSet11.Tables[0].Rows.Count - 1){
  position++;
  this.ViewState["position"] = position;
}
string id = dataSet11.Tables[0].Rows[posi-
tion].Item["au_id"];
dataView1.RowFilter = "au_id = '" + id +
"'";
TextBox1.DataBind();
Label1.DataBind();
DataGrid1.DataBind();
```

C# offers you the capability to gain more control over the SQL you use in a data adapter by supporting SQL parameters, which are much like variables that you can use in SQL statements. You can assign values to these parameters at runtime without having to alter the SQL in a data adapter.

Here's an example, the ch09_06 example in the code for this book, which lets the users select a state in a combo box, and then click a Display Authors button to display all the authors in the authors table from that state, as you see in Figure 9.28. This example works with a SQL parameter, which is assigned the state the user selects in the combo box.

In this example, a SQL parameter named @Param1 will hold the state the user has selected. Here's the SQL used in the SQL data adapter:

```
SELECT au_id, au_lname, state FROM authors
WHERE (state = @Param1)
```

Take a look at the state = @Param1 part here. This statement creates a SQL parameter named @Param1 that you can assign values to at runtime, as we'll do here. For example, if you were to assign this parameter the value CA, the SQL in the data adapter would become:

```
SELECT au_id, au_lname, state FROM authors WHERE (state = 'CA')
```

Now when you use this data adapter to fill a dataset (in particular, the dataset the other controls in the ch09_06 example are bound to), all the authors in the authors table from California will be displayed.

In the code, we start by listing the available states in the combo box. To do that, create a new SqlDataAdapter object, sqlDataAdapter1, using this SQL and the SQL DISTINCT keyword to select every unique state from the authors table (meaning no state will appear more than once):

```
SELECT DISTINCT state FROM authors
```

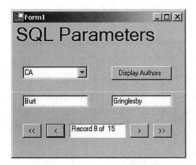

FIGURE 9.28 The Ch09_06 example.

To display the available states, generate a dataset object from sqlDataAdapter1, dataSet11, bind that dataset to the combo box's DataSource property, and bind the state field in dataSet11 to the combo box's DisplayMember property. So far, we've made all unique states in the data in dataSet11 appear in the combo box.

The next step is to create a data adapter with parameterized SQL, allowing you to set the state at runtime, and to bind a dataset using this data adapter to the remaining controls in this example, which displays an author's first and last names, as well as navigation buttons. To do this, create a new data adapter, sqlDataAdapter2, and select the au_id, au_lname, au_fname, and state fields from the authors table. To parameterize the state field, add the text "= @Param1" to the Criteria entry for that field in the Data Adapter Configuration Wizard's Query Builder, as you see in Figure 9.29.

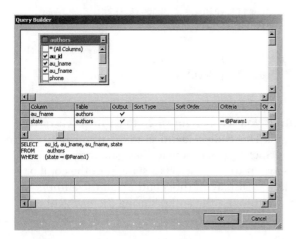

FIGURE 9.29 Creating a SQL parameter in the Query Builder.

As you can see in Figure 9.29, this generates the following parameterized SQL:

```
SELECT
    au_lname,
    au_fname,
    au_id,
    state
FROM
```

```
  authors
WHERE
  (state = @Param1)
```

When you've finished creating `sqlDataAdapter1`, choose Data, Generate Dataset, click the New radio button in the Generate Dataset dialog box that appears, and click OK to create a new dataset, `dataSet21`. Then bind the `au_fname` and `au_lname` fields from `dataSet21` to the two text boxes you see in Figure 9.28 to display the authors' first and last names.

We're almost done. We still have to set the SQL parameter in code when the user clicks the Display Authors button. In this case, we'll be working with the `sqlDataAdapter2` object's `SELECT` command, which retrieves data from a data source, and setting its SQL parameter `@Param1`, which we can access as `sqlDataAdapter2.SelectCommand.Parameters["@Param1"].Value`, to the state the user selected in the combo box. Then we use `sqlDataAdapter2` to fill the dataset bound to the text boxes and navigation buttons:

```
private void button1_Click(object sender, System.EventArgs e)
{
  sqlDataAdapter2.SelectCommand.Parameters["@Param1"].Value = comboBox1.Text;
  sqlDataAdapter2.Fill(dataSet21);
  label2.Text = "Record " +
    (((this.BindingContext[dataSet21, "authors"].Position + 1).ToString() +
    " of ") + this.BindingContext[dataSet21, "authors"].Count.ToString());
}
```

Finally, add the code for the navigation controls you see in Figure 9.28 to let the users navigate through the authors from a particular state. This code is identical to the navigation buttons' code in the previous example, ch09_05, except that here we navigate through `dataSet21`, not `dataSet11`. And you're done—when the user selects a state from the combo box in this example, ch09_06, and then clicks the Display Authors button, all the authors from that state are retrieved. The user can move through the authors using the navigation buttons you see in Figure 9.28.

In Brief

This chapter gave us our start in database handling. Here's an overview of this chapter's topics:

- ADO.NET is the main data access protocol in C#. ADO.NET centers on three primary objects—connection objects, which let you connect to data sources; data adapter objects, which store SQL statements and are responsible for fetching and storing data;

and dataset objects, which hold a copy of your data locally. ADO.NET uses a disconnected data architecture, where no connection to the data source is maintained. Connections are made when you need to get more data or update the data in the data source.

- The IDE comes with several visual tools that let you work with databases. For example, the Server Explorer lets you examine not only which database providers you can connect to, but which data connections you've made, and we've seen how to create data connections as well. To create data adapters and connection objects, you simply have to drag a data adapter from the toolbox onto a form.

- Simple-bound controls display data from a single field in a record, such as text boxes, check boxes, labels, and buttons. To bind these controls at design time, you can use the `DataBindings` property, which displays a few commonly-bound properties for each control such as the `Text` property for text boxes and labels.

- You can data-bind every property of simple-bound controls if you select the `Advanced` property in the `DataBindings` property entry. The data type of the property you're binding must be the same as the data field you're binding to.

- Complex-bound controls display data from multiple fields at once. Complex binding centers on four properties: `DataSource` (the data source), `DataMember` (the member you want to work with in a data source, usually a database table), `DisplayMember` (the field whose data you want the control to display), and `ValueMember` (the field whose data the control will return in properties like `SelectedValue`).

- You can navigate through a dataset and have bound controls update automatically as you do so in Windows forms. You use the form's `BindingContext` property, which returns a collection of `BindingManagerBase` objects, and you can use these objects to set the current record for all controls in the form. Specifically, you use the `Position` property of a `BindingManagerBase` object to set the current record, and the `Count` property to determine the total number of records.

- SQL parameters work much like variables in SQL statements. You can assign values to SQL parameters at runtime without having to change the SQL in a data adapter. All you have to do is to assign a new value to a SQL parameter in a data adapter and use that data adapter to fill a data container like a dataset.

Handling Databases in C# Code

10

Using Data Objects

There are two primary ways of working with databases in C#—with the visual tools in the IDE, and in code. We looked at the visual tools such as the Server Explorer, the Data Adapter Configuration Wizard, the Query Builder, the toolbox, and others, in the previous chapter, and you can handle a great many database tasks using those visual tools. The other way of working with databases in C# is in code, which is the way we'll do things in this chapter. Although the IDE visual tools can do a lot for you, when you really want to drill down to the details, or when you want to do things on the fly at runtime, there's no substitute for doing things yourself in code.

In order to handle databases in code, we have to become familiar with many of the ADO.NET objects, which means wading through a good amount of detail. In this chapter, we're going to work with connection objects, data adapter objects, data table objects, data row objects, dataset objects, data relation objects, and others in code. We're going to see how to connect to a database, how to put SQL into a data adapter, how to create our own database tables from scratch, storing those tables in datasets, and more.

The first task we'll cover is connecting to a data provider, reading data, and displaying that data in a data grid. Doing that in code demands knowledge of connection objects, command objects, and data adapter objects. To retrieve data from a database, you connect to the database with a connection object, assign that connection object to a command object's Connection property, assign the command object to a data adapter object's SelectCommand property, and then use the data adapter's Fill method to fill a dataset. We'll start the chapter by getting acquainted with connection, command, and data adapter objects.

Using Connection, Command, and Data Adapter Objects

Each of these objects come in four types, each in their own namespaces, depending on the data provider you're using:

- For OLE DB data providers, you use OleDbConnection, OleDbCommand, and OleDbDataAdapter objects from the System.Data.OleDb namespace.

- For SQL Server, you use SqlConnection, SqlCommand, and SqlDataAdapter objects from the System.Data.SqlClient namespace.

- For ODBC data providers, you use OdbcConnection, OdbcCommand, and OdbcDataAdapter objects from the System.Data.Odbc namespace.

- For Oracle, you use OracleConnection, OracleCommand, and OracleDataAdapter objects from the System.Data.OracleClient namespace.

We'll see how this works by taking a look at the various data objects we need—connection objects, command objects, and data adapter objects—in detail, starting with connection objects.

Using Connection Objects in Code

To gain access to the data in a data provider, you need a connection object, as we saw in Chapter 9, "Using ADO.NET and Databases." In ADO.NET, you can create and work with connections to data providers with these connection objects:

- OleDbConnection manages a connection to any data source accessible with the OLE DB protocol.

- SqlConnection manages a connection to a SQL Server, version 7.0 or later. (Optimized for use with SQL Server 7.0 or later.)

- OdbcConnection manages a connection to a data source created by using an ODBC connection string or ODBC data source name (DSN).

- OracleConnection manages a connection to Oracle databases.

We'll take a look at these various objects next.

Working with the OleDbConnection Class

You use `OleDbConnection` objects to support connections to OLE DB data providers. As with other generic data objects, you should note that not all properties, methods, and events of `OleDbConnection` objects are supported by all data providers.

To create a connection to a data provider, you need to create a *connection string* of the kind we saw in Chapter 9. Connection strings are made up of attribute/value pairs separated by semicolons like this: `Provider=SQLOLEDB.1;`. You can assign a connection string to the connection's `ConnectionString` property, or pass that string to the connection object's constructor this way:

```
string connectionString = "Provider=SQLOLEDB.1;Integrated " +
"Security=SSPI;Persist Security Info=False;Initial " +
"Catalog=pubs;Packet Size=4096;Workstation ID=STEVE;" +
"Use Encryption for Data=False";

OleDbConnection Connection1 = new OleDbConnection(connectionString);
```

As you can see, a connection string like this one is pretty obscure. If you don't know what's needed in a connection string for a specific data provider, how can you create one from scratch? As recommended in the previous chapter, you can use the visual data tools in the C# IDE to create connection strings for you. Just drag a data adapter onto a form, use it to connect to your favorite data provider, and take a look at the created connection object's `ConnectionString` property in the properties window, which will give you a template you can modify as needed. (Although we'll hard-code our connection strings in our code in this chapter, you can also store them outside your code, as in isolated storage which was discussed in Chapter 5. Doing so is a good idea if your connection string is going to change.)

When you've created a connection object and set its connection string, you open the connection with its `Open` method, and assign the opened connection object to the `Connection` property of a command object. After specifying the SQL you want in the command object, you can use that command object with a data adapter. For example, if you assign the command object to a data adapter's `SelectCommand` property (named for the SQL `SELECT` statement), that command object will be used when you call the data adapter's `Fill` method to fill a dataset. When you're through with a connection, you can call its `Close` method to close the connection.

You can find the significant public properties of `OleDbConnection` objects in Table 10.1, their significant methods in Table 10.2, and their significant events in Table 10.3.

TABLE 10.1

Significant Public Properties of OleDbConnection Objects

PROPERTY	PURPOSE
ConnectionString	Returns or sets the connection string used to connect to a database.
ConnectionTimeout	The maximum time to try to make a connection, in seconds.
Database	The name of the database to open.
DataSource	The data source (typically the location and filename to open).
Provider	The OLE DB provider's name.
ServerVersion	The version of the data server.
State	The connection's current state.

TABLE 10.2

Significant Public Methods of OleDbConnection Objects

METHOD	PURPOSE
Close	Closes the connection to the data provider.
CreateCommand	Creates an OleDbCommand object for this connection.
GetOleDbSchemaTable	Returns the current schema table.
Open	Opens a database connection.

TABLE 10.3

Significant Public Events of OleDbConnection Objects

EVENT	MEANING
InfoMessage	Happens when the provider sends a message.
StateChange	Happens when a connection's state changes.

Working with the SqlConnection Class

As you can gather from their name, SqlConnection objects connect to SQL Server (you can also use OLE DB connections with the SQL Server, but SqlConnection objects are tuned for the best performance; SQL connections to the Microsoft SQL Server are up to 70% faster than OLE DB connections). Working with SqlConnection objects is much the same as working with OleDbConnection objects in code, although the connection string you use will be different. Here's what a sample connection string might look like for a SQL connection:

```
string connectionString = "workstation id=STEVE;packet size=4096;" +
  "integrated security=SSPI;initial catalog=pubs;" +
  "persist security info=False";

SqlConnection connection1 = new SqlConnection(connectionString);
```

Because the programming interface is so similar, the significant public properties, methods, and events of the SqlConnection class are nearly the same as for the OleDbConnection class, except that the SqlConnection class doesn't support the GetOleDbSchema method, but it does support the additional methods you see in Table 10.4.

TABLE 10.4

Additional Significant Public Properties of SqlConnection Objects

PROPERTY	PURPOSE
PacketSize	Returns the size of communication packets to use, in bytes.
WorkstationId	Returns the database client ID.

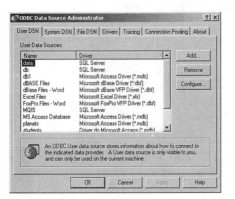

FIGURE 10.1   The ODBC Data Source Administrator.

Working with the OdbcConnection Class

You use the OdbcConnection class to connect to Open Database Connectivity (ODBC) data providers. You can create ODBC connections to nearly all data providers, including MS Access. You create and manage ODBC data sources with the ODBC Data Source Administrator, which you open from the control panel. You can see the ODBC Data Source Administrator in Figure 10.1.

In the ODBC Data Source Administrator, you give a data source a data source name, or DSN. The connection strings you use with OdbcConnection connection objects specify the DSN name. For example, if you create a DSN named books for an MS Access database named books.mdb, your connection string might look something like this:

```
string connectionString = "MaxBufferSize=2048;FIL=MSAccess;" +
"DSN=books;PageTimeout=5;UID=admin;DBQ=C:\books.mdb;DriverId=25";

odbcConnection1 = new System.Data.Odbc.OdbcConnection(connectionString);
```

The significant public properties, methods, and events of the OdbcConnection class are the same as for the OleDbConnection class, except that it doesn't support the GetOleDbSchema method, and it also supports the additional property you see in Table 10.5.

TABLE 10.5	
Additional Significant Public Properties of OdbcConnection Objects	
PROPERTY	**PURPOSE**
Driver	Returns the ODBC driver name for the connection.

Working with the OracleConnection Class

You can connect to Oracle data sources using OleDbConnection objects or OracleConnection objects; OracleConnection objects are optimized for use with the Oracle data provider. Here's how you might create an OracleConnection object and assign a connection string to its ConnectionString property:

```
string connectionString = "Data Source=Oracle8i;Integrated Security=yes;" +
"persist security info=False";

OracleConnection connection1 = new OracleConnection(connectionString);
```

As with other connection objects, the significant public properties, methods, and events of OracleConnection class are the same as for the OleDbConnection class, except that the OracleConnection class doesn't support the GetOleDbSchema method.

In code, you create a connection object, open that connection, and then use command objects, because command objects hold the actual SQL you'll use to extract data from a database. We'll take a look at command objects next. We'll also see how the entire process works in code in a few pages when we connect to a data provider and read data from it.

Using Command Objects

Command objects hold SQL. To use them, you create a connection object, and then assign that connection to a command object's Connection property. Then you store the SQL you want in the command object. Finally, you assign the command object to one of a data adapter object's four command properties: SelectCommand, UpdateCommand, InsertCommand, or DeleteCommand. The SelectCommand command object is used when the data adapter's Fill method is called, the UpdateCommand command object when the data adapter's Update method is called, and so on.

How do you store SQL in a command object? You assign SQL text to its CommandText property, or you can pass that SQL to the command object's constructor like this, where we're selecting all records in the pubs database's authors table:

```
OleDbCommand command1 = new OleDbCommand("SELECT * FROM authors");
```

You must also set the type of the command, which, for SQL statements, is `CommandType.Text` (this is also the default), and assign an open connection to the command's `Connection` property to make this `Command` object active. Here's an example:

```
OleDbCommand command1 = new OleDbCommand("SELECT * FROM authors");
```

```
command1.CommandType = CommandType.Text;
connection1.Open();
```

```
command1.Connection = connection1;
```

Now if you assign this command object to a data adapter's `SelectCommand` property, its SQL will be executed when you call the data adapter's `Fill` method. Note that you can also use these command object methods to execute commands in a database, no data adapter needed:

- `ExecuteNonQuery` executes SQL statements that do not return data rows (such as SQL `INSERT`, `DELELE`, `UPDATE`, and `SET` statements).

- `ExecuteReader` executes SQL commands that return rows, creating a data reader. More on data readers in this chapter.

- `ExecuteScalar` calculates and returns a single value, such as a sum over various records, from a database.

We'll take a look at the various command classes available next.

Working with the OleDbCommand Class

You use `OleDbCommand` objects to hold SQL statements executed in an OLE DB data provider. You can find the significant public properties of `OleDbCommand` objects in Table 10.6, and their significant methods in Table 10.7.

TABLE 10.6

Significant Public Properties of OleDbCommand Objects

PROPERTY	PURPOSE
CommandText	Returns or sets the SQL statement or stored procedure for this command to execute.
CommandTimeout	The amount of time to try a command, in seconds.
CommandType	Returns or sets the data type of the CommandText property (typically set to CommandType.Text, the default, for SQL).
Connection	Returns or sets the connection object to use.
Parameters	SQL command parameters.
UpdatedRowSource	Returns or sets how results are used in a data row when you use the Update method.

TABLE 10.7

Significant Public Methods of OleDbCommand Objects

METHOD	PURPOSE
Cancel	Cancels a command.
CreateParameter	Creates a new SQL parameter.
ExecuteNonQuery	Executes a non-row returning SQL statement, returning the number of affected rows.
ExecuteReader	Creates a data reader using the command.
ExecuteScalar	Executes the command and returns the value in the first column in the first row of the result.
Prepare	Creates a compiled version of the command.
ResetCommandTimeout	Resets the time-out value to the default.

Working with the SqlCommand Class

As you can guess, you use SqlCommand objects with SQL Server. These objects are nearly the same as OleDbCommand objects, except they're designed to be used with SQL connections. The significant public properties and methods of SqlCommand objects are the same as for OleDbCommand objects.

Working with the OdbcCommand Class

OdbcCommand objects are also similar to OleDbCommand objects, but you use them with ODBC connections. As with SqlCommand objects, the significant public properties, methods, and events of OdbcCommand objects are the same as OleDbCommand objects.

Working with the OracleCommand Class

In programming terms, OracleCommand objects are just like the other command objects, except, obviously, you use them with OracleConnection objects. The significant properties, methods, and events of the OracleCommand class are the same as for OleDbCommand objects, except there is no CommandTimeout property, and the OracleCommand class supports the additional methods you see in Table 10.8.

TABLE 10.8

Additional Significant Public Methods of OracleCommand Objects

METHOD	PURPOSE
ExecuteOracleNonQuery	Executes a SQL statement and returns the number of rows affected.
ExecuteOracleScalar	Executes the query and returns the first column of the first row in the result returned by the query as an Oracle-specific data type.

You use connection objects to connect to a data provider and assign them to command objects. Then you assign command objects to data adapters, coming up next.

Using Data Adapters in Code

When you create a connection object and use it in a command object, you can assign that command object to one of the command properties of the data adapter—SelectCommand, InsertCommand, DeleteCommand, and UpdateCommand. These commands are used as needed by the data adapter; if you plan to retrieve data only from the data source, you only need to assign a command object to the SelectCommand. Data adapters are based on the DataAdapter class, and we'll start our survey of data adapters with this class.

Working with the DataAdapter Class

The DataAdapter class is the base class for data adapters, which represent a bridge between a dataset and a database in a data provider. You can find the significant public properties of the DataAdapter class in Table 10.9, and their significant methods in Table 10.10 (this class has no non-inherited events).

TABLE 10.9

Significant Public Properties of DataAdapter Objects

PROPERTY	PURPOSE
AcceptChangesDuringFill	Returns or sets whether a data row's AcceptChanges method is called when rows are added to a table.
TableMappings	Returns the mapping between source tables and data tables. Table mappings let you use different names for tables in a dataset than their original names in the data source.

TABLE 10.10

Significant Public Methods of DataAdapter Objects

METHOD	PURPOSE
Fill	Addsor updates rows in a dataset to match those in the data source. Creates a table named "Table" by default.
FillSchema	Adds a table named "Table" to the specified DataSet object, making the table's schema match that in the data source.
GetFillParameters	Returns the parameters to use when executing a SELECT statement in SQL.
Update	Updates the data source by calling the appropriate INSERT, UPDATE, or DELETE statements for each inserted, updated, or deleted row in a dataset.

The DataAdapter class, in turn, is the base class for the DbDataAdapter class, coming up next.

Working with the DbDataAdapter Class

The DbDataAdapter class serves as the base class for the OleDbDataAdapter and SqlDataAdapter classes. You can find the significant public methods of DbDataAdapter objects in Table 10.11, and their significant events in Table 10.12.

TABLE 10.11

Significant Public Methods of DbDataAdapter Objects

PROPERTY	PURPOSE
Fill	Adds or updates rows in a dataset to match those in the data source.
GetFillParameters	Returns the parameters to use when executing a SQL SELECT statement.
Update	Updates the data source by calling the INSERT, UPDATE, or DELETE statements for each inserted, updated, or deleted row in the dataset.

TABLE 10.12

Significant Public Event of DbDataAdapter Objects

EVENT	MEANING
FillError	Happens when an error happens while performing a fill operation.

That's it for the DataAdapter and DbDataAdapter classes; now we'll take a look at the data adapter classes you actually use in code, starting with the OleDbDataAdapter class.

Working with the OleDbDataAdapter Class

The OleDbDataAdapter class represents a bridge between a dataset and an OLE DB database. You can find the significant public properties of OleDbDataAdapter objects in Table 10.13, their significant methods in Table 10.14, and their significant events in Table 10.15.

TABLE 10.13

Significant Public Properties of OleDbDataAdapter Objects

PROPERTY	PURPOSE
DeleteCommand	Returns or sets the SQL for deleting records.
InsertCommand	Returns or sets the SQL for inserting new records.
SelectCommand	Returns or sets the SQL for selecting records.
UpdateCommand	Returns or sets the SQL for updating records.

TABLE 10.14

Significant Public Methods of OleDbDataAdapter Objects

METHOD	PURPOSE
Fill	Adds or refreshes rows to a dataset to make them match the rows in a data store.

TABLE 10.15

Significant Public Events of OleDbDataAdapter Objects

EVENT	MEANING
RowUpdated	Happens when a row is updated.
RowUpdating	Happens when a row is being updated.

Working with the SqlDataAdapter Class

The `SqlDataAdapter` class is the data adapter class targeted to SQL Server. Like the other data adapter classes, the `SqlDataAdapter` class includes the `SelectCommand`, `InsertCommand`, `DeleteCommand`, and `UpdateCommand` properties you use for loading and updating data. The significant properties, methods, and events of the `SqlDataAdapter` class are the same as for the `OleDbDataAdapter` class.

Working with the OdbcDataAdapter Class

You use the `OdbcDataAdapter` class with ODBC connections and command objects. The significant properties, methods, and events of the `SqlDataAdapter` class are the same as for the `OdbcDataAdapter` class.

Working with the OracleDataAdapter Class

You use the `OracleDataAdapter` class with the Oracle data provider. Like the other data adapters, the significant properties, methods, and events of the `OracleDataAdapter` class are the same as for the `OdbcDataAdapter` class.

After you create a data adapter, you need some place to put the data you read using that adapter. You'll typically use datasets for that.

Using the DataSet Class

The dataset acts as a local repository for your data, and it'll be the target of our data operations when we retrieve data from a data provider in a few pages. As you know, you can use the `Fill` method of a data adapter to fill datasets with data, and if that dataset is bound to controls, those controls will display that new data automatically. You can find the significant public properties of `DataSet` objects in Table 10.16, their significant methods in Table 10.17, and their significant events in Table 10.18.

TABLE 10.16

Significant Public Properties of DataSet Objects

PROPERTY	PURPOSE
DataSetName	Returns or sets the dataset name.
HasErrors	Returns True if there are errors in any row in any table.
Relations	A collection of relation objects, which link tables.
Tables	Returns the tables in the dataset.

TABLE 10.17

Significant Public Methods of DataSet Objects

METHOD	PURPOSE
AcceptChanges	Accepts (that is, commits) changes made to a dataset.
Clear	Clears the dataset by removing all rows in all tables.
Copy	Copies the dataset.
GetChanges	Returns a dataset that contains all changes made to the current dataset.
GetXml	Returns the data in the dataset using XML.
GetXmlSchema	Returns the XSD schema for the dataset.
HasChanges	Indicates whether the dataset has changes that have not yet been committed.
Merge	Merges this dataset with another dataset.
ReadXml	Reads data into a dataset from XML.
ReadXmlSchema	Reads an XML schema into a dataset.
RejectChanges	Rolls back the changes made to the dataset since it was created or since the AcceptChanges method was last called.
Reset	Resets the dataset to the original state.
WriteXml	Writes the dataset's schema and data to XML.
WriteXmlSchema	Writes the dataset schema to XML.

TABLE 10.18

Significant Public Events of DataSet Objects

EVENT	MEANING
MergeFailed	Happens when a merge operation fails.

DATASETS AND XML

To see what a dataset looks like in XML, call the dataset WriteXmlSchema method to write out the XML schema for a dataset, or the WriteXml method to write out both the XML schema and the data in the dataset in XML format. You can also use the ReadXml and ReadXmlSchema methods to read data and format information back into a dataset.

Datasets can be *typed* or *untyped*—usually, they're typed, which means that C# will keep track of the data type of each field, and will object if you try to assign data of the wrong type to a field. ADO.NET uses XML to transport dataset data, and typed datasets hold their type information in XML schemas.

Note also that if you've bound a dataset to controls in your application, the user can edit the data that appears in those controls. When the user does so, the data in the dataset is also changed—but not the data in the underlying data store that the data was originally fetched from. You can determine which rows have been changed with the dataset's GetChanges method, and when you use the data adapter's Update method, those changes are sent back to the underlying database in the data provider you're working with. The data provider might make some additional changes, including updating fields that hold calculated values, and return a new dataset. In that case, you can merge those new fields into a dataset using the dataset's `Merge` method. Then you can use the `AcceptChanges` method in the dataset to accept the changes or the `RejectChanges` method to cancel the changes.

It's time for some coding—let's see all this in action. Our first example, ch10_01, creates its own connection, command, and data adapter objects, and uses them to fill a dataset in code.

Creating a Dataset in Code

The ch10_01 example creates a connection to a data source, SQL Server in this case, and then binds the data from that data source to a data grid. This example uses the `authors` table in the `pubs` database, and displays that table, as you can see in Figure 10.2.

FIGURE 10.2 The ch10_01 example.

We'll take this example apart line by line to see what makes it tick. When the user clicks the Connect to Database button you see in Figure 10.2, this application starts by creating a new dataset object named `dataset1`, passing that name to the `DataSet` constructor (note that we're using the `System.Data.SqlClient` namespace here to access the SQL Server data objects):

```
using System.Data.SqlClient;

private void button1_Click(object sender, System.EventArgs e)
{
    DataSet dataset1 = new DataSet("dataset1");
    .
    .
    .
```

We'll need a connection object to connect to the `authors` table. Here's the connection string and connection object in this example (you have to modify this connection string if you want to run this example yourself):

```
private void button1_Click(object sender, System.EventArgs e)
{
  DataSet dataset1 = new DataSet("dataset1");

  string connectionString = "workstation id=STEVE;packet size=4096;" +
    "integrated security=SSPI;initial catalog=pubs;" +
```

```
    "persist security info=False";

SqlConnection connection1 = new SqlConnection(connectionString);
    .
    .
    .
```

At this point, we have a `Connection` object, and we're working towards creating a data adapter that we'll use to get data from the database. Our next step is to use the connection object to create a command object, and then we can assign that command object to a data adapter's `SelectCommand` property in order to set the SQL the data adapter will use to fetch data from the database.

In this example, we'll create a `SqlCommand` object, giving it the SQL `SELECT * FROM authors` and set the command's type to `CommandType.Text`. After opening this new connection object, we can assign that connection object to the command object's `Connection` property like this:

```
private void button1_Click(object sender, System.EventArgs e)
{
  DataSet dataset1 = new DataSet("dataset1");

  string connectionString = "workstation id=STEVE;packet size=4096;" +
    "integrated security=SSPI;initial catalog=pubs;" +
    "persist security info=False";

  SqlConnection connection1 = new SqlConnection(connectionString);

  SqlCommand command1 = new SqlCommand("SELECT * FROM authors");
  command1.CommandType = CommandType.Text;

  connection1.Open();
  command1.Connection = connection1;
    .
    .
    .
```

Now we're ready to create the data adapter we'll need. To get the `authors` table from the database, we'll create a `SqlDataAdapter` object, and assign our command object to that adapter's `SelectCommand` property. After that, we create a `DataSet` object, `dataSet1`, and use the data adapter to fill that dataset with the `Fill` method.

There's one more thing to be aware of. When you generate a dataset from a data adapter using the IDE's Data, Generate Dataset menu item, that dataset is configured for the tables the data adapter provides. But in this example, our dataset object is new, which means that we must specify which table in the dataset we want to store data in, and we do that by passing the name "authors" to the Fill method. All we need to do after that is to bind the filled dataset to a data grid as you see in Figure 10.2:

```
private void button1_Click(object sender, System.EventArgs e)
{
  DataSet dataset1 = new DataSet("dataset1");

  string connectionString = "workstation id=STEVE;packet size=4096;" +
    "integrated security=SSPI;initial catalog=pubs;" +
    "persist security info=False";

  SqlConnection connection1 = new SqlConnection(connectionString);

  SqlCommand command1 = new SqlCommand("SELECT * FROM authors");
  command1.CommandType = CommandType.Text;

  connection1.Open();
  command1.Connection = connection1;

  SqlDataAdapter sqlDataAdapter1 = new SqlDataAdapter();

  sqlDataAdapter1.SelectCommand = command1;
  sqlDataAdapter1.Fill(dataset1, "authors");

  dataGrid1.SetDataBinding(dataset1, "authors");
}
```

And that's it—now we've connected to a database. You can see the results in Figure 10.2, where the authors table appears in the data grid when the user clicks the Connect to Database button.

Filling Datasets with Local Data

In our first example, ch10_01, we accessed the data in the authors table in the pubs example database on SQL Server. But you don't have to connect to an external data source. You can fill a dataset locally, with entirely local data—no external data connection needed.

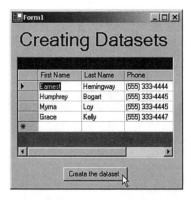

FIGURE 10.3   The ch10_02 example.

We're going to create our own database table in this example and store that table in a dataset. You can see this new example, ch10_02 in the code for this book, at work in Figure 10.3, where the data grid is displaying data for a set of customers that we've stored in a data table, which itself is stored in a dataset.

To make this work, we'll start with a look at the DataTable class.

Working with the DataTable Class

The DataTable class represents a table of data, and datasets are made up of collections of data tables. You can find the significant public properties of DataTable objects in Table 10.19, their significant methods in Table 10.20, and their significant events in Table 10.21.

TABLE 10.19

Significant Public Properties of DataTable Objects

PROPERTY	PURPOSE
ChildRelations	Returns the child relations for this table.
Columns	Returns the columns in this table.
DataSet	Returns the DataSet object this table belongs to.
HasErrors	Returns True if there are errors in any of the rows in the table.
MinimumCapacity	Returns or sets the table's starting size.
Rows	Returns the rows in this table.
TableName	Returns or sets the name of the table.

TABLE 10.20

Significant Public Methods of DataTable Objects

METHOD	PURPOSE
AcceptChanges	Accepts (that is, commits) the changes made to the table.
Clear	Clears the data in the table.
Copy	Copies the table.
GetChanges	Returns a copy of the table including changes made to the table since AcceptChanges was last called.
GetErrors	Returns rows that contain errors.
ImportRow	Imports a row into a table.
LoadDataRow	Finds and updates a row.

TABLE 10.20

Continued

METHOD	PURPOSE
NewRow	Creates a new row, with all the fields each row in the table has currently.
RejectChanges	Rolls back the changes made to the table since it was created or since AcceptChanges was called.
Select	Returns an array of rows.

TABLE 10.21

Significant Public Events of DataTable Objects

EVENT	MEANING
ColumnChanged	Happens after a value in a column was changed.
ColumnChanging	Happens while a column's value is being changed.
RowChanged	Happens after a row has been changed.
RowChanging	Happens while a row is being changed.
RowDeleted	Happens after a row was deleted.
RowDeleting	Happens while a row is about to be deleted.

In the ch10_02 example, we'll create our own data table, fill it with data, and install it in a dataset. When the user clicks the Create the Dataset button you see in Figure 10.3, we start by creating a new DataTable object. Note that we pass the name of this new table, "Customers", to the DataTable constructor:

```
private void button1_Click(object sender, System.EventArgs e)
{
    DataTable table1;
    table1 = new DataTable("Customers");
    .
    .
    .
```

This creates a new data table, table1. There's nothing in this table yet, so the next step is to configure it with the fields we want in each record. To do that, you add columns to the table using the DataColumn class. In this example, we're going to store data for various customers in the table, and then add first name, last name, phone number, and ID fields to each customer's record, using the DataColumn class.

Working with the DataColumn Class

DataColumn objects represent the columns—that is, the fields—in a data table. You can find the significant public properties of DataColumn objects in Table 10.22.

TABLE 10.22

Significant Public Properties of DataColumn Objects

PROPERTY	PURPOSE
AllowDBNull	Returns or sets whether null values are allowed.
Caption	Returns or sets the column's caption.
ColumnName	Returns or sets the column's name.
DataType	Returns or sets the column's data type.
DefaultValue	Returns or sets the column's default value used in new rows.
MaxLength	Returns or sets the maximum length of a text column.
Ordinal	Returns the column's position in the Columns collection.
ReadOnly	Returns or sets if the column is read-only.
Table	Returns the column's table.
Unique	Returns or sets if values in this column need to be unique.

When you create a column in a table, you name that column by passing its name to the DataColumn constructor. You should also set the columns data type, using the column's DataType property. Tables keep track of columns with their Columns collection, so you can add the new columns we'll create to the table with the Columns collection's Add method. In this example, we're going to create first name, last name, phone number, and ID fields for each customer's record:

```
private void button1_Click(object sender, System.EventArgs e)
{
  DataTable table1;
  DataRow row1, row2, row3, row4;
  table1 = new DataTable("Customers");

  DataColumn firstName = new DataColumn("First Name");
  firstName.DataType = System.Type.GetType("System.String");
  table1.Columns.Add(firstName);

  DataColumn lastName = new DataColumn("Last Name");
  lastName.DataType = System.Type.GetType("System.String");
  table1.Columns.Add(lastName);

  DataColumn phone = new DataColumn("Phone");
  phone.DataType = System.Type.GetType("System.String");
  table1.Columns.Add(phone);
```

```
DataColumn id = new DataColumn("ID");
id.DataType = System.Type.GetType("System.Int32");
table1.Columns.Add(id);
    .
    .
    .
```

This code has configured which fields will appear in each record in our data table. Next, we have to actually create those records, and for that, you use the DataRow class.

Working with the DataRow Class

DataRow objects correspond to the records in a data table. Using the methods of this class, you can gain access to, insert, delete, and update the records in a table. You can find the significant public properties of DataRow objects in Table 10.23, and their significant methods in Table 10.24.

TABLE 10.23

Significant Public Properties of DataRow Objects

PROPERTY	PURPOSE
HasErrors	Returns True if there are errors in the row.
Item	Returns or sets data in a specified column.
ItemArray	Returns or sets all of the data in a row.
RowError	Returns or sets a row's error description.
RowState	The current state of a row.
Table	The table that contains this row.

TABLE 10.24

Significant Public Methods of DataRow Objects

METHOD	PURPOSE
AcceptChanges	Accepts (that is, commits) the changes made to the row.
BeginEdit	Begins an edit operation.
CancelEdit	Cancels an edit operation.
ClearErrors	Clears the errors in the row.
Delete	Deletes the row.
EndEdit	Ends an edit operation.
GetChildRows	Returns the row's child rows, if any.
IsNull	Returns True if a column contains a null value.
RejectChanges	Rolls back the changes made to the table since it was created or since AcceptChanges was called.
SetColumnError	Sets the error description for a column.

You don't have to create `DataRow` objects from scratch and configure the columns in each such object before adding it to a table; you can call the table's `NewRow` method to create a `DataRow` object already configured with the correct columns for that table (the maximum number of rows a table can have, by the way, is 16,777,216). To access the data in a field in a row, you can refer to the field by name, *rowName*`["First Name"]`, or by number, *rowName*`[0]`. After you place the data you want in this new record, you can add it to the table with the table's `Rows` collection's `Add` method. Here's how we install our data in the data table in the ch10_02 example:

```csharp
private void button1_Click(object sender, System.EventArgs e)
{
  DataTable table1;
  DataRow row1, row2, row3, row4;
  table1 = new DataTable("Customers");
     .
     .
     .
  row1 = table1.NewRow();

  row1["First Name"] = "Earnest";
  row1["Last Name"] = "Hemingway";
  row1["Phone"] = "(555) 333-4444";
  row1["ID"] = 1;

  table1.Rows.Add(row1);

  row2 = table1.NewRow();

  row2["First Name"] = "Humphrey";
  row2["Last Name"] = "Bogart";
  row2["Phone"] = "(555) 333-4445";
  row2["ID"] = 2;

  table1.Rows.Add(row2);

  row3 = table1.NewRow();

  row3["First Name"] = "Myrna";
  row3["Last Name"] = "Loy";
  row3["Phone"] = "(555) 333-4445";
  row3["ID"] = 3;
```

```
    table1.Rows.Add(row3);

    row4 = table1.NewRow();

    row4["First Name"] = "Grace";
    row4["Last Name"] = "Kelly";
    row4["Phone"] = "(555) 333-4447";
    row4["ID"] = 4;

    table1.Rows.Add(row4);

    DataSet dataset1 = new DataSet();
    dataset1.Tables.Add(table1);
    dataGrid1.SetDataBinding(dataset1, "Customers");
}
```

At the end of this code, you can see how to add this new table to a dataset. You create a new `DataSet` object and add the new table to the dataset's `Tables` collection. Finally, the code binds the new dataset to a data grid. You can see the results in Figure 10.3—we've added our own data to a table, installed that table in a dataset, and bound that dataset to a data grid.

We've started drilling down to the actual cell-by-cell data in code now, and we'll continue that in the next example. The next example illustrates how to access the cell-by-cell data in the authors table, including how to retrieve the name of each column.

Reading Data Cell by Cell

When you're working with databases in code, it's important to access data on a cell-by-cell basis. To see how to gain access to the data in a database, we'll create a new example, ch10_03, which will connect to the authors table in the pubs database and display data for various authors in text boxes, as you see in Figure 10.4.

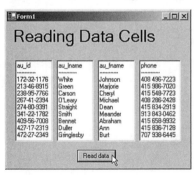

FIGURE 10.4 The ch10_03 example.

To write this example, create a new Windows application named ch10_03 now and connect a SQL data adapter to the authors table. In addition, generate a new dataset, dataSet11, to hold the entire authors table. Next, add the four multiline text boxes to the example's main form as you see in Figure 10.4, as well as the Get Data button. The text boxes will display data from the first four fields (au_id, au_lname, au_fname, and phone) in the authors table.

When the user clicks the Get Data button, we'll start by filling the dataset and displaying the name of each column in the multiline text boxes, as you see in Figure 10.4. To get the name of each column, you access the authors table as dataSet11.Tables["authors"]. This table has a Columns collection, and you can use the ColumnName property of each column to get that column's name:

```
private void button1_Click(object sender, System.EventArgs e)
{
    dataSet11.Clear();
    sqlDataAdapter1.Fill(dataSet11);

    textBox1.Text += dataSet11.Tables["authors"].Columns[0].ColumnName + "\r\n";
    textBox2.Text += dataSet11.Tables["authors"].Columns[1].ColumnName + "\r\n";
    textBox3.Text += dataSet11.Tables["authors"].Columns[2].ColumnName + "\r\n";
    textBox4.Text += dataSet11.Tables["authors"].Columns[3].ColumnName + "\r\n";

    textBox1.Text += "-----------" + "\r\n";
    textBox2.Text += "-----------" + "\r\n";
    textBox3.Text += "-----------" + "\r\n";
    textBox4.Text += "-----------" + "\r\n";
        .
        .
        .
```

Next, we want to get the actual data from the records in the authors table. You access the records in a table with the Rows collection, and you can access an item in a field in a row like this: DataSet11.Tables["authors"].Rows[0][1]. This returns the value of the second field in the first row in the authors table. Here, then, is how we loop over all the records, showing the data from the first four fields of each record in the application's text boxes:

```
private void button1_Click(object sender, System.EventArgs e)
{
    dataSet11.Clear();
    sqlDataAdapter1.Fill(dataSet11);
        .
        .
        .
    for (int rowLoopIndex = 0; rowLoopIndex <=
    dataSet11.Tables["authors"].Rows.Count - 1; rowLoopIndex++) {
        textBox1.Text += dataSet11.Tables["authors"].Rows[rowLoopIndex][0] +
            "\r\n";
    }
```

```
for (int rowLoopIndex = 0; rowLoopIndex <=
    dataSet11.Tables["authors"].Rows.Count - 1; rowLoopIndex++) {
    textBox2.Text += dataSet11.Tables["authors"].Rows[rowLoopIndex][1] +
        "\r\n";
}

for (int rowLoopIndex = 0; rowLoopIndex <=
    dataSet11.Tables["authors"].Rows.Count - 1; rowLoopIndex++) {
    textBox3.Text += dataSet11.Tables["authors"].Rows[rowLoopIndex][2] +
        "\r\n";
}

for (int rowLoopIndex = 0; rowLoopIndex <=
    dataSet11.Tables["authors"].Rows.Count - 1; rowLoopIndex++) {
    textBox4.Text += dataSet11.Tables["authors"].Rows[rowLoopIndex][3] +
        "\r\n";
}
}
```

That's all it takes to read the data in the various fields in a data table contained in a dataset. You can also write to these fields, accessing them in the same way (don't forget to call the data adapter's Update method to send the changes back to the underlying data source).

Note that you can access the data in the fields of a data row either by numeric index or by name. For example, if you're working with a row of data named row1, and the au_fname field is the third field in the row, these statements are equivalent:

```
string firstName = row1["au_fname"];
string firstName = row1[2];
```

There's another way to access the data in a dataset if you're only reading data—using data readers, which are fast, low-level data access objects.

Using Data Readers

Data readers let you read data from a data source field by field in a low-level way, and you use them when speed is an issue. You can create data readers only in code—there are no data reader objects in the toolbox. We'll take a look at data readers here in the ch10_04 example, which you can see at work in Figure 10.5. When the user clicks the Read Data button in this example, a data reader reads the data in the authors table field by field and we display that data in the text boxes you see in the figure.

FIGURE 10.5   The ch10_04
example.

There are four types of data readers—OleDbDataReader,
SqlDataReader, OdbcDataReader, and OracleDataReader—
and we'll start this topic by taking a look at them in
overview.

Working with the OleDbDataReader
Class

The OleDbDataReader class creates a data reader for use with
an OLE DB data provider. You can find the significant public
properties of OleDbDataReader objects in Table 10.25, and
their significant methods in Table 10.26.

TABLE 10.25
Significant Public Properties of OleDbDataReader Objects

PROPERTY	PURPOSE
FieldCount	Returns the number of columns in a row.
IsClosed	Returns True if a data reader is closed.

TABLE 10.26
Significant Public Methods of OleDbDataReader Objects

METHOD	PURPOSE
Close	Closes the data reader.
GetBoolean	Returns a field's data as a Boolean.
GetByte	Returns a field's data as a byte.
GetBytes	Reads a stream of bytes.
GetChar	Returns a field's data as a character.
GetChars	Reads a stream of characters.
GetDateTime	Returns a field's data as a DateTime object.
GetDecimal	Returns a field's data as a Decimal object.
GetDouble	Returns a field's data as a double-precision floating-point number.
GetFieldType	Returns the data type of a field.
GetFloat	Returns a field's data as a single-precision floating-point number.
GetGuid	Returns a field's data as a globally unique identifier (GUID).
GetInt16	Returns a field's data as a 16-bit signed integer.
GetInt32	Returns a field's data as a 32-bit signed integer.

TABLE 10.26

Continued

METHOD	PURPOSE
GetInt64	Returns a field's data as a 64-bit signed integer.
GetName	Returns the name of the given column.
GetOrdinal	Returns the column ordinal position.
GetSchemaTable	Returns an XML schema for a table.
GetString	Returns a field's data as a string.
GetValue	Returns the value of the column in its original format.
GetValues	Returns all the attribute columns in the current row.
IsDBNull	Returns True if a column contains non-existent (or missing) values.
Read	Moves to the next record and reads that record.

Working with the SqlDataReader Class

The SqlDataReader class creates a data reader for use with the SQL Server; the SqlDataReader class has the same significant public properties and methods as the OleDbDataReader class, with the additional significant methods you see in Table 10.27.

TABLE 10.27

Additional Significant Public Methods of SqlDataReader Objects

METHOD	PURPOSE
GetSqlBinary	Returns a field's data as a SqlBinary.
GetSqlByte	Returns a field's data as a SqlByte.
GetSqlDateTime	Returns a field's data as a SqlDateTime.
GetSqlDecimal	Returns a field's data as a SqlDecimal.
GetSqlDouble	Returns a field's data as a SqlDouble.
GetSqlGuid	Returns a field's data as a SqlGuid.
GetSqlInt16	Returns a field's data as a SqlInt16.
GetSqlInt32	Returns a field's data as a SqlInt32.
GetSqlInt64	Returns a field's data as a SqlInt64.
GetSqlMoney	Returns a field's data as a SqlMoney.
GetSqlSingle	Returns a field's data as a SqlSingle.
GetSqlString	Returns a field's data as a SqlString.
GetSqlValue	Returns an object of SqlDbType Variant.
GetSqlValues	Returns all the attribute columns in the current row.

Working with the OdbcDataReader Class

The `OdbcDataReader` class lets you create a data reader for use with an ODBC data provider. The `OdbcDataReader` class has the same significant public properties and methods as the `OleDbDataReader` class.

Working with the OracleDataReader Class

The `OracleDataReader` class lets you create a data reader for use with the Oracle data provider. The `OracleDataReader` class has the same significant public properties and methods as the `OleDbDataReader` class, with some additional significant methods, as you see in Table 10.28.

TABLE 10.28

Additional Significant Public Methods of OracleDataReader Objects

METHOD	PURPOSE
GetOracleBFile	Returns a field's data as an `OracleBFile` object.
GetOracleBinary	Returns a field's data as an `OracleBinary` object.
GetOracleDateTime	Returns a field's data as an `OracleDateTime` object.
GetOracleMonthSpan	Returns a field's data as an `OracleMonthSpan` object.
GetOracleNumber	Returns a field's data as an `OracleNumber` object.
GetOracleString	Returns a field's data as an `OracleString` object.
GetOracleTimeSpan	Returns a field's data as an `OracleTimeSpan` object.
GetOracleValue	Returns the value of a field in Oracle format.

Creating Data Readers in Code

You create data readers with the `ExecuteReader` method of a command object. In this example, we'll connect to the authors table using the OLE DB protocol. Here's how you create a new OLE DB data reader:

```
private void button1_Click(object sender, System.EventArgs e)
{
    string connection1String = "Provider=SQLOLEDB;" +
      "Data Source=;User ID=sa;Initial Catalog=pubs;";
    OleDbConnection connection1 = new OleDbConnection(connection1String);

    OleDbCommand command1 = new OleDbCommand("select * from authors",
      connection1);
```

```
connection1.Open();

OleDbDataReader reader1 =
    command1.ExecuteReader(CommandBehavior.CloseConnection);
    .
    .
    .
```

This data reader gives us access to the authors table. If we want to reproduce the kind of field-by-field display we saw in the previous example, ch10_04, we'll need to start by getting the name of each column in the authors table. Unfortunately, data readers are very simple data objects, designed to return data from the fields in a table, one after the next. To get the names of the columns in a table takes a little more work, but it can be done. You do that by using the data reader's GetSchemaTable method to get the XML schema for the table, which lets you retrieve the name of each column this way:

```
private void button1_Click(object sender, System.EventArgs e)
{
  string connection1String = "Provider=SQLOLEDB;" +
    "Data Source=;User ID=sa;Initial Catalog=pubs;";
  OleDbConnection connection1 = new OleDbConnection(connection1String);
    .
    .
    .
DataTable schemaTable = reader1.GetSchemaTable();

textBox1.Text += schemaTable.Rows[0][0].ToString() + "\r\n";
textBox2.Text += schemaTable.Rows[1][0].ToString() + "\r\n";
textBox3.Text += schemaTable.Rows[2][0].ToString() + "\r\n";
textBox4.Text += schemaTable.Rows[3][0].ToString() + "\r\n";

textBox1.Text += "--------------" + "\r\n";
textBox2.Text += "--------------" + "\r\n";
textBox3.Text += "--------------" + "\r\n";
textBox4.Text += "--------------" + "\r\n";
    .
    .
    .
```

Data readers return the data from field after field in your data source. You use methods like GetBoolean, GetString, and GetDouble to read the actual data from a data reader, which means you must know the data type of the field you're fetching data from. You can determine that type using the XML schema for the table so you know the data-reading method to use. Here's what that looks like in the ch10_04 example, where we're checking for both string and boolean values:

```csharp
private void button1_Click(object sender, System.EventArgs e)
{
  string connection1String = "Provider=SQLOLEDB;" +
    "Data Source=;User ID=sa;Initial Catalog=pubs;";
  OleDbConnection connection1 = new OleDbConnection(connection1String);
    .
    .
    .
  while (reader1.Read())
  {
    if (schemaTable.Rows[0][5].ToString() == "System.String") {
      textBox1.Text += reader1.GetString(0) + "\r\n";
    }

    if (schemaTable.Rows[0][5].ToString() == "System.Boolean") {
      textBox1.Text += reader1.GetBoolean(0).ToString() + "\r\n";
    }

    if (schemaTable.Rows[1][5].ToString() == "System.String") {
      textBox2.Text += reader1.GetString(1) + "\r\n";
    }

    if (schemaTable.Rows[1][5].ToString() == "System.Boolean") {
      textBox2.Text += reader1.GetBoolean(1).ToString() + "\r\n";
    }

    if (schemaTable.Rows[2][5].ToString() == "System.String") {
      textBox3.Text += reader1.GetString(2) + "\r\n";
    }

    if (schemaTable.Rows[2][5].ToString() == "System.Boolean") {
      textBox3.Text += reader1.GetBoolean(2).ToString() + "\r\n";
    }

    if (schemaTable.Rows[3][5].ToString() == "System.String")
    {
      textBox4.Text += reader1.GetString(3) + "\r\n";
    }
```

```
if (schemaTable.Rows[3][5].ToString() == "System.Boolean") {
    textBox4.Text += reader1.GetBoolean(3).ToString() + "\r\n";
  }
}
```

```
reader1.Close();
connection1.Close();
}
```

You can see the results of this code in Figure 10.5, where you see the first four fields of the records in the authors table.

Creating a Data Relation in Code

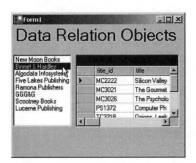

FIGURE 10.6 The ch10_05 example.

This chapter's final example will relate the data in two tables of the pubs example database—publishers and titles—together using the shared pub_id field to create a master/detail data application. This example will display publishers' names in a list box as you see in Figure 10.6 (the "master" part). When the users select a publisher, the code will display that publisher's books in a data grid (the "detail" part). To do this, we'll create a DataRelation object in code.

Datasets just hold your data in tables—they don't know anything about the relations between those tables. To set up those relations, you use DataRelation objects, which relate tables together using DataColumn objects. You can find the significant public properties of DataRelation objects in Table 10.29.

TABLE 10.29

Significant Public Properties of DataRelation Objects

PROPERTY	PURPOSE
DataSet	Returns the dataset the relation is contained in.
RelationName	Returns or sets the name of the relation.

To create the ch10_05 example, add a new SQL data adapter, sqlDataAdapter1, to a Windows form that will return the pubs database's publishers table, and another data adapter, sqlDataAdapter2, that will return the titles table. Then use the Data, Generate Dataset item to generate a new dataset, dataSet11, containing both tables. When the main form loads, we can fill the dataset from the data adapters like this:

```
private void Form1_Load(object sender, System.EventArgs e)
{
  dataSet11.Clear();
  sqlDataAdapter1.Fill(dataSet11);
  sqlDataAdapter2.Fill(dataSet11);

        .

        .

        .
```

Next, add a list box to the form for the master data, and a data grid for the detail data. Bind the list box to the pub_name field in the publishers table in dataSet11. To create our data relation between the publishers and titles tables, we'll need two DataColumn objects. The DataColumn objects will hold the shared pub_id column from both of those tables. Here's how we create those objects in code:

```
private void Form1_Load(object sender, System.EventArgs e)
{
  dataSet11.Clear();
  sqlDataAdapter1.Fill(dataSet11);
  sqlDataAdapter2.Fill(dataSet11);

  DataColumn publishersColumn;
  DataColumn titlesColumn;

  publishersColumn = dataSet11.Tables["publishers"].Columns["pub_id"];
  titlesColumn = dataSet11.Tables["titles"].Columns["pub_id"];

        .

        .

        .
```

Now we can relate the master and detail part of this application together using these DataColumn objects to create a data relation. We'll create a new data relation by passing its name—we'll call it publisherstitles—and the two column objects to the DataRelation constructor. We can install this new data relation, which shows how to relate the publishers table to the titles table, in the dataset using the Add method of the dataset's Relations collection. To display the detail data, all you have to do is bind the new data relation to a data grid like this:

```
private void Form1_Load(object sender, System.EventArgs e)
{
  dataSet11.Clear();
  sqlDataAdapter1.Fill(dataSet11);
  sqlDataAdapter2.Fill(dataSet11);
```

```
        .
        .
        .
DataRelation publisherstitles;

publisherstitles = new DataRelation("publisherstitles", publishersColumn,
    titlesColumn);

dataSet11.Relations.Add(publisherstitles);

dataGrid1.SetDataBinding(dataSet11, "publishers.publisherstitles");
}
```

You can see the results in Figure 10.6, where the new data relation object has related the publisher data in the list box to the title data in the data grid. All the user needs to do to see a publisher's titles is click the name of a publisher, which makes that publisher's titles appear in the data grid.

In Brief

Here's an overview of this chapter's topics:

- Connection objects support the connections to data sources in ADO.NET. You need a connection object, such as an `OleDbConnection`, `SqlConnection`, `OdbcConnection` or `OracleConnection` object, to connect to a database.

- When you have a connection object, you can use that object's `Open` method to open the connection, and assign the object to the `Connection` property of a command object. You store the SQL you want to execute in command objects, and you can create command objects that will select data from the data source, insert new records, delete records, and update the database. Each command object has a connection object associated with it.

- You use command objects with data adapter objects. Data adapters are responsible for handling your connection to a data source, and you can assign command objects to a data adapter object's `SelectCommand`, `DeleteCommand`, `UpdateCommand`, and `InsertCommand` properties. If just you want the data adapter to fetch data, you only need to use `SelectCommand`.

- Once you have a data adapter object, you can use its `Fill` method to fill a dataset object with data.

- You can use DataTable objects to create data tables in datasets (you can add the tables to a dataset with the Add method of the dataset object's Tables collection). You pass the name of the table to the DataTable object's constructor and use DataColumn objects to configure the fields in each record.

- When you create a data column, you pass the name of the new field to the DataColumn constructor, and set the data type of the field with the DataColumn object's DataType property. You can add the new column to a DataTable object's Columns collection using the Add method.

- To create the records in the new table, you use DataRow objects. You can create new rows with all the fields presently in the table using the table object's NewRow method. You can add the new row to a DataTable object's Rows collection using the Add method.

- You can use a DataRow object to access the value in a field in a row like this: row1["au_fname"] or row1[2].

Creating User Controls and Web User Controls

11

Creating User Controls

C# gives you the capability to build controls for both Windows and Web applications. We're going to do that in this chapter, starting with Windows custom controls, called user controls. Later in the chapter we'll see how to create custom controls for Web applications, called Web user controls.

Using Visual Studio .NET, you can create your own user controls for use in Windows forms. For example, you might want such a control to display a day planner or a mortgage amortization calculator. Building reusable user controls lets you avoid the tedium of rebuilding your day planner or mortgage calculator in multiple applications— you just need to drop your user control onto the appropriate form.

At design time, user controls appear much like mini-Windows forms, and you can add standard Windows forms controls (such as buttons in a mortgage calculator) to them to create a composite control. Or you can draw the appearance of the control yourself using its Paint event. You can also make use of the user control's built-in events, like the Click event, to support your events in your user control.

THE PAINT EVENT

The `Paint` event occurs when an object, such as a control or a form, needs to be (re)drawn. In Windows applications, the `Paint` event handler is passed a `System.Windows.Forms.PaintEventArgs` object named `e`, and you can access a `Graphics` object as `e.Graphics`. The `Graphics` class, one of the largest of the FCL classes, is used for drawing. For example, to draw a rectangle, call `e.Graphics.DrawRectangle`; to draw a line, call `e.Graphics.DrawLine`; to draw an image, call `e.Graphics.DrawImage`; to draw a filled polygon, call `e.Graphics.FillPolygon`; and so on.

We'll create an example user control now that will support a custom property, method, and event, just as you'd expect a control to do. To follow along, choose File, New Project to open the New Project dialog box that you see in Figure 11.1. This time, select the Windows Control Library item, naming this new project ch11_01, as you see in Figure 11.1 (note that you can also add a new user control to an existing application by choosing Project, Add User Control).

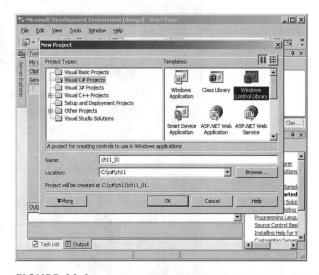

FIGURE 11.1   Creating a user control with the New Project dialog box.

Clicking the OK button in the New Project dialog box creates and opens a new user control in the IDE, as you see in Figure 11.2. As you can see in the figure, the new user control is rectangular, just like a Windows form, and in fact it acts much like a mini-Windows form. In this example, we're going to use a Windows label control to cover most of the user control, so add that label to the user control now as you see in the figure.

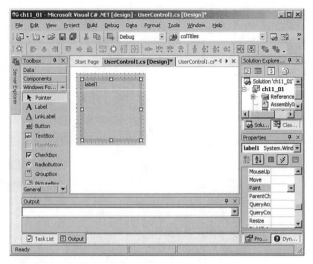

FIGURE 11.2   A user control at design time.

We'll start coding this user control by adding a new property to it; in this case, we'll add a new property named `DisplayColor` that will set the color of the label in the middle of the user control.

Giving Properties to User Controls

When you create a control for our new user control's class, assigning a value to the control's `DisplayColor` property will set the color of the control. The control's color is determined by setting the background color of the label in the center of the control. To implement the `DisplayColor` property, open the user control's code in a code designer now. As you can see in the code designer, the new user control class, `UserControl1`, is based on the `System.Windows.Forms.UserControl` class:

```
public class UserControl1 : System.Windows.Forms.UserControl
{
  private System.Windows.Forms.Label label1;
     .
     .
     .
}
```

We can create the new `DisplayColor` property like any other property, using `get` and `set` accessor methods. In this case, `DisplayColor` is going to be the color displayed by the label in this user control. To set a color, we use the label's `BackColor` property (which takes objects of the `System.Drawing.Color` class) this way:

```
public class UserControl1 : System.Windows.Forms.UserControl
{
  private System.Windows.Forms.Label label1;

  #region Component Designer generated code
     .
     .
     .
  public Color DisplayColor
  {
    get
    {
      return label1.BackColor;
    }

    set
    {
      label1.BackColor = value;
    }
  }
}
```

This code implements the DisplayColor property in the user control; now you can assign or retrieve System.Drawing.Color objects using this property. Before seeing this property at work, we'll add a new method to our control as well.

Giving Methods to User Controls

You can add methods to user controls as easily as you can add properties. As with other objects, you just add the code for the new method to the user control's class. To make that method accessible outside the control, make it a public method.

In this example, we'll add a method named DrawText, which will display the text you pass to it in the label control. That's easy enough to write; here's what that method looks like in the new user control's code:

```
public class UserControl1 : System.Windows.Forms.UserControl
{
  private System.Windows.Forms.Label label1;

  #region Component Designer generated code
     .
     .
     .
```

```
  public Color DisplayColor
  {
    get
    {
      return label1.BackColor;
    }

    set
    {
      label1.BackColor = value;
    }
  }

  public void DrawText(string text)
  {
    label1.Text = text;
  }
}
```

That adds a new method to our user control. And you can also add events, coming up next.

Giving Events to User Controls

You add events to user controls as we saw in Chapter 4, "Handling Inheritance and Delegates"—you just use a delegate and the event statement to create a new event. In this example, we'll add an event named NewText to our user control, which will occur when the text in the control changes. As we've written the user control, the only way of changing the text in the control is with the DrawText method, so we'll fire the NewText event in that method's code:

```
public class UserControl1 : System.Windows.Forms.UserControl
{
  private System.Windows.Forms.Label label1;

  #region Component Designer generated code

  public delegate void NewTextDelegate(object UserControl1, string text);

  public event NewTextDelegate NewText;

  public Color DisplayColor
  {
    get
```

```
  {
    return label1.BackColor;
  }

  set
  {
    label1.BackColor = value;
  }
}

public void DrawText(string text)
{
  label1.Text = text;
  NewText(this, text);
}
}
```

At this point, we've given our new user control a property, `DisplayColor`, a method, `DrawText`, and an event, `NewText`. With these custom items, our user control is ready to use, just as you'd use any other Windows control.

Putting User Controls to Work

In order to make our user control available to other Windows projects, it has to be compiled into .DLL form (actually a .NET assembly with the extension .DLL). To compile it, choose Build, Build Solution in the IDE. After you do, you can use this new user control in other projects by adding a reference to the control in the other project.

To see that at work, we'll create a new Windows application project now, grouping it with our user control by adding that new application to the current solution in the IDE. IDE solutions can hold multiple projects; our current solution only holds the user control project, ch11_01, but you can choose File, Add Project, New Project to add a new Windows application to this solution. Name that new application ch11_02, as you see in Figure 11.3.

This new Windows application will display our user control at runtime. Because you can't run a user control directly, you have to make the new Windows application, ch11_02, the *startup project* for the current solution. You do that by selecting that project in the Solution Explorer, right-clicking it, and then choosing Set as Startup Project. (Alternatively, select the project and choose Project, Set as Startup Project from the IDE's main menu system.)

We'll need to add our new user control to the Windows application's main form. The IDE makes it easy to do that when you add a reference to our user control, which will make our user control appear in the toolbox like any other Windows control. To add a reference to the user control, ch11_01, in the Windows application's toolbox, right-click the ch11_02 application's References item in the Solution Explorer and choose Add Reference, opening the Add Reference dialog box you see in Figure 11.4. To add a reference to the UserControls project, click the Projects tab and double-click the UserControls item, which adds that a reference to the Selected Components box at the bottom of the dialog box. Finally, click OK.

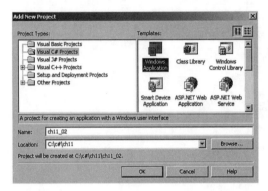

This adds the user control to the toolbox's My User Controls tab, as you see in Figure 11.5. (In earlier versions of Visual Studio .NET, the user control is added to the Windows Forms tab.) To add a user control to the main form in the ch11_02 Windows application, just drag the control from the toolbox, creating a control named userControl11 (the first object of the UserControl1 class).

FIGURE 11.3   Adding a new project to test the user control.

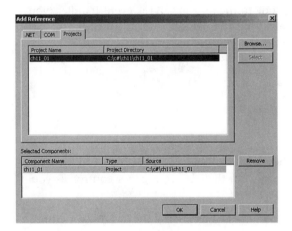

FIGURE 11.4   The Add Reference dialog box.

Note also that the properties window displays the properties of the new user control, including the custom DisplayColor property, as you see in Figure 11.5. Because we've made the type of that property System.Drawing.Color, the IDE will display drop-down lists of colors you can select for the DisplayColor property, just as it does for any property that takes System.Drawing.Color objects (such as the BackColor property of most controls). In this case, we've selected aquamarine for the DisplayColor property, which appears in the label in the center of our user control, as you can see in Figure 11.5 (in stunning black and white).

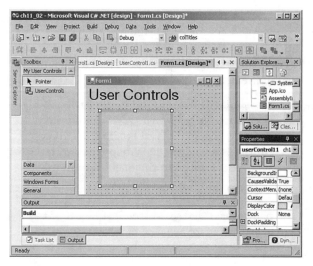

FIGURE 11.5   Adding a user control to a Windows application.

You can also call the methods of our new user control, userControl11, such as the DrawText method. To let the user call this method, add a new button with the caption Click Me! to the Windows application, ch11_02, and add this code to the button's Click event handler (you might note that as you add the code to call DrawText, the IDE's IntelliSense facility will list the type of the data you pass to DrawText, just as it would for any method built into a control you're working with):

```
private void button1_Click(object sender, System.EventArgs e)
{
    userControl11.DrawText("User Controls!");
}
```

When the user clicks the Click Me! button, the text "User Controls!" is passed to the user control's DrawText method, which displays that text in the label in the user control, as you can see in Figure 11.6.

When you change the text in the label in the user control by calling the DrawText method, the control's NewText event fires. You can add code to that event as you can any control event. Simply select the user control in the IDE, click the lightning button in the properties window to see its events, and double-click the NewText event to open its event handler in a code designer. In this case, we will make the NewText event handler for userControl11 to display the new text in a message box this way:

```
private void userControl11_NewText(object UserControl1, string text)
{
    MessageBox.Show("New text: " + text);
}
```

FIGURE 11.6 Using the DrawText method.

FIGURE 11.7 Handling the NewText event.

Now when you run the Windows application and click the Click Me! button, the NewText event occurs and that event's handler displays the new text in the message box we've added to the Windows application. You can see the results in Figure 11.7.

That's how to make use of a user control from another application in the same solution. But what if you want to use a user control in a project not in the same solution? In that case, you can still use a reference to the user control's .DLL file, ch11_01.dll. This time, the user control won't appear in the new project's toolbox by default. To add a user control to a Windows form, you can create a ch11_01.UserControl1 object in code, and then add an event handler and display the control like this:

```
ch11_01.UserControl1 uc1;

private void Form1_Load(object sender, System.EventArgs e)
{
    uc1 = new ch11_01.UserControl1();
    uc1.DisplayColor = System.Drawing.Color.Aquamarine;
    uc1.Top = 100;
    uc1.Left = 100;
    uc1.NewText += new ch11_01.UserControl1.NewTextDele-
gate(uc1_NewText);
    Controls.Add(uc1);
}
```

```
private void uc1_NewText(object sender, string text)
{
    MessageBox.Show(text);
}
```

```
private void button1_Click(object sender, System.EventArgs e)
{
    uc1.DrawText("User Controls!");
}
```

Alternatively, you can add the user control to the toolbox if you take a few extra steps. To do that, select Tools, Add/Remove Toolbox Items in the IDE, and then select the .NET Framework Components tab. Browse to and select ch11_01.dll, make sure the check box for ch11_01.dll is checked in the .NET Framework Components tab, and then click OK. The user control should appear at the bottom of the toolbox, ready for use in Windows applications like any other control. You can publish your user control in this way; just distribute its .DLL file and programmers can add it to their IDE installation's toolbox using this technique.

SHOP TALK

ACTIVEX CONTROLS AND C#

The idea behind user controls is simple: code re-use. The idea is that you write it once and use it many times. But what about working with earlier components also designed for code re-use—COM components and ActiveX controls of the kind developed with previous versions of Visual Studio? Can you use them in Visual Studio .NET? When you try to use or import these items, the main issue is one of security, something that Microsoft is desperately trying to shore up. COM components are not by nature safe (especially because they can use pointers extensively) in the same way that .NET components are, and often have to be substantially rewritten to fit in with .NET. Although it's possible to rewrite COM components for use in .NET, my experience is that you're usually better off rewriting the component's functionality using .NET code in the first place. On the other hand, ActiveX .OCX controls—designed for uses that included the Internet—were automatically made much more secure, which means that it is fairly easy to import such controls into the .NET IDE. To import an ActiveX control, select Tools, Add/Remove Toolbox Items, but this time select the COM Components tab in the Customize Toolbox dialog box, not the .NET Framework Components tab. Browse to the ActiveX control's .OCX file, make sure its check box is checked in the COM Components tab, and click OK, which adds the ActiveX control to the toolbox. (Alternatively, you can use the ActiveX importing utility, AxImp.exe, which comes with Visual Studio .NET, to import an ActiveX control into .NET this way: `AxImp controlname.ocx`. After you do, you can add the ActiveX control to the toolbox using the .NET Framework Components tab, not the COM Components tab, in the Customize Toolbox dialog box.) As with much else that motivated .NET, the issue here was security, and it turns out to be lucky that ActiveX controls were made as secure as they were, making it easy to add them to .NET applications.

That's it for our discussion on user controls, which you use in Windows applications. The other available type of user control is the Web user control, which you use in Web applications; they're coming up next.

Creating Web User Controls

Web user controls are very much like Windows user controls, with the obvious difference that they're designed for use in Web applications. Like user controls, Web user controls can be composites of other controls, or you can draw them from scratch. (Although your options

for drawing them from scratch are more limited in Web user controls because of the limita-
tions of browsers. One option is to make the Web user control display an image that you can
change when the control is clicked, activated, and so on.)

Although Web user controls are based on the `System.Web.UI.UserControl` class, which is
very different from the user control `System.Windows.Forms.UserControl` class, programming
them is similar. To demonstrate just how similar, we'll re-create the same user control we just
created as a Web user control.

To follow along, create a new Web application called ch11_03 now, and then add a Web user
control to this application by using Project, Add Web User Control. When you select this
menu item, the Add New Item dialog box opens, as you see in Figure 11.8. Accept the default
name for the new Web user control, `WebUserControl1`, by clicking Open.

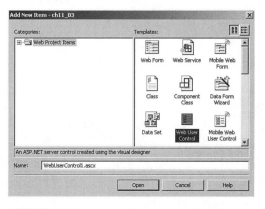

This creates the new Web user control you see
in Figure 11.9. The new Web user control's class
is `WebUserControl1`, and at design time, it looks
like a small standard Web page. We've already
added the label we'll use in this control to the
Web control, as you also see in Figure 11.9.

As far as the C# code goes, programming a Web
user control in C# is so close to programming a
user control that we can use the same code. All
we have to do is to borrow the code from our
user control example, ch11_01, and drop it into
the code designer for the new user control.
Here's what that looks like in
WebUserControl1.ascx.cs:

FIGURE 11.8 The Add New Item dialog box.

```
public class WebUserControl1 : System.Web.UI.UserControl
{
    protected System.Web.UI.WebControls.Label Label1;

    #region Web Form Designer generated code

    public delegate void NewTextDelegate(object UserControl1, string text);

    public event NewTextDelegate NewText;

    public Color DisplayColor
    {
        get
```

```
    {
        return Label1.BackColor;
    }


    set
    {
        Label1.BackColor = value;
    }
}


public void DrawText(string text)
{
    Label1.Text = text;
    NewText(this, text);
}
}
```

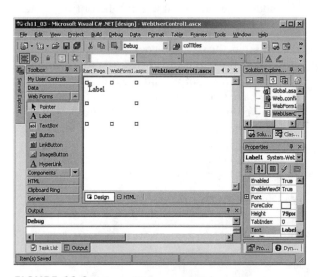

FIGURE 11.9   A new Web user control.

This implements the DisplayColor property, the DrawText method, and the NewText event in our Web user control. It was as simple as that.

This is the point where things start to differ from user controls. As you recall, all we had to do to make a user control available to other projects was to compile it. The IDE can't work that closely with the Web server, however, which means that you have to follow a different procedure to add our Web user control to the ch11_03 Web application.

Here's what you do: Open the Web application's main form in a form designer, and then drag the WebUserControl1.ascx entry from the Solution Explorer onto that form, adding the Web user control, `WebUserControl11`, to the form as you see in Figure 11.10. Because the Web user control has not been compiled, the IDE doesn't know what it will look like at runtime, so it gives it a generic button-like appearance at design time, as you can see in the figure.

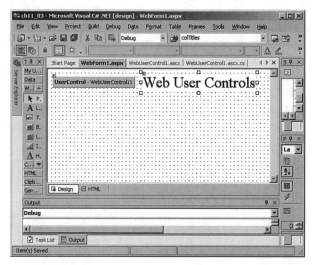

FIGURE 11.10   Adding a Web user control to a Web application.

Dragging this control to the Web form creates a new Web user control, `WebUserControl11`, in the Web application's main Web form, WebForm1.aspx. Here's what this new control looks like in ASP.NET, in WebForm1.aspx:

```
<%@ Page language="c#" Codebehind="WebForm1.aspx.cs" AutoEventWireup="false"
  Inherits="ch11_03.WebForm1" %>
<%@ Register TagPrefix="uc1" TagName="WebUserControl1"
  Src="WebUserControl1.ascx" %>
<!DOCTYPE HTML PUBLIC "-//W3C//DTD HTML 4.0 Transitional//EN" >
<HTML>
  <HEAD>
   <title>WebForm1</title>
   <meta name="GENERATOR" Content="Microsoft Visual Studio .NET 7.1">
   <meta name="CODE_LANGUAGE" Content="C#">
   <meta name=vs_defaultClientScript content="JavaScript">
   <meta name=vs_targetSchema
     content="http://schemas.microsoft.com/intellisense/ie5">
  </HEAD>
```

```
<body MS_POSITIONING="GridLayout">

  <form id="Form1" method="post" runat="server">
<asp:Label id=Label1 style=
  "Z-INDEX: 101; LEFT: 204px; POSITION: absolute; TOP: 10px"
runat="server" Font-Size="X-Large">Web User Controls</asp:Label>
<uc1:WebUserControl1 id=WebUserControl11 runat="server"></uc1:WebUserControl1>
  </form>
 </body>
</HTML>
```

On the other hand, because this control will not actually be compiled until runtime, the IDE does not automatically add the user control, WebUserControl11, to the "code-behind" file for our Web application, WebForm1.aspx.cs. To use this control in code, you have to declare it in WebForm1.aspx.cs like this:

```
public class WebForm1 : System.Web.UI.Page
{
  protected System.Web.UI.WebControls.Label Label1;

  protected WebUserControl1 WebUserControl11;

    .
    .
    .
```

That adds the Web user control to our code designer, which means you can work with the control's properties, methods, and events in code. Note that because the control hasn't been compiled, you can't work with its properties in the properties window at design time. You can, however, set properties (such as setting the DisplayColor property to System. Drawing.Color.aquamarine) when the Web form containing the control loads, which we'll do in the ch11_03 example like this:

```
private void Page_Load(object sender, System.EventArgs e)
{
  WebUserControl11.DisplayColor = System.Drawing.Color.Aquamarine;
}
```

As in the user control example we saw earlier today, we can also add a button with the caption Click Me! to call the DrawText method, except this time we'll use that method to display the text "Web User Controls!" (not "User Controls!") in the label in our Web user control:

```
private void Button1_Click(object sender, System.EventArgs e)
{
```

```
WebUserControl11.DrawText("Web User Controls!");
}
```

The `DrawText` method will also fire the `NewText` event in the Web user control. In our Web application, we can connect an event handler, `WebUserControl11_NewText`, to that event. To do that, add this code to the `InitializeComponent` method in the Web Form Designer generated code in WebForm1.ascx.cs:

```
private void InitializeComponent()
{
  this.Button1.Click += new System.EventHandler(this.Button1_Click);
  this.Load += new System.EventHandler(this.Page_Load);
  this.WebUserControl11.NewText += new
    ch11_03.WebUserControl1.NewTextDelegate(WebUserControl11_NewText);
}
```

All that's left is to write the event handler `WebUserControl11_NewText`. In that event handler, we'll display the new text in our Web user control in a text box this way:

```
private void WebUserControl11_NewText(object sender, string text)
{
  TextBox1.Text = text;
}
```

And that's all we need. We've been able to duplicate the work we did with the `UserControls` example earlier, but this time we're using a Web user control.

You can see this example at work in Figure 11.11. When you click the Click Me! button, the new text is displayed in the Web user control and the text box, as you see in that figure.

FIGURE 11.11   Using a Web user control.

That rounds off our discussion on user controls and Web user controls. When it comes to code reuse, it's hard to beat these types of custom-built controls—you write them once and you can use them in dozens of applications.

In Brief

In this chapter, we looked at user controls for Windows applications and Web user controls for Web applications. Here's an overview of this chapter's topics:

- User controls and Web user controls are custom controls that specialize in code reuse. You can create composite controls using standard controls, and/or design the appearance of a control from scratch.

- User controls are based on the `System.Windows.Forms.UserControl` class. They are designed for use in Windows forms, and they support properties, methods, and events like any standard control.

- Web user controls are much like standard user controls, except they're designed to be used in Web applications. These controls are based on the `System.Web.UI.UserControl` class. The process of creating Web user controls in code is very similar to how you create user controls.

- The way you add Web user controls to a Web form is substantially different from the corresponding user controls; you drag a Web user control directly from the Solution Explorer to a Web form.

Creating Windows Services, Web Services, and Deploying Applications

Creating Windows Services

There are three programmer-to-programmer topics in this chapter: Windows services, Web services, and how to deploy applications using Windows installer (.MSI) files. All these issues are important ones, and we'll use them to round off the GUI-oriented application coverage. We'll start with Windows services.

Windows services are not typically front-line applications that the user runs and interacts with. Instead, they provide support services, often for device drivers, such as printer device drivers, audio devices, data providers, CD creation software, and so on. As such, Windows services don't need a real user interface as you see in standard Windows applications. They often do have a control panel-like interface that the users can open by clicking or right-clicking an icon in the taskbar, however. (You can create taskbar icons in Windows applications using the `NotifyIcon` control from the Windows Forms tab in the toolbox.) Users can customize, and even start or stop, a Windows service using that control panel. Other Windows applications can interact with the service at runtime; for example, SQL Server uses a Windows service to make it accessible to other applications.

We'll see how to create a working Windows service in this chapter. In the FCL, Windows services are based on the `ServiceBase` class, and that class gives us most of the support we'll need. When you write a Windows service, you should override the `OnStart` and `OnStop` methods—even though their names imply they are event handlers, they're actually methods. These methods are called when the service starts and stops. You might also want to override the `OnPause` and `OnContinue` event handlers to handle occasions where the service is paused and resumed.

SHOP TALK

ABUSING WINDOWS SERVICES

Currently, there is a great deal of abuse of Windows services, and it's getting so bad that sooner or later there's going to be a user revolt. Too many software manufacturers just decide that the user's computer has nothing better to do than to continuously run their software, and so you find Windows services that do nothing else besides check—once a second—whether the software manufacturer's software is running, or printer drivers that run as a Windows service, also polling once a second and displaying multiple taskbar icons and pop-ups. Some one-time-use applications, like a few tax programs, appear to install Windows services that run continuously as long as the user has the computer. Other manufacturers use Windows services to gather information about the user's work habits, installed software, and/or accessed files to send over the Internet without the user's knowledge.

Because Windows services can be invisible, they've been incredibly abused. If you look in the Service Control Manager tool that we'll discuss in this chapter, you may find a dozen or so Windows services running that you've never heard of before. It's very important to resist this temptation to monopolize the user's machine. If you need to poll your device driver or service, you can start a `Timer` object (see Chapter 7, "Creating C# Windows Applications") when the service's `OnStart` method is called, but don't use this technique to wrest control from the user more than just occasionally, unless you specifically let the user know what's going on. Many users, when told what some formerly unknown Windows services are doing, consider them no better than viruses.

You can configure Windows services to start automatically when the computer starts, or you can start them manually using an administration tool built into Windows, the Service Control Manager (SCM).

We'll see how this works in practice now. You can see an example, ch12_01, in the code for this book, and we'll take that application apart here. To follow along, create a new Windows service project. Choose File, New, Project in the IDE, and select the Windows Service icon in the Templates box of the New Project dialog box. Give this new service the name ch12_01 and click OK. This creates the new Windows service project in Figure 12.1; the default name for this new service is "Service1".

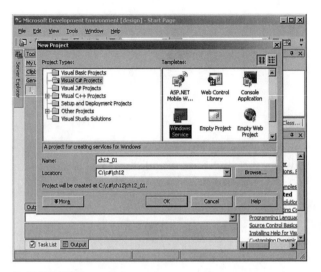

FIGURE 12.1   A new Windows service.

In our Windows service, we are going to write to our Windows service's event log when the OnStart and OnStop methods are called. To handle an event log, you must specify or create an *event source*. An event source registers your application with the event log as a source of data so the event log can listen for that data. You can give the event source as any string, but the name must be unique among other registered sources.

In this example, we're going to register our event log in the Windows service's constructor, which you can find in the Component Designer generated code region of the Windows service's code, Service1.cs. That constructor looks like this now:

```
public Service1()
{
    // This call is required by the Windows.Forms Component Designer.
    InitializeComponent();

    // TODO: Add any initialization after the InitComponent call
}
```

In this example, we create an event source named "CSSource1". After the new source is created, we assign its name to the eventLog1 object's Source property like this:

```
public Service1()
{
    // This call is required by the Windows.Forms Component Designer.
    InitializeComponent();
```

```
   if (!System.Diagnostics.EventLog.SourceExists("CSSource1"))
   {
       System.Diagnostics.EventLog.CreateEventSource("CSSource1",
           "currentLog1");
   }

   eventLog1.Source = "CSSource1";
}
```

Now we're ready to write to our event log when the service starts and stops. You can do that in the OnStart and OnStop methods, which look like this in Service1.cs currently:

```
protected override void OnStart(string[] args)
{
    // TODO: Add code here to start your service.
}

protected override void OnStop()
{
    // TODO: Add code here to perform any tear-down necessary to
    // stop your service.
}
```

To write text to a Windows service's event log, you can use the log's WriteEntry method. In this case, we'll insert a message into the log indicating that the service started or stopped, like this:

```
protected override void OnStart(string[] args)
{
    eventLog1.WriteEntry("Starting ch12_01.");
}

protected override void OnStop()
{
    eventLog1.WriteEntry("Stopping ch12_01.");
}
```

When our Windows service starts, our code will write "Starting ch12_01." to event log currentLog1, and when the service stops, our code will write "Stopping ch12_01." to the log.

We've created our Windows service. To install that service, we'll need an installer, so click the Service1.cs[Design] tab now to open the designer for Service1. Make sure that eventLog1 in that designer does *not* have the focus (we want to create an installer for the service itself, not the event log object in the service), and then click the Add Installer link in the description section of the properties window (this link is visible at bottom right in Figure 12.2).

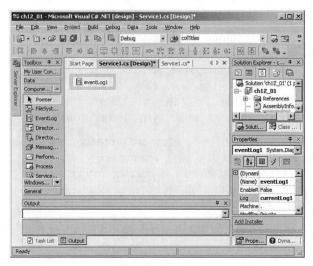

FIGURE 12.2 Adding an event log to a Windows service.

This creates `ProjectInstaller.cs` with two objects in it, `serviceProcessInstaller1` and `serviceInstaller1`, as you see in Figure 12.3.

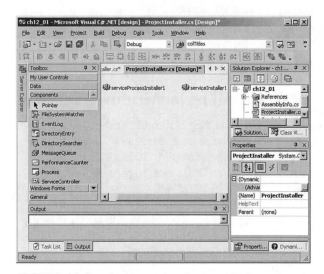

FIGURE 12.3 Creating an installer for a Windows service.

ServiceInstaller objects inform Windows about a service by writing Windows Registry values for the service to a Registry subkey under the HKEY_LOCAL_MACHINE\System\ CurrentControlSet\Services Registry key. The service is identified by its ServiceName value in this subkey. ServiceProcessInstaller objects handle the individual processes started by our service.

When you install a Windows service, you have to indicate which account it should run under. In this example, we'll do that by clicking the serviceProcessInstaller1 object to give it the focus and setting its Account property to LocalSystem. Besides LocalSystem, you can also set this property to LocalService, NetworkService, or User. When you set Account to User, you must set the Username and Password properties of the serviceProcessInstaller1 object to configure this object for a specific user account.

Now click the serviceInstaller1 object and make sure its ServiceName property is set to the name of this service, Service1 (it should already be set that way). You use the ServiceInstaller1 object's StartType property to indicate how to start the service. Here are the possible ways of starting the service, using values from the ServiceStartMode enumeration:

- ServiceStartMode.Automatic—The service should be started automatically when the computer boots.

- ServiceStartMode.Disabled—The service is disabled (so it cannot be started).

- ServiceStartMode.Manual—The service can only be started manually (by either using the Service Control Manager, or by an application).

USING MANUAL STARTUP WHILE DEVELOPING WINDOWS SERVICES

A Windows service with errors in it that starts automatically on boot can make Windows unstable, so be careful when testing Windows services. Until you're sure a service is working correctly, it's best to keep its start mode Manual, making sure it doesn't start again automatically if you need to reboot. (If you get into a loop where a problematic Windows service is starting automatically when you boot and causing Windows to hang, press and hold the F8 key while booting so Windows comes up in safe mode.)

The safest of these while testing a new Windows service is Manual, so set the StartType property of the ServiceInstaller1 object to Manual now.

Installing a Windows Service

The next step is to build and install our new Windows service, Service1. To build the service, select Build, Build ch12_01, which creates ch12_01.exe. To actually install the service in Windows, you can use the InstallUtil.exe tool that comes with the .NET Framework. In Windows 2000, for example, you can find InstallUtil.exe in the

C:\WINNT\Microsoft.NET\Framework\xxxxxxxx directory, where xxxxxxxx is the .NET Framework's version number.

Here's how you install ch12_01.exe using InstallUtil.exe at the DOS command prompt (note that the command line here is too wide for the page, so it's split into two lines):

```
C:\WINNT\Microsoft.NET\Framework\xxxxxxxxx>installutil
c:\c#\ch12\ch12_01\bin\Debug\ch12_01.exe

Microsoft (R) .NET Framework Installation utility Version xxxxxxxxxx
Copyright (C) Microsoft Corporation 1998-2002. All rights reserved.

Running a transacted installation.

Beginning the Install phase of the installation.
See the contents of the log file for the
c:\c#\ch12\ch12_01\bin\debug\ch12_01.exe assembly's progress.
The file is located at c:\c#\ch12\ch12_01\bin\debug\ch12_01.InstallLog.
Installing assembly 'c:\c#\ch12\ch12_01\bin\debug\ch12_01.exe'.
Affected parameters are:
    assemblypath = c:\c#\ch12\ch12_01\bin\debug\ch12_01.exe
    logfile = c:\c#\ch12\ch12_01\bin\debug\ch12_01.InstallLog
Installing service Service1...
Service Service1 has been successfully installed.
Creating EventLog source Service1 in log Application...

The Install phase completed successfully, and the Commit phase is beginning.
See the contents of the log file for the
c:\c#\ch12\ch12_01\bin\debug\ch12_01.exe assembly's progress.
The file is located at c:\c#\ch12\ch12_01\bin\debug\ch12_01.InstallLog.
Committing assembly 'c:\c#\ch12\ch12_01\bin\debug\ch12_01.exe'.
Affected parameters are:
    assemblypath = c:\c#\ch12\ch12_01\bin\debug\ch12_01.exe
    logfile = c:\c#\ch12\ch12_01\bin\debug\ch12_01.InstallLog

The Commit phase completed successfully.

The transacted install has completed.

C:\WINNT\Microsoft.NET\Framework\xxxxxxxxx>
```

Now our Windows service has been installed. If InstallUtil hadn't been able to install the new service without problems, it would have rolled back the installation and removed the non-working service.

AUTO-INSTALLING A WINDOWS SERVICE

You can also deploy Windows services with setup programs in C#; we'll cover setup programs at the end of this chapter. You create setup programs with setup projects, and to install a Windows service, you add a *custom action* to a setup project. In the Solution Explorer, right-click the setup project, select View, and then select Custom Actions, making the Custom Actions dialog box appear. In the Custom Actions dialog box, right-click the Custom Actions item and select Add Custom Action, making the Select Item in Project dialog box appear. Double-click the Application Folder in the list box, opening that folder. Select Primary Output from *ServiceName* (Active), where *ServiceName* is the name of your service, and click OK. The primary output (that is, the Windows service itself) is added to all four custom action folders—Install, Commit, Rollback, and Uninstall.

Our new Windows service is installed, but not yet started, because we chose manual startup. In this case, we'll use the Service Control Manager to start our service. The SCM is part of Windows; for example, in Windows 2000, you can start the SCM this way:

- In Windows 2000 Server, you select Start, select Programs, click Administrative Tools, and click Services.

- In Windows 2000 Professional, right-click the My Computer icon on the desktop and select the Manage item in the menu that pops up. In the dialog box that appears, expand the Services and Applications node and click the Services item.

You can see the Service Control Manager in Figure 12.4, and you can see our newly installed service, Service1, listed in the SCM in the figure.

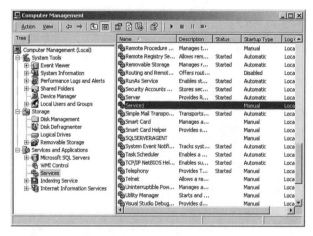

FIGURE 12.4 The Service Control Manager.

To start our new service, right-click Service1 in the Service Control Manager now and select the Start item in the menu that appears. Doing so starts the service, as you see in Figure 12.5, where Service1 is listed as Started.

To stop the service, right-click Service1 in the Service Control Manager and select the Stop item.

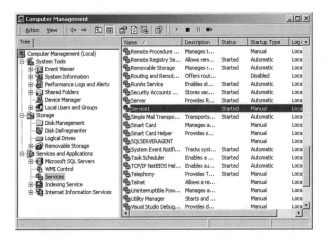

FIGURE 12.5   Starting a Windows service.

We've been able to start and stop our new service, so it should have written to our event log, currentLog1. You can check whether it has from inside the IDE; you just open the Server Explorer's Event Logs node as you see in Figure 12.6, and take a look at the entry for CSSource1 in currentLog1. Here, you can see our service's two entries—Starting ch12_01. and Stopping ch12_01.—in the event log in the Server Explorer in Figure 12.6. (If you don't see the messages there, or messages don't appear when you start and stop the service a number of times, refresh the event log by right-clicking currentLog1 in the Server Explorer and selecting the Refresh item.) And that's it—the Windows service is a success.

Our Windows service did exactly what it was supposed to—it wrote to an event log when it was started and stopped. Now that you can run code in a Windows service, you can see this is only the beginning. You can get the service's code started when the OnStart method is called, and run it in the background, supplying its service for as long as needed.

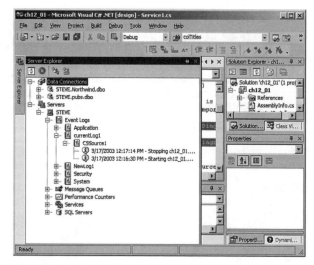

FIGURE 12.6   The Server Explorer.

Uninstalling a Windows Service

You can uninstall a Windows service, removing it from the SCM, with InstallUtil.exe; just use the /u option to uninstall. Here's what you see when you uninstall the Windows service—notice that the command line is the same except for the /u:

```
C:\WINNT\Microsoft.NET\Framework\xxxxxxxxxx>installutil
c:\c#\ch12\ch12_01\bin\Debug\ch12_01.exe /u


Microsoft (R) .NET Framework Installation utility Version xxxxxxxxxx
Copyright (C) Microsoft Corporation 1998-2002. All rights reserved.


The uninstall is beginning.
See the contents of the log file for the
c:\c#\ch12\ch12_01\bin\debug\ch12_01.exe assembly's progress.
The file is located at c:\c#\ch12\ch12_01\bin\debug\ch12_01.InstallLog.
Uninstalling assembly 'c:\c#\ch12\ch12_01\bin\debug\ch12_01.exe'.
Affected parameters are:
    assemblypath = c:\c#\ch12\ch12_01\bin\debug\ch12_01.exe
    logfile = c:\c#\ch12\ch12_01\bin\debug\ch12_01.InstallLog
Removing EventLog source Service1.
Service Service1 is being removed from the system...
Service Service1 was successfully removed from the system.
```

The uninstall has completed.

C:\WINNT\Microsoft.NET\Framework*xxxxxxxxxx*>

Interacting with Windows Services from Other Applications

We've seen how to run a Windows service in the background, but how do you connect to that Windows service from another application? All you need to do is drag a `ServiceController` object from the `Components` tab of the `Toolbox` to a form in a Windows application, creating a new object, serviceController1. Then you set these properties in the properties window for this object:

- `MachineName`—The name of the computer that hosts the service, or "." for the local computer.

- `ServiceName`—The name of the service you want to work with.

Now using the power of the Windows service becomes easy—you can use the properties and methods exposed by the Windows service as though they were properties and methods of the serviceController1 object. For example, here's how you might use the CanStop and ServiceName properties of a Windows service as connected to by serviceController1:

```
if (serviceController1.CanStop)
{
    MessageBox.Show(serviceController1.ServiceName + " can be stopped.");
}
```

You can also create a `ServiceController` object in code. To do that, you add a reference to the System.ServiceProcess DLL by right-clicking the current project in the Solution Explorer and selecting Add Reference. Then, click the .NET tab in the Add Reference dialog box, select System.ServiceProcess.dll and click Select. Finally, click OK to close the Add Reference dialog box. Also, you should include a using statement in your application's code for the System.ServiceProcess namespace. Now you can access the properties and methods that are built into a Windows service using the new ServiceController object like this:

```
using System.ServiceProcess;
        .
        .
        .
ServiceController controller1 = new ServiceController("Service1");

if (controller1.CanStop)
{
```

```
    MessageBox.Show(controller1.ServiceName + " can be stopped.");
}
```

That's all it takes to access a Windows service from code. (Note that you can even implement events in a Windows service, and, using `ServiceController` objects, handle those events in other applications.)

Next, we'll take a look at the properties, methods, and events of a few of the important Windows services classes to round off this topic.

Working with the ServiceBase Class

The `ServiceBase` class is the base class for Windows services, and you can find the significant public properties of `ServiceBase` objects in Table 12.1, and their significant protected methods in Table 12.2 (note that although the items in Table 12.2 look like events, they're actually methods you can override).

TABLE 12.1

Significant Public Properties of ServiceBase Objects

PROPERTY	PURPOSE
AutoLog	Sets whether to record in the event log automatically.
CanPauseAndContinue	Returns or sets whether the service can be paused and continued.
CanShutdown	Returns or sets whether the service should be informed when the computer shuts down.
CanStop	Returns or sets whether the service can be stopped.
EventLog	Returns the event log.
ServiceName	Returns or sets the name of the service.

TABLE 12.2

Significant Protected Methods of ServiceBase Objects

METHOD	PURPOSE
OnContinue	Called when a service continues (after it was paused).
OnPause	Called when a service is paused.
OnShutdown	Called when the system shuts down.
OnStart	Called when the service starts.
OnStop	Called when a service stops running.

Working with the EventLog Class

The EventLog class supports access to Windows event logs used by Windows services; you can find the significant public static methods of EventLog in Table 12.3, the significant public properties of EventLog objects in Table 12.4, their significant methods in Table 12.5, and their significant events in Table 12.6.

TABLE 12.3

Significant Public Static Methods Properties of the EventLog Class

METHOD	PURPOSE
CreateEventSource	Creates an event source to let you write to a log.
Delete	Deletes a log.
DeleteEventSource	Deletes an event source.
Exists	Returns true if a log exists.
GetEventLogs	Returns an array of event logs.
SourceExists	Checks whether an event source exists.
WriteEntry	Writes an entry to the log.

TABLE 12.4

Significant Public Properties of EventLog Objects

PROPERTY	PURPOSE
Entries	Returns the contents of the log.
Log	Returns or sets the name of the log.
LogDisplayName	Returns the log's display name.
MachineName	Returns or sets the name of the log's computer.
Source	Returns or sets the source name to use when writing to the log.

TABLE 12.5

Significant Public Methods of EventLog Objects

METHOD	PURPOSE
BeginInit	Begins initialization of a log.
Clear	Clears all the entries in a log.
Close	Closes the log.
EndInit	Ends initialization of a log.
WriteEntry	Writes an entry in the log.

TABLE 12.6

Significant Public Events of EventLog Objects

EVENT	PURPOSE
EntryWritten	Happens when data is written to a log.

Working with the ServiceProcessInstaller Class

As we've already seen, ServiceProcessInstaller objects let you install specific processes in a Windows service. You can find the significant public properties of objects of the ServiceProcessInstaller class in Table 12.7, their significant methods in Table 12.8, and their significant events in Table 12.9.

TABLE 12.7

Significant Public Properties of ServiceProcessInstaller Objects

PROPERTY	PURPOSE
Account	Returns or sets the type of account for the service.
HelpText	Returns help text.
Installers	Returns the service's installers.
Parent	Returns or sets the parent installer.
Password	Returns or sets the password for a user account.
Username	Returns or sets a user account.

TABLE 12.8

Significant Public Methods of ServiceProcessInstaller Objects

METHOD	PURPOSE
Install	Installs a service, writing information to the Registry.
Rollback	Rolls back an installation, removing data written to the Registry.
Uninstall	Uninstalls an installation.

TABLE 12.9

Significant Public Events of ServiceProcessInstaller Objects

EVENT	PURPOSE
AfterInstall	Happens after an installation.
AfterRollback	Happens after an installation is rolled back.
AfterUninstall	Happens after an uninstallation.
BeforeInstall	Happens before installation.
BeforeRollback	Happens before installers are rolled back.

TABLE 12.9

Continued

EVENT	PURPOSE
BeforeUninstall	Happens before an uninstallation.
Committed	Happens after all installers have committed installations.
Committing	Happens before installers commit installations.

Working with the ServiceInstaller Class

You use ServiceInstaller objects to install Windows services, and you can find the significant public properties of objects of this class in Table 12.10, their significant methods in Table 12.11, and their significant events in Table 12.12.

TABLE 12.10

Significant Public Properties of ServiceInstaller Objects

PROPERTY	PURPOSE
DisplayName	The display name for this service.
HelpText	Help text for the installers.
Installers	Returns the installers.
Parent	Returns or sets the parent installer.
ServiceName	The name of this service.
ServicesDependedOn	Specifies services that must be running in order to support this service.
StartType	Specifies when to start this service.

TABLE 12.11

Significant Public Methods of ServiceInstaller Objects

METHOD	PURPOSE
Commit	Commits an installation.
Install	Installs the service by writing data to the Registry.
Rollback	Rolls back a service's data written to the Registry.
Uninstall	Uninstalls the service.

TABLE 12.12

Significant Public Methods of ServiceInstaller Objects

EVENT	PURPOSE
AfterInstall	Happens after the installers have installed.
AfterRollback	Happens after the installations are rolled back.
AfterUninstall	Happens after all the installers finish their uninstallations.
BeforeInstall	Happens just before the each installer's Install method runs.
BeforeRollback	Happens before the installers are rolled back.
BeforeUninstall	Happens before the installers uninstall.
Committed	Happens after all the installers commit their installations.
Committing	Happens before the installers commit their installations.

That completes our look at Windows services; next up are Web services.

Creating Web Services

We've seen Windows services, and many people are familiar with them on a day-to-day basis. But what about Web services? They're less familiar than Windows services to most people, but the idea is the same—they're code components—on Web servers this time—that your code can call and that can return data, much as you'd work with a Windows service.

For example, Web services can connect to databases, letting you retrieve data from data sources, and you can connect to Web services from either Windows or Web applications. Using Web services, you can implement custom logic such as performing a credit check before approving a loan. Web services are often used as middle-tier business objects, which work with and transfer data in three-tier data Web applications.

Writing the Web Service

As an example, we're going to create a three-tier data application here. This example is going to use its middle tier—our Web service—to connect to the authors example database and fetch or update data from that database. The lowest tier is a Windows application, the middle tier is our Web service that fetches or updates data on demand (although note you can also implement business rules, such as only returning authors for whom you have books in stock, in the middle tier), and the top tier is the authors database in SQL Server.

This Web service example is named ch02_12. In Web services, you can implement methods callable from Windows or Web applications (and, in fact, from applications running on other platforms as well); in this example, we're going to write two methods: GetAuthors to return a dataset holding the authors table, and UpdateAuthors to update that table as needed.

We're going to use a Windows application to call these Web service methods, and we're going to use a data grid to display the authors table. As long as the user's machine is connected to the Internet, our operations will appear as though they're taking place entirely in the Windows application.

To follow along, create a new Web service project named ch12_02 with File, New, Project, selecting the ASP.NET Web Service icon. Create the new Web service project you see in Figure 12.7.

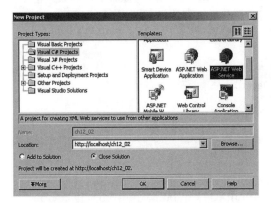

The default name of our new Web service is Service1, and we'll keep that name. The C# code for this service is stored in Service1.asmx.cs, and in that file you'll see that this new Web service is derived from the WebService class:

```
public class Service1 :
System.Web.Services.WebService
{
    public Service1()
    {
        .
        .
        .
```

FIGURE 12.7 A new Web service project.

Because we intend to use the authors database, we'll need to connect to it. As we've done before, drag a SqlDataAdapter object from the toolbox; in this case, drag that object onto the Web service designer. Doing so opens the Data Adapter Configuration Wizard; use that tool to connect the data adapter to the authors table. Finally, use Data, Generate Dataset to create a new dataset class, DataSet1 (no dataset object are created, just the class DataSet1). This is the dataset class we'll use to access the authors table in the Web service. (Alternatively, you can connect and create a dataset in code, storing the connection string in the project's Web.config file.)

How does the Windows application connect to this new Web service? The Web service will expose methods that we'll write, and the Windows application can call those methods after we create a reference to our Web service. To expose methods in a Web service, you use the [WebMethod] attribute. For example, in the GetAuthors method, we want to return a dataset filled with the authors table, so we add this code to Service1.asmx.cs now:

```
[WebMethod]
public DataSet1 GetAuthors()
{
    DataSet1 authors = new DataSet1();
```

```
    sqlDataAdapter1.Fill(authors);
    return authors;
}
```

This code makes the `GetAuthors` method return a dataset object of our new `DataSet1` class that will hold the `authors` table. As you can see, all we need to do is to create a new object of that class and use the data adapter to fill the object before returning it to the calling code.

The `UpdateAuthors` method, which updates the `authors` table when the user makes changes in the data grid, is easy to write. We'll pass this method a dataset holding the changed records in the `authors` table and update the `authors` table using the data adapter's `Update` method like this:

```
[WebMethod]
public DataSet1 UpdateAuthors(DataSet1 UpdatedRecords)
{
    sqlDataAdapter1.Update(UpdatedRecords);
    return UpdatedRecords;
}
```

We've created our two Web methods, `GetAuthors` and `UpdateAuthors`, at this point. To make this Web service available to our Windows application, you can build the Web service now using Build, Build ch12_02 in the IDE. Our Web service is ready for use.

Writing a Windows Application to Connect to Our Web Service

The next step involves writing the Windows application that will call the Web service's `GetAuthors` and `UpdateAuthors` methods. To create this Windows application, add a new Windows Application project to the current solution with File, Add Project, New Project. (This application doesn't have to be part of the current solution to connect to the Web service. You can add a reference to the Web service in any Windows application.)

Select the Windows Application icon in the Add New Project dialog box, name this new Windows application ch12_03, and click OK to create the Windows application as you see in Figure 12.8. Also, make this Windows application the startup project by selecting it in the Solution Explorer and using Project, Set as StartUp Project.

Now that we've created our Windows application, the next step is to connect to the Web service, which you do by adding a Web reference to the Web service. Right-click the ch12_03 entry in the Solution Explorer and select Add Web Reference, opening the Add Web Reference dialog box. This dialog box lists the available Web services. To add a reference to a Web service, you can enter the URL for the service's .VSDISCO (Visual Studio Discovery) file in the Add Web Reference dialog box's Address box. You can also browse to the service by clicking the link in the Add Web Reference dialog box for the server you want and then clicking the name of the service, which is Service1 in this example.

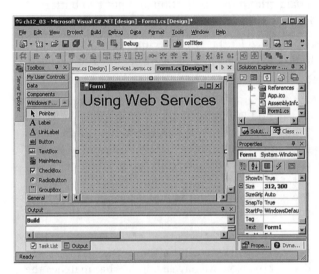

FIGURE 12.8 A new Windows application.

When you select a Web service this way, that Web service appears in the Add Web Reference dialog box, as you see in Figure 12.9, where the Add Web Reference dialog box is displaying the Service1 Web service. To add a Web reference to this service to the Windows application, click the Add Reference button.

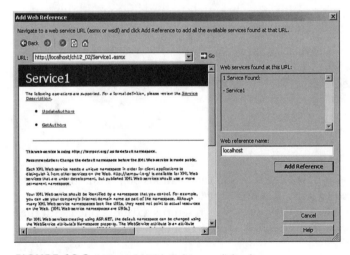

FIGURE 12.9 The Add Web Reference dialog box.

At this point, we have a Web reference to Service1, which means our Windows application will know how to find the GetAuthors and UpdateAuthors methods. To put those methods to work in the Windows application, add a data grid to the application and put two buttons above the data grid with the captions Get Authors and Update Authors.

To handle data from the Web service, we'll need to let the Windows application know about the DataSet1 class in the Web service. To do that, drag a new DataSet object—not a data adapter—from the Data tab of the toolbox to the Windows application. When you do, the Add DataSet dialog box opens.

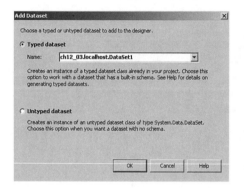

In the Add DataSet dialog box, make sure the Typed Dataset radio button is selected, and select the dataset class in our Web service, DataSet1, from the drop-down list. Note that the fully qualified name of DataSet1 is ch12_03.localhost.DataSet1, which is the way it appears in the Add DataSet dialog box, as shown in Figure 12.10.

To create a new dataset object of the DataSet1 class, dataSet11, click the OK button in the Add DataSet dialog box. Now we have a dataset that matches the DataSet1 class in the Web server, which means we can use that dataset as a repository for the data sent to us from the Web service. We bind dataSet11 to the data grid in the Windows application by setting the data grid's DataSource property to dataSet11, and its DataMember property to authors.

FIGURE 12.10   The Add DataSet dialog box.

We want to fill dataSet11 with data when the user clicks the Get Authors button. When the user clicks that button we'll start by creating an object, service1, of our Web service:

```
private void button1_Click(object sender, System.EventArgs e)
{
    ch12_03.localhost.Service1 service1 = new ch12_03.localhost.Service1();
    .
    .
    .
}
```

Using this new object, service1, you now have access to the methods built into our Web service. For example, if you wanted to fetch data using the GetAuthors method, you just have to call that method like this: service1.GetAuthors(), which returns a dataset filled with the authors table. You can store the data from that dataset in dataSet11 with the Merge method like this:

```
private void button1_Click(object sender, System.EventArgs e)
{
    ch12_03.localhost.Service1 service1 = new ch12_03.localhost.Service1();
    dataSet11.Merge(service1.GetAuthors());
}
```

That's how the process works—you create a new object corresponding to the Web service, much as you would with any reference added to your application. Then you can use that object's methods to call the Web service directly.

Besides the `GetAuthors` method, we can also call the `UpdateAuthors` method when the user clicks the Update Authors button. When the user makes changes in the data grid, those changes are sent to our local dataset. We need to send those changes back to the data store when the user clicks the Update Authors button. You can do that by creating a dataset holding just the changed records using the dataset's `GetChanges` method and the `DataSet` `Merge` method:

```
private void button2_Click(object sender, System.EventArgs e)
{
    ch12_03.localhost.DataSet1 update1 = new ch12_03.localhost.DataSet1();
    update1.Merge(dataSet11.GetChanges());
          .
          .
          .
}
```

We'll call the Web service's `UpdateAuthors` method to update the `authors` table. That method returns the changed records, and we will merge them back into the Windows application's dataset object, making sure those records will no longer be marked as newly changed:

```
private void button2_Click(object sender, System.EventArgs e)
{
    ch12_03.localhost.Service1 service1 = new ch12_03.localhost.Service1();
    ch12_03.localhost.DataSet1 update1 = new ch12_03.localhost.DataSet1();
    update1.Merge(dataSet11.GetChanges());
    dataSet11.Merge(service1.UpdateAuthors(update1));
}
```

Finally, add a data grid to the Windows application and bind it to `dataSet11` to show our results. That completes the code we need for both the Web service and the Windows application that connects to it. Run this example now and click the Get Authors button. When you do, the `authors` table is retrieved from the Web service and displayed in the bound data grid, as you see in Figure 12.11.

FIGURE 12.11   Connecting to a Web service from a Windows application.

In addition, when you edit the data in the data grid and click the Update Authors button, those changes will be sent back to the data store. And that's it—we've created a Web service and connected to that Web service in code from a Windows application. As far as the user is concerned, the whole connection process to the Web service was transparent. Web services like this are great for many uses. Employees out in the field using Web services, for example, can connect immediately to the latest version of the home office's business logic as posted to the Internet.

Working with the WebService Class

As we've seen, the System.Web.Services.WebService class is the base class for Web Services. You can find the significant public properties of objects in the Webservice class in Table 12.13.

TABLE 12.13

Significant Public Properties of Webservice Objects

PROPERTY	PURPOSE
Application	The HTTP Application object for the HTTP request.
Context	The HttpContext object for the HTTP request.
Server	The HttpServerUtility object for the HTTP request.
Session	The HttpSessionState object for the HTTP request.
User	The ASP.NET server User object.

Deploying Your Applications

When you create a .NET application, you can often copy it to another .NET machine simply by copying the .EXE file. On the other hand, installing most real applications isn't that simple; there's usually much more to install than just an .EXE file. You might want to add items to the machine's Start menu, and so on. The best way to install C# applications on .NET machines is to create a Microsoft Installer (.MSI) file, and we'll see how to create such a file here.

To install an application, all you have to do is to copy the .MSI file to the target machine and double-click it. The Microsoft Windows Installer will do the rest, as we'll see. You can also use a setup.exe program, which we'll also create here, to run the .MSI file for you.

Creating a Deployable Application

The IDE lets you create deployment files easily. To see how this works, we're going to create an .MSI file for a Windows application, ch12_04. This super-advanced application displays a message box with the text "Thanks for choosing ch12_04!" when the user clicks a Click Me! button. That's all ch12_04 does:

```
private void button1_Click(object sender, System.EventArgs e)
{
MessageBox.Show("Thanks for choosing ch12_04!");
}
```

This application appears in Figure 12.12 at design time, where you can see the Click Me! button in the main form.

FIGURE 12.12   The ch12_04 application.

To create a deployment package for ch12_04, we'll need an .EXE file for the application, so select Build, Build ch12_04 to create ch12_04.exe. The goal is to create an .MSI file for this application, and to deploy it.

Creating an Installer File

You can create an installer file with a new type of project, a deployment project, which we'll call ch12_05. To create ch12_05 and add it to the current solution (which contains only ch12_04 at the moment), select File, Add Project, New Project, opening the Add New Project dialog box, which you see in Figure 12.13.

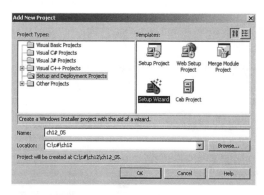

FIGURE 12.13   Creating a deployment project with the Add New Project dialog box.

FIGURE 12.14   The Setup Wizard, first pane.

The ch12_05 project is going to be a deployment project, not a standard C# project, so select the Setup and Deployment Projects folder in the Project Types pane of the Add New Project dialog box, and the Setup Wizard icon in the Templates pane. There are various options for deployment projects, but the Setup Wizard lets you create them in the quickest way. We'll give this new deployment project the name ch12_05, as you see in Figure 12.13. Click OK to open the first pane of the Setup Wizard, as shown in Figure 12.14.

The first pane of the Setup Wizard introduces the wizard; click Next to move to the pane you see in Figure 12.15. As mentioned , the Setup Wizard supports various types of deployment projects, including those for Windows and Web applications. We're going to deploy a Windows application, so select the Create a Setup for a Windows Application radio button.

Click Next to open the third pane in the Setup Wizard, which appears in Figure 12.16.

The third pane lets you specify what files you want to deploy. You can deploy just the application (the check box labeled Primary Output from ch12_04), or the application and its documentation, or just the source code, and so forth. In this example, we will deploy all items for the ch12_04 application, so select all the items, as shown in Figure 12.16.

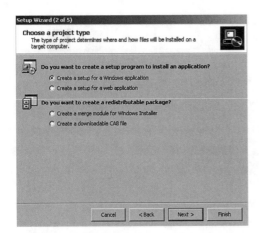

FIGURE 12.15 The Setup Wizard, second pane.

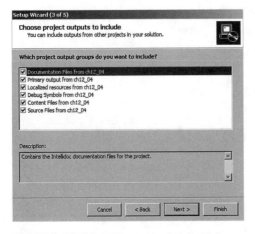

FIGURE 12.16 The Setup Wizard, third pane.

Clicking Next again moves you to the fourth pane of the Setup Wizard, shown in Figure 12.17. In this pane, the Setup Wizard lets you add other files to be deployed, such as additional documentation, license information, contact information, and so on.

In this example we're not going deploy any additional files, so just click the Next button to move to the fifth and final pane of the Setup Wizard, shown in Figure 12.18. This pane of the Setup Wizard summarizes what the wizard will do; click Finish to create the installer file.

Clicking Finish closes the Setup Wizard, and you'll see the file structure of the setup project, as shown in Figure 12.19. It's easy to move files around to different target locations in the user's machine just by dragging them. You can specify the name of the application that the Windows installer displays by setting the setup project's ProductName property, and you can also set the Manufacturer property to the name of your company.

We've now created our deployment project. To create the .MSI file, select Build, Build ch12_05 in the IDE, creating ch12_05.msi. This is our deployment file; all you need to do is to copy it to the target machine. Double-clicking that file on the target machine opens the Windows installer, as you see in Figure 12.20.

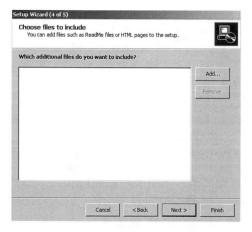

FIGURE 12.17   The Setup Wizard, fourth pane.

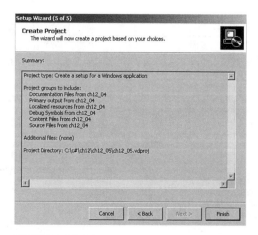

FIGURE 12.18   The Setup Wizard, fifth pane.

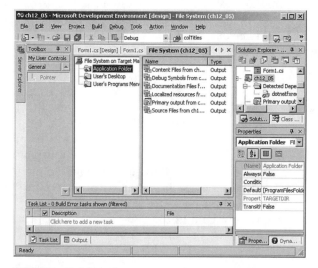

FIGURE 12.19   The setup project in the IDE.

Besides creating the .MSI file, building the deployment project also creates the files setup.exe and setup.ini in the same directory as the .MSI file. If you copy all three files to the target machine and place them in the same directory, the user only has to run setup.exe, which will launch the .MSI file automatically.

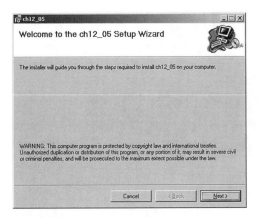

FIGURE 12.20 The Windows installer, first pane.

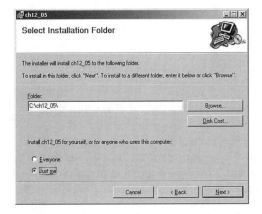

FIGURE 12.21 The Windows installer, second pane.

Click Next in the Windows installer, making its second pane appear, as shown in Figure 12.21. This pane lets you indicate where to install the application.

Clicking Next twice more installs the application, as you see in Figure 12.22. That's it; you've now installed the application, ch12_04, using the installer file ch12_05.msi.

To complete the test, double-click the newly installed ch12_04.exe file, running that application as you see in Figure 12.23.

At this point, we've created a Windows application, an installer for that application, and used the installer to install the application on a target machine. In this case, we installed a Windows application, but the whole process is much the same for Web applications. To create an installer for Web applications, select the Create a Setup for a Web Application option in the second pane of the Setup Wizard.

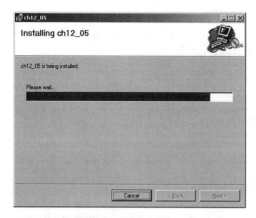

FIGURE 12.22   Installing ch12_04 using the ch12_05 installer project.

FIGURE 12.23   Running ch12_04.

In Brief

In this chapter, we looked at three important topics—Windows services, Web services, and how to deploy applications. Here's an overview of this chapter's topics:

- Windows services run in the background, and you have the option of starting them automatically when the computer starts. These services are typically used to configure device drivers such as those that handle printers, CD creation software, audio devices, and data providers like SQL Server. You can give a Windows service a user interface, which often resembles a control panel that opens when the user clicks or right-clicks a taskbar icon. You can create a taskbar icon with the NotifyIcon control in the IDE's toolbox.

- You can create Windows services in the IDE and the IDE will write much of the C# code you need. Windows services are based on the ServiceBase class. To implement your Windows service, you override various methods of the ServiceBase class, including OnStart and OnStop, to handle Windows service actions.

- To install Windows services, you need an installer for every service you want to install. That involves using both the ServiceProcessInstaller and ServiceInstaller classes in C#.

- You can use a Windows service's StartType property to indicate when the service should start. ServiceStartMode.Automatic means that the service should be started automatically when the computer is booted, ServiceStartMode.Disabled means that it cannot be started, and ServiceStartMode.Manual means that the service can only be started manually (by using the Service Control Manager or by an application).

- You can interact with a Windows service in an application with an object of the `ServiceController` class. You can call the methods of the service using an object of this class.

- Web services expose methods that can be called by other code across the Internet. In C#, Web services are based on the `WebService` class. To expose methods from a Web service, you declare them with the `[WebMethod]` attribute.

- You can call the Web methods of Web services if you first add a Web reference to that service. You can do that by right-clicking a project in the Solution Explorer, selecting Add Web Reference, and browsing to the Web service you want in the Add Web Reference dialog box. When you have a Web reference to a Web service, you create a new object corresponding to that service and call the Web methods of that object.

- To deploy your application, you can create .MSI (Microsoft Installer) files using a setup and deployment project. To create a deployment package for a project, you add a setup and deployment project to the current solution.

- After your setup project has been created, you build it to create the .MSI file you can deploy to target machines (if they're running the .NET Framework). On the target machine, double-click the .MSI file to open it in the Windows installer. Alternatively, you can also use the setup.exe and setup.ini files created by building the deployment project to install the application.

Understanding C# Assemblies and Security

All About Assemblies

The best way to describe an assembly is that it's the fundamental unit of deployable code in the .NET Framework. That may sound awkward, but it's still the best way to describe assemblies. The .EXE and .DLL files you create are assemblies, and each assembly is a collection of files held internally and appearing to the users to be a single file. The term *assembly* was introduced because you can produce deployable code in both EXE and DLL format, and the term assembly covers them both.

Assemblies were also designed to alleviate "DLL Hell," which occurs when a new application loads a new version of a DLL file, overwriting the previous version. Such an action can break earlier applications that relied on the original DLL. Because assemblies maintain version information that can be accessed by the CLR, different versions of an assembly can co-exist side by side without overwriting any resources like DLL files.

Assemblies can contain many files inside them, including resources like image files. The assembly's code is stored in *code modules*, in MSIL format. Although the assemblies you can create with C# in the IDE can only contain a single module, we'll see how to build multi-module assemblies in this chapter (the assemblies you create using C++, not C#, in the IDE can actually produce multi-module assemblies).

We're also going to look at the internal structure of assemblies in this chapter. In fact, to describe their own internal structure, assemblies include metadata in a *manifest*, which describes the assembly and its contents. The manifest describes the types and methods in the assembly, and we're going to get some first-hand knowledge of that in this chapter. The manifest holds the assembly's name, version, a list of the types and the resources in the assembly, and a map connecting the name of a type to its code. There's also a list of the assemblies this assembly references, including the name of the referenced assemblies, their version numbers, their *cultures* (a culture refers to data such as language and text display details), and their creators. Each assembly also has a version number, which labels not only the assembly, but everything in the assembly as well. In other words, all the types in an assembly change version numbers when you change the assembly's version number. Security permissions, which we'll take a look at later in the chapter, are granted on the assembly level.

Internally, assemblies can also have one—but only one—entry point, which calling code will call first. These entry points are WinMain (for Windows EXEs), Main (for standard code like console application EXEs), or DLLMain (for DLLs, usually called if you want to initialize some aspect of the DLL). Assemblies also provide security boundaries—an assembly is the scope boundary for the types it contains and types that cannot cross assembly boundaries. You cannot have a type definition span two assemblies, but you can use a reference to a type in another assembly.

That's all the overview we need for the moment; let's get to some code. In our first example, we'll create an assembly and then take a look at what's inside.

Creating an Assembly

Any .NET EXE or DLL is an assembly, so as soon as we create either of these items, we've created an assembly. In this chapter's first example, we'll do a little more with assemblies than we have in the past; here, we'll set the assembly's version and title using *assembly attributes*. Assembly attributes let you set metadata in an assembly, and these attributes are divided into the following types:

- Assembly identity attributes
- Informational attributes
- Assembly manifest attributes
- Strong name attributes

Table 13.1 lists the assembly identity attributes, Table 13.2 the informational attributes, Table 13.3 the assembly manifest attributes, and Table 13.4 the strong name attributes.

TABLE 13.1

Assembly Identity Attributes

ASSEMBLY IDENTITY ATTRIBUTE	PURPOSE
AssemblyCultureAttribute	Indicates the culture that the assembly supports.
AssemblyFlagsAttribute	Sets various assembly attributes, such as whether the assembly can be run side-by-side.
AssemblyVersionAttribute	Holds assembly version number in the format *major.minor.build.revision,* for example, 1.2.5.0. The CLR uses this value to perform binding operations in assemblies with strong names.

TABLE 13.2

Informational Attributes

INFORMATIONAL ATTRIBUTE	PURPOSE
AssemblyCompanyAttribute	A company name.
AssemblyCopyrightAttribute	Copyright information.
AssemblyFileVersionAttribute	String value specifying the Win32 file version number (usually defaults to the assembly version).
AssemblyInformationalVersionAttribute	Version information that is not used by the CLR.
AssemblyProductAttribute	Product information.
AssemblyTrademarkAttribute	Trademark information.

TABLE 13.3

Assembly Manifest Attributes

ASSEMBLY MANIFEST ATTRIBUTE	PURPOSE
AssemblyConfigurationAttribute	The configuration of the assembly, such as Retail or Debug.
AssemblyDefaultAliasAttribute	A default alias to be used by referencing assemblies. This value provides a human-friendly name when the name of the assembly itself is not human-friendly (such as a GUID value).
AssemblyDescriptionAttribute	Short description of the assembly.
AssemblyTitleAttribute	A human-friendly name for the assembly.

TABLE 13.4

Strong Name Attributes

STRONG NAME ATTRIBUTE	PURPOSE
AssemblyDelaySignAttribute	True if delay signing (with a public key) is being used.
AssemblyKeyFileAttribute	Name of the file that contains the public key (if using delay signing) or both the public and private keys.
AssemblyKeyNameAttribute	Specifies the key container containing the key pair passed to the constructor of this attribute.

You can see our first example in Listing 13.1, where we're setting the assembly's version to 1.0.0.0 and its title to "Example ch13_01". Note that we're using the System.Reflection namespace here to include the predefined assembly attributes.

LISTING 13.1   Using Assembly Attributes (ch13_01.cs)

```
using System;
using System.Reflection;

[assembly:AssemblyVersionAttribute("1.0.0.0")]
[assembly:AssemblyTitleAttribute("Example ch13_01")]

class ch13_01
{
  public static void Main()
  {
    System.Console.WriteLine("No worries!");
  }
}
```

Running ch13_01.exe just displays the text "No worries!" in a console window, but taking a look at the assembly itself is more interesting. To examine the assembly, use the ILDASM tool that comes with Visual Studio, ildasm.exe. (ILDASM is automatically in your path if you use the Visual Studio command prompt. Just select Start, Programs, Microsoft Visual Studio .NET, Visual Studio .NET Tools, Visual Studio .NET Command Prompt.) Use File, Open in this tool to open ch13_01.exe, as you see in Figure 13.1. As you can see in the figure, the Main method appears in our assembly. Double-clicking the MANIFEST entry opens the manifest for the ch13_01 assembly.

Here's what the assembly's manifest looks like. Note in particular that the name of the assembly (given with the .assembly entry) is ch13_01, that we've set the title of the assembly to "Example ch13_01", and that the assembly's version number (given with the .VER entry) is indeed 1.0.0.0:

```
.assembly extern mscorlib
{
 .publickeytoken = (B7 7A 5C 56 19 34 E0 89 )  // .z\V.4...ver 1:0:5000:0
}
.assembly ch13_01
{
 .custom instance void
[mscorlib]System.Reflection.AssemblyTitleAttribute::.ctor(string) =
```

```
( 01 00 0F 45 78 61 6D 70 6C 65 20 63 68 31 33 5F  // ...Example ch13_
30 31 00 00 )                        // 01..
  // --- The following custom attribute is added automatically,
  // do not uncomment -------
  // .custom instance void [mscorlib]
  // System.Diagnostics.DebuggableAttribute::.ctor(bool, bool) =
  // ( 01 00 00 01 00 00 )
  .hash algorithm 0x00008004
  .ver 1:0:0:0
}
.module ch13_01.exe
// MVID: {52521874-3C35-485B-B070-EA321722834D}
.imagebase 0x00400000
.subsystem 0x00000003
.file alignment 512
.corflags 0x00000001
// Image base: 0x07090000
```

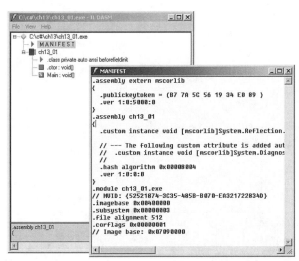

FIGURE 13.1   Using ILDASM on an assembly.

These kinds of assembly attributes are set routinely in Visual Studio projects in the AssemblyInfo.cs file, created automatically for every project that creates an assembly. For example, here's what AssemblyInfo.cs looks like for the ch12_04 project we saw in the previous chapter:

```
using System.Reflection;
using System.Runtime.CompilerServices;

//
// General Information about an assembly is controlled through the following
// set of attributes. Change these attribute values to modify the information
// associated with an assembly.
//
[assembly: AssemblyTitle("")]
[assembly: AssemblyDescription("")]
[assembly: AssemblyConfiguration("")]
[assembly: AssemblyCompany("")]
[assembly: AssemblyProduct("")]
[assembly: AssemblyCopyright("")]
[assembly: AssemblyTrademark("")]
[assembly: AssemblyCulture("")]


//
// Version information for an assembly consists of the following four values:
//
//    Major Version
//    Minor Version
//    Build Number
//    Revision
//
// You can specify all the values or you can default the Revision
// and Build Numbers by using the '*' as shown below:

[assembly: AssemblyVersion("1.0.*")]


//
// In order to sign your assembly you must specify a key to use. Refer to the
// Microsoft .NET Framework documentation for more
// information on assembly signing.
// Use the attributes below to control which key is used for signing.
//
// Notes:
//   (*) If no key is specified, the assembly is not signed.
//   (*) KeyName refers to a key that has been installed in the Crypto Service
//       Provider (CSP) on your machine. KeyFile refers to a file which
//       contains a key.
//   (*) If the KeyFile and the KeyName values are both specified, the
```

```
//    following processing occurs:
//    (1) If the KeyName can be found in the CSP, that key is used.
//    (2) If the KeyName does not exist and the KeyFile does exist, the key
//       in the KeyFile is installed into the CSP and used.
//  (*) In order to create a KeyFile, you can use the
//    sn.exe (Strong Name) utility.
//    When specifying the KeyFile, the location of the KeyFile should be
//    relative to the project output directory which is
//    %Project Directory%\obj\<configuration>. For example, if your KeyFile
//    is located in the project directory, you would specify the
//    AssemblyKeyFile attribute as
//    [assembly: AssemblyKeyFile("..\\..\\mykey.snk")]
//  (*) Delay Signing is an advanced option - see the Microsoft .NET Framework
//    documentation for more information on this.
//
[assembly: AssemblyDelaySign(false)]
[assembly: AssemblyKeyFile("")]
[assembly: AssemblyKeyName("")]
```

Storing Multiple Modules in an Assembly

Assemblies can contain several modules, and we're going to create a multi-module assembly next. An assembly includes a hash code for each module, which is a numeric representation of the module's code used for version verification. The Visual Studio IDE can't create multi-module assemblies for C#, although it can for C++, so we're going to use the command-line compiler, csc, in this example.

This example shows how to link several modules into the same assembly. In this case, we're going to define a string-handling class, ch13_02, in one module, and use it in another. In ch13_02.cs, we'll define the ch13_02 class in a namespace called MultiModule and give that class a property named Text that will hold a string of text:

```
namespace MultiModule
{
  class ch13_02
  {
    string privateText;

    public string Text
    {
      get
```

```
    {
        return privateText;
    }
    set
    {
        privateText = value;
    }
}
    .
    .
    .
```

We'll also give this class a public method, `LowerCase`, which will convert the stored string to lowercase and return it, as you see in Listing 13.2.

LISTING 13.2   Defines the ch13_02 Class (ch13_02.cs)

```csharp
using System;

namespace MultiModule
{
  public class ch13_02
  {
    string privateText;

    public string Text
    {
      get
      {
        return privateText;
      }
      set
      {
        privateText = value;
      }
    }

    public string LowerCase()
    {
      return privateText.ToLower();
    }
  }
}
```

We're going to use `ch13_02` objects in a new module, ch13_03.cs. In this module, we'll use the `MultiModule` namespace and create a new object of the `ch13_02` class named `stringer`:

```
using System;
using MultiModule;

class ch13_03
{
  public static void Main()
  {
    ch13_02 stringer = new ch13_02();
    .
    .
    .
```

Now we can assign the text "`No Worries!`" to the string object's `Text` property and convert that text to lowercase with the `LowerCase` method just before displaying it, as you see in Listing 13.3.

LISTING 13.3   Using the ch13_02 Class (ch13_03.cs)

```
using System;
using MultiModule;

class ch13_03
{
  public static void Main()
  {
    ch13_02 stringer = new ch13_02();
    stringer.Text = "No Worries!";
    Console.WriteLine(stringer.LowerCase());
  }
}
```

We'll also include some manifest information for the assembly we're going to build in a third file, ch13_04.cs, which you can see in Listing 13.4.

LISTING 13.4   Defines the ch13_03 Assembly (ch13_04.cs)

```
using System.Reflection;

[assembly: AssemblyTitle("Example ch13_02")]
[assembly: AssemblyVersion("1.0.0.0")]
```

To compile the first module, ch13_02.cs, use the /t:module switch like this:

```
C:\>csc /t:module ch13_02.cs
```

This creates the file ch13_02.netmodule. The code in ch13_03.cs makes use of the ch13_02 class defined in ch13_02.netmodule, so we'll use the /addmodule switch to include the needed code from ch13_02 when we compile ch13_03:

```
C:\>csc /addmodule:ch13_02.netmodule /t:module ch13_03.cs
```

This creates ch13_03.netmodule. All we need is the final module, created from ch13_04.cs, which holds the manifest information for this assembly:

```
C:\>csc /t:module ch13_04.cs
```

This creates ch13_04.netmodule. To link these modules into one assembly, which we'll call ch13_03.exe (because Main is in ch13_03.cs), you use the assembly linker, al, which comes with Visual Studio, al.exe (where *xxxxxxxxxx* is the .NET version number). Here's how we create our assembly. Note the /main switch, which lets you specify the entry point for the assembly, the /out switch, which lets you name the output file, and the /t:exe switch, which specifies that the type of this assembly is an .EXE file:

```
C:\>al ch13_02.netmodule ch13_03.netmodule ch13_04.netmodule
/main:ch13_03.Main /out:ch13_03.exe /t:exe
```

This links our modules into the same assembly and creates ch13_03.exe. When you run ch13_03.exe, you see that the text is indeed converted to lowercase:

```
C:\>ch13_03
no worries!
```

You can see the three modules we've put into this assembly in the assembly's manifest:

```
.module extern ch13_03.netmodule
.assembly extern mscorlib
{
 .publickeytoken = (B7 7A 5C 56 19 34 E0 89 )        // .z\V.4..
 .hash = (AB 74 A6 A8 1D E6 70 59 FD BE DE D7 9F 2F E3 E4 // .t....pY...../..
     7B 27 2C 18 )                 // {',.
 .ver 1:0:5000:0
}
.assembly ch13_03
{
 // --- The following custom attribute is added automatically,
 // do not uncomment -------
```

```
// .custom instance void
// [mscorlib]System.Diagnostics.DebuggableAttribute::.ctor(bool,
// bool) = ( 01 00 00 01 00 00 )
.custom instance void
[mscorlib]System.Reflection.AssemblyTitleAttribute::.ctor(string) =
( 01 00 0F 45 78 61 6D 70 6C 65 20 63 68 31 33 5F  // ...Example ch13_
  30 32 00 00 )                    // 02..
.hash algorithm 0x00008004
.ver 1:0:0:0
}
.file ch13_02.netmodule
.hash = (18 D5 D4 B6 C8 44 12 C3 82 EB E4 24 75 F1 2D 5C  // .....D.....$u.-\
   4C 4D 8A 49 )                    // LM.I
.file ch13_03.netmodule
.hash = (1A 36 CC F6 E8 B6 5D 5A D9 65 2C 9F 8C 9D D8 F5  // .6....]Z.e,.....
    1C A3 BC AB )
.file ch13_04.netmodule
.hash = (24 D5 92 AC AB 32 33 7C 3B CA D6 18 1B 0B 01 BD  // $....23|;.......
    E6 5A 10 C4 )                   // .Z..
.module ch13_03.exe
// MVID: {9B78128A-5400-4CA1-ADA6-C24F67494F1C}
.imagebase 0x00400000
.subsystem 0x00000003
.file alignment 512
.corflags 0x00000001
// Image base: 0x07090000
```

It's also worth noting that you can load any kind of file into an assembly using the /embed switch. For example, here's how you can include a .JPG file in an assembly.

```
C:\>al ch13_02.netmodule ch13_03.netmodule ch13_04.netmodule
/embed:ch13_03.jpg /main:ch13_03.Main /out:ch13_03.exe /t:exe
```

You can build a DLL instead of an EXE using the /out and /t:library switches like this, which converts ch13_02.cs into ch13_02.dll:

```
C:\>csc /out:ch13_02.dll /t:library ch13_02.cs
Microsoft (R) Visual C# .NET Compiler version xxxxxxxxx
for Microsoft (R) .NET Framework version xxxxxxxxx
Copyright (C) Microsoft Corporation 2001-2002. All rights reserved.
```

You can then add a reference to the ch13_02.dll DLL (instead of the earlier module ch13_02.netmodule) when you compile the file that uses it, ch13_03.cs:

```
C:\>csc /r:ch13_02.dll /t:module ch13_03.cs
Microsoft (R) Visual C# .NET Compiler version xxxxxxxxxx
for Microsoft (R) .NET Framework version xxxxxxxxxx
Copyright (C) Microsoft Corporation 2001-2002. All rights reserved.
```

Now you can link ch13_03.netmodule and ch13_04.netmodule into ch13_03.exe:

```
C:\>al ch13_03.netmodule ch13_04.netmodule /main:ch13_03.Main
/out:ch13_03.exe /t:exe
Microsoft (R) Assembly Linker version xxxxxxxxxx
for Microsoft (R) .NET Framework version xxxxxxxxxx
Copyright (C) Microsoft Corporation 2001-2002. All rights reserved.
```

And that creates ch13_03.exe as before, except that this time, we created and used a DLL. You can make also make use of DLLs like ch13_02.dll in the IDE, and that's coming up next.

Working with DLLs in the IDE

Can you use the ch13_02.dll file in the IDE? Yes. In the IDE, you create a new console project, ch13_05. You then right-click the References node in the Solution Explorer, select the Add Reference menu item, and add a reference to ch13_02.dll. Now you can use the same code as was used in ch13_03.cs to interact with ch13_02.dll in the IDE console project, as you see in Listing 13.5.

LISTING 13.5   Using a DLL (ch13_05.cs)

```
using System;
using MultiModule;

namespace ch13_05
{
  /// <summary>
  /// Summary description for Class1.
  /// </summary>
  class Class1
  {
    /// <summary>
    /// The main entry point for the application.
    /// </summary>
    [STAThread]
    static void Main(string[] args)
    {
```

LISTING 13.5 Continued

```
        ch13_02 stringer = new ch13_02();
        stringer.Text = "No Worries!";
        Console.WriteLine(stringer.LowerCase());
    }
  }
}
```

That's all it takes—now you're using the new DLL in the IDE console application code you see in Listing 13.5. This application runs as before, displaying "No Worries!" in a console window.

You can also create DLLs in the IDE, of course. To do that, create a new project, ch13_06, in the IDE, selecting the Class Library icon in the Templates box, as you see in Figure 13.2.

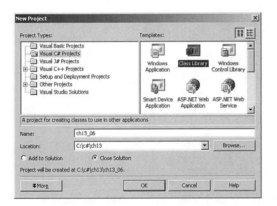

FIGURE 13.2   Creating a new DLL project.

This new project will create a DLL, ch13_06.dll, when you build it. We can make the code in this DLL match the code in our current DLL, ch13_02.dll, by giving the new ch13_06 class a Text property and a LowerCase method, as you see in Listing 13.6.

LISTING 13.6   Creating a DLL (ch13_06.cs)

```
using System;

namespace MultiModule
{
    /// <summary>
    /// Summary description for Class1.
```

LISTING 13.6   Continued

```
/// </summary>

public class ch13_06
{
   string privateText;

   public string Text
   {
      get
      {
         return privateText;
      }
      set
      {
         privateText = value;
      }
   }

   public string LowerCase()
   {
      return privateText.ToLower();
   }
}
}
```

That's all we need; now build ch13_06.dll by choosing Build, Build ch13_06 from the IDE. We can use this new, IDE-built DLL, ch13_06.dll, just as we used our earlier command-line—built DLL, ch13_02.dll. To do that, just open the ch13_05 console project in the IDE, add a reference to ch13_06.dll, and use this code:

```
static void Main(string[] args)
{
   ch13_06 stringer = new ch13_06();
   stringer.Text = "No Worries!";
   Console.WriteLine(stringer.LowerCase());
}
```

So far, the assemblies we've been creating are *private assemblies,* used by only one application. Even the DLLs we've created are intended to be stored in an application's directory structure and used by only one application. But you can also create *shared assemblies,* which can be used by multiple applications.

Creating Shared Assemblies

Usually, assemblies are private, which means they are meant to be used by only one application. But you might have a DLL intended for use by several applications, in which case you could make it shared.

Shared assemblies are stored in the *Global Assembly Cache* (GAC), and you'll find familiar assemblies like System and System.Data there. Assemblies in the GAC are usually DLLs, and applications share access to these assemblies. Note that you *should not* place assemblies in the GAC unless there is a pressing reason to do so, and you're using those assemblies in multiple applications. It's a very bad idea to fill up the GAC for no good reason.

You can see the GAC in several ways. You can select Start, Programs, Administrative Tools, Microsoft .NET Framework 1.1 Configuration to open the .NET Configuration 1.1 tool, select the Assembly Cache node, and click the View List of Assemblies in the Assembly Cache link to see the GAC. Or you can simply browse to the c:\WINNT\Assembly folder in the Windows Explorer, which will turn the Windows Explorer into a GAC viewer, as you see in Figure 13.3.

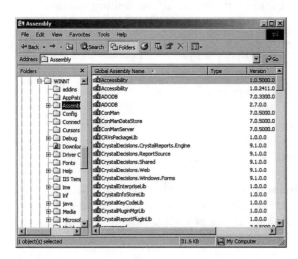

FIGURE 13.3   The Global Assembly Cache.

To share an assembly, you add it to the GAC. And to do that, you must sign it with a *strong name*.

Signing Assemblies with Strong Names

Shared assemblies use strong names, based on public key encryption. Signing an assembly with a strong name ensures that the assembly can't be tampered with, and relies on both a public and a private key; you encrypt data with the private key, and people can use the public key to decrypt that data so they can be sure the assembly has not been tampered with.

You can create a public/private key pair to sign an assembly with the sn tool, sn.exe. For example, here's how you might create such a pair and store them in a file named key.snk:

```
C:\>sn -k key.snk

Microsoft (R) .NET Framework Strong Name Utility Version xxxxxxxxx
Copyright (C) Microsoft Corporation 1998-2002. All rights reserved.

Key pair written to key.snk
```

This gives you the key pair you need to sign an assembly. You can sign an assembly with a strong name in the IDE by opening the assembly's AssemblyInfo.cs file and finding this line:

```
[assembly: AssemblyKeyFile("")]
```

To use our key pair file key.snk, change this line to point to that file, something like this:

```
[assembly: AssemblyKeyFile("C:\\c#\\ch13\\key.snk")]
```

At the command line, you can use the /keyfile switch like this to sign an assembly with a strong name:

```
C:\>al ch13_03.netmodule ch13_04.netmodule /main:ch13_03.Main
/out:ch13_03.exe /t:exe /keyfile:key.snk
Microsoft (R) Assembly Linker version xxxxxxxxx
for Microsoft (R) .NET Framework version xxxxxxxxx
Copyright (C) Microsoft Corporation 2001-2002. All rights reserved.
```

You can check if an assembly has been signed with a strong name with the sn -T switch (note that the switches you use with sn are case-sensitive. sn -T is not the same as sn -t). Here, for example, we can see that signing ch13_06.dll has given it the public key token (which is an abbreviated form of the public key) 1b525656c70396e6:

```
C:\>sn -T ch13_06.dll

Microsoft (R) .NET Framework Strong Name Utility Version xxxxxxxxx
Copyright (C) Microsoft Corporation 1998-2002. All rights reserved.

Public key token is 1b525656c70396e6
```

SHOP TALK

USING CERTIFICATE AUTHORITIES

Signing an assembly with a strong name isn't enough if you're going to distribute the assembly commercially on the Internet (as when you create a .CAB file for download). If you've worked in a commercial environment that creates code modules for distribution on the Web, you know that you usually want a true digital certificate (from certificate authorities like www.verisign.com or www.thawte.com, which charge fees) before distributing those modules. Signing an assembly with a strong name isn't enough in such cases—that kind of signature shows that the assembly hasn't been tampered with, but you need to *code sign* your assemblies to indicate who built it, using a digital certificate. Once again, security on the Internet was the big issue. Microsoft's partial answer for developers who wanted to sign their own code was to introduce Microsoft *Authenticode*, which lets you code sign your own .CAB, .CTL, .DLL, .EXE, and .OCX files. Visual Studio comes with code signing tools: You use the Certificate Creation Tool, makecert.exe, to create your own digital certificate. You then convert that certificate into a Software Publisher's Certificate (SPC) with the cert2spc.exe tool. You can check the code signature on an assembly by trying to download it in Internet Explorer, or with the with chktrust.exe tool that comes with Visual Studio. Finally, you can use the SignCode tool to actually code sign your assembly. Note that signing your assemblies using your own certificates won't be as well respected as those from the larger companies like VeriSign. If you're going to release code for downloading on the Internet, I'd recommend getting a digital certificate from one of the well-known certification companies.

Signing the assembly, ch13_06.dll, with a strong name means we can add it to the GAC, which we'll do next.

Adding Assemblies to the Global Assembly Cache

There are several ways to add an assembly to the GAC. You can use the gacutil.exe tool with the /i switch to install ch13_06.dll in the GAC. You do so like this:

```
C:\>gacutil /i ch13_06.dll

Microsoft (R) .NET Global Assembly Cache Utility. Version xxxxxxxxxx
Copyright (C) Microsoft Corporation 1998-2002. All rights reserved.

Assembly successfully added to the cache
```

You can also select Start, Programs, Administrative Tools, Microsoft .NET Framework 1.1 Configuration to open the .NET Configuration 1.1 tool, select the Assembly Cache node, and then click the Add an Assembly to the Assembly Cache link. Then you browse to the assembly and click the Open button.

The easiest way, however, is to simply drag the assembly into the WINNT\Assembly directory in the Windows Explorer. After you've added an assembly to the GAC, you can see it in the GAC viewer, as you see in Figure 13.4. Note that this assembly's public key token, 1b525656c70396e6, also appears in the GAC viewer, as for the other assemblies in the GAC.

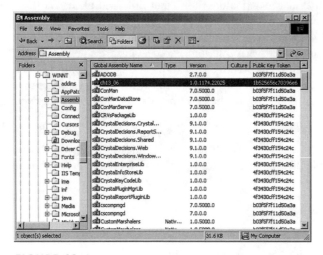

FIGURE 13.4   Adding an assembly to the Global Assembly Cache.

Now that you've added ch13_06.dll to the GAC, you can share it between assemblies, much like System.dll or System.Data.dll, which come with .NET—no longer is this DLL purely local. To delete ch13_06.dllfrom the GAC, right-click it and select the Delete item, or use the /uf switch with gacutil.exe: gacutil /uf ch13_06.dll.

Now it's time to turn to another important topic—security.

Implementing Security in C#

One of the important aspects of programming assemblies is to understand and handle security. Security is an increasingly important issue to Microsoft so we'll take a look at this issue in the rest of this chapter, starting with using pointers in C#.

Using Pointers

You can use pointers in C++, but not in C# by default. If you're a C++ programmer, you know that a pointer holds the address and type of a programming entity, such as a variable or a method. Pointers are a problem if you're trying to be secure, because hackers can sometimes use them to point and modify various locations in your code far beyond your original intentions. (On the day of this writing, for example, Microsoft just issued a patch for all Windows versions back to Windows 98 for a "critical security issue" in Microsoft Outlook and Internet Explorer having to do with a security hole that can be exploited by hackers using pointers to access code past the data buffers they were intended for.) For that reason, Java doesn't even support pointers. C# doesn't support them by default (and it's best not to if security is an issue), but you can use them if you work with the unsafe and fixed keywords.

Here's an example, ch13_07.cs. In this case, we'll use pointers to copy five integers from one byte buffer to another in our code. We start by creating our byte buffers, Source and Target, and placing five integers into Source:

```
static void Main(string[] args)
{
  byte[] Source = new byte[20];
  byte[] Target = new byte[20];

  for(int loopIndex = 0; loopIndex < 5; ++loopIndex)
  {
    Source[loopIndex] = (byte) loopIndex;
  }
  .
  .
  .
```

Each integer in Source is four bytes long, so we will copy the data in Source to Target in four-byte chunks. You can use pointers only in a context marked *unsafe* in C#. You can mark a type or class member unsafe using the keyword unsafe, so we'll use that keyword in the declaration of the Main method here, indicating that we're going to use pointers in that method.

You also need a fixed statement, because you can only work with pointers inside that statement in C#. In this example, we're going to create two pointers, one to point to the source buffer and one to the target. You use the fixed statement to fix pointers in memory so that the garbage collector doesn't automatically move them behind your back. You pass the pointers you want to fix to the fixed statement, which makes those pointers read-only. On the other hand, we need pointers we can write to, so inside the fix statement we'll copy those read-only pointers to read/write pointers and copy our data from Source to Target like this:

```
static unsafe void Main(string[] args)
{
  byte[] Source = new byte[20];
  byte[] Target = new byte[20];

  for(int loopIndex = 0; loopIndex < 5; ++loopIndex)
  {
    Source[loopIndex] = (byte) loopIndex;
  }

  fixed (byte* pSourceFixed = Source, pTargetFixed = Target)
  {
  byte* pSource = pSourceFixed;
  byte* pTarget = pTargetFixed;

    for (int loopIndex = 0 ; loopIndex < 20 ; loopIndex++)
    {
      *((int*)pTarget) = *((int*)pSource);
      pSource += 4;
      pTarget += 4;
    }
  }
    .
    .
    .
```

All that's left is to display the integers copied into the Target buffer, and you can see how that works in Listing 13.7.

LISTING 13.7   Using Pointers (ch13_07.cs)

```
class ch13_07
{
  static unsafe void Main(string[] args)
  {
    byte[] Source = new byte[20];
    byte[] Target = new byte[20];

    for(int loopIndex = 0; loopIndex < 5; ++loopIndex)
    {
      Source[loopIndex] = (byte) loopIndex;
    }
```

LISTING 13.7 Continued

```
    fixed (byte* pSourceFixed = Source, pTargetFixed = Target)
    {
      byte* pSource = pSourceFixed;
      byte* pTarget = pTargetFixed;

      for (int loopIndex = 0 ; loopIndex < 20 ; loopIndex++)
      {
        *((int*)pTarget) = *((int*)pSource);
        pSource += 4;
        pTarget += 4;
      }
    }

    for(int loopIndex = 0; loopIndex < 5; ++loopIndex)
    {
      System.Console.Write(Target[loopIndex] + " ");
    }
  }
}
```

When you compile this example, ch13_07.cs, you must use the /unsafe switch:

```
C:\>csc /unsafe ch13_07.cs
```

And that's it. You've used pointers in a C# program. When you run the program, you see that the integers were indeed copied over from Source to Target:

```
C:>ch13_07
0 1 2 3 4
```

One place where pointers are essential is when you have to call a Windows API function that uses them. To interact with Windows API functions directly in C#, you can use the [DllImport] attribute to indicate where the program can find those functions. For example, to import that Windows API function CreateFile, which is in the Windows system DLL kernel32.dll, you can use this code in a .CS file, but outside any method (make sure to include System.Runtime.InteropServices as well, as shown here):

```
using System.Runtime.InteropServices;

[DllImport("kernel32", SetLastError=true)]
static extern unsafe IntPtr CreateFile(
string FileName,
```

```
uint DesiredAccess,
uint ShareMode,
uint SecurityAttributes,
uint CreationDisposition,
uint FlagsAndAttributes,
int hTemplateFile
);
```

After importing `CreateFile`, you can call it to create a Windows file handle for a new file like this:

```
const uint GENERIC_READ = 0x80000000;
const uint OPEN_EXISTING = 3;
IntPtr handle;
handle = CreateFile(FileName, GENERIC_READ, 0, 0, OPEN_EXISTING, 0, 0);
```

You can use a Windows file handle like this to read from a file, using the `ReadFile` API function. To call that function, you need to pass a pointer to the data buffer you want filled with data and a pointer to an integer which will hold the number of bytes read:

```
[DllImport("kernel32", SetLastError=true)]
static extern unsafe bool ReadFile(
IntPtr hFile,
void* pBuffer,
int NumberOfBytesToRead,
int* pNumberOfBytesRead,
int Overlapped
);
```

That means you should call `ReadFile` in an unsafe context, as in this method:

```
public unsafe int Reader(byte[] buffer, int index, int count)
{
  int number = 0;
  fixed (byte* p = buffer)
  {
    if (!ReadFile(handle, p + index, count, &number, 0))
    return 0;
  }
  return number;
}
```

Setting Security Permissions

You can grant or deny access to assemblies using *permissions*. There are three kinds of permissions, each with a specific purpose:

- Code access permissions represent access to a protected resource or the capability to perform a protected operation.

- Identity permissions indicate that code has credentials that support a particular kind of identity.

- Role-based security permissions indicate whether a user has a particular identity or is a member of a specified role.

Code access permissions are used to protect resources and operations from unauthorized use. All code access permissions can be requested or demanded in code, and the runtime decides which permissions, if any, to grant the code. You can see the code access permissions in Table 13.5.

TABLE 13.5

Code Access Permissions

PERMISSION CLASS	PERMISSION
DirectoryServicesPermission	Allows access to the System.DirectoryServices classes.
DnsPermission	Allows access to Domain Name System (DNS).
EnvironmentPermission	Allows reading or writing of environment variables.
EventLogPermission	Allows read or write access to event log services.
FileDialogPermission	Allows access to files that have been selected by the user in an Open dialog box.
FileIOPermission	Allows code to read, append, or write files or directories.
IsolatedStorageFilePermission	Allows access to private virtual file systems.
IsolatedStoragePermission	Allows access to isolated storage.
MessageQueuePermission	Allows access to message queues through the managed Microsoft Message Queuing (MSMQ) interfaces.
OleDbPermission	Allows access to databases using OLE DB.
PerformanceCounterPermission	Allows access to performance counters.
PrintingPermission	Allows access to printers.
ReflectionPermission	Allows access to information about a type at runtime.
RegistryPermission	Allows the code to read, write, create, or delete Registry keys and values.
SecurityPermission	Allows the code to execute, assert permissions, call into unmanaged code, skip verification, and so on.
ServiceControllerPermission	Allows access to running or stopped services.

TABLE 13.5

Continued

PERMISSION CLASS	PERMISSION
SocketPermission	Allows access to sockets.
SqlClientPermission	Allows access to SQL databases.
UIPermission	Allows access to user interface functionality.
WebPermission	Allows the code to use connections on a Web address.

Identity permissions hold characteristics that identify an assembly. The CLR grants identity permissions to an assembly based on the information it discovers about the assembly. For example, one identity permission represents the strong name an assembly must have, another represents the Web site where the code must have come from, and so on. You can see the identity permissions in Table 13.6.

TABLE 13.6

Identity Permissions

PERMISSION CLASS	IDENTITY
PublisherIdentityPermission	Permission based on the software publisher's digital signature.
SiteIdentityPermission	Permission based on the Web site where the code came from.
StrongNameIdentityPermission	Permission based on the strong name of the assembly.
URLIdentityPermission	Permission based on the URL where the code came from.
ZoneIdentityPermission	Permission based on the zone where the code originated.

There are also role-based permissions, and roles are groups of users. At this point, the PrincipalPermission class is the only role-based security permission supplied by the .NET Framework class library. PrincipalPermission is a security permission that you can use to determine whether a user has a given identity or is a member of a given group.

We'll take a look using code access permissions in the following few examples.

Asking for Minimum Permission

In our first example, ch13_08.cs, we'll simply request the minimum file I/O permissions that this application needs to run. To request code access permissions for the assembly, you use an assembly attribute, [assembly:FileIOPermissionAttribute] in your code. In this case, we'll request permission to read and write files in a directory named c:\ch13_08, as you see in ch13_08.cs in Listing 13.8.

LISTING 13.8   Requesting Minimum Code Access Permissions (ch13_08.cs)

```
using System;
using System.IO;
using System.Security.Permissions;

[assembly:FileIOPermissionAttribute(SecurityAction.RequestMinimum,
 All="c:\\ch13_08")]

class ch13_08
{
  public static void Main()
  {
    FileStream filestream = File.Create("c:\\ch13_08\\ch13_08.txt");
    StreamWriter streamwriter = new StreamWriter(filestream);
    streamwriter.WriteLine("No worries!");
    streamwriter.Flush();
    streamwriter.Close();
  }
}
```

When you run ch13_08.exe, it'll create a file named ch13_08.txt with the text "No worries!" in it. So far so good—now how about restricting what permissions you can get for ch13_08.exe in code? To do that, you can use *code groups*.

Restricting Permission with Code Groups

When you create a code group, you act as an administrator, defining permissions for various assemblies. If an assembly is part of a code group, the code group grants the assembly a set of permissions that has been given to that code group. For example, we'll see how to add our ch13_08.exe application to a code group and restrict its permissions now.

How can you add assemblies to a code group? You do that by specifying the *membership condition* for the group; any code that meets the membership condition is included in the group (each code group has just one membership condition). You can see the possible membership conditions in Table 13.7.

TABLE 13.7

Membership Conditions

MEMBERSHIP CONDITION	MEANING
All code	Membership matches all code.
Application directory	Membership matches the application's installation directory.
Cryptographic hash	Membership matches an MD5, SHA1, or other cryptographic hash.
Software publisher	Membership matches the public key of a valid Authenticode signature.
Site membership	Membership matches the HTTP, HTTPS, and FTP site from which code came.
Strong name	Membership matches a cryptographically strong signature.
URL	Membership matches the URL from which the code came.
Zone	Membership matches the zone from where the code came.

After an assembly is identified as part of a code group, it is granted the permissions in the code groups' associated *permission set*. You can use any of the built-in permission sets with a code group—Nothing, Execution, FullTrust, Internet, LocalIntranet, and SkipVerification—or you can create your own permission set.

To see how all this works, we'll take a look at creating a code group now to see how to restrict the security example we just wrote, ch13_08.exe. We'll use the .NET Framework Configuration tool for this purpose. Select Start, Programs, Administrative Tools, Microsoft .NET Framework 1.1 Configuration to open the configuration manager, as shown in Figure 13.5.

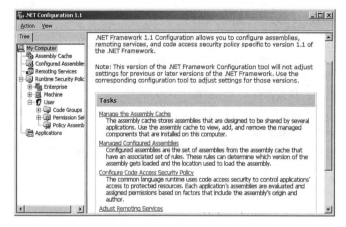

FIGURE 13.5   The .NET Framework Configuration tool.

Expand the Runtime Security Policy node in the .NET Framework Configuration tool, and then the User node, and then the Permission Sets node to see the available pre-built permission sets for the current user: Nothing, Execution, FullTrust, Internet, LocalIntranet, and SkipVerification. We're going to create a new permission set here to deny assemblies file I/O access, so right-click the Everything permission set now and select Duplicate to create a copy of that permission set, which will be called Copy of Everything.

Select the Copy of Everything permission set and click the Rename Permission Set link in the right pane of the configuration tool. Change the name of this permission set to No Files and click OK, creating the new No Files permission set you see in Figure 13.6.

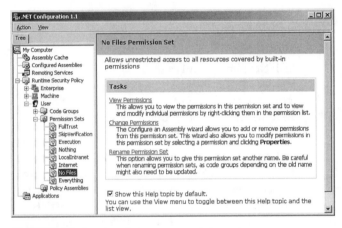

FIGURE 13.6   Creating a new permission set.

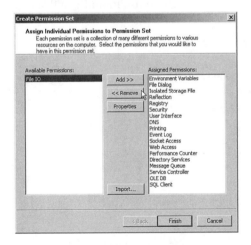

FIGURE 13.7   Changing a permission set's permissions.

To set the permissions for this new permission set, click the Change Permissions link in the right pane of the configuration tool to open the Create Permission Set dialog box you see in Figure 13.7. Select the File IO permission and click the Remove button, as you see in the figure, and then click Finish. At this point, our new permission set has all the standard permissions in it except File I/O.

To create a new code group with this permission set, expand the Code Groups folder and click the All Code group, and then click the Add a Child Group link to open the Create Code Group dialog box you see in Figure 13.8. Because we're only going to restrict ch13_08.exe here, name the new code group ch13_08 and click Next.

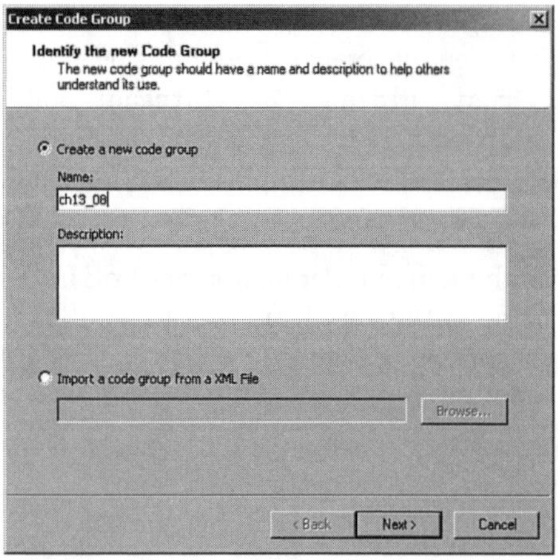

FIGURE 13.8   Creating a code group.

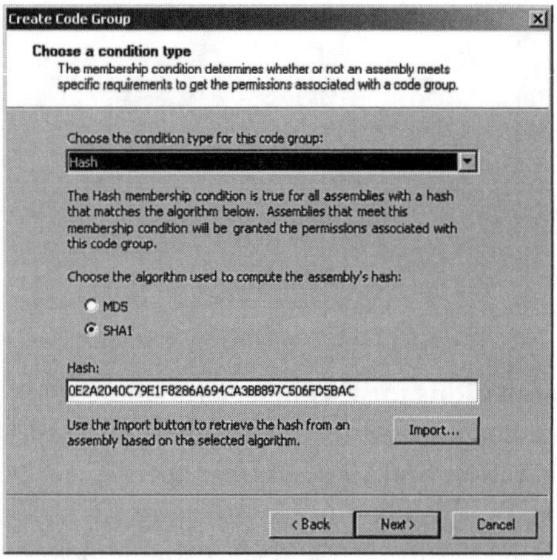

FIGURE 13.9   Identifying an assembly.

To identify the ch13_08.exe assembly, we'll use a hash membership condition in this code group. Select Hash in the Choose the Condition Type for this Code Group drop-down list, and then click SHA1 as the type of hash. Click the Import button, browse to ch13_08.exe, and click Open. This will display the hash used to identify ch13_08.exe in the Create Code Group dialog box, as you see in Figure 13.9. Now we've created a new code group that will contain only one assembly, ch13_08.exe.

Now click Next to specify the permission set for this new code group. In this case, select the No Files permission set as you see in Figure 13.10.

Click Next and then Finish to create the new code group, ch13_08. To make this code group active, right-click the code group now and select the Properties item to open the ch13_08 Properties dialog box you see in Figure 13.11.

Click the top check box in the ch13_08 Properties dialog box, labeled "This policy level will only have the permissions from the permission set associated with this code group" and click OK. This restricts the permissions available to ch13_08.exe so that it can't execute any file I/O operations. You can see how that works now—try to run it, and you'll see this error:

```
C:\>ch13_08
```

```
Unhandled Exception: System.Security.Policy.
PolicyException:
Required permissions cannot be acquired.
```

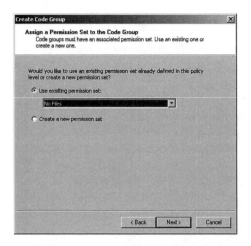

FIGURE 13.10   Specifying a permission set.

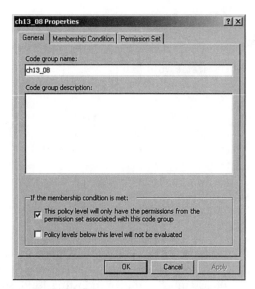

FIGURE 13.11   The ch13_08 Properties dialog box.

In this way, we've created a code group with one assembly in it, assigned the code group a custom permission set, and restricted the actions the assembly can take. As you can see, security in .NET is real, and you can use it to control assemblies as you want.

Making Permission Levels Optional

Our permission example requested minimum permissions that it needed to run, but you can also request optional permissions that you would like but don't need. You can see how this works in Listing 13.9, where we've modified ch13_08.cs to ask for File I/O to the directory c:\ch13_08 if it can get it.

LISTING 13.9   Requesting Optional Code Access Permissions (ch13_08.cs, Second Version)

```
using System;
using System.IO;
using System.Security.Permissions;

[assembly:FileIOPermissionAttribute(SecurityAction.RequestOptional,

All="c:\\ch13_08")]
```

LISTING 13.9 Continued

```
class ch13_08
{
  public static void Main()
  {

    FileStream filestream = File.Create("c:\\ch13_08\\ch13_08.txt");
    StreamWriter streamwriter = new StreamWriter(filestream);
    streamwriter.WriteLine("No worries!");
    streamwriter.Flush();
    streamwriter.Close();
  }
}
```

Unfortunately, we've denied file I/O permission to ch13_08.exe (although you'll have to update the code group's hash that it uses to identify ch13_08.exe after modifying the ch13_08 assembly as shown in Listing 13.9), so this new version of ch13_08.exe won't run. But in this case, the code won't automatically simply halt—you can handle this problem with a try/catch block in your code and recover from it, because you've indicated that this permission request is optional.

Requesting a Permission Set

In fact, evenif your assembly isn't part of a code group, you can request that it be assigned one of the pre-built permission sets, Nothing, Execution, FullTrust, Internet, LocalIntranet, or SkipVerification, using PermissionSetAttribute. For example, the code in Listing 13.10 is requesting Internet permission.

LISTING 13.10 Requesting Permission Sets (ch13_08.cs, Third Version)

```
using System;
using System.IO;
using System.Security.Permissions;

[assembly:PermissionSetAttribute(SecurityAction.RequestMinimum,
 Name="Internet")]

class ch13_08
{
  public static void Main()
  {
    FileStream filestream = File.Create("c:\\ch13_08\\ch13_08.txt");
```

LISTING 13.10   Continued

```
    StreamWriter streamwriter = new StreamWriter(filestream);
    streamwriter.WriteLine("No worries!");
    streamwriter.Flush();
    streamwriter.Close();
  }
}
```

Requiring Permission Levels

To maintain security, you can also require that code calling your assembly meets certain minimum permission levels. The code in Listing 13.11 shows how this works, where we're requiring that code linking to ours has unrestricted File I/O permission. Note that you require this type of permission on the class or method level, not on the assembly level (which would use an assembly attribute).

LISTING 13.11   Requiring Permission Levels (ch13_08.cs, Fourth Version)

```
using System;
using System.IO;
using System.Security.Permissions;

[FileIOPermissionAttribute(SecurityAction.LinkDemand, Unrestricted=true)]
class ch13_08
{
  public static void Main()
  {
    FileStream filestream = File.Create(@"c:\\ch13_08\\ch13_08.txt");
    StreamWriter streamwriter = new StreamWriter(filestream);
    streamwriter.WriteLine("No worries!");
    streamwriter.Flush();
    streamwriter.Close();
  }
}
```

Encrypting Files

Our last security topic in this chapter will cover how to encrypt and decrypt data files using the Triple Data Encryption Standard (DES) algorithm. This algorithm is supported in the FCL with the TripleDESCryptoServiceProvider class; when you encrypt data, you use an encryption key and an initialization vector, both of which can be handled as byte arrays, and you use them later as well to decrypt that data.

Here's how it works. You first create a `CryptoStream` stream and then configure it. Then you can pass that stream to a `StreamReader` or `StreamWriter` constructor and work with standard stream readers or stream writers.

Here's an example, ch13_09.cs in the code for this book. In this example, we'll encrypt the text `"No worries!"` and write it out to disk, and then read it back in with the decryption example coming up, ch13_10.cs. We first create a new `CryptoStream` object using the `CreateEncryptor` method of the `TripleDESCryptoServiceProvider` class. You can pass a specific encryption key and an initialization vector to the `CreateEncryptor` method if you want. However, if you don't want to—and we won't here—`CreateEncryptor` creates a random encryption key and an initialization vector for you. After creating our `CryptoStream` object, we'll pass it to a `StreamWriter` constructor. Then we'll use the stream writer to write the text `"No worries!"` to an encrypted file, secret.dat:

```
public static void Main()
{
  TripleDESCryptoServiceProvider cyptoProvider =
    new TripleDESCryptoServiceProvider();

  FileStream fileStream = File.Create("c:\\c#\\ch13\\secret.dat");

  CryptoStream cryptoStream = new
    CryptoStream(fileStream, cyptoProvider.CreateEncryptor(),
    CryptoStreamMode.Write);

  StreamWriter streamWriter = new StreamWriter(cryptoStream);

  streamWriter.WriteLine("No worries!");
  streamWriter.Close();
    .
    .
    .
```

The decrypting program needs the encryption key and an initialization vector, so we'll store those in a separate file, secret.key, as you see in ch13_09.cs, Listing 13.12.

LISTING 13.12   Encrypting Data (ch13_09.cs)

```
using System.IO;
using System.Security.Cryptography;

class ch13_09
{
  public static void Main()
```

LISTING 13.12 Continued

```
    {
        TripleDESCryptoServiceProvider cyptoProvider =
          new TripleDESCryptoServiceProvider();

        FileStream fileStream = File.Create("c:\\c#\\ch13\\secret.dat");

        CryptoStream cryptoStream = new
          CryptoStream(fileStream, cyptoProvider.CreateEncryptor(),
          CryptoStreamMode.Write);

        StreamWriter streamWriter = new StreamWriter(cryptoStream);

        streamWriter.WriteLine("No worries!");
        streamWriter.Close();

fileStream = File.Create("c:\\c#\\ch13\\secret.key");

        BinaryWriter binaryWriter = new BinaryWriter(fileStream);

        binaryWriter.Write(cyptoProvider.Key);
        binaryWriter.Write(cyptoProvider.IV);
        binaryWriter.Close();

        System.Console.WriteLine("Data encrypted, key stored.");
    }
}
```

When you run ch13_09.cs, you'll see the message "Data encrypted, key stored." and the files secret.dat and secret.key will be created. If you take a look at secret.dat, all you'll see is gibberish:

```
C:\>type secret.dat
∞_^``bET&:_,<=
```

Now it's time to decrypt that gibberish.

Decrypting Files

At this point, we have an encrypted file, secret.dat, and a file holding our encryption key and initialization vector (only the people authorized to do the encrypting and decrypting should have access to the encryption key and an initialization vector). To decrypt secret.dat, we need the encryption key (24 bytes) and initialization vector (8 bytes) from secret.key; we can read them in using a BinaryReader and assign them to a TripleDESCryptoServiceProvider object's Key and IV properties like this:

```
public static void Main()
{
  TripleDESCryptoServiceProvider cyptoProvider =
    new TripleDESCryptoServiceProvider();

  FileStream fileStream = File.OpenRead("c:\\c#\\ch13\\secret.key");

  BinaryReader binaryReader = new BinaryReader(fileStream);

  cyptoProvider.Key = binaryReader.ReadBytes(24);
  cyptoProvider.IV = binaryReader.ReadBytes(8);
    .
    .
    .
```

Now we can create a new CryptoStream object and use that object to create a StreamReader object to read in the encrypted data:

```
public static void Main()
{
  TripleDESCryptoServiceProvider cyptoProvider =
    new TripleDESCryptoServiceProvider();

  FileStream fileStream = File.OpenRead("c:\\c#\\ch13\\secret.key");

  BinaryReader binaryReader = new BinaryReader(fileStream);

  cyptoProvider.Key = binaryReader.ReadBytes(24);
  cyptoProvider.IV = binaryReader.ReadBytes(8);

  fileStream = File.OpenRead("c:\\c#\\ch13\\secret.dat");

  CryptoStream cryptoStream = new
    CryptoStream(fileStream, cyptoProvider.CreateDecryptor(),
    CryptoStreamMode.Read);

  StreamReader streamReader = new StreamReader(cryptoStream);
    .
    .
    .
```

All that's left is to read in the encrypted data, which will be decrypted automatically, and to display the resulting text, as you see in ch13_10.cs, Listing 13.13.

LISTING 13.13   Decrypting Data (ch13_10.cs)

```
using System.IO;
using System.Security.Cryptography;

class ch13_10
{
  public static void Main()
  {
    TripleDESCryptoServiceProvider cyptoProvider =
      new TripleDESCryptoServiceProvider();

    FileStream fileStream = File.OpenRead("c:\\c#\\ch13\\secret.key");

    BinaryReader binaryReader = new BinaryReader(fileStream);

    cyptoProvider.Key = binaryReader.ReadBytes(24);
    cyptoProvider.IV = binaryReader.ReadBytes(8);

    fileStream = File.OpenRead("c:\\c#\\ch13\\secret.dat");

    CryptoStream cryptoStream = new
      CryptoStream(fileStream, cyptoProvider.CreateDecryptor(),
      CryptoStreamMode.Read);

    StreamReader streamReader = new StreamReader(cryptoStream);

    System.Console.WriteLine(streamReader.ReadLine());

    streamReader.Close();
  }
}
```

Here's what you see when you run ch13_10.cs. As you can see, we've been able to recover our encrypted data:

```
C:\c#\ch13>ch13_10
No worries!
```

And that's it—now we're using encryption and decryption.

In Brief

In this chapter, we looked at assemblies and security issues. Here's an overview of the topics:

- Assemblies are the fundamental unit of deployment, security, and versioning in C#. A great deal of metadata about the assembly can be found in the assembly's manifest. You can set assembly attributes, such as `AssemblyVersionAttribute`, in code. Assemblies are .EXE or .DLL files.

- You can store multiple modules in the same assembly using the assembly linker, al.exe. You can't create multi-module assemblies using C# in the IDE yet.

- Shared assemblies must have a strong name, and they can be stored in the Global Assembly Cache (GAC). You can generate strong names with the sn tool, and you can add assemblies to the GAC with the gacutil tool, or by dragging them into the `WINNT\Assembly` folder in the Windows Explorer.

- To use pointers in a C# application, you need to use the `unsafe` and `fixed` keywords. You also need to compile them with the `/unsafe` switch.

- You can set permission levels for assemblies with the .NET Framework Configuration tool, creating code groups and assigning them permission sets.

- You can encrypt data using the `TripleDESCryptoServiceProvider` class. When you encrypt data, you use an encryption key and an initialization vector, both of which are used later to decrypt that data. You can create a `CryptoStream` stream and pass it to `StreamReader` or `StreamWriter` constructors, allowing you to work with standard stream readers or stream writers to handle data in a transparent fashion.

Using Attributes and Reflection

14

Handling Metadata in C#

In the previous chapter, we started discussing *metadata*, the information a module can store about its types, code, methods, and so on. In this chapter, we're going to continue discussing metadata as we turn to attributes and reflection.

As we've seen throughout the book, *attributes* let you specify metadata, including directives to the compiler, in your code. You can read this metadata yourself with tools like ILDASM and others, and you can also access it in code, as we're going to see. *Reflection*, introduced in this chapter, is a set of techniques that allows an application to read and work with its own metadata. Custom attributes of the kind we'll see in this chapter can be very useful in the reflection process. One reflection technique, *reflection emit*, lets you actually create methods on the fly, from scratch (you're responsible for writing them in MSIL). We're going to see how that works in this chapter.

We'll start with attributes. There are two kinds of attributes in C#—built-in and custom—and we'll take a look at the built-in ones first.

Built-in Attributes

You use attributes to connect metadata, including compiler directives, to an element in your code. There are plenty of attributes built into C#, and we've already seen a number of them in this book. For example, this attribute lets you indicate that a method is a Web method, accessible from a Web service:

```
[WebMethod]
```

This attribute lets you indicate that a class can be serialized:

```
[Serializable]
```

This attribute indicates that you want to import a DLL; in this case, kernel32.dll:

```
[DllImport("kernel32", SetLastError=true)]
```

Note the syntax in this case. We're passing text to the DLLImport attribute, followed by the expression SetLastError=true.

ATTRIBUTES ARE CREATED WITH CLASSES

It probably won't surprise you to learn that attributes are created with classes in C#, and the values you pass to an attribute are passed to its constructor. Additional *name=value* pairs let you set the values of properties built into the attribute's class. More on this when we create our own custom attributes in a page or two.

We also saw that you can use attributes to specify metadata about specific elements, as here, where we're setting the version and title of an assembly:

```
[assembly:AssemblyVersion
Attribute("1.0.0.0")]
[assembly:AssemblyTitleAttribute("Example
ch14_01")]
```

Also note that the attributes here are prefixed with the text assembly:, which is an attribute *target*.

Specifying Attribute Targets

Sometimes, it might not be clear what the target of an attribute is. For example, if you use an attribute just before a method, does it apply to the method or to the assembly as a whole? To make sure that the target of an attribute is clear to the compiler, you can specify one of a set of predefined targets like this:

```
[target : attribute-list]
```

Here are the parts of this attribute:

- *target*—The target of the attribute.
- *attribute-list*—A list of applicable attributes.

You can see the predefined targets for attributes, as defined in the AttributeTargets enumeration, in Table 14.1.

TABLE 14.1

Predefined Attribute Targets

DECLARATION	TARGET(S)
All	Any application element
Assembly	An assembly
Class	A class
Constructor	A constructor
Delegate	A delegate
Enum	An enumeration
Event	An event
Field	A field
Interface	An interface
Method	A method
Module	A module
Parameter	A parameter
Property	A property
ReturnValue	A return value
Struct	A structure (that is, a value type)

Conditional Attributes

Attributes can contain directives to the compiler, and one consequence of that is that besides standard attributes, you can also use *conditional attributes*. Conditional attributes are much like the preprocessor directives we saw in Chapter 1, "Essential C#," although they're designed exclusively for use in method declarations. These attributes determine whether a symbol has been defined, and if so, include the following code at compile time. Here's how you use them in general:

```
[Conditional(conditionalSymbol)]
```

In this case, `conditionalSymbol` is a symbol you can define with the #define preprocessor directive. Here's an example, the Debugger class, where we'll include code for use only when we're debugging. If you define a symbol you name DEBUGGING in this code (using the #define preprocessor directive), the method following the [Conditional] attribute, which displays a debugging message, is included at compile time:

```
#define DEBUGGING
using System;
using System.Diagnostics;
```

```
public class Debugger
{
  [Conditional("DEBUGGING")] public static void Write(string text)
  {
   System.Console.WriteLine(text);
  }
}
```

Now you can call Debugger.Write in other code; if DEBUGGING is defined, that method will display the text passed to it. If the #define DEBUGGING line is commented out, calling Debugger.Write won't display any text. You can see this at work in ch14_01.cs, Listing 14.1.

LISTING 14.1   Creating a Custom Conditional Attribute (ch14_01.cs)

```
#define DEBUGGING
using System;
using System.Diagnostics;

public class Debugger
{
  [Conditional("DEBUGGING")] public static void Write(string text)
  {
   System.Console.WriteLine(text);
  }
}

class ch14_01
{
  static void Method1()
  {
   Debugger.Write("Now in Method1.");
   Method2();
  }

  static void Method2()
  {
   Debugger.Write("Now in Method2.");
  }

  public static void Main()
  {
   Method1();
```

LISTING 14.1   Continued

```
    System.Console.WriteLine("Did it work?");
  }
}
```

Here's what you see when you run ch14_01.cs as it appears in Listing 14.1:

```
C:\>ch14_01
Now in Method1.
Now in Method2.
Did it work?
```

If you comment out the #define DEBUGGING line in the code, you'll see this instead:

```
C:\>ch14_01
Did it work?
```

Creating Custom Attributes

You can also create your own custom attributes for storing metadata in a module or assembly (but not as new compiler directives). To create a new attribute, you use (surprise!) an attribute—the AttributeUsage attribute:

```
[AttributeUsage(
  validon,
  AllowMultiple=allowmultiple,
  Inherited=inherited
)]
```

Here are the parts of this attribute:

- validon—Gives the language element(s) with which the attribute can be used. This item is a combination of AttributeTargets values (see Table 14.1), ORed together. The default value is AttributeTargets.All.

- allowmultiple (optional)—If true, the attribute is *multiuse*, which means you can use it multiple times for the same element. Default is false (single-use).

- inherited (optional)—If true, the attribute is inherited by derived classes. The default is false, which means not inherited.

Here's an example of a custom attribute. In this case, we'll create an attribute named Author that will let us store data about the author of a section of code. We'll allow this attribute to be used on classes, constructors, fields, methods, and properties. Here's how to specify that using the [AttributeUsage] attribute:

```
[AttributeUsage(AttributeTargets.Class |
  AttributeTargets.Constructor |
  AttributeTargets.Field |
  AttributeTargets.Method |
  AttributeTargets.Property,
  AllowMultiple = true)]
```

We'll derive our new attribute, Author, from the System.Attribute class, giving it a constructor and properties to hold the code author's name, code creation time, and any comments the author wants to leave:

```
[AttributeUsage(AttributeTargets.Class |
  AttributeTargets.Constructor |
  AttributeTargets.Field |
  AttributeTargets.Method |
  AttributeTargets.Property,
  AllowMultiple = true)]
public class Author : System.Attribute
{
  private string privateText;
  private string privateTime;
  private string privateName;

  public Author(string name, string time)
  {
    privateName = name;
    privateTime = time;
  }

  public string Text
  {
    get
    {
      return privateText;
    }
    set
    {
      privateText = value;
    }
  }
}
```

```
    public string Time
    {
      get
      {
        return privateTime;
      }
    }

    public string Name
    {
      get
      {
        return privateName;
      }
    }
}
```

Now we'll use this new attribute in code. You pass values to the attribute's constructor corresponding to the author's name and the time the code was authored. And you can also set the read/write Text property by assigning text to the property name Text, as you see in ch14_02.cs, Listing 14.2.

LISTING 14.2   Creating Custom Attributes (ch14_02.cs)

```
using System;
using System.Reflection;

[AttributeUsage(AttributeTargets.Class |
  AttributeTargets.Constructor |
  AttributeTargets.Field |
  AttributeTargets.Method |
  AttributeTargets.Property,
  AllowMultiple = true)]
public class Author : System.Attribute
{
  private string privateText;
  private string privateTime;
  private string privateName;

  public Author(string name, string time)
  {
    privateName = name;
```

LISTING 14.2   Continued

```
      privateTime = time;
    }

    public string Text
    {
      get
      {
        return privateText;
      }
      set
      {
        privateText = value;
      }
    }

    public string Time
    {
      get
      {
        return privateTime;
      }
    }

    public string Name
    {
      get
      {
        return privateName;
      }
    }
  }

[Author("Cary Grant", "11/25/48")]
[Author("Grace Kelly", "11/25/48", Text="Hi Cary!")]
public class Displayer
{
  public void Display()
  {
    System.Console.WriteLine("No worries!");
  }
}
```

LISTING 14.2   Continued

```
public class ch14_02
{
  public static void Main()
  {
    Displayer displayer = new Displayer();
    displayer.Display();
  }
}
```

If you run ch14_02.cs, you won't see any sign of the new attribute:

```
C:>ch14_02
No worries!
```

FIGURE 14.1   A custom attribute in ILDASM.

However, if you take a look at ch14_02.exe in ILDASM, you can see the new Author attributes, as shown in Figure 14.1.

In fact, there's a way for code to read its own metadata of the type stored in this custom attribute—you can use reflection.

Using Reflection

Reflection is a set of techniques that lets code read and work with its own metadata, or that of other code, and it's supported by classes in the System.Reflection namespace, such as System.Reflection.MemberInfo (which is the class that we're going to use to read metadata from the custom Author attributes we just created). There are four parts to reflection:

- *Accessing metadata* of the kind stored in attributes.

- *Discovering and examining types*, including creating objects from those types.

- *Late binding*, also called *dynamic invocation*, which lets you create objects on the fly and use their properties and methods.

- *Reflection emit*, which lets you create new types at runtime and use those types in your code.

We'll take a look at each of these four techniques in the remainder of this chapter.

Accessing Metadata

We'll start our discussion of reflection by extracting metadata from the Author attributes we created in the previous example. We can read those attributes at runtime with the System.Reflection.MemberInfo class's GetCustomAttributes method, which works like this:

```
public abstract object[] GetCustomAttributes
(Type attributeType, bool inherit)
```

Here are the arguments you pass to this method:

- *attributeType*—The type of attributes you want.

- *inherit*—Specifies whether to search the inheritance chain to find attributes.

For example, to access the properties of the [Author] attributes we created in ch14_02.cs, we can create a MemberInfo object and call that object's GetCustomAttributes method to get an array of Author attribute objects:

```
public static void Main()
{
  object[] attributes;
  Displayer displayer = new Displayer();
  displayer.Display();

  System.Reflection.MemberInfo memberInfo = typeof(Displayer);
  attributes = memberInfo.GetCustomAttributes(typeof(Author), false);
    .
    .
    .
```

These Author attribute objects support the properties we've built into them—Name, Time, and Text—so we can loop over each Author attribute object and display those properties as you see in ch14_03.cs, Listing 14.3.

LISTING 14.3   Reading Metadata (ch14_03.cs)

```
using System;
using System.Reflection;
```

LISTING 14.3 Continued

```
[AttributeUsage(AttributeTargets.Class |
  AttributeTargets.Constructor |
  AttributeTargets.Field |
  AttributeTargets.Method |
  AttributeTargets.Property,
  AllowMultiple = true)]
public class Author : System.Attribute
{
  private string privateText;
  private string privateTime;
  private string privateName;

  public Author(string name, string time)
  {
    privateName = name;
    privateTime = time;
  }

  public string Text
  {
    get
    {
      return privateText;
    }
    set
    {
      privateText = value;
    }
  }

  public string Time
  {
    get
    {
      return privateTime;
    }
  }

  public string Name
  {
    get
    {
```

LISTING 14.3   Continued

```
        return privateName;
      }
    }
}

[Author("Cary Grant", "11/25/48")]
[Author("Grace Kelly", "11/25/48", Text="Hi Cary!")]
public class Displayer
{
  public void Display()
  {
    System.Console.WriteLine("No worries!");
  }
}

public class ch14_03
{
  public static void Main()
  {
    object[] attributes;
    Displayer displayer = new Displayer();
    displayer.Display();

    System.Reflection.MemberInfo memberInfo = typeof(Displayer);
    attributes = memberInfo.GetCustomAttributes(typeof(Author), false);

    foreach(Object attribute in attributes)
    {
      Author author = (Author) attribute;
      System.Console.WriteLine("Author = {0}", author.Name);
      System.Console.WriteLine("Time = {0}", author.Time);
      System.Console.WriteLine("Text = {0}", author.Text);
      System.Console.WriteLine();
    }
  }
}
```

Here's what you see when you run ch14_03, showing the attribute metadata as you see here:

```
C:\>ch14_03
No worries!
Author = Cary Grant
```

```
Time = 11/25/48
Text =

Author = Grace Kelly
Time = 11/25/48
Text = Hi Cary!
```

Next we're going to take a look at how to discover and examine types at runtime using reflection.

Discovering and Examining Types

Reflection lets you examine an assembly and discover what types the assembly defines. You can also get more information about a type at runtime by examining that type in some detail. We'll take a look at how to discover a type first.

Discovering Types

You can discover defined types by loading an assembly with the `Assembly.Load` method, which creates an `Assembly` object, and using the `GetTypes` method of that object, which returns an array of `Type` objects:

```
public static void Main()
{
  Assembly assembly = Assembly.Load("ch14_03");
  Type[] types = assembly.GetTypes();
    .
    .
    .
```

After you have an array of `Type` objects, you can loop over each type and display it using a foreach loop, as you see in ch14_04.cs, Listing 14.4, where we're discovering the types defined in the ch14_03.exe assembly.

LISTING 14.4 Discovering Types (ch14_04.cs)

```
using System;
using System.Reflection;

public class ch14_04
{
  public static void Main()
```

LISTING 14.4   Continued

```
  {
     Assembly assembly = Assembly.Load("ch14_03");
     Type[] types = assembly.GetTypes();

     System.Console.WriteLine("{0} types discovered.", types.Length);

     foreach(Type type in types)
     {
        System.Console.WriteLine("Type = {0}", type);
     }
  }
}
```

Here's what you see when you run ch14_04.cs:

```
C:\>ch14_04
3 types discovered.
Type = Author
Type = Displayer
Type = ch14_03
```

Examining Types

You can also use the `Type.Getmembers` method to get all the *members* of a type, which is invaluable if you're trying to discover more about a type at runtime. For example, you can see how to get all the members of the `System.Console` class, and their types (method, property, and so on) in ch14_05.cs, Listing 14.5.

LISTING 14.5   Examining Types (ch14_05.cs)

```
using System;
using System.Reflection;

public class ch14_05
{
  public static void Main()
  {
     Type type = Type.GetType("System.Console");

     MemberInfo[] memberInfos = type.GetMembers();
```

LISTING 14.5   Continued

```
    foreach (MemberInfo member in memberInfos)
    {
     System.Console.WriteLine("{0}: {1}", member.MemberType, member);
    }
  }
}
```

And here's what you see when you run ch14_05.cs, listing the types in `System.Console`:

```
C:\>ch14_05
Method: Int32 GetHashCode()
Method: Boolean Equals(System.Object)
Method: System.String ToString()
          .
          .
          .
Method: Void WriteLine(UInt64)
Method: Void WriteLine(System.Object)
Method: Void WriteLine(System.String)
Method: Void WriteLine(System.String, System.Object)
          .
          .
          .
Property: System.IO.TextWriter Error
Property: System.IO.TextReader In
Property: System.IO.TextWriter Out
```

Note that you get not only the type of members this way, such as `Method` or `Property`, but you get the argument types you pass to methods and their return types as well. If you want to see only the methods of a type, you can call `type.GetMethods` instead of `type.GetMembers`.

Some assemblies have hundreds of members, and you can use the `Type.FindMembers` method to filter only the ones you want. For example, you can find all members beginning with "Write" in `System.Console` using this method. Here's how you use this method formally:

```
public virtual MemberInfo[] FindMembers(
  MemberTypes memberType,
  BindingFlags bindingAttr,
  MemberFilter filter,
  object filterCriteria
)
```

Here are the parameters you pass to this method:

- *memberType*—A MemberTypes object indicating the type of member to search for.

- *bindingAttr*—One or more BindingsFlag elements to specify what kinds of members you want to look for. The BindingsFlag enumeration is covered shortly.

- *filter*—The delegate that does the actual comparisons, returning true if a member matches *filterCriteria* and false otherwise. You can use the pre-built FilterAttribute, FilterName, and FilterNameIgnoreCase delegates.

- *filterCriteria*—The search criteria. You can use the fields of FieldAttributes, MethodAttributes, and MethodImplAttributes enumerations, as well as text that includes wildcards.

Here are the members of the BindingsFlag enumeration you can OR together for the *bindingAttr* parameter:

- DeclaredOnly

- FlattenHierarchy

- IgnoreCase

- IgnoreReturn

- Instance

- NonPublic

- Public

- Static

- ExactBinding

- OptionalParamBinding

- CreateInstance

- GetField

- SetField

- GetProperty

- SetProperty

- InvokeMethod

- PutDispProperty

- PutRefDispProperty

For example, you can see how to find all public, static methods of System.Console that start with "Write" in ch14_06.cs, Listing 14.6. Note in particular that we're using the Type.FilterName predefined delegate to indicate that we're going to supply a filter name, which members much match; in this example that filter name is "Write*".

LISTING 14.6   Filtering Members (ch14_06.cs)

```
using System;
using System.Reflection;

public class ch14_05
{
  public static void Main()
  {
    Type type = Type.GetType("System.Console");

    MemberInfo[] memberInfos =
        type.FindMembers(MemberTypes.Method,
        BindingFlags.Public |
        BindingFlags.Static,
        Type.FilterName, "Write*");

    foreach (MemberInfo member in memberInfos )
    {
      Console.WriteLine("{0}: {1}", member.MemberType, member);
    }
  }
}
```

Here's what you see when you run ch14_06, listing all the members that begin with "Write" in System.Console:

```
C:\>ch14_06
Method: Void WriteLine()
Method: Void WriteLine(Boolean)
Method: Void WriteLine(Char)
Method: Void WriteLine(Char[])
Method: Void WriteLine(Char[], Int32, Int32)
Method: Void WriteLine(System.Decimal)
Method: Void WriteLine(Double)
Method: Void WriteLine(Single)
Method: Void WriteLine(Int32)
Method: Void WriteLine(UInt32)
```

```
Method: Void WriteLine(Int64)
Method: Void WriteLine(UInt64)
Method: Void WriteLine(System.Object)
Method: Void WriteLine(System.String)
Method: Void WriteLine(System.String, System.Object)
Method: Void WriteLine(System.String, System.Object, System.Object)
Method: Void WriteLine(System.String, System.Object,
  System.Object, System.Object)
Method: Void WriteLine(System.String, System.Object,
  System.Object, System.Object, System.Object, ...)
Method: Void WriteLine(System.String, System.Object[])
Method: Void Write(System.String, System.Object)
Method: Void Write(System.String, System.Object, System.Object)
Method: Void Write(System.String, System.Object, System.Object, System.Object)
Method: Void Write(System.String, System.Object, System.Object,
  System.Object, System.Object, ...)
Method: Void Write(System.String, System.Object[])
Method: Void Write(Boolean)
Method: Void Write(Char)
Method: Void Write(Char[])
Method: Void Write(Char[], Int32, Int32)
Method: Void Write(Double)
Method: Void Write(System.Decimal)
Method: Void Write(Single)
Method: Void Write(Int32)
Method: Void Write(UInt32)
Method: Void Write(Int64)
Method: Void Write(UInt64)
Method: Void Write(System.Object)
Method: Void Write(System.String)
```

Using Late Binding

Late binding is the process of waiting until runtime to bind a method to an object. With late binding, you don't have to specify what object you're going to work with until the code is actually running. This is a useful skill because you can create an instance of an assembly (such as Microsoft Access or Excel) and invoke its methods using late binding.

Here's an example. Say you have a class named `Calculator` with a method named `Addem` that adds two integers:

```
public class Calculator
{
  public virtual long Addem(int x, int y)
  {
    return x + y;
  }
}
```

Now say you want to invoke the `Addem` method at runtime using late binding. We'll start by creating a new instance of the `Calculator` type using the `Activator` class's `CreateInstance` method. We could just create a `Calculator` object in code with `new`, of course, but we're demonstrating the `CreateInstance` method here because you can use this method to create objects from external assemblies and other remote objects:

```
Type calculatorType = Type.GetType("Calculator");
Object calculator = Activator.CreateInstance(calculatorType);
```

In fact, the `Activator` class specializes in creating objects from assemblies and other external objects; here are its static members, which you use for this purpose:

- `CreateComInstanceFrom`—Creates an instance of a COM object.

- `CreateInstance`—Creates an instance of the specified type.

- `CreateInstanceFrom`—Creates an instance using an assembly file.

- `GetObject`—Creates a proxy for a currently running remote object, server-activated object, or Web service.

To call the `Addem` method of the new `calculator` object, we need to indicate which parameters this method takes, which we can do by creating a `Type` array:

```
Type[] parameterTypes = new Type[2];
parameterTypes[0]= Type.GetType("System.Int32");
parameterTypes[1]= Type.GetType("System.Int32");
```

We also need to create a `MethodInfo` object holding information about the method we're about to call. You're free to specify the name of the method at runtime, which is what late binding is all about:

```
Type type = Type.GetType("Calculator");
MethodInfo methodInfo = type.GetMethod("Addem", parameterTypes);
```

And we need to set up an array with the data we want to pass to this method; in this case, we'll add 2 and 3:

```
Object[] parameters = new Object[2];
parameters[0] = 2;
parameters[1] = 3;
```

Finally, you can call the Invoke method of the MethodInfo object to invoke the Addem method, as you see in ch14_07.cs, Listing 14.7.

LISTING 14.7   Late Binding (ch14_07.cs)

```
using System;
using System.Reflection;

public class Calculator
{
  public virtual long Addem(int x, int y)
  {
    return x + y;
  }
}

class ch14_07
{
  public static void Main()
  {
   Type calculatorType = Type.GetType("Calculator");
   Object calculator = Activator.CreateInstance(calculatorType);

   Type[] parameterTypes = new Type[2];
   parameterTypes[0]= Type.GetType("System.Int32");
   parameterTypes[1]= Type.GetType("System.Int32");

   Type type = Type.GetType("Calculator");
   MethodInfo methodInfo = type.GetMethod("Addem", parameterTypes);

   Object[] parameters = new Object[2];
   parameters[0] = 2;
   parameters[1] = 3;

   System.Console.WriteLine("Addem(2, 3) = {0}",
     methodInfo.Invoke(calculator, parameters));
  }
}
```

Here are the results you see when you run ch14_07:

```
C:\>ch14_07
Addem(2, 3) = 5
```

As you can see, we've been able to late-bind a method, specifying which method of an object to bind at runtime, not at compile time. In this way, late binding lets you customize your code at runtime. In fact, the fourth reflection technique, reflection emit, lets you customize your code entirely at runtime, by writing it from scratch.

Using Reflection Emit

Reflection emit is the process of creating your own types and code at runtime. When you use reflection emit, you create not only a type, but also the members of that type—and compile them on the fly, "emitting" the MSIL code for the new type. Note that this is an advanced technique, and the code here is going to get a little involved. Not many programmers use reflection emit.

To get an idea of the kinds of problems reflection emit can solve, take a look at ch14_08.cs, Listing 14.8. In that example, we'll use a method named CountLoop to count from 1 to 30:

```
public int CountLoop(int n)
{
  int total = 0;

  for(int loopIndex = 1; loopIndex <= n; loopIndex++)
  {
    total++;
  }

  return total;
}
```

This method relies on a loop to execute, which is fairly fast, but it can't beat a custom method like this, which does the same thing as CountLoop, but uses addition:

```
public int CountSimple()
{
  return 1 + 1 + 1 + 1 + 1 + 1 + 1 + 1 + 1 + 1 +
    1 + 1 + 1 + 1 + 1 + 1 + 1 + 1 + 1 + 1 +
    1 + 1 + 1 + 1 + 1 + 1 + 1 + 1 + 1 + 1;
}
```

This second method, named CountSimple, just counts to 30 by adding one 30 times. We'll keep track of how fast it takes CountLoop and CountSimple to count to 30 using a TimeSpan object, as you see in Listing 14.8. Note that because computers don't take long to count to 30, we'll count to 30 10,000,000 times to get a time we can actually measure.

LISTING 14.8   Comparing Counting Methods (ch14_08.cs)

```
using System;
using System.Diagnostics;

public class Counter
{
  public int CountLoop(int totalCount)
  {
    int total = 0;

    for(int loopIndex = 1; loopIndex <= totalCount; loopIndex++)
    {
      total++;
    }

    return total;
  }

  public int CountSimple()
  {
    return 1 + 1 + 1 + 1 + 1 + 1 + 1 + 1 + 1 + 1 +
      1 + 1 + 1 + 1 + 1 + 1 + 1 + 1 + 1 + 1 +
      1 + 1 + 1 + 1 + 1 + 1 + 1 + 1 + 1 + 1;
  }
}

public class ch14_08
{
  public static void Main()
  {
    Counter counter = new Counter();
    int total = 0;

    DateTime begin = DateTime.Now;
    for (int loopIndex = 0; loopIndex < 10000000; loopIndex++)
    {
      total = counter.CountLoop(30);
```

LISTING 14.8 Continued

```
    }
    TimeSpan duration = DateTime.Now - begin;

    System.Console.WriteLine("Looped to {0} 10,000,000 times in {1} milliseconds.",
        total, duration.TotalMilliseconds);

    begin = DateTime.Now;
    for (int loopIndex = 0; loopIndex < 10000000; loopIndex++)
    {
        total = counter.CountSimple();
    }
    duration = DateTime.Now - begin;

    System.Console.WriteLine("Counted to {0} 10,000,000 times in {1} milliseconds.",
        total, duration.TotalMilliseconds);
    }
}
```

Here are the results. As you can see, the custom method is far faster than using a loop:

```
C:\>ch14_07
Looped to 30 10,000,000 times in 901.296 milliseconds.
Counted to 30 10,000,000 times in 40.0576 milliseconds.
```

The whole idea behind reflection emit is to be able to create custom methods like
CountSimple on the fly. It's not an easy thing to do, because you're responsible for doing a lot
of work—including creating the MSIL for the custom method—but it can be done.

This new example will be called ch14_09.cs. For the sake of reference, we'll include the
Counter class we just created and its CountLoop method in this example so we can see how
much faster the method we create on the fly is. In this example, we use reflection emit to
create the other method, CountSimple, from scratch.

Like the previous version of CountSimple, we're going to count to 30 by adding 1 + 1 + 1 .. +
1, but we're going to write this new version of CountSimple at runtime. We'll do this by creating a new class, Reflector, and then calling Reflector.CountSimple(30) to count to 30.

The Reflector class's CountSimple method will call a new method we'll write, Emitter,
which will return an AssemblyBuilder object that lets you create assemblies. These assemblies
will have a built-in method named GeneratedCountSimple, which will be our custom counting method. Because we're generating a new assembly on the fly, C# will have no idea which
parameters that assembly's GeneratedSimple method takes and what its return type is. To

give the compiler this information, we'll create an interface, `ICounter`, with one method, `GeneratedSimple`:

```
public interface ICounter
{
  int GeneratedCountSimple();
}
```

All we have to do in our new version of `CountSimple` is use the `AssemblyBuilder` object's `CreateInstance` method to create a new assembly, store that assembly in an `ICounter` object, call its `GeneratedCountSimple` method, and return the result that method gives us:

```
public class Reflector
{
  ICounter counter = null;

  public int CountSimple(int totalCount)
  {
    if (counter == null)
    {
      AssemblyBuilder assemblyBuilder = Emitter(totalCount);
      counter = (ICounter) assemblyBuilder.CreateInstance("Counter");
    }

    return (counter.GeneratedCountSimple());
  }
  .
  .
  .
```

That's it for `CountSimple`. The only question now is how to create the `Emitter` method, which returns the `AssemblyBuilder` object that lets us create assemblies supporting the `GeneratedCountSimple` method. To create a new `AssemblyBuilder`, we start by giving the assemblies we'll create a name, `CounterAssembly`, using an `AssemblyName` object. Next, we create the `AssemblyBuilder` object we'll return from this method, using the current application domain's `DefineDynamicAssembly` method. You can get the current application domain using the static `Thread.GetDomain` method (more on threads and how to use the `Thread` class in Chapter 15, "Using Multithreading and Remoting"):

```
AssemblyBuilder Emitter(int totalCount)
{
  AssemblyName assemblyName = new AssemblyName();
  assemblyName.Name = "CounterAssembly";
```

```
AssemblyBuilder assemblyBuilder = Thread.GetDomain().DefineDynamicAssembly(
  assemblyName, AssemblyBuilderAccess.Run);
```

To structure the assemblies built by this assembly builder, we create a `ModuleBuilder` and `TypeBuilder` object that will create a new type named `Counter`:

```
ModuleBuilder moduleBuilder = assemblyBuilder.DefineDynamicModule("Module1");

TypeBuilder typeBuilder =
  moduleBuilder.DefineType("Counter", TypeAttributes.Public);

typeBuilder.AddInterfaceImplementation(typeof(ICounter));
```

Now we will create the `GeneratedCountSimple` method in the new `Counter` type. To create this method, we will create a `MethodBuilder` object, `generatedMethod`, using the `TypeBuilder` class's `DefineMethod` method. Note that we have to specify the parameter types and return type of this new method like this:

```
Type[] paramTypes = new Type[0];
Type returnType = typeof(System.Int32);

MethodBuilder generatedMethod =
  typeBuilder.DefineMethod("GeneratedCountSimple",
    MethodAttributes.Virtual |
    MethodAttributes.Public, returnType, paramTypes);
```

Now it's time to generate the actual MSIL code for the new `GeneratedCountSimple` method. You can do that with an object of the `ILGenerator` class, and in this case, we'll just generate the MSIL to keep adding 1 to a running sum as many times as we're supposed to in this new, generated method. Here's where we use the actual `Emit` method:

```
ILGenerator ilGenerator = generatedMethod.GetILGenerator();
ilGenerator.Emit(OpCodes.Ldc_I4, 0);

for (int loopIndex = 1; loopIndex <= totalCount; loopIndex++)
{
  ilGenerator.Emit(OpCodes.Ldc_I4, 1);
  ilGenerator.Emit(OpCodes.Add);
}

ilGenerator.Emit(OpCodes.Ret);
```

Our newly generated method, stored in `generatedMethod`, is simply made up of anonymous MSIL. To give it a name and the coding characteristics we'll need, we'll use the `TypeBuilder`

class's DefineMethodOverride method to override this anonymous method using the
ICounter interface's GeneratedCountSimple method. After that, our AssemblyBuilder object is
complete, and we return it from the Emitter method like this at the end of the Emitter
method:

```
MethodInfo methodInfo = typeof(ICounter).GetMethod("GeneratedCountSimple");

typeBuilder.DefineMethodOverride(generatedMethod, methodInfo);
typeBuilder.CreateType();

return assemblyBuilder;
}
```

That's it—the Emitter method returns a new AssemblyBuilder object, and calling that
object's CreateInstance will create an assembly with the customized GeneratedCountSimple
method that will do our counting in the simplest way. All that remains is to put this new
customized method to work and to compare it to the looping method, CountLoop. You can
see the code that does that in ch14_09.cs, Listing 14.9.

LISTING 14.9   Using Reflection Emit (ch14_09.cs)

```
using System;
using System.Threading;
using System.Reflection;
using System.Reflection.Emit;

public class Counter
{
  public int CountLoop(int totalCount)
  {
    int total = 0;

    for(int loopIndex = 1; loopIndex <= totalCount; loopIndex++)
    {
      total++;
    }
    return total;
  }
}

public class Reflector
{
  ICounter counter = null;
```

LISTING 14.9   Continued

```
public int CountSimple(int totalCount)
{
  if (counter == null)
  {
    AssemblyBuilder assemblyBuilder = Emitter(totalCount);
    counter = (ICounter) assemblyBuilder.CreateInstance("Counter");
  }

  return (counter.GeneratedCountSimple());
}

AssemblyBuilder Emitter(int totalCount)
{
  AssemblyName assemblyName = new AssemblyName();
  assemblyName.Name = "CounterAssembly";

  AssemblyBuilder assemblyBuilder =
    Thread.GetDomain().DefineDynamicAssembly(
    assemblyName, AssemblyBuilderAccess.Run);

  ModuleBuilder moduleBuilder =
    assemblyBuilder.DefineDynamicModule("Module1");

  TypeBuilder typeBuilder =
    moduleBuilder.DefineType("Counter", TypeAttributes.Public);

  typeBuilder.AddInterfaceImplementation(typeof(ICounter));

  Type[] paramTypes = new Type[0];
  Type returnType = typeof(System.Int32);

  MethodBuilder generatedMethod =
    typeBuilder.DefineMethod("GeneratedCountSimple",
    MethodAttributes.Virtual |
    MethodAttributes.Public, returnType, paramTypes);

  ILGenerator ilGenerator = generatedMethod.GetILGenerator();
  ilGenerator.Emit(OpCodes.Ldc_I4, 0);

  for (int loopIndex = 1; loopIndex <= totalCount; loopIndex++)
  {
```

LISTING 14.9   Continued

```
        ilGenerator.Emit(OpCodes.Ldc_I4, 1);
        ilGenerator.Emit(OpCodes.Add);
    }

    ilGenerator.Emit(OpCodes.Ret);

    MethodInfo methodInfo =
        typeof(ICounter).GetMethod("GeneratedCountSimple");

    typeBuilder.DefineMethodOverride(generatedMethod, methodInfo);
    typeBuilder.CreateType();

    return assemblyBuilder;
  }
}

public interface ICounter
{
  int GeneratedCountSimple();
}

public class ch14_09
{
  public static void Main()
  {
    int total = 0;

    Counter counter = new Counter();

    DateTime begin = DateTime.Now;
    for (int loopIndex = 0; loopIndex < 10000000; loopIndex++)
    {
      total = counter.CountLoop(30);
    }
    TimeSpan duration = DateTime.Now - begin;

    System.Console.WriteLine(
      "Looped to {0} 10,000,000 times in {1} milliseconds.",
      total, duration.TotalMilliseconds);

    Reflector reflector = new Reflector();
```

LISTING 14.9 Continued

```
    begin = DateTime.Now;
    for (int loopIndex = 0; loopIndex < 10000000; loopIndex++)
    {
        total = reflector.CountSimple(30);
    }
    duration = DateTime.Now - begin;

    System.Console.WriteLine(
        "Counted to {0} 10,000,000 times in {1} milliseconds.",
        total, duration.TotalMilliseconds);
    }
}
```

Here are the results you see when you run ch14_09. As you can see, the custom method we wrote on the fly using reflection emit is indeed much faster than the looping method:

```
C:\>ch14_09
Looped to 30 10,000,000 times in 871.2528
milliseconds.
Counted to 30 10,000,000 times in 280.4032
milliseconds.
```

And that's it—we've created a custom method on the fly using reflection emit, creating the method's actual MSIL, and then called that method. An advanced technique to be sure, and not for everyone—but very impressive.

A LITTLE ABOUT SPEED

Why is the custom reflection emit CountSimple method here slower than the previous CountSimple method, which used the code return 1 + 1 .. + 1? If you're familiar with the way compilers optimize, you know that the compiler simply added the long 1 + 1 .. + 1 expression in that code to 30 when it compiled that code (as you can verify with ILDASM), so no counting was actually performed in the previous CountSimple method. Actually, the MSIL code we created to increment a value thirty times is about as fast as you can go in .NET programming.

In Brief

In this chapter, we took a look at two important topics—attributes and reflection. Here's an overview of this chapter's coverage:

- Attributes let you specify metadata, including directives to the compiler, in your code. Reflection is a set of techniques that lets an application read and work with its own metadata. Reflection is made up of four parts: accessing metadata, discovering and examining types, late binding, and reflection emit.

- You can create your own custom metadata attributes with the `[AttributeUsage]` attribute, which you use on the class that holds the support code for the attribute. You can pass data to that class's constructor when you use the custom attribute, as well as set property values, like `Text` in this example we saw: `[Author("Grace Kelly", "11/25/48", Text="Hi Cary!")]`.

- You can extract metadata from attributes, such as the `System.Reflection.MemberInfo` class's `GetCustomAttributes` method at runtime.

- There are various techniques that let you discover types at runtime. For example, you can load an assembly with the `Assembly.Load` method, creating an `Assembly` object. You can then call the `GetTypes` method of that object, returning an array of `Type` objects.

- Late binding means that you don't have to specify which object you're calling a method on until runtime. You can call the `Invoke` method of `MethodInfo` objects to support late binding.

- Reflection emit is the process of generating your own code at runtime. (As we've seen in this chapter, that means creating our own MSIL and running it, a rather involved process.)

Using Multithreading and Remoting

15

Working with Multiple Threads

This chapter, which winds up our C# survey, is on two important topics: *multithreading* and *remoting*. We'll tackle multithreading first, and turn to remoting—the process of sending types and objects across application and machine boundaries—in the second half of the chapter.

As you might already know, a *thread* is a stream of execution in your code, and C# programs can support multiple threads. Using multithreading (also called *free threading*), your code can be doing one thing with the user and another behind the scenes, such as working on some long, involved calculation. In this way, your code won't appear to freeze as that long calculation is performed. There are thousands of uses for threads, of course—you might be working on the Internet while the user is working on something else, for example, or backing up data, or waiting to access a shared resource that other applications are using at the moment. Any time you want your application to be performing multiple tasks at the same time, think of multithreading as a possibility.

By default, each application is given a single thread, the *main thread* (to access the main thread, use the Thread class's CurrentThread property), but you can create others. Behind the scenes, however, creating new threads and letting them handle various tasks is a great idea. We're going to see how that works here. You create new threads using the Thread class. You can see the Thread class's significant public properties in Table 15.1, and its significant public methods in Table 15.2.

SHOP TALK

USER INTERFACE THREAD SAFETY

Here's an issue that you won't find discussed in enough depth in the C# documentation—not all threads are created equal. You should only work with user-interface elements like forms and controls ina .NET application's main thread (it's OK to use other threads to display text in console applications). In other words, user interface elements are not *Thread Safe*. The main thread has a lot of code to work with the user interface built into it; if you start working with user interface elements in another thread as well, there will be a conflict between threads sooner or later and your application is going to hang. This doesn't always happen every time you run the application, and in the past it's provided some non-repeatable bugs that took me a long time to find because the application code ran to dozens of pages (and it wasn't clear that a worker thread was calling main thread UI code). So, for example, if you want to undertake some complex calculation but want to let the user stop that calcualtion by clicking a button, you can handle the calculation in a new thread, and the button click in the main thread. Thread safety is one of those sticky issues that Microsoft has been working on for years with various programming models, such as the aprartment-threading model, which confines threads to "apartments," and which is not as powerful as true multithreading, We'll discuss more about thread safety when we synchorniczie our threads later in the chapter.

TABLE 15.1

Significant Public Properties of the Thread Class

PROPERTY	PURPOSE
CurrentCulture	Returns or sets the culture of the current thread.
CurrentThread	Returns the currently running thread.
IsAlive	True if the thread is active.
IsBackground	Returns or sets whether a thread is a background thread.
IsThreadPoolThread	Returns a value that indicates whether a thread belongs to a thread pool.
Name	Returns or sets the name of the thread.
Priority	Returns or sets the scheduling priority of a thread.
ThreadState	Returns the state of the current thread.

TABLE 15.2

Significant Public Methods of the Thread Class

METHOD	PURPOSE
Abort	Terminates a thread and raises a ThreadAbortException in the thread on which it is invoked.
GetDomain	Returns the domain in which the current thread is running.
GetDomainID	Returns a unique application domain identifier for the thread.
Interrupt	Interrupts a thread if it is in the WaitSleepJoin thread state.
Join	Returns only when a thread terminates.
MemoryBarrier	Synchronizes memory operations.
ResetAbort	Cancels an Abort requested for the thread.
Resume	Resumes operation in a thread that was suspended.
Sleep	Stops the current thread for the given number of milliseconds.
Start	Starts a thread's code executing.
Suspend	Suspends the thread until Resume is called.

We'll put the Thread class to work here, starting a few new threads and using them to demonstrate what you can do.

Creating and Starting Multiple Threads

In our first example, we'll create two new threads and use them to display text in a console application. One thread will type "No worries." 20 times, and the other will type "No Problems." 20 times. We start this new example, ch15_01.cs, by creating an object and calling a method named StartThreads from Main because we can't use only static methods in this example:

```
static void Main()
{
  ch15_01 app = new ch15_01();

  app.StartThreads();
}
```

In the `StartThreads` method we'll create two new threads, `thread1` and `thread2`, using the Thread class's constructor. Threads operate on the method level in C#, which means you pass the name of the method that holds a thread's code using a `ThreadStart` delegate to the Thread constructor (those methods will be named `NoWorries` and `NoProblems` here). After you've created a new thread, you call the thread's `Start` method to start executing the code in the thread's method:

```
public void StartThreads()
{
  Thread thread1 = new Thread(new
ThreadStart(NoWorries));
  Thread thread2 = new Thread(new
ThreadStart(NoProblems));

  thread1.Start();
  thread2.Start();
}
```

In the `NoWorries` method, we can print `"No Worries."` in the console window 20 times:

```
public void NoWorries()
{
  for (int loopIndex = 0; loopIndex < 20; loopIndex++)
  {
    System.Console.WriteLine("No Worries.");
  }
}
```

Similarly, in the `NoProblems` method, we can print `"No Problems."` in the console window 20 times, as you see in ch15_01.cs, Listing 15.1.

LISTING 15.1   Creating Two Threads (ch15_01.cs)

```
using System.Threading;

class ch15_01
{
  static void Main()
  {
```

LISTING 15.1   Continued

```
    ch15_01 app = new ch15_01();

    app.StartThreads();
  }

  public void StartThreads()
  {
    Thread thread1 = new Thread(new ThreadStart(NoWorries));
    Thread thread2 = new Thread(new ThreadStart(NoProblems));

    thread1.Start();
    thread2.Start();
  }

  public void NoWorries()
  {
    for (int loopIndex = 0; loopIndex < 20; loopIndex++)
    {
      System.Console.WriteLine("No Worries.");
    }
  }

  public void NoProblems()
  {
    for (int loopIndex = 0; loopIndex < 20; loopIndex++)
    {
      System.Console.WriteLine("No Problems.");
    }
  }
}
```

Now when you run this example, the machine will give some time to thread1 and then some time to thread2. Computer processing time is divided into *slices*, so thread1 will get some time, and then thread2 will, and then back to thread1, and so on. Here's what you might see when you run this example:

```
C:\>ch15_01
No Worries.
No Worries.
No Worries.
No Worries.
No Worries.
No Worries.
No Worries.
No Worries.
No Worries.
No Worries.
No Worries.
No Problems.
No Problems.
No Problems.
No Problems.
No Problems.
No Problems.
No Problems.
No Problems.
No Problems.
No Problems.
No Problems.
No Problems.
No Problems.
No Problems.
No Problems.
No Problems.
No Problems.
No Problems.
No Problems.
No Problems.
No Worries.
No Worries.
No Worries.
No Worries.
No Worries.
No Worries.
No Worries.
No Worries.
No Worries.
```

As you can see, thread1 got some time to run, and then thread2 did, and then back to thread1, and so on.

Sleeping, Aborting, Suspending, Resuming, and Joining Threads

Besides the Start method, threads also have other methods that let you control their behavior:

- Sleep—Makes a thread stop executing for a specified number of milliseconds.
- Abort—Aborts a thread.
- Suspend—Suspends a thread until you call Resume.
- Resume—Resumes a suspended thread's execution.
- Join—Returns only when the thread it's called on terminates.

We'll put these methods to work in a new example, ch15_02.cs. In this case, we'll have three threads, which will display "No Worries.", "No Problems." and "No Troubles." 20 times each. After creating these threads, we name them with the Thread class's Name property, and start thread1:

```
Thread thread1 = new Thread(new ThreadStart(NoWorries));
Thread thread2 = new Thread(new ThreadStart(NoProblems));
Thread thread3 = new Thread(new ThreadStart(NoTroubles));

thread1.Name = "Thread 1";
thread2.Name = "Thread 2";
thread3.Name = "Thread 3";

thread1.Start();
    .
    .
    .
```

thread1 just displays "No Worries." 20 times. After starting thread2 (which types "No Problems." 20 times), however, we'll make the main thread sleep three milliseconds and then abort this thread:

```
thread1.Start();

thread2.Start();
Thread.Sleep(3);
thread2.Abort();
    .
    .
    .
    .
```

Aborting a thread terminates its execution immediately. You can determine when a thread was aborted by catching a ThreadAbortException exception in the thread's code. Here's how that looks in the code for thread2, where we'll show a message when the thread is aborted:

```
public void NoProblems()
{
  try
  {
    for (int loopIndex =0; loopIndex < 20; loopIndex++)
    {
      System.Console.WriteLine("No Problems.");
    }
  }
  catch (ThreadAbortException)
  {
    System.Console.WriteLine("Thread {0} was aborted.",
      Thread.CurrentThread.Name);
  }
  finally
  {
    System.Console.WriteLine("Thread {0} is done.",
      Thread.CurrentThread.Name);
  }
}
```

CATCHING THREAD INTERRUPTIONS

Besides ThreadAbortException, you can also catch ThreadInterruptedException, which occurs when a thread is interrupted by another thread.

Note also the finally block in this code, which also appears in the code for thread1 and thread3, and will type a message when each thread terminates.

After starting and aborting thread2 in Main, we'll start thread3, which types "No troubles." 20 times. We'll then suspend it, wait 10 milliseconds, and then resume that thread:

```
thread3.Start();
thread3.Suspend();
Thread.Sleep(10);
thread3.Resume();
```

To make sure all three threads have finished, we'll call their Join methods, as you see in ch15_02.cs, Listing 15.2. A thread's Join method won't return until the thread is done executing (at which point its stream of execution "joins" the main thread again).

LISTING 15.2 Suspending and Working with Two Threads (ch15_02.cs)

```
using System.Threading;

class ch15_02
{
  static void Main()
  {
    ch15_02 app = new ch15_02();

    app.StartThreads();
  }

  public void StartThreads()
  {
    Thread thread1 = new Thread(new ThreadStart(NoWorries));
    Thread thread2 = new Thread(new ThreadStart(NoProblems));
    Thread thread3 = new Thread(new ThreadStart(NoTroubles));

    thread1.Name = "Thread 1";
    thread2.Name = "Thread 2";
    thread3.Name = "Thread 3";

    thread1.Start();

    thread2.Start();
    Thread.Sleep(3);
    thread2.Abort();

    thread3.Start();
    thread3.Suspend();
    Thread.Sleep(10);
    thread3.Resume();
```

LISTING 15.2   Continued

```
    thread1.Join();
    thread2.Join();
    thread3.Join();

    System.Console.WriteLine("All threads finished.");
  }

  public void NoWorries()
  {
    Thread.Sleep(10);
    try
    {
      for (int loopIndex =0; loopIndex < 15; loopIndex++)
      {
        System.Console.WriteLine("No Worries.");
      }
    }
    catch (ThreadAbortException)
    {
      System.Console.WriteLine("{0} was aborted.",
        Thread.CurrentThread.Name);
    }
    finally
    {
      System.Console.WriteLine("{0} is done.",
        Thread.CurrentThread.Name);
    }
  }

  public void NoProblems()
  {
    try
    {
      for (int loopIndex =0; loopIndex < 20; loopIndex++)
      {
        System.Console.WriteLine("No Problems.");
      }
    }
    catch (ThreadAbortException)
    {
      System.Console.WriteLine("{0} was aborted.",
```

LISTING 15.2   Continued

```
        Thread.CurrentThread.Name);
    }
    finally
    {
      System.Console.WriteLine("{0} is done.",
        Thread.CurrentThread.Name);
    }
  }

  public void NoTroubles()
  {
    try
    {
      for (int loopIndex =0; loopIndex < 15; loopIndex++)
      {
        System.Console.WriteLine("No Troubles.");
      }
    }
    catch (ThreadAbortException)
    {
      System.Console.WriteLine("{0} was aborted.",
        Thread.CurrentThread.Name);
    }
    finally
    {
      System.Console.WriteLine("{0} is done.",
        Thread.CurrentThread.Name);
    }
  }
}
```

Here are the results you see when you run ch15_02.cs. Note that thread2 was aborted as we requested, that thread1 finishes before the suspended thread3, that all threads report when they're done, and the program only finishes when all three threads are done. (Also note that your results will depend on how your machine's scheduler is working and how big the resulting time slices are. You might have to adjust the time the code sleeps to see thread2 aborted, for example.)

```
C:\>ch15_02
No Problems.
No Problems.
No Problems.
```

```
Thread 2 was aborted.
Thread 2 is done.
No Worries.
No Worries.
No Worries.
No Worries.
No Worries.
No Worries.
No Worries.
No Worries.
No Worries.
No Worries.
No Worries.
No Worries.
No Worries.
No Worries.
No Worries.
Thread 1 is done.
No Troubles.
No Troubles.
No Troubles.
No Troubles.
No Troubles.
No Troubles.
No Troubles.
No Troubles.
No Troubles.
No Troubles.
No Troubles.
No Troubles.
No Troubles.
No Troubles.
No Troubles.
Thread 3 is done.
All threads finished.
```

BACKGROUND THREADS

You can also set a thread's `IsBackground` property to `true`, making it a background thread. Background threads are the same as foreground threads, except that an application doesn't need to wait for background threads to terminate before finishing.

Now that we have multiple threads executing in the same program, there's a possibility that they might interfere with each other if they both work with the same object. The way out of that is to *synchronize* your threads.

Synchronizing Threads

In this section, we'll take a look at the kind of problems conflicting threads can create. Say you have an integer variable named counter, and two threads are both trying to increment that variable. Each thread also has some other work to do (which we'll simulate by sprinkling a few Sleep statements in the code), so between the time thread1 reads counter and stores its value in a local variable, increments its value, and then assigns the new value back to counter, thread2 might have already done the same thing. This means that thread1 will wipe out thread2's work (conflicting access to a shared resource like this is called a *race condition*). Because both threads are sharing the same object, counter, they conflict. You can see the code that will cause conflicts of this type in ch15_03.cs, Listing 15.3.

LISTING 15.3   Two Unsynchronized Threads (ch15_03.cs)

```
using System.Threading;

class ch15_03
{
  int counter = 0;

  static void Main()
  {
    ch15_03 app = new ch15_03();

    app.StartThreads();
  }

  public void StartThreads()
  {
    Thread thread1 = new Thread(new ThreadStart(CounterMethod1));
    thread1.Name = "Thread 1";
    thread1.Start();

    Thread thread2 = new Thread(new ThreadStart(CounterMethod2));
    thread2.Name = "Thread 2";
    thread2.Start();

    thread1.Join();
    thread2.Join();

    System.Console.WriteLine("All threads finished.");
  }
```

LISTING 15.3   Continued

```
public void CounterMethod1()
{
  while (counter < 20)
  {
    int localCounterValue = counter;
    if(localCounterValue < 20){
      Thread.Sleep(50);
      localCounterValue++;
      Thread.Sleep(10);
      counter = localCounterValue;

      System.Console.WriteLine("Counter = {0} in {1}",
        counter, Thread.CurrentThread.Name);
    }
  }
  System.Console.WriteLine("{0} done. ", Thread.CurrentThread.Name);
}

public void CounterMethod2()
{
  while (counter < 20)
  {
    int localCounterValue = counter;
    if(localCounterValue < 20){
      localCounterValue++;
      Thread.Sleep(10);
      counter = localCounterValue;
      Thread.Sleep(5);

      System.Console.WriteLine("Counter = {0} in {1}",
        counter, Thread.CurrentThread.Name);
    }
  }
  System.Console.WriteLine("{0} done. ", Thread.CurrentThread.Name);
}
}
```

You can see the two threads interfering with each other when you run ch15_03. Note, for example, that after thread2 increments counter a few times, thread1 sets it back to 1, and thread2 starts all over:

```
C:\>ch15_03
Counter = 1 in Thread 2
Counter = 2 in Thread 2
Counter = 3 in Thread 2
Counter = 4 in Thread 2
Counter = 5 in Thread 2
Counter = 1 in Thread 1
Counter = 1 in Thread 2
Counter = 2 in Thread 2
Counter = 3 in Thread 2
Counter = 4 in Thread 2
Counter = 5 in Thread 2
Counter = 6 in Thread 2
Counter = 2 in Thread 1
Counter = 2 in Thread 2
Counter = 3 in Thread 2
Counter = 4 in Thread 2
Counter = 5 in Thread 2
Counter = 6 in Thread 2
          .
          .
          .
Thread 2 done.
Counter = 16 in Thread 1
Counter = 17 in Thread 1
Counter = 18 in Thread 1
Counter = 19 in Thread 1
Counter = 20 in Thread 1
Thread 1 done.
All threads finished.
```

Clearly, our two threads are interfering with each other. So how do we fix the problem? Our first fix is to use a *lock*.

Using a Lock to Synchronize Threads

A lock marks a *critical section* in your code, which is a code that you don't want other threads to interrupt. To use a lock, you use the .NET lock statement by passing this statement the object you want locked (which will be the current object, this, in this example). The code you put into the lock statement is run only by the current thread. Other threads will wait until you're done, removing the conflict in ch15_03.cs. You can see the new version of the code, using the lock statement, in ch15_04.cs, Listing 15.4.

LISTING 15.4   Using a Lock (ch15_04.cs)

```csharp
using System.Threading;

class ch15_04
{
  int counter = 0;

  static void Main()
  {
    ch15_04 app = new ch15_04();

    app.StartThreads();
  }

  public void StartThreads()
  {
    Thread thread1 = new Thread(new ThreadStart(CounterMethod1));
    thread1.Name = "Thread 1";
    thread1.Start();

    Thread thread2 = new Thread(new ThreadStart(CounterMethod2));
    thread2.Name = "Thread 2";
    thread2.Start();

    thread1.Join();
    thread2.Join();

    System.Console.WriteLine("All threads finished.");
  }

  public void CounterMethod1()
  {
    while (counter < 20)
    {
      lock(this)
      {
        int localCounterValue = counter;
        if(localCounterValue < 20){
```

LISTING 15.4 Continued

```
            Thread.Sleep(50);
            localCounterValue++;
            Thread.Sleep(10);
            counter = localCounterValue;


System.Console.WriteLine("Counter = {0}
in {1}",
            counter, Thread.Current-
Thread.Name);
        }
    }
  }
    System.Console.WriteLine("{0} done.
", Thread.CurrentThread.Name);
  }

  public void CounterMethod2()
  {
    while (counter < 20)
    {
      lock(this)
      {
        int localCounterValue = counter;
        if(localCounterValue < 20){
          localCounterValue++;
          Thread.Sleep(10);
          counter = localCounterValue;
          Thread.Sleep(5);

          System.Console.WriteLine("Counter = {0} in {1}",
            counter, Thread.CurrentThread.Name);
        }
      }
    }
    System.Console.WriteLine("{0} done. ", Thread.CurrentThread.Name);
  }
}
```

USING INTERLOCKED.INCREMENT AND INTERLOCKED.DECREMENT

Besides the other techniques that we'll take a look at here that you can use to synchronize threads, it's also worth mentioning that using threads to increment or decrement a counter is such a common operation that C# includes the `Interlocked.Increment` and `Interlocked.Decrement` methods to do just that. You pass these methods a reference to an integer or long variable, and these methods will increment or decrement that variable while being careful to avoid conflicts with other threads. While discussing thread conflicts, note that events provide a good way of communicating between threads, and through that kind of communication, you can eliminate conflicts.

When you run this new version of the code, the two threads no longer conflict, as you can see:

```
C:\>ch15_04
Counter = 1 in Thread 1
Counter = 2 in Thread 2
Counter = 3 in Thread 1
Counter = 4 in Thread 2
Counter = 5 in Thread 1
Counter = 6 in Thread 2
Counter = 7 in Thread 1
Counter = 8 in Thread 2
Counter = 9 in Thread 1
Counter = 10 in Thread 2
Counter = 11 in Thread 1
Counter = 12 in Thread 2
Counter = 13 in Thread 1
Counter = 14 in Thread 2
Counter = 15 in Thread 1
Counter = 16 in Thread 2
Counter = 17 in Thread 1
Counter = 18 in Thread 2
Counter = 19 in Thread 1
Counter = 20 in Thread 2
Thread 2 done.
Thread 1 done.
All threads finished.
```

Using a Monitor to Synchronize Threads

Another way to synchronize threads is to use a *monitor*. Using a monitor, you can specify which parts of your code need to be synchronized with other threads. To start synchronization with other threads, you call Monitor.Enter, and pass this method an object to synchronize on (we'll use this here). When you leave the critical section, you can call Monitor.Exit. You can see this in a new version of the code, ch15_05.cs, in Listing 15.5, which uses both Monitor.Enter and Monitor.Exit to synchronize the two threads.

LISTING 15.5   Using a Monitor (ch15_05.cs)

```
using System.Threading;

class ch15_05
{
  int counter = 0;
```

LISTING 15.5 Continued

```
static void Main()
{
  ch15_03 app = new ch15_05();

  app.StartThreads();
}

public void StartThreads()
{
  Thread thread1 = new Thread(new ThreadStart(CounterMethod1));
  thread1.Name = "Thread 1";
  thread1.Start();

  Thread thread2 = new Thread(new ThreadStart(CounterMethod2));
  thread2.Name = "Thread 2";
  thread2.Start();

  thread1.Join();
  thread2.Join();

  System.Console.WriteLine("All threads finished.");
}

public void CounterMethod1()
{
  while (counter < 20)
  {
    Monitor.Enter(this);
    int localCounterValue = counter;
    if(localCounterValue < 20){
      Thread.Sleep(50);
      localCounterValue++;
      Thread.Sleep(10);
      counter = localCounterValue;
      System.Console.WriteLine("Counter = {0} in {1}",
        counter, Thread.CurrentThread.Name);
    }
    Monitor.Exit(this);
  }
  System.Console.WriteLine("{0} done. ", Thread.CurrentThread.Name);
}
```

LISTING 15.5   Continued

```
public void CounterMethod2()
{
  while (counter < 20)
  {
    Monitor.Enter(this);
    int localCounterValue = counter;
    if(localCounterValue < 20){
      localCounterValue++;
      Thread.Sleep(10);
      counter = localCounterValue;
      Thread.Sleep(5);

      System.Console.WriteLine("Counter = {0} in {1}",
        counter, Thread.CurrentThread.Name);
    }
    Monitor.Exit(this);
  }
  System.Console.WriteLine("{0} done. ", Thread.CurrentThread.Name);
}
}
```

USING THE MUTEX CLASS

You can also use a *mutex object*, which is much like a monitor, to protect a shared resource from access by multiple threads at the same time. Only one thread at a time can own a mutex object. The state of a mutex object is *signaled* when it is not owned by any thread, or *nonsignaled* when it is owned. To create a mutex object in C#, you use the Mutex class.

When you run ch15_05.cs, you get the same results as when using the lock statement in ch15_04.cs. The threads are synchronized successfully once again.

It's also worth noting that the Monitor class has two additional methods—Wait and Pulse. The Wait method tells the CLR that you're willing to wait until continuing processing so that other threads can get some work done. When the active thread calls the Pulse method, threads that are waiting are called.

Remoting: Passing Types and Objects Across Boundaries

The final topic in this chapter is *remoting*. Remoting is the technique of passing types or objects across process or machine boundaries using a process called *marshalling* (which is the general name for the technique of moving types or objects across programming boundaries).

In this topic, we'll create a server and client application to pass types and objects between processes on the same machine, but you can as easily pass them between processes on different machines.

In order to move types and objects across process boundaries, we're going to use two FCL classes—MarshalByRefObject, which marshals types and objects, and HttpChannel, which allows us to communicate between processes using port numbers. (HttpChannel handles firewalls well, but if firewalls are not an issue, you can also use TcpChannel, which is often faster.) You can see the significant public methods of MarshalByRefObject in Table 15.3, the significant public properties of the HttpChannel class in Table 15.4, and the significant public methods of the HttpChannel class in Table 15.5.

TABLE 15.3

Significant Public Methods of the MarshalByRefObject Class

METHOD	PURPOSE
CreateObjRef	Creates an object that can generate a proxy used to communicate with a remote object.

TABLE 15.4

Significant Public Properties of the HttpChannel Class

METHOD	PURPOSE
ChannelData	Returns channel-specific data.
ChannelName	Returns the name of the current channel.
ChannelPriority	Returns the priority of the current channel.
IsFixedSize	Returns true if the number of properties in the current channel object is fixed.
IsReadOnly	Returns true if the collection of properties in the current channel object is read-only.
IsSynchronized	Returns true if the current dictionary of channel object properties is synchronized.
Item	Returns or sets a channel property associated with the specified key. This property is the indexer for the HttpChannel class.
Keys	Returns an ICollection of keys with which the channel properties are associated.
Properties	Returns an IDictionary of the channel properties associated with the current channel.
Values	Returns an ICollection of the values of the properties associated with the current channel object.

TABLE 15.5

Significant Public Methods of the HttpChannel Class

METHOD	PURPOSE
StartListening	Makes the current channel start listening for requests.
StopListening	Makes the current channel stop listening for requests.

COMMUNICATING BETWEEN PROCESSES IN C++ AND C#

In languages like C++, you can also communicate between processes using *memory mapping*, which allows you to share memory between two processes. Memory mapping, with its heavy emphasis on pointers, is not available in C#.

In the first example, the server will provide a type to the client, which will create objects of that type. The type we'll remote will have only one method—ToCaps, which takes a string argument, capitalizes that string, and returns it. Although the object is used locally in the client, its code executes in the server.

In this example, we'll use this object to send a text string from the client to the server across process boundaries, and code in the server will then send the capitalized text back to the client. It's useful to create an interface in this case to tell the client how the object that it's remoting works, so in this example, we'll implement the ICaps interface that you see in Listing 15.6, ch15_06.cs.

LISTING 15.6   A Remoting Interface (ch15_06.cs)

```
public interface ICaps
{
  string ToCaps(string text);
}
```

To compile ch15_06.cs into ch15_06.dll, use this command (or, of course, create a DLL project in the IDE):

```
C:\>csc /t:library ch15_06.cs
```

Now we're ready to create the server that will remote the ICaps type to the client.

Creating the Server

There are two types of servers you can use for remoting in .NET—*well-known* and *client-activated* servers. The difference is that connections to client-activated servers are permanent as long as a session lasts, and connections to well-known servers are created each time the client sends a message to the server. This example uses a well-known server object.

In turn, there are two types of well-known servers—*singleton* and *single-call*. Singleton servers handle connections to clients with a single object, whereas single-call servers handle requests from the client with a new object for each request. Single-call servers are useful when you have a lot of clients that need to be handled, but in this case, we have only one client so we'll use a singleton server.

To create a type to be marshaled, we'll construct a class, Capitalizer, which inherits MarshalByRefObject and implements the ICaps interface:

```
public class Capitalizer : MarshalByRefObject, ICaps
{
    .
    .
    .
}
```

This class simply implements the ToCaps method, which accepts a string, capitalizes it, and returns it:

```
public class Capitalizer : MarshalByRefObject, ICaps
{
    public string ToCaps(string inText)
    {
        System.Console.WriteLine("Got the text: \"{0}\"", inText);
        string outText = inText.ToUpper();
        System.Console.WriteLine("Sending back the text: \"{0}\"", outText);
        return outText;
    }
}
```

This is the type we'll remote to the client.

Actually setting up the server is easy; all we have to do is register the Capitalizer type (so that you can create objects of that type in the client) and let .NET know that we'll be providing services on a particular port. In this case, we'll use port 65432 in the current machine for our server:

```
public static void Main()
{
    HttpChannel channel = new HttpChannel(65432);
    ChannelServices.RegisterChannel(channel);
    .
    .
    .
}
```

To register the Capitalizer type, indicating that it's available from this server, you can use the RemotingConfiguration class's RegisterWellKnownServiceType method. Here's how we do that, indicating that we are creating a singleton well-known server, and establishing an *endpoint* (named EndPoint1 here), which is the name the remoting service associates with the type we'll provide:

```
public static void Main()
{
  HttpChannel channel = new HttpChannel(65432);
  ChannelServices.RegisterChannel(channel);

  Type capitalizerType = Type.GetType("Capitalizer");

  RemotingConfiguration.RegisterWellKnownServiceType
    (capitalizerType, "EndPoint1", WellKnownObjectMode.Singleton);
    .
    .
    .
}
```

And that's all it takes—now the server runs by itself, until the application is terminated. To
let it run for a while, we'll display a message, `"Server is running, press Enter to quit."`,
and end the application when the user presses Enter, as you see in Listing 15.7, ch15_07.cs.

LISTING 15.7   A Remoting Server (ch15_07.cs)

```
using System;
using System.Runtime.Remoting;
using System.Runtime.Remoting.Channels;
using System.Runtime.Remoting.Channels.Http;

public class Capitalizer : MarshalByRefObject, ICaps
{
  public string ToCaps(string inText)
  {
    System.Console.WriteLine("Got the text: \"{0}\"", inText);
    string outText = inText.ToUpper();
    System.Console.WriteLine("Sending back the text: \"{0}\"", outText);
    return outText;
  }
}

public class ch15_07
{
  public static void Main()
  {
    HttpChannel channel = new HttpChannel(65432);
    ChannelServices.RegisterChannel(channel);
```

LISTING 15.7   Continued

```
    Type capitalizerType = Type.GetType("Capitalizer");

    RemotingConfiguration.RegisterWellKnownServiceType
      (capitalizerType, "EndPoint1", WellKnownObjectMode.Singleton);

    System.Console.WriteLine("Server is running, press Enter to quit.");
    System.Console.ReadLine();
  }
}
```

To build the server, you have to reference ch15_06.dll, where the ICaps interface is defined. Create the server, ch15_07.exe, like this (or in the IDE by adding a reference to ch15_06.dll in a console project):

```
C:\>csc /t:exe /r:ch15_06.dll ch15_07.cs
```

Next we'll create the client application that will communicate with the server.

Creating the Client

The client is going to connect to the server on the port we've designated, 65432, and so gain access to our Capitalizer class, which implements the ICaps interface. We start creating the client by creating a new HttpChannel object and registering it as we did in the server:

```
public static void Main()
{

  HttpChannel channel = new HttpChannel();
  ChannelServices.RegisterChannel(channel);
    .
    .
    .
```

This time, however, we indicate which port to use when we connect to our server, referring to the server with the URL http://localhost:65432/EndPoint1. Here's how we connect to the server and create a marshaled object from the type our server provides:

```
public static void Main()
{

  HttpChannel channel = new HttpChannel();
  ChannelServices.RegisterChannel(channel);
```

```
MarshalByRefObject marshalledObject =
   (MarshalByRefObject) RemotingServices.Connect
   (typeof(ICaps), "http://localhost:65432/EndPoint1");
   .
   .
   .
```

We're almost home. We've created a marshaled object, but it's still anonymous. To let the C# compiler know what members are available in this object, we'll cast it into a new ICaps variable, capper:

```
try
{
  ICaps capper = (ICaps) marshalledObject;
  .
  .
  .
```

Now you can use this new object, capper, in the client's code. In this case, we'll call the ToCaps method of this object to capitalize the text "No worries.", as you see in the client's code, ch15_08.cs, Listing 15.8.

LISTING 15.8 A Remoting Client (ch15_08.cs)

```
using System;
using System.Runtime.Remoting;
using System.Runtime.Remoting.Channels;
using System.Runtime.Remoting.Channels.Http;

public class ch15_08
{
  public static void Main()
  {

    HttpChannel channel = new HttpChannel(0);
    ChannelServices.RegisterChannel(channel);

    MarshalByRefObject marshalledObject =
      (MarshalByRefObject) RemotingServices.Connect
      (typeof(ICaps), "http://localhost:65432/EndPoint1");

    try
    {
      ICaps capper = (ICaps) marshalledObject;
```

LISTING 15.8   Continued

```
      string outText = "No worries.";
      System.Console.WriteLine("Sending this text: \"{0}\"", outText);
      string inText = capper.ToCaps(outText);
      System.Console.WriteLine("Got this text back: \"{0}\"", inText);
    }
    catch(System.Exception e)
    {
      System.Console.WriteLine(e.Message);
    }
  }
}
```

That completes the client. Compile it like this (or by adding a reference to ch15_06.dll to a console project in the IDE):

```
C:\>csc /t:exe /r:ch15_06.dll ch15_08.cs
```

Through marshalling, you can use the capper object in the client, but its code will run on the server. The server and client are two different processes, so they'll run in different DOS sessions. Start the server, ch15_07.exe, in one DOS session, and the client, ch15_08.exe, in another. When the server starts, you'll see this in its DOS window:

```
C:\>ch15_07
Server is running, press Enter to quit.
```

When the client starts, you'll see this in its DOS window:

```
C:\>ch15_08
Sending this text: "No worries."
```

By calling the ToCaps method, the client sends the text "No worries." to the server, which capitalizes that text and sends it back, as it indicates in its DOS window:

```
C:\>ch15_07
Server is running, press Enter to quit.
Got the text: "No worries."
Sending back the text: "NO WORRIES."
```

The client gets back its text capitalized, and displays the results this way:

```
C:\>ch15_08
Sending this text: "No worries."
Got this text back: "NO WORRIES."
```

Congratulations; you've just handled remoting in a client/server relationship.

What if you wanted to create a new server object each time a client sent a request? You can use a single-call server instead; just change this line in the server:

```
RemotingConfiguration.RegisterWellKnownServiceType
  (capitalizerType, "EndPoint1", WellKnownObjectMode.Singleton);
```

to this:

```
RemotingConfiguration.RegisterWellKnownServiceType
  (capitalizerType, "EndPoint1", WellKnownObjectMode.SingleCall);
```

Sending an Object to the Client

In our server example, we exported an entire type using `RegisterWellKnownServiceType`. But what if you just wanted to export an object, not a type? You can do that with `RemotingServices` class's `Marshal` method. You can see a new version of our server in Listing 15.9, ch15_09.cs, where we create a new object of the `Capitalizer` class and send the actual object. The code that's different from our previous version of the server is highlighted.

LISTING 15.9   Sending an Object (ch15_09.cs)

```
using System;
using System.Runtime.Remoting;
using System.Runtime.Remoting.Channels;
using System.Runtime.Remoting.Channels.Http;

public class Capitalizer : MarshalByRefObject, ICaps
{
  public string ToCaps(string inText)
  {
    System.Console.WriteLine("Got the text: \"{0}\"", inText);
    string outText = inText.ToUpper();
    System.Console.WriteLine("Sending back the text: \"{0}\"", outText);
    return outText;
  }
}

public class ch15_09
{
  public static void Main()
  {
```

LISTING 15.9 Continued

```
    HttpChannel channel = new HttpChannel(65432);
    ChannelServices.RegisterChannel(channel);

    Capitalizer capitalizer = new Capitalizer();
    RemotingServices.Marshal(capitalizer, "EndPoint1");

    System.Console.WriteLine("Server is running, press Enter to quit.");
    System.Console.ReadLine();
  }
}
```

There's another way to communicate as well. You can use the Simple Object Access Protocol, SOAP.

Using SOAP for Remoting

SOAP is a popular XML protocol for transferring data on the Internet, and you can also use it in .NET for remoting objects. To do that, you use the System.Runtime.Serialization. Formatters.Soap namespace. We'll create the server and client we've been using in this chapter again using SOAP messaging now.

Creating the Server

In the server, we create a new object of our Capitalizer class to remote, and get a reference to that object with the RemotingServices class's Marshal method. Then we create a file named soap.txt, which will hold the SOAP message read by the client and use it to connect to the server, and use a SoapFormatter object to serialize our object reference to the file soap.txt:

```
public static void Main()
{
  HttpChannel channel = new HttpChannel(65432);
  ChannelServices.RegisterChannel(channel);

  Capitalizer capitalizer = new Capitalizer();

  ObjRef objref = RemotingServices.Marshal(capitalizer);

  FileStream filestream = new FileStream("soap.txt", FileMode.Create);
```

```
SoapFormatter soapformatter = new SoapFormatter();

soapformatter.Serialize(filestream, objref);

filestream.Close();
    .
    .
    .
```

Now it's up to the client to read soap.txt and connect. We'll wait while that happens, using System.Console.ReadLine, as you see in ch15_10.cs, Listing 15.10.

LISTING 15.10   SOAP Server (ch15_10.cs)

```csharp
using System;
using System.IO;
using System.Runtime.Remoting;
using System.Runtime.Remoting.Channels;
using System.Runtime.Remoting.Channels.Http;
using System.Runtime.Serialization.Formatters.Soap;

public class Capitalizer : MarshalByRefObject, ICaps
{
  public string ToCaps(string inText)
  {
    System.Console.WriteLine("Got the text: \"{0}\"", inText);
    string outText = inText.ToUpper();
    System.Console.WriteLine("Sending back the text: \"{0}\"", outText);
    return outText;
  }
}

public class ch15_10
{
  public static void Main()
  {
    HttpChannel channel = new HttpChannel(65432);
    ChannelServices.RegisterChannel(channel);

    Capitalizer capitalizer = new Capitalizer();

    ObjRef objref = RemotingServices.Marshal(capitalizer);
```

LISTING 15.10   Continued

```
    FileStream filestream = new FileStream("soap.txt", FileMode.Create);

    SoapFormatter soapformatter = new SoapFormatter();

    soapformatter.Serialize(filestream, objref);
    filestream.Close();

    System.Console.WriteLine("soap.txt created. Press Enter to quit.");
    System.Console.ReadLine();
  }
}
```

Creating the Client

In the client, we want to read the SOAP message in soap.txt and connect to the server. To do that, we'll need a SoapFormatter object, which we create like this:

```
public static void Main()
{
  HttpChannel channel = new HttpChannel();
  ChannelServices.RegisterChannel(channel);

  FileStream filestream = new FileStream ("soap.txt", FileMode.Open);
  SoapFormatter soapformatter = new SoapFormatter();
      .
      .
      .
```

Now all we need to do is to use our new SoapFormatter object's Deserialize method to create our ICaps object, which we can use as before, as you see in ch15_11.cs, Listing 15.11.

LISTING 15.11   SOAP Client (ch15_11.cs)

```
using System;
using System.IO;
using System.Runtime.Remoting;
using System.Runtime.Remoting.Channels;
using System.Runtime.Remoting.Channels.Http;
using System.Runtime.Serialization.Formatters.Soap;

public class ch15_11
{
```

LISTING 15.11   Continued

```
public static void Main()
{
  HttpChannel channel = new HttpChannel();
  ChannelServices.RegisterChannel(channel);

  FileStream filestream = new FileStream ("soap.txt", FileMode.Open);
  SoapFormatter soapformatter = new SoapFormatter();

  try
  {
    ICaps capper = (ICaps)soapformatter.Deserialize(filestream);

    string outText = "No worries.";
    System.Console.WriteLine("Sending this text: \"{0}\"", outText);
    string inText = capper.ToCaps(outText);
    System.Console.WriteLine("Got this text back: \"{0}\"", inText);
  }
  catch(System.Exception e)
  {
    System.Console.WriteLine(e.Message);
  }
}
}
```

The new SOAP server, ch15_10.cs, and the new SOAP client, ch15_11.cs, work as before. This time, however, you're using SOAP to do your remoting. As you can see, remoting gives you a number of useful options to communicate between running processes.

In Brief

In this chapter, we took a look at multithreading and remoting. Here's an overview of the topics:

- *Multithreading* is all about hosting multiple threads in addition to an application's main thread, and using them as multiple streams of execution. You can create new threads with the Thread class. This class has various methods you can use to control threads: Start, Suspend, Resume, Sleep, Join, Abort, and so on.

- You can give a thread its own code by placing that code in a method, which you pass to the Thread constructor. Do not handle user interface elements like forms or controls in any thread but the main one.

- You can synchronize threads with `lock` and `Monitor` statements, avoiding conflict when threads use shared resources.

- *Remoting* is the technique of passing objects across process or machine boundaries. By basing a class on `MarshalByRefObject`, you can export that type from the server to the client. And you can use the `HttpChannel` to communicate between the server and the client.

- You can also send an object (not just a type) from the server to the client. In that case, you use the `RemotingServices.Marshal` method.

- SOAP provides another mechanism for remoting. You can use the `SoapFormatter` class in the server to serialize an object to disk, for example, and this same class's `Deserialize` method to connect to the server.

And That's It

And that's it—that completes our survey of C#. We've come far in this book, from the very basics up through OOP, inheritance, delegates, streams, indexers, collections, Windows and Web applications, ADO.NET and databases, user controls and Web user controls, Windows Services, Web Services, deployment, assemblies and security, attributes and reflection, and now multithreading and remoting. We've become acquainted with all of these topics and dozens more in this book. In a programmer-to-programmer treatment like this, the idea is not to drag in all the beginning material from scratch, but to give you what you need as a knowledgeable programmer to hit the ground running. There's an incredible richness here for you to exploit—all that's left is to put it to use. Happy programming.

Index

SYMBOLS

A

C

How can we make this index more useful? Email us at indexes@samspublishing.com

How can we make this index more useful? Email us at indexes@samspublishing.com

data adapter objects, 393-395
Data Adapter Preview dialog box, 364
data adapters (ADO.NET), 346
   configuring, 355
   creating, 352-356, 381
   datasets, 347
   previewing data, 364
   SQL parameters, 380
data applications
   creating, 347
      data connections, 348-355
      datasets, 356-359
   running, 359
   security, 360
data binding, 367
   complex data binding, 373-376
   simple data binding, 368-372
data connections
   creating, 348-349
   deleting, 351
   selecting, 352
   testing, 350
   versus connection objects, 348
Data Form Wizard, 379
data grids, 357-359, 375
Data Link properties dialog box (Server Explorer), 349-350
data members. See fields
data objects, 385
   command objects, 390-392
   connection objects, 386-390
   data adapter objects, 393-395
   data reader objects, 408-410
   dataset objects, 395, 402-405
Data property dialog boxes, 303
data providers, 387
data reader objects, 408-410
data readers, 407, 410-413
data relation objects, 413
data relations, 413-415
data sources, 389

data storage
   boolean types, 21
   decimal types, 20
   floating-point types, 20
   integral types, 20
   isolated storage, 218-221
   Web applications, 317-320
data tables
   columns, 402-403
   DataRow objects, 404
   datasets (ADO.NET), 401
   field data, 404-407
   installing data, 404-407
data transfer streams, 188
   asynchronous, 195-197, 204-209
   buffered streams, 192-193
   Internet streams, 209-211
   isolated storage, 218-221
   network I/O, 197-204
   reading/writing, 188-195
data views, 365-367. See also datasets
DataAdapter objects, 393
Database property, 388
databases
   accessing data, 405-407
   relational databases, 360-362
DataBind method, 359
DataBindings property, 369-372
DataColumn objects, 402
DataMember property, 373
DataRelation objects, 413
DataRow objects, 403-405
DataSet objects, 395-396, 400-405
DataSet property, 400, 413
DataSetName property, 365
datasets (ADO.NET), 347, 395. See also data views
   controls, 396
   creating, 356, 397-399
   data
      displaying, 357
      filling with local, 399
      filtering, 365-366

How can we make this index more useful? Email us at indexes@samspublishing.com

DataSet objects, 395

dataset objects, 395, 400-405

DataTable objects, 400

DbDataAdapter objects, 393

deserializing, 213

EventLog objects, 445-446

events

declaring, 176

subscribing to, 175-179

exception objects, 75-77

FontInfo object, 324

ICounter object, 522

late binding, 516-519

marshaled objects, 553-554

methods, binding to, 516-519

ModuleBuilder object, 523

mutex objects, 548

non-serialized data handling, 216-217

OdbcCommand objects, 392

OdbcConnection objects, 346, 389-390

OdbcDataAdapter objects, 395

OdbcDataReader objects, 410

OleDbCommand objects, 391-392

OleDbConnection objects, 346, 387-388

OleDbDataAdapter objects, 394

OleDbDataReader objects, 408

OracleCommand objects, 392

OracleConnection objects, 346, 390

OracleDataAdapter objects, 395

OracleDataReader objects, 410

Request objects, 320-321

Response object, 321

serializing, 212-215

Service Controller object, 443-444

ServiceBase objects, 444

ServiceController objects, 443

ServiceInstaller objects, 447-448

ServiceProcessInstaller objects, 446-447

SoapFormatter object, 559

SqlCommand objects, 392

SqlConnection objects, 346, 388-389

SqlDataReader objects, 409

SqlDbDataAdapter objects, 395

Type objects, 511

TypeBuilder object, 523

Web services objects, 454

WebService objects, 454

Windows services objects, 444-448, 454

ODBC Data Source Administrator, 389

OdbcCommand objects, 392

OdbcConnection objects, 346, 389-390

OdbcDataAdapter objects, 395

OdbcDataReader objects, 410

OleDbCommand objects, 391-392

OleDbConnection objects, 346, 387-388

OleDbDataAdapter objects, 394-395

OleDbDataReader objects, 408-409

OleDbPermission (code access permissions), 485

OnContinue event, 434

OnContinue method, 444

OnPause event, 434

OnPause method, 444

OnShutdown method, 444

OnStart method, 435-436, 444

OnStop method, 435-436, 444

OOP (object-oriented programming)

access modifiers, 97-99

classes, creating, 93-95

constructors

copy constructors, 107-109

creating, 105-106

declaring, 107

overloading, 124-125

destructors, creating, 117-119

encapsulation, 93, 97

fields

creating, 99

initializing, 100

garbage collector, 117-122

inheritance, 138-140

boxing/unboxing value types, 150-151

calling base classes, 141-143

interfaces, 155-166

nested classes, 152-155

new keyword, 139, 145

override keyword, 145

P

PacketSize property, 389
pageLayout property, 311
Paint event, 418
parameters
  bindingAttr parameter, 514
  delegates
    declaring, 166-167
    multicasting, 172-174
    static delegates, 171-172
    static methods, 167-168
    subscribing to events, 175-179
  delegates, 168-170
  filter parameter, 514
  filterCriteria parameter, 514
  memberType parameter, 514
  versus arguments, 60
Parameters property, 391
params keyword, 63
Parent property, 446-447
Parse method, 31
passing
  arguments to methods, 63-64
  data to methods, 59-63
Password property, 446
PasswordChar property, 284
passwords
  text box passwords, 284
  Web server text boxes, 326
Path variables, setting, 9
PerformanceCounterPermission (code access permissions), 485
permission sets, 488
  creating, 489
  permissions, changing, 489
  requesting, 492
  specifying, 490
permissions
  assembly permissions, 485
    requesting minimum code access permissions, 486-487
    requesting optional code access permissions, 491

requesting (code groups), 488
requiring permission levels, 493
restricting (code groups), 487-491
code access permissions, 485-487, 491
identity permissions, 485-486
role-based security permissions, 485-486
picture boxes, 288
ping utility, 200
pointers, 14, 22, 482
  fixed keyword, 481
  fixed statements, 481
  security, 481
  unsafe keyword, 481
  Windows API functions, 483-484
polymorphism, 137, 148-150, 169-170
ports, 200
Position property, 378-379
positioning picture box images, 288
pre-built regular expressions, 85
pre-defined attribute targets, 500
precedence (operators), 40
Prepare method, 392
preprocessor directives, 46-47
previewing data in data adapters (ADO.NET), 364
PrincipalPermission (role-based security permissions), 486
PrintingPermission (code access permissions), 485
Priority property, 530
private assemblies, 476
private keyword, 98, 140
properties
  (id) property, 314
  AcceptButton property, 302
  AcceptChangesDuringFill property, 393
  Account property, 446
  AllowDBNull property, 402
  Application property, 454
  Array object properties, 224
  ArrayList class properties, 234
  AutoLog property, 444
  AutoPostBack property, 317, 328, 333
  BackColor property, 288
  background property, 311

Q – R

SiteIdentityPermission (identity permissions), 486

SizeMode property, 288

sizing picture box display areas, 288

sizing handles, 272

Sleep method, 531, 535

sleeping threads, 535

sn tool, creating public/private key pairs, 478

SOAP, 557-560

SoapFormatter object, 559

SoapFormatter objects, 559

Socket class, 198-199

SocketPermission (code access permissions), 486

sockets, 197

Solution Explorer, 298, 423

Solution Explorer window (Visual Studio IDE), 10

Sort method, 231

Sorted property, 287-289

sorting
arrays, 231-232
combo boxes, 289
list boxes, 287

Source byte buffer, 481

source code files
naming, 10
self-documenting, 34-35

Source property, 445

SourceExists method, 445

spaghetti code, 57

specifying
attribute targets, 500
membership conditions, 487
permission sets, 490

SQL
command objects, 390-391
ISO specifications, 352
parameters, 380-381
writing statements, 353-355

SqlClientPermission (code access permissions), 486

SqlCommand objects, 392

SqlConnection objects, 346, 388-389

SqlDataReader objects, 409

SqlDbDataAdapter objects, 395

Stack class, 240

stacks, 239-242

standard ports, 200

Start method, 531

starting
multiple threads, 532-535
timers, 292
Windows applications, 274
Windows services, 438-441

StartListening method, 549

StartThreads method, 532

StartType property, 447

State property, 388

StateChange event, 388

statements, 36
break statements, 54-55
C# statements, 17
class statements, 94
compound statements, 36
conditional statements, 40
continue statements, 54-55
event statement, 176
fixed statements, 481
goto statements, 56-57
if statements, 37, 41-42
interface statements, 155
lock statements, 543-546
return statements, 60
switch statements, 43-45
try-catch statements, 67
using statements, 17

static classes, 182-184

static constructors, 115

static delegates, 171-172

static fields, 111-113

static members, 517

static methods
creating, 113-114
delegates, 167-168
this keyword, 114

static properties, 115-117

StopListening method, 549

How can we make this index more useful? Email us at indexes@samspublishing.com

T

Other Related Titles

ASP.NET Kick Start
by Stephen Walther
0-672-32476-8
$34.99 US/$54.99 CAN

Microsoft Direct3D Programming Kick Start
by Clayton Walnum
0-672-32498-9
$34.99 US/$54.99 CAN

ASP.NET Data Web Controls Kick Start
by Scott Mitchell
0-672-32501-2
$34.99 US/$54.99 CAN

Managed DirectX 9.1 Kick Start
by Tom Miller
0-672-32596-9
$34.99 US/$54.99 CAN

Microsoft Visual Basic .NET 2003 Kick Start
by Duncan Mackenzie
0-672-32549-7
$34.99 US/$54.99 CAN

All prices are subject to change.

Microsoft .NET Compact Framework Kick Start
by Erik Rubin and Ronnie Yates
0-672-32570-5
$34.99 US/$54.99 CAN

SAMS
www.samspublishing.com

Other Related Titles